DEPTH CALLS TO DEPTH

Spiritual Direction and Jungian Psychology in Dialogue

John Ensign

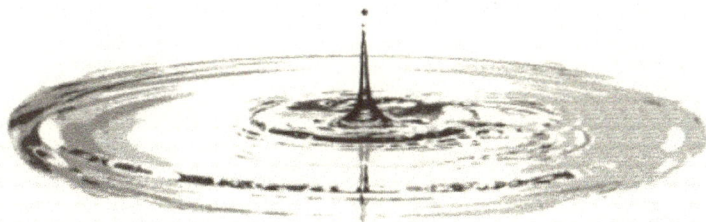

CHIRON PUBLICATIONS • ASHEVILLE, NORTH CAROLINA

www.ChironPublications.com

Interior and cover design by Danijela Mijailovic
Printed primarily in the United States of America.

ISBN 978-1-68503-133-6 paperback
ISBN 978-1-68503-134-3 hardcover
ISBN 978-1-68503-135-0 electronic
ISBN 978-1-68503-136-7 limited edition paperback

Library of Congress Cataloging-in-Publication Data

Names: Ensign, John (Psychologist), author.
Title: Depth calls to depth : spiritual direction and Jungian psychology in dialogue / John Ensign.
Description: Asheville, North Carolina : Chiron Publications, [2023] | Includes bibliographical references. | Summary: "Depth Calls to Depth: Jungian Psychology and Spiritual Direction in Dialogue draws on the author's dual background as a certified Jungian analyst and psychologist as well as a spiritual director with a master's degree in theology. Over the last several decades, spiritual direction has moved beyond its monastic origins to become a major force in contemporary spirituality. Its emphasis on direct spiritual experience offers a natural parallel to Jung's model of psychospiritual healing. This book describes how Jungian dreamwork can enhance the practice of spiritual direction. There is much interest in Jung's thought in spiritual circles but little informed understanding of the details of his model and its application to work with individuals. In an effort to meet this need, chapters alternate between descriptions of Jung's approach, augmented by extensive case material and accounts of spiritual direction sessions. In this way, the book combines a comprehensive summary of Jung's main ideas and methodologies with vignettes that illustrate their practical application. Larger issues regarding the relationship between psychology and spirituality are discussed as well as Jung's complicated relationship with the Christian tradition. The author's background in Ignatian spirituality and the work of mystics like Meister Eckhart allow him to demonstrate how these approaches can bridge gaps between the Christian and Jungian models of spiritual growth. Parallels to 12-Step spirituality also are explored"-- Provided by publisher.
Identifiers: LCCN 2023009478 (print) | LCCN 2023009479 (ebook) | ISBN 9781685031336 (paperback) | ISBN 9781685031343 (hardcover) | ISBN 9781685031350 (ebook)
Subjects: LCSH: Jungian psychology--Religious aspects--Christianity. | Christianity--Psychology. | Spiritual direction--Christiantiy.
Classification: LCC BR110 .E57 2023 (print) | LCC BR110 (ebook) | DDC 261.5/15--dc23/eng/20230413
LC record available at https://lccn.loc.gov/2023009478
LC ebook record available at https://lccn.loc.gov/2023009479

For Fred Maples, S.J., with gratitude and admiration.

There are two main images of the pastor in the New Testament: the shepherd who leads the flock to safe pasture and the fisherman who casts his nets into the depths to see what emerges. Fr. Maples is both a trusted guide and a fearless explorer.

Deep calls to deep at the thunder of your cataracts.
All your waves and billows have gone over me.

Psalm 42:7

The river is within us, the sea is all about us.

T. S. Eliot, "The Dry Salvages"
from *The Four Quartets*

Contents

Acknowledgments

Of the thanks due to the many people who have helped bring this book to fruition, pride of place goes to LeeAnn Pickrell. Ms. Pickrell is not only an editor extraordinaire who can clarify the murkiest passage and parse the most tangled prose, she has been a trusted collaborator in the creative process and proved instrumental in guiding it to completion. A profound debt of a different kind is owed to an inspired spiritual director and Jungian analyst, Fred Maples, SJ, who not only piloted me through the storms of middle life but also taught me whatever I know of bringing Jung's vision to spiritual direction. Other guides too numerous to name include the many friends, relatives, clients, and directees who have shared their lives and struggles with me through the decades. A special thanks goes to Susan Calfee, Jungian analyst, and close friend of many decades, who kindly plodded through a ragged draft of the manuscript and gave me invaluable guidance in its improvement. A profound thank you also goes to Steven Herrmann, Jungian analyst and noted author, who also read rough drafts and mentored me on the process of birthing books and with whom I spent pleasurable hours discussing Meister Eckhart. Thanks as well to Dick Jaco and George Thoma, my brothers in the vagaries of the spiritual path, and the members of my Shalem peer support group, with whom I shared many of the dilemmas and ideas that led to the creation of the book.

Throughout my life, I have been especially fortunate in the teachers and mentors who have generously shared their time and knowledge. Sadly, many have passed ahead of me into the beyond, including Arthur Lynip, who first woke my spirit's sleep; Leon Willis, who showed me how to be a gentle man in a sometimes-harsh world; and my beloved spiritual teacher, Dan Jorgensen. Of the many healers who have tutored me—Western, Eastern, and Traditional—my heartfelt thank you goes out to "Gramma" Mai Chang, who not only took me under her shamanic wings but also welcomed my family into hers. I am forever grateful for the training I received through the C. G. Jung Institute of San Francisco during the long process of becoming an analyst. I am grateful as well for the luxury of being able to return to the University of San Francisco in middle age to study theology and wish to extend particular thanks to the late Dan Kendall, SJ, and Vincent Pizzuto, PhD, who read the first iteration of this book as a master's thesis in 2007. I also am profoundly indebted for the training I received at the Shalem Institute for Spiritual Formation, the Center for Ignatian Spirituality in Sacramento, and the Bread of Life Center in Sacramento and its founder, Sandra Lommasson.

The mental spaciousness needed for writing—let alone spiritual growth—was made possible by the opportunity for extended retreats. A special thanks goes out to Colleen Gregg, MA, director of the Mercy Retreat Center in Auburn, California, my friend, and companion on the spiritual path. I am particularly grateful for the meditation retreats provided by Dan Jorgensen and Claudia Hansson and the guidance and instruction I received from both. The Curl of the Wave community that developed from these retreats has provided me a spiritual family complete with treasured brothers and sisters on the path. A very different kind of home was offered by the now-defunct Cross Court Gym where I did much of the heavy reading for the book on various machines of torture, tomes that provided welcome distraction from the pain in my legs.

On a more serious note, I am forever grateful for the love and support of my children, Olivia, and Michael, who gamely volunteered to read early drafts, and my daughter-in-law and tech guru, Valerie. My final and greatest gratitude goes to my wife, Katherine, my heart and life companion, whose inspiring example and unflagging support has accompanied me all these years.

Credits

Chapter 1
Introduction

"So, is this a psychological issue or a spiritual one?" The speaker, an experienced spiritual director in her sixties, was describing a session with a directee to our peer consultation group. There was a long silence. A couple of people glanced at me sidelong while I stared into the carpet. I had many thoughts about the question but no good answer. None of us did and it hung there awhile before we moved on. It is an issue I encounter frequently as a spiritual director and Jungian analyst, a therapeutic approach that emphasizes the relationship between psychology and spirituality.

A quick look at the spiritual direction literature confirms that the field is struggling with the same question with no consensus in sight. When I trained as a spiritual director, the common wisdom held that the two domains were entirely separate and needed to stay that way. There were good reasons, including the fear that directors would go beyond their area of competence, although a case could be made that more psychological knowledge might help them avoid doing so.

Unfortunately, we could not escape the problem that easily. There is no getting away from psychology. Toss it out the door and it comes in through the window, like the standard dream of locking the house against an intruder and turning to find him standing behind you. Our cultural worldview is shaped by psychology, and there is no such thing as a non-psychological approach to spiritual direction, only unconscious psychological views and assumptions.

Put metaphorically, psychology provides the lens through which we see ourselves, other people, and the divine. Just as someone viewing the world through a fractured lens sees the same crack running through everything they look at, distortions arising from early relationships affect how directees experience not only themselves and those around them but also the image of God they bring to the encounter. Because the same difficulties show up across relationships, many directees need an approach that integrates psychology and spirituality. I will describe one such approach over the course of these pages and track how it unfolded in the life of a directee struggling to reconcile his childhood faith with his adult perspective.

But first, a little background. I was already a mid-career therapist when a series of life-changing experiences led me to train in spiritual direction. As a mental health professional, I was viewed with a certain degree of suspicion and admonished to keep psychology out of spiritual direction, two disciplines with radically different aims and methods. However, I could not help noticing crossover. Some of my therapy clients were also in spiritual direction and brought back what sounded to me like psychological interpretations, often delivered with a certitude that left me uneasy. I found myself wondering how exploring the impact of family history on a directee's current relationships differed from what happens in counseling. If erecting a conceptual firewall between the two fields was supposed to keep directors from doing therapy, it did not seem to be working.

I noticed the language used by spiritual directors was saturated with psychological constructs, from codependency to the inner child. These passed unnoticed, partly because the ideas are ubiquitous in the culture and partly because they did not fit the way psychology was being framed in the conversation. Characterizing a field as diverse as psychology is problematic even for therapists, but depictions in the spiritual direction literature often look more like a *New Yorker* cartoon than the actual practice of psychotherapy. References to the traditional psychoanalytic, or Freudian, model predominate. That was the prevailing model back when mental health professionals first began cross training as spiritual directors. Now it represents somewhat of a time warp in the field.

Arguing from that perspective, a common refrain in training seminars is that whereas spiritual direction centers on an individual's relationship with God, therapy focuses on the therapist through transference of childhood conflicts to the therapeutic encounter. There is an optimistic assumption that less frequent meetings and a prayerful attitude will allow spiritual directors to avoid psychological projections, despite the fact these underlie every human interaction, including prayer life. Prayerful attention notwithstanding, spiritual direction does not exist in a cultural vacuum and always brings a worldview to the encounter. Directors tend to rely on one or more favored modalities, from Enneagram to SoulCollage, and each carries underlying assumptions about the human personality that, on closer examination, bear the mark of psychology.

But if spiritual direction turns psychology into a convenient caricature, psychology returns the favor with interest. Secular critics delight in hauling religion before the docket of psychology to analyze God's motives and decide whether they fit their picture of how "He" should act. I once attended a seminar where a group of psychologists concluded that Jesus was probably a grandiose paranoid schizophrenic. This war between disciplines has no winners.

Spirituality cannot be reduced to psychology, but it cannot be separated from it either, which is why the either/or question posed in the group could not be answered. Every culture has theories about what makes people tick, from the four humors of medieval philosophy to elaborate categorizations of spirit activity in traditional cultures. Throughout most of human existence, these explanatory systems interwove seamlessly with the religious frameworks in which they were grounded and which they justified in turn. In the classic spirituality literature, such models of human nature comprise a spiritual anthropology, an implicit or explicit set of assumptions that shape how we see ourselves and our encounters with God. Like any theoretical system, they reflect the social and technological context in which they arise and need to be reformulated as culture changes, like Thomas Aquinas's brilliant reworking of Scholastic Theology that laid the groundwork for several centuries of theological thought.

The sharp division between spirituality and psychology I encountered during training is starting to soften, but spiritual direction still lacks a comprehensive model of the human personality and its relationship to divine reality, something pre-psychological ages took for granted. In practical terms, this means that directors tend to switch back and forth between religious and psychological language.

The problem is compounded by the fact that psychology does not have a unified model of human personality either. Not only do psychological models disagree among themselves, but therapists flit promiscuously between paradigms, citing chemical imbalances and poor boundaries in the same breath. Confusion is amplified when psychology trickles down into the culture. Like pornography and spirituality, we know what psychology is until we are asked to define it. The closer you look the more confusing things get. The constructs that undergird our psychological self-understanding reflect diverse, sometimes contra-dictory, models drawn from biological, developmental, cognitive, relational, and sociological schools of thought. Yet for all their limitations, we cannot live without psychological explanations. I once worked on a community-based treatment team that decided diagnostic categories were stigmatizing and banned them from staff meetings. But we still needed a way to communicate about clients and the descriptions we substituted turned out to be veiled psychiatric diagnoses whose content ranged from euphemistic gobbledygook—"she has an incredibly unique take on the world"—to the downright snarky— "a junkie hustler who's just looking to cash in on his abusive childhood."

For better or worse, psychology is our default setting. It pervades our thinking in subtle ways we do not recognize. The psychological paradigm is so familiar we do not even notice it, like the old joke about fish not tasting water. Once you start looking for it, psychology shows up everywhere. And despite its avowed secularism, psychology permeates our spirituality like the proverbial white on rice. This is less sinister than it sounds since psychology and spirituality are merely two aspects of our unified human experience. Put more poetically, psyche and spirit yearn to be joined. Without spirituality, psychology takes itself far too seriously, confusing its limitations with the boundaries of the universe. And a spirituality that does not speak to the real-life problems of actual people quickly becomes ethereal and ungrounded.

We are a single being, and healing needs to happen on all levels of experience, within and between individuals as well as in a culture whose splits manifest in personal problems. A spiritual practice that does not address the impact of individuals' unique psychological histories on who they are and the wounds they carry remains theoretical, a set of maxims instead of a relationship. Worse, it can discourage them from seeking God's presence in the messiness of everyday life instead of relegating it to past events or reducing it to rules and formulas.

The approach I will use is one of the few that addresses psychology and spirituality in an integrated and systematic manner, the system developed by the Swiss psychiatrist Carl Jung. Sixty years after his death, his work still offers the most comprehensive model of the complicated relationship between the two domains. Jung's name is already familiar to most readers. It crops up from time to time in the spiritual direction literature, although the picture presented there is usually superficial, at times distorted. Jung is easy to misunderstand: his ideas are complex, and his writing can be hard to follow. There is a method to his meandering as he circles around a topic, but for the casual reader the effect can be bewildering.

Given the vast and contradictory nature of the psyche, Jung chose to approach it from multiple angles, which left him saying different things in different contexts. Jung's ideas evolved over time, and, not unlike scripture, his writings can be used to *proof text* almost anything with quotes to back it up. His relationship to Christianity is especially complicated and defies easy categorization. This ambiguity tempts his Christian supporters to gloss over his more negative comments, which Christian detractors seize with glee. I will explore these issues later and their implications for adapting this approach to spiritual direction. Although comprehensive treatment of his model is beyond the scope of this book, I will sketch the broad outlines of his mature thought as it pertains to spiritual direction, considering parallels with Christian thought and ways it stands in tension.

On a technical note, I have been referring to Jungian psychology but that's not strictly accurate since generations of practitioners have helped develop the tradition, sometimes diverging from Jung on important points. He himself suggested the name *analytic psychology* to contrast his approach with the *psychoanalytic psychology* initiated by Freud and his inner circle. Unfortunately, the term did not catch on in the broader culture, so I will follow common usage in referring to Jungian psychology, with the understanding that Jungians differ widely among themselves.

Jung was unique among early psychological theorists in taking religion seriously. For him, it was not a defense against reality but its ultimate expression. Every psychological difficulty was at root a spiritual problem.[1] His basic premise, like that of this book, was that psychology cannot be separated from spirituality, any more than spirituality can be separated from psychology since God is always seen in terms of human experience and relationships.[2]

From a Jungian perspective, spirituality and psychology are not so much different circles on a Venn diagram that overlap in spiritual direction, as they are two dimensions of our unified human experience. In his search for healing for himself and his patients, Jung was startled to

---

[1] C. G. Jung, 1928. "Psychoanalysis and the Cure of Souls," *Psychology and Religion,* CW 11, ¶¶497–499.
[2] Jung, 1938/1940. "Psychology and Religion" (The Terry Lectures), CW 11, ¶144.

encounter an active force within the personality that he conceptualized as a religious drive. This impulse toward spiritual development seemed to have a life of its own as it drew the *small self* of ordinary awareness toward the deeper levels of psyche. For him this was not a theoretical construct but a living reality whose creativity surprised him and continues to amaze me after nearly forty years in the field.

Just as Sigmund Freud, his older contemporary, found symbolic representations of conflicts surrounding sexuality and aggression in the dreams of his patients, Jung discovered this journey of inner transformation was represented in symbols drawn from an individual's unique life experience. These images, which manifested in dreams, waking fantasies, and outer events, became a major focus of his work. In his view, they pointed the way forward on life's journey and highlighted the emotional patterns that blocked access to an inner wholeness he referred to as the *Self*. For Jung, the Self bore not only the imprint of the divine but also a direct connection with it that finds expression in so-called God-images.[3]

I have introduced several concepts that need unpacking, a job for future chapters, but this brief foray into Jung's approach gives a sense of how it set him apart from his fellow psychologists and why it offers a natural bridge between psychology and spiritual direction. The goal is not to provide a grand synthesis of the two but rather demonstrate why spiritual directors may find some Jungian techniques and ideas helpful to their work.

Perhaps the closest analogue in the religious literature is the approach to spiritual direction associated with the sixteenth-century mystic Ignatius of Loyola. Ignatian spirituality will surface repeatedly in the pages ahead, both as a methodology and a natural point of comparison with Jung that highlights the complex relationship between psychology and spirituality. For now, I will concentrate on two aspects of his thought that are particularly relevant to Jungian thought: Ignatius's dedication to encountering God in every situation and his use of imagination in spiritual direction, including techniques like "application of the senses" to enter directly into the personal meaning of a sacred text.[4]

---

[3] Jung, 1942/1948. "A Psychological Approach to the Dogma of the Trinity," CW 11, ¶¶230–231.
[4] Ignatius of Loyola, *The Spiritual Exercises of Saint Ignatius*, 60, ¶¶121–125.

As articulated in his *Spiritual Exercises,* the quest to find God in all things deepens awareness of God's pervasive presence in outer experience while personalizing the believer's inner relationship with the symbols, stories, and rituals of revealed religion. Using a Gospel narrative or a religious image as an object of reflection, retreatants engage in a multistep process of imagination or fantasy, meditation and contemplation, colloquy with a sacred figure, and reflection back on their experience and its meaning for their lives. The imagination is given free rein to enter the scene using all the senses, not just the flare of torches but the sour smell of fear emanating from panicked disciples. Participants may move into the narrative from any perspective, whether as Judas, Jesus, or a bystander. Additional characters or scenes may be added as the spirit leads. For instance, Ignatius liked to imagine himself as a small boy serving Mary and Joseph on their flight to Egypt[5] and encouraged directees to open a dialogue with Christ as he hung on the cross, an example of a *colloquy.*[6] Multiple modalities are engaged as directees meditate on the meaning of a scripture passage and enter the scene imaginatively through a contemplative process emphasizing sensation and feeling. Allowing its imagery to expand as fully as possible, they observe their response to the story through introspective awareness of internal stirrings that show up in emotions, images, promptings, and bodily sensations. In the last stage of the process, directees move yet more deeply into the divine presence and open fully to God's movement within them before reflecting on the experience and its application to daily life.

The process happens on multiple levels, bringing together the play of imagination and emotion, memories, and images from a directee's personal history, as well as sacred texts, symbols, and prayerful reflection to bring the experience more fully into consciousness. Retreatants engage God in a highly personal way, whether through internal dialogue or imaginative participation in the events of the Gospels. Ignatius advocated careful discernment in interpreting the encounter but had no problem opening the most sacred symbols and religious figures to individual experience. There is an implicit recognition that each person has a unique perspective on God, just as members of a family see each other differently. His dedication to following individual experience wherever it led was

---

5 Ignatius, 58–59, ¶114.
6 Ignatius, 42, ¶53.

truly revolutionary. More startling still was his trust in the subjective dimension of religious reality. Believers were encouraged to track God's movement within them through emotional reactions and spontaneous images. Like a reflection on water, the contours of God's presence in that moment were revealed in their own internal responses.

Ignatius was fearless in his willingness to take seriously the promptings and images arising from this focused reflection, an elevated view of human capacity that brought him to the attention of the Inquisition. Viewed in hindsight, his decision to shift the focus of spiritual practice from the revealed text to the believer's response seems surprisingly modern, anticipating the Kantian "turn to the subject" that shaped Jung's work. Other aspects of Ignatius's thought remind us he was very much a man of his time, including attributing the internal stirrings experienced by directees to the influence of good and bad spirits.[7] This view is largely out of sync with our current cultural understanding, in which the demons who tormented the solitary mystic have moved inside as psychological forces.

Despite such differences, parallels to Jung are apparent even from this brief description. Although sometimes critical of Ignatius, Jung engaged deeply with his thought. In many ways, Jung's methodology can be seen as a more radical extension of Ignatius's pioneering work, which also emphasized the subjective dimension of religious response. Among Jung's most important innovations was applying to the emerging field of psychology the age-old belief that the divine nature is experienced through the prism of personality, a view shared by Ignatius and other mystics. Leaving aside the awkward fact that it is our only frame of reference, this allows us to see God in terms we can relate to. The question of how humans go about experiencing something beyond perception or comprehension has preoccupied theologians throughout Christian history. Most have argued for a process of analogy, in which we extrapolate from our experience to something infinitely beyond it. This assumes an intimate correspondence between God and human beings made in the divine image, a continuity fully realized in the Incarnation. In the absence of direct sight, approaching God through human analogies elevates imagination to a central organ of perception. Like Ignatius, Jung prioritized the role of imagination and direct personal experience in

---

[7] Ignatius, 126–128, ¶¶328-336.

establishing connection with the deepest levels of reality. His emphasis on subjective experience runs counter to the modern tendency to downplay imagination in favor of empirically verifiable external sensations, as though these are not also constructed imaginatively.

But Jung and Ignatius share more than a methodology. Operating within a psychological framework, Jung demonstrated a similar dedication to finding the holy in everyday life without losing touch with either side of the equation—divine presence or ordinary existence. This struggle to keep both poles in sight—elevated spirituality and messy human life—is shared by spiritual direction and other forms of applied spirituality. Like Ignatius, Jung was less interested in grasping religious symbols conceptually than entering fully into the images and allowing them to work within the deeper levels of consciousness. He criticized Ignatius, not entirely fairly, for artificially restricting the scope of imaginative engagement to the symbols and texts of revealed religion.[8] By enlarging the range of sources for reflection to include dreams, spontaneous images, relationships, and events of daily life, Jung sought to increase awareness of spiritual depths in all aspects of existence.

His clinical experience also led him to conclude there was an overarching continuity across human experience. Tensions in the larger culture surfaced as psychological difficulties, just as cultural divisions represented the accumulation of individual conflicts. Jungians recommend treating dreams as life and life as a dream, by which they mean taking inner images seriously and looking for the symbolic dimensions of outer experience. The relationship between the different parts of ourselves is shaped by our outer relationships and shapes them in turn. By the same token, core patterns that emerge as internal images derive from the deepest level of reality and reflect our personal relationship to it. Like Ignatius before him, Jung discovered that conscientious and humble reflection on inner and outer manifestations of these deep patterns opens us to a level of reality that guides us toward wholeness. In Christian terms, God's spirit within the believer illuminates areas of woundedness, comforting, correcting, and inviting changed attitudes and behavior.

In the chapters ahead, I will explore how Jung's model can shed light on the integration of the psychological and spiritual dimensions of human

---

[8] Jung, 1954. "Letter to Père Lachat," *The Symbolic Life*, CW 18, ¶1548; Jung, 1935/1953. "Psychological Commentaries on the Tibetan Book of the Dead," CW 11, ¶854.

experience that happens in spiritual direction. Following the same directee over the course of several years grounds the discussion in an actual human life, revealing how dreams and spontaneous images presaged spiritual developments that manifested over time in the outer world. The faith journey of the directee, whom I will call Mark, offers a good example of how seemingly intractable personal conflicts can provide a window on unresolved issues within the larger culture. His painful inward struggle gave him access to perhaps the only place where these divisions can find resolution. In this way, his journey illustrates the Jungian axiom that fully engaging on a personal level with problems that cannot be resolved within the larger cultural framework allows new solutions to emerge. Because dream images played a central role in this directee's faith journey, I will concentrate on his reflections in the narrative. Dreamwork is by no means the only avenue for Jungian work, let alone spiritual direction. However, in his case a series of striking dreams offered a way out of a seeming impasse, where personal issues interwove with conflicts in the larger religious culture that he had internalized. The perspective I bring to spiritual direction is informed by both Jungian psychology and Ignatian spirituality, a dual orientation that has shaped my approach to the dream material presented in the pages that follow. In practical terms, this meant using dreams as objects of spiritual reflection, much as Ignatius did with sacred texts, a technique that raises issues I will discuss in later chapters.

I will explore developments in the life of this directee in considerable detail, but for now a brief overview may help frame his journey within a larger conceptual framework. Like many people I have seen in spiritual direction, he was raised in a Fundamentalist household but left the church as a teenager. He followed a meandering spiritual path typical of seekers from his generation before connecting with a progressive form of Protestant Christianity after a series of deep religious experiences in middle life.

To his surprise, the intense engagement with traditional Christianity that marked his childhood picked up where it had left off, and he found himself caught between two irreconcilable positions. An "inner Evangelical" showed up in dreams as well as feelings of subtle contempt for fellow congregants in his new church. (Although the Evangelical tradition has a complex and varied history, in recent American history it has become largely identified with the theological fundamentalist and socially conservative milieu in which both Mark and I were raised, which is how I will use the word *Evangelical* in the pages that follow.) This side of him held a very literal view of religious truth that was abhorrent to his intellectual day world self, who viewed his renewed Christian faith with amused skepticism.

Over the course of several years, my task as a director was to help create space for both voices, a task aided and complicated by my own similar background. What began as a struggle between conservative and progressive Christianity opened into a new perspective that preserved both traditions. In Jungian terms, this kind of creative solution reflects the *transcendent function* that arises in the psyche when people are caught between apparently irreconcilable opposites and must await the emergence of an ampler viewpoint able to encompass both.[9] At the same time, the split between thinking and feeling—between his rational day world self and deep emotional attachment to the Christianity of his childhood—came together in a new kind of heartfelt knowing. The experience carried with it a sense of personal connection reminiscent of his childhood relationship with God, yet very different from it. Although specifics of the graced reconciliation he experienced cannot be generalized to painful divisions within the larger religious culture, they nevertheless point toward a possible path of healing.

A few practical points need to be addressed in closing, beginning with the question every book must ask, who is the intended audience? Spiritual directors, of course, along with others who serve in a similar capacity. More generally, it may be useful to people interested in the relationship between spirituality and psychology, including those with a particular interest in Jung. Here a caveat is needed.

What follows is not intended as a comprehensive, let alone scholarly, treatment of Jung's approach, which evolved over his long career, or the vast range of subsequent Jungian thought. Written for an informed lay audience, the book offers a broad survey of Jung's major ideas and their potential application to spiritual direction from the sometimes-idiosyncratic perspective of one Jungian practitioner. This brings up yet another caveat. The aim is not to turn spiritual directors into Jungians but rather to suggest approaches and ways of thinking that may be useful in that setting. Despite overlap, spiritual direction and Jungian analysis come out of quite different traditions and have different goals. Few directors are

---

[9] Jung, 1921/1971. *Psychological Types,* CW 6, ¶¶827–829.

equipped to address serious psychological issues, and most analysts lack a thorough and sympathetic grounding in the Christian tradition. To help bridge this gap, the book will pay particular attention to Jung's relationship with Christianity, including points of tension and ways his ideas may be adapted to spiritual direction with a Christian orientation. Those sections reflect my personal take on Jung's contributions as I seek, like many of his readers, to differentiate between central elements of his approach and the specific conclusions to which they led him as an individual.

A second issue has to do with dreams and dreamwork. There is an ongoing debate in the scientific community regarding dreams—what they are, what function they serve, and whether they have meaning. Without wading into these deep waters, the premise of this book is that something valuable happens when we view dreams as meaningful and engage with them in a serious way.

So, does this mean treating dreams as gospel, especially since I talked about using Ignatian methods for reflecting on scripture? Unlike sacred texts whose universality speaks across time, dreams always come to a particular person in a particular situation and provide a detailed picture of processes unfolding in that person's inner and outer life. This gives them great power in pinpointing issues specific to the individual, although some dreams may also address concerns in the larger culture. Dream contents can be deeply spiritual but may simply reflect nervousness about an upcoming presentation or replay a traumatic event the dreamer is trying to come to terms with. Dreams look at things from a different angle than everyday awareness, and incorporating this perspective can deepen our understanding, although a dream's meaning is not always clear since they also speak another language. Finally, some dreams convey a guiding force that draws us toward greater awareness, perhaps even a divine voice.

Like the parallel debates in the psychological community, the issue of dreams has been a source of controversy in the spiritual literature. Questions regarding the status of dreams and imagination have surfaced frequently over the course of Christian history, including concerns over Ignatius's decision to view the images and emotions arising from imaginative reflections as a form of divine communication. Both testaments of the Christian Bible contain examples of God speaking through dreams, from Jacob's grand vision linking heaven and earth to detailed economic policies outlined in the Pharaoh's dreams and the practical advice received by Peter, the magi, and Joseph. As in most spiritual traditions, there is little differentiation between dreams and visions. This makes sense from a Christian perspective since God is always speaking to us, whether we are asleep or awake.

Jung had a similar idea. He believed the divine voice communicates through dreams, spontaneous images, relationships, and outer events, and that paying attention to a dream's message increases awareness of spiritual movement in all facets of life. I will track how these modes of communication converged in the life of the directee, along with prayer and revealed religion, while keeping in mind that God's voice is always heard through human ears.

This brings me to the third point. The practice of spiritual direction has moved far beyond its origins in Catholic religious institutions. It is not only an ecumenical Christian phenomenon but has been adopted by other faith traditions and individuals with no formal religious affiliation. In a parallel way, Jung had a particularly intense relationship with Christianity, based on his upbringing, but spoke to a broad religious audience and drew on a wide range of sources, including Jewish, Islamic, Buddhist, and Hindu texts and images. By contrast, this book is written from a primarily Christian viewpoint. Beyond the simple fact that this is the only perspective I am remotely qualified to speak from, other practical considerations dictated the choice, including the Christian nature of the dream material and issues faced by the directee. Many aspects of his journey mirror those found in other religious traditions. In psychological terms, his journey can be viewed as a "case study" whose implications apply to a variety of spiritual settings.

Similar issues arise regarding our parallel backgrounds. Like me, the directee is a white male from an Evangelical background who struggled with its limitations. This strengthened some aspects of our work together but meant that issues of marginalization entered the dialogue obliquely, as when the directee reflected on his mixed motives as an advocate for the poor.

I originally had intended to include material from multiple directees with diverse backgrounds but settled on the current format for several reasons. The first involved access to an unusually comprehensive set of dreams that track in depth the dreamer's spiritual odyssey across time. Serendipitously, this material also offered a good vehicle for exploring Jung's deep engagement with Christianity and his complex relationship to the Christian tradition. A third reason is more conceptual and has to do with the nature of books of this kind. When drawing from multiple sources, there is a tendency to "cherry-pick" material that cleanly illustrates the theory being discussed. Things are far sloppier in real life and working with dreams, images, and events in the life of a single directee gives, I believe, a better sense of that messiness. Rather than treating theoretical constructs as real things that individual examples serve to illustrate, the idea is to start with a directee's actual experience and then see how Jung's ideas might help illuminate what we encounter there.

Consequently, the narrative will alternate between spiritual direction sessions and more theoretical material. Although these chapters inter-relate, some readers may be frustrated there is not a more systematic effort to integrate the two. It may help to think of them as parallel paths, the directee's journey and my reflections on the larger questions it raises, as we walk down opposite sides of the same canyon, calling back and forth across the river, sometimes in sight of one another and sometimes not.

Being present for a directee's spiritual journey is always a journey for the director as well. In this way, spiritual direction is a joint venture between partners whose viewpoints never entirely converge but together fill out the picture like two camera angles on the same vista. This rambling approach follows a method that Jung called *circumambulation,* an image derived from walking a labyrinth or around a Buddhist stupa.[10] Although it can feel like talking in circles, the hope is that looking at something from all sides yields a fuller picture than linear exposition. Finally, excerpts from direction sessions are offered with the full permission of the directee and changes have been made to preserve anonymity. Unfortunately, the need for confidentiality sometimes precludes disclosing details that would give a fuller picture of his situation and correspondences between his inner and outer life. With these provisos in mind, let's meet the directee.

---

[10] Jung, 1951/1968. *Aion,* CW 9ii, ¶352.

Chapter 2
Unless an Egg Falls to the Ground

What struck me most on meeting the directee whom I will call Mark was his quiet intensity. He had called a few days earlier after receiving my name from a former directee he met at an AA (Alcoholics Anonymous) meeting. After a couple minutes on the phone, I suggested we make an appointment to meet so we could get a sense of the fit between us, but he said he had some questions first. He inquired about my credentials, an issue that more typically comes up with therapy clients, and I wondered if there had been a mix-up. Mark assured me he was looking for spiritual direction, something he had never done before and asked how it worked. I did my best to answer, and he decided to set up a meeting, although he was clearly less than satisfied with my rather rambling explanation.

The window in my office looks out on the street so I watched him coming up the walkway when he arrived for our session a few days later. A balding man with a ponytail and a walrus mustache, he wore wrinkled slacks and a patterned shirt. He appeared to be in late middle age, with an air of rumpled professionalism. He looked every inch the community organizer he turned out to be. We shook hands in the waiting room, and I brought him back to my office where we exchanged pleasantries. His manner was casual, almost deferential, but I had the distinct feeling I was being evaluated and not entirely passing the test.

The big question hanging over initial meetings is what brings people to spiritual direction and what they hope to find. Before I could ask, let alone pause for a moment of reflective silence, Mark began telling me his life story, leaning forward in his chair, and gesturing with his hands. That was when I noticed his intensity. His account was unusually clear and insightful, full of wry observations and offhand humor. Obviously, he had thought deeply about his life and the patterns running through it. At the same time, there was something slightly distanced about the narrative, like a touching anecdote that has been repeated many times.

Twenty minutes into the session, I refocused him gently, saying we would definitely return to his story if he decided to work with me, but for today I wanted to make sure we got to what was happening in his life now and what he hoped to get from spiritual direction. I half expected him to bristle at the interruption but instead he paused, his expression thoughtful as he clearly struggled for words. In contrast to his earlier fluidity, he had a hard time articulating his answer beyond a vague sense of disquiet and dissatisfaction. After another long silence, he added tentatively, "It's like I'm running out of runway and haven't taken off yet, if that makes any sense."

I hear this sentiment frequently from middle-aged therapy clients, although seldom so vividly expressed, and I wondered how God fit into this—the omnipresent question in spiritual direction. Before I could find a way to ask, Mark answered the question by describing a series of startling experiences that seemed to have come out of nowhere, although they made perfect sense in the context of the life history that he had been trying to give me.

I learned a great deal about the details of Mark's life over the next several years, as old events took on new meanings and he reevaluated what had once seemed certain. I will explore some of those memories in future chapters but for now I will summarize the broad outlines of his biography. His life began in the rural community where his father pastored a small church, despite lacking formal theological training. The family moved frequently in Mark's early years before settling in a midsize city. His father had changed professions by then but continued to serve as a lay minister in a local Fundamentalist congregation. Family life centered around the church, which provided a link to their earlier rural life. Mark was deeply religious from an early age and showed promise as a preacher himself, delivering short sermons to the assembled children in his vacation Bible school when he was in fifth grade.

He did well in school, but his home life was chaotic. His father was bipolar, at times abusive. Mark was the eldest child and his overwhelmed mother turned to him for support. By his account, things really began falling apart about the time he entered adolescence. The massive cultural changes of the late 1960s reached the town where the family lived, bringing drugs and new ideas. His father's condition deteriorated, and his mother and father divorced, something unthinkable in their religious subculture. Doubts crept in and Mark began searching out alternate perspectives, an isolated intellectual quest that continued into the present.

"Just one more alienated Evangelical boy reading Camus and Ram Dass and thinking I was so unique," he told me wryly. "And Kerouac, of course, which is even more embarrassing."

His new attitude did not go over well at the church, which had become increasingly entrenched as the culture eroded out from under it. He moved into a new crowd at school and began using drugs, starting a long drift toward addiction that lasted through his early forties.

At some indiscernible point, he simply put away his Christianity— "mothballed in a cedar trunk in the back closet," as he phrased it—where it waited untouched until the spiritual upheaval of his mid-fifties that ultimately brought him into direction. Despite disavowing his childhood faith, he remained obsessed with spirituality and read widely in the field. Although self-educated when it came to religion (like his father, he realized to his chagrin), his reading list included dense scholarly texts on subjects ranging from Tibetan Buddhism to biblical hermeneutics. He tried on several religious traditions, from Western Occultism to secular Sufism, but never stayed long in any spiritual community.

He "took the scenic route through college," working odd jobs to support himself. As Mark described it, he stumbled into a position as a community organizer while attempting to establish himself as a freelance political journalist and went on to build a successful career in community-based service agencies where he moved into an advocacy role with individual clients.

In his mid-thirties, he married a woman whom I will call Jennifer. Their relationship was sometimes tumultuous, marked by periodic crises. The first came when the couple was unable to conceive, despite a long course of medical interventions that led to increasing conflict. Mark, who had been ambivalent about children from the first, strenuously opposed his wife's subsequent desire to adopt. The resulting tensions never completely resolved but were somewhat muted when she began helping care for the children of a niece who was experiencing drug and psychiatric problems. Her deepening involvement with them led to a new round of conflict in the relationship. It also reintroduced Christianity into Mark's life when Jennifer insisted they take the children to church. In hindsight, he realized God had never actually left but merely gone underground, resurfacing in various guises. Part of my work with Mark in the early stages of spiritual direction involved tracking the continuity between these occasional sightings. He unearthed many, but for now I will just note a couple of the most salient.

One occurred during a psychedelic experience in early adolescence. He had taken LSD with a couple friends and wandered off by himself, winding up in a grove of trees where he lay on the ground, staring up into the shimmering leaves above him. The woods had been his place of sanctuary growing up and he had experienced moments of God's presence there as far back as he could remember. Some of his most vivid childhood memories were of dawdling home through the darkening trees as evening fell, hearing turtledoves call in the distance.

"It's that same feeling of homecoming when you first come onto acid," he told me. "Forget the bells and whistles and floating ice cream cones, that feeling of recognition was always what mattered to me, instantly knowing you're back in the real place and on some level, you've been there all along. The same feeling I used to get on Communion night as a kid. That was my favorite time at church; the organ played softly in the hushed sanctuary—there wasn't quiet in our congregation otherwise—and I had the same swelling sense of meaning and return, although I didn't have words for it. Once I told my mother that I saw Jesus sitting next to me, but she said that kind of thing didn't happen anymore."

This sense of divine presence had been especially palpable to Mark during that long afternoon as he lay on his back staring up into the shifting leaves. "It wasn't about the acid," he told me. "I was already starting to come down by then anyway. It was more knowing that God was still there even if I wasn't, just as real as ever." Mark climbed atop a stone outcropping and shouted, "I love you God!" just as his friends appeared, having come looking for him. The phrase became a punchline among the group, though people eventually forgot where it came from, but the experience remained with Mark for the rest of his life.

Another watershed experience came in his forties, soon after he got sober. He attended a professional conference and found himself at loose ends on a Saturday afternoon, skipping the cocktail party and killing time before a dinner where he knew there would be heavy drinking. Walking in the rundown urban neighborhood around the hotel, he passed an old Catholic church and went inside, thinking he might find an AA meeting. He did not but a service was in progress, and he slipped into an empty pew at the back of the sanctuary. The acoustics were so poor that it took him a moment to realize the priest was speaking in a foreign language, Portuguese he found out later. Mark was waiting for an unobtrusive moment to slip out when the familiar feeling of homecoming washed over him. "I think it helped that I couldn't understand the language," he told me, "Which meant nobody said anything stupid to jar me out of the moment, or if they did, I didn't know it." When Communion came, he found himself walking forward with the others. "I couldn't have stopped myself if I tried," he explained a little defensively. "I didn't want to be disrespectful, but no thunderbolts came so I guess it was OK."

All these years later, the moment remained vivid in a way he could not articulate. For whatever reason, there was something deeply moving about shuffling forward with a group of strangers, just another guy in the crowd, surrounded by other people and for once not feeling separate. He felt intensely bonded to those around him and awed by their beauty, almost more than he could stand. There were serious little kids with their arms crossed for a blessing, a mother and son guiding an old man with a walker. After receiving Eucharist, he went out the back without waiting for the rest of service. A summer rain spattered the hot streets, and he could smell the wet pavement. Drifting in a kind of dream and totally in the moment, not knowing where he was going but certain of the direction, Mark wandered awhile as the rain petered out and the streets grew dark. The familiar sensation of fullness faded, although he tried to hang onto it. "Only to come crashing down to earth in a deserted strip mall. Like always happens," he added bitterly. "Talk about a perfect image." He angled out to a main boulevard and caught a cab back to the hotel where he ordered room service and sat in his room watching TV, "everything dry and stupid again."

"I went to Catholic churches a couple times after I got home," he went on, "even tried out different languages, Latin for God's sake, knowing I was just being superstitious. An Episcopalian church for good measure after a guy at a meeting called it user-friendly Catholicism. But it was all just dry and stupid, not the kind of Christian I'm not, as an old stoner friend from Sunday School days used to say whenever anybody talked about New Age religion. Looking back, I can see I missed the point, like my grandfather's joke about remembering a good fishing spot by marking it on the side of the boat."

In the end, Mark wound up filing the experience away with the other random flashes of meaning that did not pan out. The whole "Christian thing," as he dubbed it at the time, went back underground and stayed there until Jennifer asked him to accompany her to church on weekends when she had the kids. Things got off to a rocky start. The church was everything he remembered from childhood, minus the yelling and enthusiastic singing, and he numbed out, scanning the kids for signs of restlessness so he could take them out in the courtyard to play.

When the homecoming feeling came a few weeks after they started attending, it blindsided him. The denomination Jennifer had chosen celebrated Communion twice a month and he had been underwhelmed by these services, which felt more awkward than anything, but this time something was different. People had barely started filing forward when the familiar feeling swept over him, so strong he fought to keep from sobbing. Jennifer rolled her eyes at him when he stood to go with them, thinking he was being sarcastic, then saw his face and shot him a worried look. She said later she wondered if he had relapsed or was feeling guilty about an affair or something. "I imagine it did seem completely out of character," Mark grinned, "especially since I'd never said anything about the night in the cathedral or trying churches after I got back, just told her I was going to an AA meeting."

He brushed off Jennifer's nervous inquiries when they got to the car and waited anxiously to see whether it would happen the next time they went to church, but the service was "as meaningless as ever." He concluded that the wave of homecoming had been another of his one-off spiritual experiences. Then a couple weeks later it happened again, not even on Communion day. Just to make things completely confusing, he felt the rest of the service "was dumb as ever," and on the way home he railed about vapid sermons and the minister's ignorance regarding social issues until Jennifer begged him to stop.

After that, he cycled between moments of meaning that came out of nowhere and disappeared just as suddenly, not only in church but also walking in the park or simply driving to work. As I came to know Mark better over the next few months, I realized this was a life-long pattern—promising beginnings that never quite came to fruition and then left him desolate. That was what brought him to spiritual direction in the first place, although it took a while to put into words. He felt at a crossroads and did not know why.

"My life's fine on paper," he told me. "But I always feel like there's something more I should be doing, something big I can't seem to reach." In fact, there was much to celebrate in Mark's current life, which made his dissatisfaction even more bewildering. After the tumultuous years of his twenties and thirties, once he got into recovery, his life had stabilized. His work was engaging, if demanding, and offered more financial security than he had ever known. Despite areas of ongoing conflict, his home life was generally satisfying. Mark was not in therapy now but had found it helpful previously in dealing with relationship issues and the aftershocks of his chaotic childhood. He still had his moods but hadn't been seriously suicidal for years and no longer felt acutely depressed and angry all the time. Despite these positive developments, he felt plagued by an amorphous sense of unease. The flashes of significance that lit the sky and faded like fireworks offered both relief and disappointment, the solution and the problem, leaving him reading frantically and going to spiritual workshops, attending church in hopes it would happen again and feeling generally frustrated.

From a psychological perspective, Mark's pattern of promising beginnings that never quite panned out and his gnawing worry about running out of runway illustrate what Jungians call the puer dilemma.[11] Puer, which is short for puer aeternus or eternal youth, refers to the restless energy and sense of boundless possibilities that mark adolescence. Individuals who carry this stance into midlife often have a teenage quality, with all the pluses and minuses of that intense developmental phase. On the one hand, they display an appealing openness to new concepts and innovations, often accompanied by spontaneity and humor. On the other, they can be self-centered and prone to drama; the fear of settling gives their commitments a tentative feel. It takes hard work to turn flashes of insight into reality and their creativity can have the ungrounded quality associated with the image of a flying youth like Icarus or Peter Pan. The dilemma part of the puer dilemma has to do with the compromises required to turn brilliant ideas into accomplishments. Choosing one possibility means forsaking all others, in the words of the marriage vow, and eliminating options can feel like a kind of death—which in fact it is. What's doable always pales in comparison to what's imaginable. And while it is intoxicating to float in endless possibilities, time is a limited resource.

---

[11] Marie-Louise von Franz, *The Problem of the Puer Aeternus*.

Life in Neverland remains provisional, forever waiting for a future that never comes, with a growing risk that nothing will ever get solidified, like Mark's image of outrunning the runway.

Jung structured his theories in terms of opposites and the counterpoint to the youthful puer is the senex, or old man who upholds the established order.[12] There is much to be said for tradition, but the dark side of the conventional viewpoint is sometimes portrayed as a devouring father who cuts off emerging possibilities, like the Gospel story of Herod's Slaughter of the Innocents.

These two characters, puer and senex, usually appear together in myth and fiction. Common movie tropes include the aging cop and the defiant teenager, the head nun and the rebellious Catholic schoolgirl, the revolutionary and the military interrogator. Their drama plays out on the national stage during periods of upheaval, often with tragic results. Stability and innovation are both necessary to community life, and successful societies find ways to hold the two extremes in dynamic tension. On an individual level, the puer and senex can be pictured as aspects of the personality that lie on opposite poles of a continuum. A balance must be struck between fluid creativity and the structure needed to ground possibilities in practical reality. The fulcrum of this balance tends to shift over the life span; an attitude of open-ended exploration appropriate to a twenty-something can wear thin by fifty. This was graphically illustrated for me some years ago when a longtime "deadhead" called for psychotherapy following the death of the bandleader. She was a highly intelligent and creative woman in her late forties who, despite her youthful appearance, suddenly found herself faced with the reality of aging. She felt torn between preserving the freedom of her nomadic lifestyle and her desire for career and family. "I've done a lot of cool shit but never got around to having a life," she complained plaintively, "or maybe that's what life is."

Unlike her, Mark had managed to build a solid presence in the larger society after some initial stumbles. But despite outward successes, he had a similar sense of unrealized talents. As his life trajectory became increasingly clear, he found himself preoccupied with making his mark in the world and the diminishing likelihood of stellar achievements. Like the

---

[12] Andrew Samuels, Bani Shorter, and Fred Plaut, *A Critical Dictionary of Jungian Analysis*, 137.

nightmare image in the Peter Pan story of a pursuing crocodile who has swallowed an alarm clock, he had a nagging awareness of the inexorable advance of time. He felt his abilities were being underutilized in all aspects of his life and worried that he would never find his true calling, a weight of unrealized potential that he wryly described with the classic movie phrase: "I coulda been a contendah." At the same time, he knew intellectually that no mere job could satisfy this sense of unfulfilled mandate, which therapy had led him to associate with ways in which he carried the unlived dreams of his depressed mother. Feeling the clock ticking, he grieved over missed chances and dithered over present possibilities, all of which seemed inadequate. Early in our work together, he brought in a Tarot card that summarized the quandary for him, the Five of Cups, in which a man fixes his attention on three spilled goblets in front of him while ignoring the two full ones standing behind him.

In his spiritual life, this burden of dreams surfaced in a vague sense of being called but not knowing to what. Like seekers throughout the ages, part of what drew him to the spiritual quest was a yearning for intense experience that would lift him out of his humdrum existence. He described embarrassing fantasies of picturing himself as a great spiritual teacher, despite lacking a solid connection to any religious tradition or faith community. After the experience in the Portuguese church, he turned his considerable intellectual gifts to mastering the history of Christian spirituality. The journal entries he brought to our direction sessions oscillated between cerebral reflections on his latest reading and accounts of intense spiritual experiences that punctuated his pervasive sense of pointlessness. Over time, I came to visualize his spiritual life as an archipelago of volcanic peaks separated by vast expanses of empty sea.

In contrast to his early religious training, he felt little connection with the traditional Christian emphasis on relationship with God, experiencing his encounters in largely impersonal terms, what he called "the feeling of the real." All else paled by comparison and he was fond of repeating a line from T. S. Eliot's "Four Quartets" about the "waste sad time stretching before and after" these flashes of meaning. Although he was too polite to say so, I suspect he saw our sessions in similar terms, moments of real helpfulness with long dull stretches in between.

Despite jettisoning his religious faith as a teenager, Mark remained deeply involved with Christianity, as the story of his spiritual ambush in a random urban church makes clear. At the same time, he felt conflicted regarding nearly every aspect of the Christian faith, including core beliefs about the nature of God and God's relationship with human beings. As often happens, his picture of God was colored by negative experiences of church authority and darker aspects of his religious upbringing. In Mark's case, this inevitable contamination was intensified by the long shadow of his minister father.

In Jungian terms, God took on the complexion of a senex, a murderous Herod out to strangle the innocent baby Jesus. But it was not just a matter of projecting his childhood image of God onto Christianity as a whole and Christian settings where he found himself. Both positions existed inside him, senex and puer, although the latter lay much closer to the surface. The childhood faith he had walked away from and the rebellious teenager who did the walking were still fighting it out.

Christianity, like every religious tradition, can be viewed as an endless struggle between structure and spontaneity. Mark identified his spiritual life with sudden surges of feeling, an amorphous wind that blows where it will, but his inner Nicodemus, the Pharisee who represents the established order in the Gospel story, needed to have his say as well. The religious faith he had put away as a child retained the flat certainty of childhood and any attempt to humanize it felt wrong, "not the kind of Christian I'm not," as he put it. This split between the two halves of his inner experience made it hard for him to land anywhere, especially since it happened beneath the level of conscious awareness. Initial dreams have a way of laying out the crucial issues and hinting at the road ahead. A dream he brought to our second session neatly captures his dilemma and points the way out of this impasse.

I carry a bag I have taken from those trying to harm us. I am on a mission and seem to be the good guys. We are on a tour of the Holy Land. We walk through what looks like the old city, a scary maze of dark streets. Others carry knives but I walk in an unprotected way. A Palestinian woman greets me warmly. I hide the bag under my sweatshirt, despite the heat. It contains three eggs, among other objects. One is cracked and I throw it away and then throw another from the bus as we drive to make the bag less bulky. Later, I learn that one of the eggs contains the secret, like a magic ring, and will explode and destroy the world if dropped. By luck, I kept the right one. I consider going back to see what was in the others but decide that is impractical.

The hour was nearly over when he brought up the dream, and I told him we could return to it the next time if he wanted. In the meantime, I encouraged him to reflect on it further by writing down his initial reactions and giving the dream a name, which became the title of this chapter. The phrase he chose, "Unless an Egg Falls to the Ground," refers to Jesus's saying about how a grain of wheat cannot produce unless it falls to the ground and dies.[13] As expected, the associations he shared at our next meeting were mainly intellectual in nature. These included an internet image of the cosmic egg as the source of life and new possibilities, Lenin's remark that no omelet is made without breaking eggs, the magic ring of power in Tolkien's trilogy, and an enigmatic icon in which Mary of Egypt holds up an egg to which she points with the other hand. A more personal association involved a youthful visit to Israel where he wandered Jerusalem alone by night, the memory that provided the context for the dream.

I encouraged him to deepen his relationship with the dream's images by holding them in contemplative silence, paying particular attention to emotions and physical sensations. After several minutes of quiet reflection, Mark opened his eyes, and we began exploring how his internal reactions resonated with his day world experience. He had been especially struck by a familiar feeling of righteousness at being one of the "good guys," despite considerable ambiguity in the dream regarding the bag's origin and whose side he was on. The trite action movie phrase reminded him of his tendency to get embroiled in conflicts, bringing to them a moral certainty that he sometimes found embarrassing afterward. Mark said he no longer got in fistfights—something I had trouble imagining given his cerebral demeanor—but he often regretted his irritability with family members, coworkers, and other drivers, reactions that seemed to explode out of nowhere.

This brittle bellicosity contrasted with the comfortable feeling arising from his unprotected stance later in the dream, a sensation he associated with the "homecoming" moments in which he experienced a permeating sense of wellbeing. Being set in the Holy Land located the dream in the arena of his spiritual life, where he often felt like a tourist. His fear of walking alone through a maze of dark streets reminded him of his uneasy relationships with others, his pervasive feeling of loneliness, and a global

---

[13] John 12:24.

sense of being at sea in his life. He had no personal associations to the Palestinian woman but resonated viscerally with her warmth and the smiling eyes that drew him like an icon. The dream's conclusion left him agitated and physically uncomfortable. Moving deeper into this sensation, he realized that the image touched a deep fear of having thrown away great possibilities through carelessness, like the fairytale motif of tossing away the magic beans. He connected immediately with a paralyzing fear of making a mistake and the abyss of self-blame and second guessing into which it plunged him.

I encouraged Mark to take these images into his daily "reflection time," much the way that meditation in the Christian tradition involves mulling over a sacred text. (I had begun using this phrase after he objected to the word prayer, which reminded him of his Evangelical childhood, despite its prominent place in AA philosophy.) In our next session, he recounted a second dream that advanced the plot.

> *A woman I know in another context, in which she had authority, is a waitress in a restaurant. It looks like a coffee shop but is apparently quite exclusive and expensive. I drop by in the evening and join a group of friends. She brings me a menu and says she will highlight which entrees are available, as the restaurant closes in fifteen minutes, at 8:00. I have difficulty making sense of the menu. She offers a dish made with three eggs that has been rejected at another table, saying it costs $27, market price. I balk at the price and say I don't want it and won't order tonight but will come by another time. She agrees and adds that I do many things right, but her one criticism is that I don't seem to familiarize myself with the menu. This seems silly to me, and I smile as I join my friends at what is now an outdoor table at a downscale place by the beach, like the Seahorse.*

A few of Mark's personal associations may be helpful. He connected the looming pressure of closing time to his perennial worry he had missed his calling and was running out of time. Despite this sense of urgency, his decision to put off uncomfortable choices felt disturbingly familiar. So did his condescending smile in response to the waitress's admonition to familiarize himself with the menu, although he usually managed to keep such reactions to himself. The mention of a downscale burger joint where he used to drink with friends reminded him of the dark places his addiction took him and how he still romanticized the seamy side of life despite knowing better. Other themes that emerged during his subsequent reflection on the dream included discovering unexpected value in what had been judged worthless, like the Gospel passage about the rejected stone becoming the cornerstone. Seen in this light, the egg dish refused at another table reminded him of his decision in the earlier dream to throw out an egg that seemed "cracked" or crazy. "Appearances can be deceptive!!" he wrote in his journal. What looked like an ordinary coffee shop was an exclusive restaurant, in contrast to the cheap places where he drank with friends and always spent more than intended, often on cocaine.

Living with these two dreams over the next few weeks, it became clear to Mark that he was being asked to internalize whatever was represented by the image of the three eggs. Something external to him was being assimilated into his very being in a way that reminded him of receiving Communion. His inability to pin down the precise meaning of the image, despite repeated internet searches, mirrored the frustrating ambiguity that surrounded this unmarked crossroads in his life. The waitress's claim that he was not familiarizing himself with the menu was especially galling given the amount of effort he poured into his spiritual reading. Like most dream images, the critique resisted systematic interpretation, but he found himself remembering times when he had rejected possibilities out of hand without bothering to investigate them. He described the sensation accompanying these memories as a funny mix of big arrogance over not needing anybody's advice and a tiny feeling, "I couldn't possibly do that anyway." The intimation that he was not willing to pay the price irked him when he was giving his all to spiritual life and the process of discernment. I encouraged him to reflect further on the question and at our next session he described getting in touch with an embarrassing fear that something real was happening that might demand sacrifice. "You shoulda warned me that this stuff actually works," he quipped. "So much for informed consent."

Looking back on the dreams some months later, Mark saw them as harbingers of a deeper level opening in his spiritual journey and his resistance to entering it. In coming chapters I will track the tension between his search for God's will and the fear that he might find it, an all-too-human ambivalence he characterized as "wash my fur but don't get me wet."

Before concluding, it is worth noting the intimate interpenetration of personal psychology, religious symbols, and universal spiritual struggles observable in the dream images and the internal processes to which they point. Ambivalence over the cost of discipleship is a central motif in spiritual life, echoed in mystical accounts throughout the ages. For Mark, the universal human resistance to being relativized by the divine presence was intensified by a developmental struggle I have framed as the puer dilemma, in which grounding grand potentialities in quotidian reality means surrendering the illusion of unlimited possibilities. Coming to terms with this unavoidable loss requires facing ourselves in all our embarrassing humanness. In Jungian terminology that I will explicate in future chapters, the way to Self lies through the shadow.

Chapter 3

Is Not/Is Too: Spirituality and Psychology I

This book was conceived in a crowded airport lobby. Let me explain. It happened nearly ten years ago. Ten-thirty in the morning, Denver time, and I had been up since two. I had a ninety-minute layover and was searching for a quiet spot to do my morning readings, but dangling TV screens were everywhere. The only empty seat lay smack in front of one and a panel discussion was in progress. The presenters had finished talking by the time I sat down, and the moderator was wandering around the audience getting reactions. I was doing my best to tune out the chatter when he said something about religion, pulling me forward in my seat like a crack pipe draws an addict.

"God will not be mocked," intoned a gaunt man in the first row as the camera moved in for a close-up. His eyes locked mine and I glanced around nervously, wondering if I had wandered into a Twilight Zone. "God is real," the man continued, "and his nature is revealed in scripture."

"And the witness in our heart," the woman beside him added, glancing over nervously to see if she had overstepped.

The moderator pointed the microphone at a young woman who was gesturing in frustration behind the gaunt man. "It's all in your mind," she burst. "God's all in your mind!" People around her nodded in agreement, but I couldn't help wondering, so where else would God manifest?

"It's just the unconscious," her companion explained. "That's all God is."

And that's circular, the teacher in me objected, tautological if you want to be technical about it. One of those beard-stroking statements that repeats what you already know, like saying water is a wet substance. Unconscious refers to whatever I am not aware of, a kind of verbal placeholder, and since God is beyond comprehension that includes most of God most of the time. But her pronouncement made perfect sense to a good share of the audience, who nodded sagely. "Word magic," I muttered and smiled reassuringly at the couple beside me. Thinking you know what something is just because you give it a name.

All this by 10:40 and I had my meditation text without even opening the missal. It was hard to know where to start. One level of the dialogue was *ontological* and *epistemological,* what is and how we know it, respectively, another *sociological* with the splits in the culture on full display. Actually, not so much a dialogue as spliced monologues, I decided as the discussion ground on, people talking past each other with increasing vehemence. Two perspectives were coalescing and neither had much patience for the other.

"You just want a big daddy in the sky," a young man with a nose ring jeered. The usual clichés but just below the surface lurked fundamental questions that have preoccupied spiritual questers for centuries.

Is God out there or in here or both? A projected part of ourselves or the source of who we are, and how would we know the difference? Does this ultimate source have a personality or is that just a function of anthropomorphic wiring? And how does psychology fit into the discussion, beyond a handy way to dismiss religion by labeling it? If human beings are made in God's image, whatever that means, does our own psychology tell us anything about divine nature? If not, where else do we start looking?

The questions just kept multiplying, filling the page in my journal. Everyone seemed so sure of themselves, but for me the uncertainties outnumbered the answers, starting with do we know God or not? Yes and no, I decided, depending on what you mean by *know*. Scripture has plenty to say about God but keeps insisting that no one knows God but God, and the main experience of biblical characters who do meet God is that "he" acts in ways that confuse and surprise them.

"I'm spiritual without being religious," a young woman with a matching nose ring piped up. I hear this sentiment occasionally from directees, and it always intrigues me. Who would disagree that spirituality is more than religious creeds and symbols? But no matter how you mix and match, those same beliefs and religious images are the basic building blocks of any spiritual practice, the content that gives spirituality shape. I remember a friend from college who joined a commune dedicated to living in accordance with Black Elk's vision, the Bhagavad Gita, the Four Noble Truths, and the Sermon on the Mount.

Put another way, spirituality is a vast continent and religions are the roads running through it. Every faith tradition has unique strengths and viewing the terrain from another religious perspective lets us see our own with new eyes. At the same time, spiritual teachers across the spectrum warn that people who pick and choose pieces of different faith traditions run the risk of only selecting the easy parts that reinforce what they want to believe, like the old jibe about cafeteria Catholics. Students of religion describe a universal struggle between established dogma and individual experience, law and spirit, the knowers and the seekers. Interpretation of sacred texts veers back and forth between the literal and the metaphorical, eternal truth and things said for a particular time and place. Growing up, we used to tweak our teetotaling Baptist elders with Paul's admonition to Timothy to drink a little wine for the stomach, just as today's teenagers no doubt ask their Sunday School teachers, so if head coverings for women are cultural, what about same-sex marriage?

"It's what I said the first time," the young woman in the second row blurted, interrupting my musings. "God's all in your mind."

"No honey," the gaunt man answered patiently, "God loves you and has a wonderful plan for your life if you'd only give him a chance."

"That's absurd," she shot back, "it's all wishful thinking and money-grubbing."

"It isn't ..." he began.

She interrupted him. "But it is! It's just your mind!"

I could see heads bobbing in the audience, first one group and then the other, and pictured the crowd breaking into call-and-response like a scene from a musical, the classic playground argument of is not/is too. As usual, I felt split down the middle. The young woman is right about God's voice coming through the unconscious, I decided, but that does not mean they are the same thing; the medium is not necessarily the message.

Now I am doing it too, I thought, treating the unconscious like a something when it is just a negative boundary construct. And the smug young man with the big daddy comment? Well, of course, we build our image of God from our own experience—what we fear and long for. How else would we visualize what's beyond conceptualization? That's part of what spiritual direction is for, helping people claim their spiritual baggage. And the old man who looks like a prophet from central casting? He's right too. Every image of divinity comes from somebody's revealed text and figuring how to relate to them has been a primary concern of human beings since we came down out of the trees, probably before.

We lined up to board, and I shuffled down the aisle to my seat, still pondering. Is God reducible to psychology as the young woman claimed or totally separate, wholly other in the language I grew up with? As the city dropped away beneath us, a new and uncomfortable thought began bouncing around my brain. Leaving aside the overheated verbiage, this is the same question that interrupts my sleep, the one that just will not go away.

The question about the tangled relationship between psychology and spirituality, to be precise, my two hats as a helper. Partly it depends on what you mean by psychology. Spirituality too, but let's start with the field I am supposed to know about, even taught for a while. So, what is psychology, Mr. Psychologist?

A million different things, when you stop to think about it, but why not begin with what I used to tell my intro class. The very first day, right after roll call, when we addressed the all-important question: what is psychology? Or in the hedged language of academia, what constitutes the central characteristics of the psychological paradigm?

I pictured writing out the words on a white board, the faint squeak and chemical smell of the marker. It had been years since I taught in the training program, but the handout was still living happily in the cloud, I discovered once the captain's voice came over the PA to say we had reached our cruising altitude and electronic devices were permitted. I scrolled down to the handout at the end and skimmed through the text, wincing at non sequiturs and typos I hadn't noticed at the time.

Lecture I: Central Characteristics of the Psychological Paradigm from a Clinical Perspective

Characteristic One: Multidimensional. The seeming monopoly of conscious awareness and personal choice is relativized by non-conscious forces operating within the individual. A core assumption shared by schools as diverse as depth psychology and cognitive/behavioral therapy is that actions and beliefs reflect forces and learned responses beyond immediate awareness.

Characteristic Two: Developmental. Current neuropsychological research supports the emphasis most psychological schools place on the role of early experience in shaping thought, emotion, perception, and behavior. This assumes a developmental approach to human growth, in which unfolding physical, cognitive, and emotional abilities create windows of maximum receptivity to outside influences. Development occurs unevenly along multiple dimensions: biological, emotional, psychological, relational, and cognitive, and progresses through a sort of dialogue between external situations and changing biological capacities.

Characteristic Three: Relational. Relationships play a crucial role in the initial formation of core perspectives and subsequent reworking of their limitations. Just as they provide the context in which these response sets are established, relationships offer the best place for healing their distortions, whether with a partner, children, a friend, or a therapist. Unfortunately, relationships also can reinforce maladaptive schemas, so that it sometimes seems as though individuals walk around auditioning for the lead in their traumatic script. Such stuck places are where a focused and accepting relationship like the one offered by therapy can be especially helpful in identifying problematic patterns and facilitating change.

Characteristic Four: Affective/Emotional. Positive change is facilitated by an accepting and attuned feeling tone in key relationships, including therapy. This attitude creates an atmosphere in which polarized aspects of experience can be reconciled, which leads to greater internal awareness and a more balanced and open stance toward the world. Psychology's emphasis on the feeling tone of these important relationships highlights the role of emotion in how humans perceive and interpret the world. Our neurological system is programed for relationship and literally programed by it. Many neural pathways can only be activated during interactions with caregivers during a specific life stage and the feeling tone of these exchanges creates the lens through which the individual views the world. Accessing and identifying feelings, an important function of psychotherapy, allows them to be integrated into conscious awareness. Increased emotional integration lends nuance and coherence to individuals' experience of the world and eases the tendency toward rigidity or disorganization that marks many psychological difficulties. Improved accuracy and flexibility in reading and responding to the world unfolds through relationships and folds back into relationships in turn, making them more satisfying.

Characteristic Five: Experiential. The therapeutic process is experiential and rooted in a biological substratum. Tracking internal experience through interoception (moment-by-moment focus on bodily sensations, emotions, and thoughts) helps create a framework for psychological integration and management of mood disturbances. The gaze of therapy is dual, with one eye turned outward on relationships and how clients move through the world while the other looks inward to capture the play of thoughts, memory, sensation, and fantasy. Tracking the ongoing flow of emotions, thoughts, and perceptions helps establish the base of self-awareness needed to change old patterns. The last few decades have witnessed increased interest in facilitating direct experience of the shifting and embodied nature of human awareness through techniques like mindfulness and incorporation of non-verbal strategies to access internal experience through art and movement therapies.

Characteristic Six: Cultural. Psychological development and functioning cannot be separated from the larger cultural and societal context. Factors like gender, ethnicity, immigration status, economic class, and sexual orientation are crucial in understanding the worldviews of the client and therapist, as well as the interaction between them. For much of its short history, psychology has focused on individual and familial aspects of development at the expense of the larger social milieu. In recent decades, this deficiency has been balanced by increased awareness of the impact of culture, broadly defined to include factors like ethnicity, gender, religion, sexual identity, and economic status. The multicultural movement that began as an effort to be sensitive to cultural dimensions of clients' experience soon broadened to include the clinician since both bring social markers into the room that mirror patterns in the larger society. The heightened awareness of power dynamics emerging from the civil rights and feminist movements brought attention to the cultural context in which the therapeutic encounter occurs and social realities that encompass both client and clinician. Inherent power differences are intensified by the highly structured and often cerebral nature of the therapeutic interaction, a stylized way of relating that gives the therapist a "home court advantage."

***

Glad I quit teaching, I decided, struggling to focus as I forced myself to plod through the handout a second time. No doubt my former students would agree. Psychology gets sliced lots of different ways, but assuming these categories have at least some validity, how does spirituality compare along the same parameters? I reclined my seat and stared out the airplane window at the clouds before returning to my keyboard, typing frenetically, and toggling occasionally between documents to remind myself what the handout said.

***

Multidimensional

In the context of psychology, multidimensionality basically means we happen on multiple dimensions at once. Internal forces interact with each other constantly at a level below awareness. External ones as well, to the extent we can separate them. The whole tradition of applied spirituality would definitely endorse that one. Teresa of Ávila and her buddy John of the Cross as well as Luther, Cassian, even the Apostle Paul with his plaintive lament about doing what he would not do. Unseen forces are a major concern of every spiritual system and pretty much all of them describe opening our narrow and distorted self-focus to a larger awareness. The whole point of Ignatian spirituality is being sensitive to subtle internal movements so that God has free rein to release what's restricted and loosen the chains of limiting expectation. The same goal as psychological healing, but psychology is pretty much clueless when it comes to the impact of spiritual forces. Not just clueless but contemptuous, or at least subtly condescending.

Developmental

Psychology and spirituality both see the person in developmental terms. There are literally thousands of models of spiritual development. Spiritual practitioners mature in faith over the course of their lives, and religious traditions evolve in response to cultural shifts. Images of God change with society, from lord of the manor to the man upstairs, and metaphors for spiritual life morph with technology, from sheep herding to computer processing.

If psychology is clueless about the spiritual dimensions of human experience, spiritual systems falter when it comes to human development over the lifespan. Here psychology shines, both in terms of identifying developmental stages—what to expect from a girl of twelve or a man of seventy—and the impact of individual history on psychological development. The people encountered in a day are all at different stages in their lives with very different backgrounds and personalities. To complicate things further, development tends to be uneven across different life domains so somebody can function like a thirty-year-old intellectually and a ten-year-old in relationships or vice versa. That makes a huge difference when it comes spiritual direction. Most spiritual guides have good intuitions but no systematic model of human development. Things get especially complicated around psychological wounding, which shapes personality and relationships, including the one with God. That's where Jung stands out, arguably the only psychological theorist with a fully articulated model that integrates psychological and spiritual development.

Relational

Relationships are important in shaping personality and facilitating personality change. Religion also stresses the role of relationship in catalyzing transformation, whether with a divine being or an inspired teacher in non-theistic approaches like Buddhism. Spiritual writers offer lots of suggestions for working with different kinds of personalities and their implications for spiritual development. Systems like the Enneagram provide sophisticated models of different personality types and the relationship patterns associated with each. What's missing is a nuanced way to understand individual human beings in all their complexity and the impact of important relationships and life events on a given person with a particular life situation and constellation of personality traits. There is often a kind of impatience when you raise the issue, as a job best left to psychology, as though the permutations of relationship and personality are beneath the notice of spirituality.

This is especially odd in the case of Christianity, which focuses on the individual and is deeply relational in orientation. The Incarnation means God entered psychology as a particular human being, an infant dependent on his mother's love. Not just for survival but to unfold as a functioning person who could talk, manage his bowels and feelings, and take other people into account. The story did not end in the manger because God was also a nine-year-old in need of playmates, a twelve-year-old who tried his parents' patience with his nonchalant response when they finally located him after three days of frantic searching, and a thirty-three-year-old who told his friends he eagerly desired to share a last meal with them before his torturous death.

Emotional

This category stresses the centrality of emotion in psychology. From a psychological viewpoint, emotion is what determines salience, enabling us to sort through the vast array of stimuli bombarding us so we can focus on what's most important. Psychology is especially good at examining the nuances of emotion and ways that feeling can distort interpretations of people and situations (looking at the world through shit-smeared glasses, an old supervisor of mine used to say). In psychotherapy, emotion is the lodestar that orients the client and clinician. No matter how brilliant a therapist's interpretation may be, if it does not feel right to the client, it probably is not. And whatever the problems between a couple, if there is sufficient goodwill to enter into the partner's emotional world and feel their experience, the relationship can usually find a way forward. Psychological research strongly suggests we make our decisions based on emotion and figure out our reasons afterward.

This happens in religious conversion and religious belief in general, from Paul knocked off his horse to my nine-year-old self stunned to find myself walking forward in the stifling frame church to be prayed over by the elders. Emotion is key to religious experience and spiritual direction. Ignatius is called the mystic of moods for his meticulous attention to shifting feelings of desolation and consolation in trying to discern between different kinds of spiritual stirrings. A quick look at Psalms demonstrates that the whole range of human emotions are woven into scripture: love, hate, anger, exultation, despair, guilt, revenge, shame, terror, and trust. Religious worship explicitly cultivates emotion using all the senses, plays on it, critics say, with music and sonorous phrases, stirring messages, and comforting rituals.

Experiential

Experience is everything when it comes to psychology and psychological change, the goal, and the method. A major aim of therapy is helping people become aware of what's going on inside and around them. The handout talked about a dual gaze that encompasses both. This requires cultivating what's sometimes called an *observing ego* that can track the ongoing flow of thoughts, memory, emotions, and sensations without being completely caught up in them (keeping one toe out of the emotional river, I sometimes explain to clients). Developing this capacity creates a kind of meta-awareness that increases their freedom in choosing how to respond to situations as they come up.

Here too, spirituality and psychology find common ground, beginning with the fact that psychology addresses this goal with mindfulness techniques that were developed in spiritual settings. Spirituality is nothing if not experiential; it is sometimes defined as having direct *experience* of God instead of *ideas* about God. In John's Gospel, the Samaritan woman's neighbors told her we do not believe because of what you told us but because we saw for ourselves. Psychology's emphasis on nonverbal dimensions of experience is strongly echoed in religious ritual and practice. Although religious dogma sometimes downplays physical aspects of life, spiritual practice is deeply embodied. Across the religious spectrum, contemplative practices deepen awareness of our intimate connection with the natural world. Religious rituals are participatory on all levels, appealing to sight, hearing, touch, and smell with pageantry and incense, and involving the body with prostrations, kneeling, and hand gestures.

Cultural

This last category stipulates that people are deeply embedded in culture and cannot be understood apart from it. As a social institution, religion is intimately intertwined with culture and often has a strong ethnic component, with all the pluses and minuses of group identification. Like all social entities, religious institutions mirror the ambivalent qualities of the individuals who comprise them. They provide a powerful source of solidarity and communal identity, but their shadow side emerges in religious chauvinism that can give rise to violence. Religion is a powerful voice for both radical change and preservation of the status quo, often at the same time. Like the election in Central America when a Marxist priest and a fascist priest were both running for office. Conservatives and progressives find scriptural backing on every issue, from income disparity to birth control, often with little regard to the original cultural context.

Christianity, Buddhism, and Islam proved particularly adaptable in moving across cultures, assuming different forms in different places, from the rich iconography of Tibetan Buddhism to the radical iconoclasm of Zen. The resulting syncretism drives purists mad and makes for interesting overlays, like the Guatemalan campesino who pointed to a roadside shrine and told me, "The Spanish call him San Simon but we still use the old name," that of a particularly raucous Mayan deity worshiped with rum and cigars who happened to have the same feast day. From this perspective, spirituality provides an overarching structure that reorganizes existing social patterns and reinterprets old belief systems, although the inherent conservatism of religious institutions can make them cling to outworn mores long after the culture has moved on.

***

I paused to read back over what I had written with a sinking feeling. This compare and contrast is not getting us anywhere, I decided. Juggling abstractions, my own kind of word magic. Psychology and spirituality share some structural components but so what? Both may talk about unseen forces, but they mean very different things. And construing the world in developmental and relational terms is just being human.

Okay, so let's forget categories. How about a clever metaphor that captures their relationship, like separate but adjacent fields growing equally nutritious though entirely different crops? That's the standard party line, although neither side really believes the equally nutritious part. Despite their overlap, psychology and spirituality certainly appear to be doing different things. The differences are most evident at the extremes, like patients with panic disorders who just need a quick round of cognitive behavioral therapy—although even that has a way of dropping into existential depths.

But what on earth would spirituality look like apart from a human personality, with all its hurt feelings and job issues? Okay then, how about two aspects of a unitary process of growth and development? Except one does not necessarily translate into the other, like advanced meditators I have seen for eating disorders and the constant drip of sex scandals, not just in the Catholic Church but also in dharma centers and ashrams. Tibetans say not to choose a lama from your same valley, and a prophet is not without honor except in his hometown. Even the Apostle Paul had issues if you read between the lines—whatever his mysterious thorn in the flesh may have been.

So how about mutually supportive structures, like parallel train tracks that never meet but between them take us where we need to go? Except they will not stay apart! I felt a sudden urge to stand up and wave my arms in frustration like the young woman on the talk show. Like a legally separated couple who keeps sneaking back together, they hook up in spiritual practice and spiritual direction, daily life for that matter. Not to mention the fact that Jesus spent much of his time healing people who'd carry a psychiatric diagnosis today.

I had already shut down my laptop in discouragement when the captain's voice came on the overhead to tell us to turn off electronic devices, that we were beginning our descent and the weather in Sacramento was ungodly hot. So maybe I have been thinking about this all wrong, I mused, as farmland gave way to suburbs on the ground below. Overcomplicating things as usual, we murder to dissect, as Wordsworth said. Suppose psychology and spirituality are just two ways of looking at the same thing—person actually—and the split between them is a function of our limited thinking.

We are created in God's image, according to the Bible, and God's story is all mixed up with ours. How can you separate spiritual life from being a personality living in the world, the domain of psychology? The whole point of Incarnation is God happening in human form and walking among us, subject to the same pushes and pulls, so we can find God in our own draws and drives and sorrows and joys.

Spirituality cannot help incorporating culture because people live in society and every religious system operates from culturally based psychological model, from astrology to Christian Science, whether its adherents know it or not. Those models lag in the culture during times of change, and right now our spiritual anthropology does not fully reflect how we see ourselves, as psychological beings shaped by personal history and the confluence of developmental and cultural forces.

At this point we still lack a comprehensive theory that can integrate psychology and religion with each other and our scientific models, which are in flux themselves. Which leaves spiritually oriented people with lousy options. We can live in a split world, cobble together our own makeshift system, or do our best with the existing models. And there the pickings are slim.

Naturally I am partial to Jung's spiritually oriented model of psychological development (or psychologically oriented model of spiritual development), but he has limitations too. His basic premise is simple: the divine voice speaks within and learning to hear the guidance emerging from our sustaining depths allows us to encounter it in a personal way. "The witness in our hearts," in the language of the woman in the television audience whose words sank without a ripple in the polarized crowd, prompting our longings and recalling what's forgotten or dimly remembered.

But the divine voice's work goes beyond simply nudging us along. Like the householder in the parable who brings out treasures old and new, it rummages its storehouse of symbols for just the right guiding image. If the old treasures in the parable are traditional sacred symbols and the new ones are novel images specific to the person, both serve as signposts on the road home, to mix metaphors. Any good teacher knows to use examples drawn from the lives of her students and tailored to their unique experience, which is exactly what the inner teacher does. I have watched it happen in my own dreams and those of clients, but how do you communicate what that's like to someone who has not seen it in action? The way it unfolds in individual lives is truly miraculous but incomprehensible without knowing the person and what those images mean. The indwelling spirit blows where it will but who can describe its movements? Without direct experience whatever you say is just so much abstraction, the same problem as trying to prove religion.

The plane touched down with a bump, jarring me out of my revery. I felt a superstitious urgency to solve the conundrum before disembarking, but the answer did not come until nearly two months later and then it was gnomic as an oracle. I was washing dishes when the phrase "show don't tell" swam into awareness, apropos of nothing, the standard advice to beginning students in creative writing programs. I waited politely for clarification, but it did not arrive for several more years when Mark's bundle of dreams dropped into my lap.

Chapter 4
Finding God in the Ditch

Once Mark made up his mind to work with me, he approached our sessions with great seriousness. He arrived early to go over his notes in the waiting room and began each hour with a list of topics he wanted to cover, including recent dreams and questions from his reading. Being with him felt often like drinking out of a firehose, and I sometimes had trouble keeping up, especially when he shared dense passages about spiritual books from his journal. Mark was clearly frustrated with my efforts to slow the pace of our sessions and pause periodically for reflection but said nothing, even when I tried to broach the topic.

His dreams came in torrents, and it was impossible to look at them all in an hour, which also left him frustrated. Those dreams are a primary focus in this chapter and others that follow, although they were not the only aspect of our work together. There are several reasons for this. Mark's dreams are unusually comprehensive and depict major developments in his inner and outer life with a vividness that's hard to capture in any other way. At the same time, they provide a good window on Jung's distinctive way of working with spiritual material, and my discussion will approach them from that perspective, using language and concepts that will be clarified in future chapters. The final reason for concentrating on dreams is practical and has to do with their central place in Mark's inner life. God's movement shows up differently for different people, and I suspect part of the reason dreams played such an important role for him was their ability to bypass his intellect and go straight to the heart of the matter. He had a natural affinity for symbolic work and booked our first appointment after checking online and discovering I was also a Jungian analyst. He had some familiarity with Jung's ideas, which proved a mixed blessing. I was wary of being drawn into theoretical discussions, given his tendency to intellectualize, and my failure to provide the kind of conceptual explication offered in this book soon became another source of frustration.

Like his interest in Jung, Mark's spiritual reading provided a helpful framework but accentuated his tendency to stay stuck in his head. He read voraciously and the titles varied wildly, from process theology to texts from the *Philokalia,* a compilation of early Eastern Orthodox writings, a reading list organized around his determination to integrate the Christianity of his childhood with his current spiritual perspective. His literary intake was truly astounding, and he told me with evident pride that his wife once remarked he inhaled spiritual literature the way her teenaged students ate pizza.

With my encouragement, he began setting aside a brief time of silent reflection before starting his morning reading, during which he did not so much collect his thoughts as simply observe the internal weather that day. Also at my suggestion, he ended most evenings with an "examination of consciousness" modeled on the Ignatian *examen of conscience,*[14] a practice that reminded Mark of the daily inventory recommended in AA. After briefly reviewing the events of the day, he would scan for moments when he felt God's presence and his response to the invitation.

"I know what you're doing," he told me with a grin, "and just for the record that's not prayer." When I expressed puzzlement, he told me that as a child he had been adept at elaborate public prayers, full of thees and thous, which he now realized were mainly a way to show off. His private prayer during that time had been largely petitionary, long lists of concerns and requests addressed to what he now called the "Santa Claus God." Despite his dismissive tone, when I inquired further into his early prayer life, he acknowledged there also had been spontaneous times of simply talking to God while still insisting this was not prayer. Clearly Mark's childhood experience had left a bad taste in his mouth, and the whole concept of prayer felt tainted for him. "I don't mind hanging out with God but I'm not praying," he told me earnestly, a phrase that evolved into a running joke between us.

This struggle to find an authentic way of connecting with the holy was a central theme throughout our work together. Previous chapters described Mark's split experience of Christianity. There was something morally repugnant about finding himself back in a Christian context and

---

[14] Ignatius of Loyola, *Spiritual Exercises,* 38, ¶43.

he said the whole thing felt stupid and unreal apart from those random moments of clarity and meaning that brought tears to his eyes.

This inner conflict coalesced around three major themes that recurred throughout his journal. The most central involved what it meant to have a personal relationship with God at this point in his life. As a child, he had experienced Jesus as a companion and protector but that seemed suspicious to him now. "I think it was mainly psychological," he told me, "an imaginary friend who knew what it was like to have a punitive father." His current experience of God was more diffuse, a place or state that came over him in unpredictable ways, but he sometimes longed for the kind of intimate connection he had felt in childhood.

A second preoccupation had to do with his relationship with scripture and the model of literal inspiration he had grown up with. Here, too, his experience was split. "I get the historical/critical method and source analysis and everything modern biblical criticism has to offer," he told me, "I really do. I know it's important but part of me can't help wondering—and it feels stupid to say—what's gonna be left of the sweater once you start pulling the threads?"

A third concern revolved around the meaning of Jesus's death. "Even as a kid I had trouble wrapping my head around the idea that Jesus died for my sins so I can go to heaven," he told me. "Vicarious atonement never really grabbed me, even back then, but there's something compelling in the idea of sacrificial death. It's like the Zen saying about a red-hot ball you can't swallow and can't cough up. I can't take it in, and I can't let it go." Mark paused a moment before continuing. "Actually, that's a little hyperbolic, even for me. Maybe not so much a red-hot ball as something stuck in my craw. That's a real thing, you know, lots of birds have a sort of bag on the esophagus where they hold food before swallowing it. My grandmother raised chickens, and they sometimes get this condition called sour crop, crop's the same as craw, when they can't digest their food and it just sits there. Pretty soon it starts rotting and if apple vinegar doesn't clear it up you have to massage the gunk out manually. Sorry for the gross analogy but that's how Christianity feels sometimes, like it's stuck in my throat and I can't swallow and can't get rid of it."

These were big theological issues, to say the least, and Mark realized there was something grandiose about his determination to resolve them. At the same time, he was clearly disappointed I could not offer more insight on them or the books he was reading. Perhaps partly in response, his focus during sessions gradually shifted to situations in his life. Increasingly dissatisfied at work, he obsessed over where his future ministry lay and whether it would offer a way out his current employment. Things had grown more difficult in his personal life as well. He described increasing conflict in his marriage and recurrent episodes of depression that brought a feeling of inner deadness. His heart literally ached, a pressure in his chest that sometimes made it hard to breath. "The spiritual path is a tease," he complained, "like when you walk the labyrinth. The first few steps head straight for the center, and you think you're almost there but the longer you walk the farther away you get."

I encouraged him to discuss this discouragement with God during his times of reflection, carefully avoiding the word *prayer*. I also suggested paying particular attention to the texture of what he called his "God moments." These were brief times when he felt ambushed by joy, "consolation without prior cause" in Ignatian terms, sudden flashes of vitality and joy that arrived on their own timetable.[15]

A couple months into our work together, Mark had two dreams he found especially gripping. They seemed to shed light on the issue, or at least clarify his situation. His first impulse on waking was to look up the images on the internet, a method he called consulting "Guru Google," but he remembered that I had encouraged him to sit with them first, paying attention to his sensations and emotions. Despite his lack of artistic talent, he found that his reflection on them was enhanced by sketching the images with colored markers, something I had suggested. The first dream was quite short.

> *I am walking downhill with my Evangelical sister, involved in a theological disagreement. I point out God as a ditch dug in a straight line across a barren landscape. This isn't rhetoric but literally true, in line with the prophecy about John the Baptist. The ditch is about 18" wide and a couple feet deep, as though for irrigation or a water pipe.*

As Mark sat quietly with the dream, the image of the ditch took on a life of its own. I encouraged him to experience the dream with all his senses, like the Ignatian method of *imaginative prayer*. He had grown up around

---

[15] Ignatius, 128, ¶336.

farming and the scene was vivid for him. The dusty heat of midday and the smell of water, the play of light on its dull brown surface and the gushing sound as it spilled into a new row. There was something deeply stirring about watching it flow, cool and vivifying, the only thing moving in the hot stillness.

I asked him how God was the ditch, noting that the dream equated them, and he looked at me with a startled expression. On reflection, Mark said he found the question intellectually appealing but a little shocking to his "inner Evangelical." I pointed out that the dialogue between these two parts of himself was the context of the dream itself, framed as a theological dispute between his Evangelical sister and the dreamer. I speculated that the opening image seemed to suggest that returning to the religious world of his childhood felt like going downhill to the part of him engaged in serious theological debate, although this was the very place where he felt stuck.

Resting with this dilemma for a few minutes, Mark reported that the progressive Christian in him applauded how the dream shifted away from paternal images of God. He knew that conflicts with his minister father played a big part in his difficulty relating to God in personal terms, but to the Evangelical side of him, seeing God as a ditch was beneath comment. Although he felt absurd saying it, Mark even worried that simply entertaining the idea might be blasphemy against the Holy Spirit, the unforgivable sin when he was growing up. On the other hand, the banality of the image bothered the liberal side of him as well. "It's like a Monty Python bit," he confessed ruefully. "God as a muddy ditch. Plus, I keep remembering the stupid joke about busy ditches." I looked confused, and he glanced down, embarrassed, then continued. "I forget the details but it's something sexist about dizzy blonds and the Panama Canal. One is a busy ditch and the other, well anyway ..."

His remaining reflections on the dream were more cerebral in tone. He had grown up in dry country and resonated with the water imagery that permeates the scriptures, from the tree planted beside the river to Jesus's offer of living water. He had never really thought about all the bible passages that describe God in terms of natural phenomena, from rocks and trees to mountains and wind, but the dream seemed to be insisting that he take them literally. Seeing God in the running water and the dirt that contained it reminded him of Paul's image of holding treasure in earthen vessels. He struggled without success to assign precise meaning to the ditch's dimensions, and I encouraged him to let the image keep its mysteries and rest with the big picture. In keeping with a common dream pattern, it vacillated between two alternatives, an irrigation ditch associated with farming and a water pipe Mark linked to construction sites he had worked on as a young man. Taken together, they implied the living water was available for all creation, plants as well as people.

The dream's oblique mention of John the Baptist is typical of how passing allusions build a web of interlocking images. Given his upbringing, Mark recognized at once the underlying reference to Isaiah's prophecy about rivers in the desert and a path across the wasteland, which the Gospel writers applied to John's role in preparing the way for Jesus's ministry. Mark had mixed feelings about the figure of John the Baptist. As a disaffected teenager in the Baptist church, he got sick of pointed comparisons to his own long hair and questions about eating grasshoppers, based on John the Baptist's diet of locusts and wild honey. Reconnecting with Christianity as an adult, he saw John as a role model, a fearless advocate for social justice in defiance of the established order.

"There's something tragic about his position," Mark told me, "A transitional figure caught between the old dispensation and the new." He warmed to the topic as he spoke, becoming briefly tearful when he described the moment John declares that Jesus must increase while he must decrease.

Mark found the dream's implicit promise that the Messiah was coming into his life at once thrilling and unsettling. Personalizing prophecy felt exciting but a bit much, naive to the progressive Christian in him and blasphemous to his inner Evangelical. I encouraged him to locate these reactions in his body, and he described the first as heady giddiness, the second as a fluttery hollowness in his chest.

The second dream was more complicated:

My mother and I are walking on a dirt road, accompanied by another man about my age. Although it doesn't look like it, I know this is the road on the land behind the house where I grew up. A path branches off to the left, headed for the beach (not factual). It has tire tracks on it and seems overused. My mother points out a new road a few hundred yards further. As we approach, a fierce brown dog bars the path. I notice he is tied to a picnic bench with a bright, braided rope. We approach the turn and find three middle-aged blond women, perhaps sisters, and three dogs blocking the turn-off. I know they are dead, like the resuscitated woman in American Gods.[16] The man with us attacks one, then nearly severs the head of another with a metal spatula. She merely pauses and readjusts her head, her neck healing. I know they intend to kill us and give a speech, thanking them for making the situation clear and apologizing for our behavior. They offer to let my mother and me go if we abandon the other man. I refuse but say I will die so the other two can escape. My mother refuses the deal. I ask for mercy, and they agree, saying they are dedicated to the Virgin Mary and so must be merciful, especially given our attitude of self-sacrifice.

This dream also placed Mark back in his childhood environment, now accompanied by his mother and an unknown man his current age. As often happens, the setting both was and was not the world he had known as a child, the old place seen from a new perspective. The wild land behind his house had been his refuge as a child. He felt a deep affinity with nature and had experiences there which he now viewed as mystical, although back then they seemed completely unrelated to his religious life in church. As with the earlier dream, his associations linked references to water with a new spiritual dimension in his life. His childhood home lay far from any beaches, but when he lived near the ocean later in his life, Mark experienced a similar rush of the holy when he crested the hill above the shoreline, catching the sound of faraway breakers and the first whiff of sea air.

In the mythological amplification provided by "Guru Google," the watery depths are typically associated with the unknown, the unconscious in psychological parlance, a source of monsters and new life. The branching paths in the dream reminded him of the Robert Frost poem about two roads diverging in the woods and the Gospel saying about the narrow road to life and the broad highway to destruction. On reflection, this recalled the current struggle to find his true path, a "straight gate" in the King James translation of his childhood.

In the dream, it appears that the old road worn with use no longer works for him, and his mother obligingly points out a new path. At this

---

[16] Gaiman, *American Gods*.

point, the dream has finished setting the stage and introduces the issue or difficulty it will explore. From a childish perspective, the problem is resolved: what could go wrong with mommy's advice? Lots, apparently. When Mark put himself back in the dream, the subsequent complications felt somehow unfair, like his earlier complaint about the path veering away from the center when he walked the labyrinth.

In a heady montage of Greek mythology, he associated the women with the three Fates who spin, measure, and cut the thread of life. The reference echoed his fear that life was passing him by while he searched for his calling. The braided rope holding the dog reminded him of the thread of life spun by the Fates, and its unspooling had an ambivalent quality, protecting the dreamer from harm but preventing the dog from running free. I had trouble following this last part, which had to do with Mark's mixed feelings about the increased security adulthood offered, but it rang true to him. That was the real test, of course, since the point was not arriving at the true interpretation but connecting with the deep patterns that he had difficulty accessing.

He linked the brown dog who becomes three dogs with internet images of Cerberus, the three-headed guardian of the underworld, after rejecting the idea of the Trinity. In psychological terms, guardians at the threshold depict the difficulties associated with transition to a new way of being. The three women in the dream are themselves dead, like underworld rulers in many mythologies, perhaps another indication of an outworn attitude. In the novel referenced by the dream, a deceased woman is brought to life with a magic talisman and becomes an animated corpse with uncanny powers. This zombie image suggests unnatural perseverance of an old pattern that has continued past its time and needs to die. Mark's reference to Cerberus evokes the classic theme of descent into the underworld, a journey of death and rebirth undertaken by heroes like Gilgamesh and Orpheus.

Translated into personal psychology, the theme of descent connotes the painful dying to self that happens when the egocentric perspective surrenders to the larger whole, the process that had moved him to tears when describing John the Baptist. The motif of descent into the underworld shows up in Christian imagery as the harrowing of hell, in which Jesus enters the realm of death and brings back captives. I kept these musings to myself as Mark struggled to connect the dream with his daily life, using emotions and personal associations as a sort of bridge. Although it was not apparent at the time, his downhill trajectory in the first dream and the difficulties encountered in the second pointed toward a coming descent into a time of darkness and suffering.

This dream is typical in its use of objects and characters to depict internal attitudes. These may be at odds with the conscious perspective, as witnessed by Mark's embarrassment over his dream association to a sexist joke. Frustrated at encountering an obstacle in his way, the dreamer's male companion attacks the women. Mark associated this aggressive reaction with his irritation over difficulties in the spiritual path and his tendency to lash out at perceived enemies. The description sounded vague, so I probed further. He rambled about problems at work and then described with obvious shame blowing up at his wife and coworkers as well as heated confrontations with strangers when he felt disrespected, incidents that sometimes became physical, despite what he had told me at our first meeting. In Jungian terms, his male companion represented the *shadow*, or the denied aspect of himself relegated to the unconscious, the part he cannot see or does not want to look at. It causes problems for all of us whenever it pops out of its hole and our first impulse is to deny its existence or blame the damage on someone else, like Adam passing the buck to Eve.

In keeping with this urge to deny the shadow, the women offer to spare Mark's life and allow him to continue the journey with his mother, if he abandons his obnoxious companion. The dreamer declines, despite the headaches caused by this troublesome part of himself. His refusal to jettison it and continue alone with his mother suggests a new psychological and spiritual maturity.

Like Hamlet, the archetypal puer in Western literature, Mark tended to vacillate between passive dithering and impulsive aggression. In Shakespeare's claustrophobic family drama, these bursts of violence have an adolescent quality, like a teenager fighting to define himself against his parents. Mark could be similarly princely in his expectation that others make allowances for him, especially women. But at this point in his life, childish dependence and ineffectual adolescent piques—the options offered by the fellow travelers who represented aspects of himself—were not working anymore, and he needed to grow up and come to terms with the dark side of himself. In contrast to his companion's failed attempt at murderous violence, the dreamer heroically presents himself as a ransom for the others, echoing Mark's earlier comment about the compelling nature of sacrificial death. Reflecting on the dreamer's offer raised intense emotion in Mark as he remembered his childhood identification with the suffering of Jesus, which gave meaning to his own experience of abuse. Looking back, he not only felt deep sadness for his younger self but also found its attitude a little morbid and melodramatic.

His dream mother appears to share this sentiment and nixes the deal, indicating that another form of sacrifice is needed. Attacking, placating, and negotiating are useless in the face of mortality, and he throws himself on the women's mercy. This seems to be the right approach, and they relent, citing their dedication to the Holy Mother.

As often happens, the dream draws on religious imagery outside Mark's own experience, whether in his Evangelical childhood or the progressive Protestant church he now attended. His lack of prior history with the image of Mary gives it an open-ended quality, something new and flexible. At this point in the dream, he appears to have passed the test, another common mythic motif that comes up frequently in dreams. The women seem mollified by his balanced self-sacrifice and his refusal to deny unpleasant parts of himself in a bid for transcendence. The dream ends on an unresolved note, however, and I encouraged him to continue it forward, one of several techniques for engaging the unconscious through what Jungians call *active imagination*.[17] He doubted this would work but quickly found himself picturing a new ending:

> *I ask about proceeding down the road, wondering if it is my path. The women say it is a rocky road to death and the ocean. I must leave my ID and clothes and go alone, separating from the other two and placing myself under the protection of Mary.*

As often happens, Mark's initial dreams anticipated many elements of our subsequent journey together. Just as walking the labyrinth enacts the spiritual path in miniature, they offered a holographic image of the road ahead. I chose not to comment on these emerging patterns, and we concentrated on the images instead, paying particular attention to his emotional reactions and how these expressed themselves in his body. This tends to be a place where transformative processes manifest with force,

---

[17] C. G. Jung, 1955–56/1970. *Mysterium Coniunctionis*, CW 14, ¶706.

and noticing them can be revelatory, especially for someone as cerebral as Mark.

In a common dream motif, the images interweave elements from his history and personal psychology to depict his individual spiritual path. Full exploration of Mark's associations would lead too far into personal material so I will keep to a few observations. His mother had been his silent ally in childhood, and he still looked to women to care for him. Not surprisingly, the sense of specialness that led him to resent following rules at work also caused problems in his marriage. Seen in this light, moving from reliance on his personal mother to walking alone under the protection of internal maternal guidance represents developmental growth. The shift also suggests being born again spiritually, like Jesus's reframe of Nicodemus's question about literal return to the mother's womb. From a traditional Jungian perspective, the figure of the Virgin Mother provided Mark an archetypal image of the maternal and represented the aspect of his internal experience that gave birth to God within his awareness.

Mark's reflections on the dream resonated with the larger issues that preoccupied him, especially questions surrounding his personal relationship with God and the meaning of sacrifice. Like the ditch dream, it challenged his childhood images of God, including traditional masculine imagery shadowed by the difficult relationship with his father. In contrast to his companion's stereotypically male attempt to seize control by lashing out aggressively, the dreamer assumes a stance of self-surrender consistent with Mary's attitude in the Gospel account of the Annunciation. For Mark, relinquishing ego control meant moving away from the combative intellectualism of the theological debater in the first dream, another stereotypically male pattern. Fear over surrendering this position of power surfaced in the image of "beheading," perhaps even the implied reference to "dizzy bitches" in the joke he was too embarrassed to finish.

Here his new religious attitude finds expression in feminine imagery as he places himself under the protection of the Holy Mother. He associated this more receptive stance with Mary's assent to the work of the Holy Spirit in God's slow growth within her. The long and uncomfortable slog of gestation has a very different tone than the dreamer's dramatic offer to die for the others. In theological terms, relinquishing personal heroics means relying on Christ's sacrifice instead of one's own effort. Jung, like many of the Christian mystics he admired, saw this process of ego relativization as a slow death for the small self. In the active imagination that dreamed the dream forward, Mark is called to leave behind outer vestiges of identity. He must shed his driver's license and the clothes that define his standing in the world, placing himself under the protection of the Holy Mother. "Treading naked and alone the rocky road to death and the oceanic womb of life," he wrote in his journal, "but what does that mean in real life?" As usual, my lack of clear answers left him frustrated, as did my suggestion that he ponder these ambiguities in his heart like Mary.

I need to touch on a couple issues in closing. The first is my failure to offer Mark the kind of conceptual gloss provided here. Although this may seem disingenuous, even cruel, there were good reasons for the omission. The first is that much of what has been outlined here simply was not evident at the time and only became clear as the patterns hinted at in the dreams surfaced in Mark's life. They are laid out here to show how dreams can anticipate and guide the spiritual path, but the actual practice of dreamwork often feels like groping around in the dark. To the extent I had inklings of these larger patterns, I knew that handing Mark a tidy bundle of conceptual insight wouldn't be helpful. That's true for most people but especially him, given the split between his intellectual understanding and the volatile dynamics playing out in his life. Although both of us lacked the kind of clarity available in hindsight, the intimations he gained by grappling with dream images nudged him along the path in ways his conscious awareness could not have seen, a process he called "brailling" his way. From a Jungian standpoint, these dream images emerged in the context of a growing relationship between his everyday self and deeper levels of the psyche. Consequently, they had the quality of a dialogue rather than an oracle, an ongoing conversation in which he participated. And as any therapist knows, nothing shuts down dialogue quicker than "mansplaining."

The second issue involves a very different kind of difficult conversation. Visualizing Mark's receptive attitude as a female figure raises sticky questions about the meaning of gender in unconscious material, a contentious area in Jungian theory. The topic will resurface in later chapters, along with equally messy questions surrounding racial imagery in dreams. From a traditional Jungian standpoint, viewing women as "other" to his male identity allowed Mark to project unconscious aspects of himself onto them.[18] As might be expected, the potential for distortion is both enormous and inevitable. Confusion between male projections and flesh-and-blood women haunts many relationships, not to mention public policy. In Jung's writings, the issue is further complicated by his reliance on introspection in formulating his theories, including his experience of the "inner feminine" or *anima*.[19] This sometimes led to unfortunate assumptions about the "true" nature of women when he forgot his own historically conditioned perspective and the impossibility of a gender-neutral vantage point.[20] In response to these difficulties, some Jungians have proposed treating masculinity and femininity as symbolic constructs separate from biological sex, on the order of yin and yang.[21] Like every approach to gender, making femininity equally available to men and women raises its own paradoxes. I once heard a male Jungian argue that he understood the feminine better than the women in the room based on a well-developed relationship with his personal anima.

Other contemporary Jungians stress the culturally conditioned nature of all gender expressions and imagery,[22] although treating gender as a social construct divorced from biological sex raises its own complications. Leaving such questions for gender theorists, it is generally safest to interpret gendered images in dreams in terms of a given individual's symbolic system, which has roots in her or his personal history and cultural background. But as you've seen in Mark's material, sometimes dream images fall outside the dreamer's experience and need to be elucidated in light of the meanings they carry in other contexts. His reflections on the figure of Mary occurred against the vast backdrop of meanings associated with her in Western culture and the Christian tradition. From this perspective, the Virgin Mary represented one facet of Mark's experience of women and the gender expressions available in the culture. By providing a sacred image of maternal care that conveyed

---

[18] Jung, 1951/1968. *Aion*, CW 9ii, ¶42.

[19] Jung, *Memories, Dreams, Reflections,* 181–182.

[20] Jung, 1928. "The Relations between the Ego and the Unconscious," *Two Essays on Analytical Psychology,* CW 7, ¶¶330–335.

[21] Gareth Hill, *Masculine and Feminine;* Andrew Samuel, *The Plural Psyche;* June Singer, *Androgyny.*

[22] Susan Rowland, *Jung: A Feminist Revision;* Estella Lauter and Carol Schreier Rupprecht, *Feminist Archetypal Theory;* Demaris Wehr, *Jung and Feminism;* Hill, *Masculine and Feminine.*

the same sense of wellbeing he experienced during his "God moments," it offered an alternative to his longstanding pattern of seeking mothering from women in his life.

From a Jungian standpoint, the image of Mary embodies for many people an experience of a powerful feminine presence that manifests within the unconscious to guide them toward wholeness. As a collective religious symbol, the figure helps balance predominately masculine images of God in the culture. For Mark, like many others, these male images were overlaid with negative associations that interfered with his connection to God. Although the figure of Mary fell outside his own religious framework, its image of spiritual mothering lent a human face to his experience of divine nurturance. In terms of his spiritual growth, it pointed toward a more receptive stance able to tolerate uncertainty, the attitude traditionally associated with Mary. Over time, this emerging attitude of patient surrender helped offset the oscillation between intellectualism and inarticulate emotionality that marked his relationships with God and people in his life.

Chapter 5
Bridging the Chasm:
Spirituality and Psychology II

I grew up during the height of the Cold War. The world was divided by an Iron Curtain, and, in the case of Berlin, a concrete wall topped with concertina wire. On one side lay democracy and freedom, on the other godless communism. Things were not quite that simple, of course, but to a child it all made sense in a fairytale kind of way. At school, we prepared for nuclear war with "duck-and-cover" drills, where we crouched beneath our desks with our eyes shut tight, hands clasped behind our necks, and forearms shielding our ears from the blast. The thought of an ultimate showdown between the forces of good and evil was nothing new or even all that scary, right in line with Pastor Carpenter's sermons about the end times and God coming in glory to separate the sheep from the goats.

This apocalyptic view of history was among the many aspects of my background that resonated with Mark's, although for the most part my memories of that world were more positive than his. The church was literally our home away from home. Between Sunday School, church, evening church, youth group, prayer meetings, workdays, and youth outings, we sometimes wound up at church five days a week. Our church was a family, with all the same intimacy and bickering. Community life was intensely relational and so was our worship, a faith centered around a noisy relationship with Christ that dictated every part of life. Besides making scripture a kind of second language for me, this visceral sense of personal connection with God was probably the richest legacy of my religious upbringing, another place where I related to Mark.

Our bond as a community was enhanced by our keen awareness of being set apart, "a peculiar people" in the language of the King James Bible that we mocked as teenagers, adding under our breath *and boy are they peculiar* as we looked out over the congregation from the back of the church. The battle lines were clear, however. Outside the charmed circle of the church the world was a hostile place for Christians. "Whose side do you choose?" we sang in Sunday School. The choice, with its eternal consequences, was up to each of us; we were either in or we were out, in heaven or in hell. "One door and only one / And yet the sides are two," went another song, "I'm on the inside / On which side are you?" Or, in the amended version we sang as kindergartners outside the teacher's hearing, pointing at each other and giggling: "I'm on the inside and you're going to hell."

The mandate was clear. "Be not unequally yoked together with un- believers," Paul admonished us in II Corinthians 6:14, his cinematographic metaphor illustrated in my Sunday School bulletin with a cartoon of an ox and a pygmy goat hitched to a plow going around in circles. Keeping our distance from non-Christians was easier said than done when we all went to the same school and played together afterward. We knew in a theoretical way that our buddies were damned to eternal hellfire but that did not affect our friendships. As Christians, we were used to this kind of compartmentalization, dimly aware of that mental split but not the larger crack running right down the middle of our religious universe, stark as the chasm between communism and capitalism. We could not see it for the same reason we do not notice air, intrinsic to the medium itself.

On one side lay the Sunday world where bread fell from the sky and Jesus walked on water. On the other, everyday existence defined by science, a superpower whose territory was expanding at an exponential rate. There miracles did not happen anymore, apart from the occasional faith healing, although God could always make the sun stand still again if He really wanted to. Like the Soviets, science had a nasty habit of encroachment, and this chronic threat gave us a defensive edge. "God said it, I believe it, and that settles it," went the mantra we repeated in Sunday School.

However, we still had to navigate the tricky border between our two modes of being. Like all bicultural individuals, we shifted frame in response to subtle and largely unconscious cues. The elders prayed over you on Sunday, but you still saw the doctor on Monday. And just as the Roman Empire persecuted Christians but made the roads safe for evangelistic journeys, the reign of science was a mixed blessing. Biology was a poison with healing properties: good when it came to medicine but bad when it led to evolution. Chemistry and engineering were theologically neutral and whatever problems they raised could be solved with more science. Nuclear physics had saved the world for democracy but might well bring on the Apocalypse. Which was not necessarily a bad thing for us Christians, of course, and the two domains intersected when Pastor Carpenter preached on the Cuban Missile Crisis and signs of the end times. Evangelicals were not especially political back then, hard as that is to picture now, although we scanned the news zealously for signs of the Tribulation that would set the stage for the Second Coming described in I Corinthians 15:2 when the last "trumpet shall sound, and the dead shall be raised incorruptible, and we shall be changed."

Back then, psychology did not come up much in Christian circles. Although it did not explicitly challenge our faith the way biology did, it was also a lot less useful. And like the real sciences, it was best left to the experts. Psychotherapy was still a new phenomenon in the culture, so we viewed it with the wariness accorded any innovation. The best educated among us probably knew there were good grounds for suspicion. The ruling psychological paradigm at the time saw God as a projection of human needs and wishes, as Freud intimated in *The Future of an Illusion*,[23] just another example of how the foolishness of the wise gets things backward but then what do you expect? To the extent we engaged them at all, such issues were a mere side skirmish in a larger war whose main front was the pitched battle between a literal reading of the creation story and scientific theories regarding the origins of the Earth and human life. Both sides argued from proofs the other found laughable. We had the real answers, but scientists could not hear them, like Paul's complaint that the Gospel of Christ was "foolishness to the Greeks" who thought they were too sophisticated for such nonsense. And although science claimed to deal in hypothesis and probability, its message was still abundantly clear; under its leadership all would be revealed with time. This optimistic faith in the power of explanation extended to psychology during what could be called the golden age of insight, when understanding unconscious patterns was the *sine qua non* of transformation.

Looking back, I find it hard to remember the luster science carried back then. The gifts it bestowed were still too new to take for granted, and the lay public hadn't yet bumped up against its limitations. For my parents' generation, the technological changes over the course of their lifetime were literally magical. Across the culture, belief in science bordered on

---

[23] Sigmund Freud, *The Future of an Illusion.*

the religious, a truth as unquestionable as democracy. We Christians held two faiths without realizing it, the kind of thing missionaries described sadly during fundraisers. In hindsight, it is clear we were struggling with what has since been called *modernity*. The word gets defined in various ways, though it generally refers to a world view in which free individuals make rational choices based on empirical facts. We absorbed modernity's core tenants without even realizing it and tailored our faith accordingly. Technically we still believed God predestined ahead of time exactly who was saved and who got damned, but practically speaking the choice was ours to make—you either believed or you did not. And those miraculous events in the Bible that scientists choked over? Walking on water and turning water to wine were exceptions that proved the rule. Everything happened according to scientific laws except when it did not, and anyway, that sort of thing did not happen anymore.

In the end, miracles were physical events like any others a scientist might study, except they happened to be special. Christianity was a fact, like gravity, and everything in the Bible was literally true, empirical data in the language of science. The seven days of creation in the Genesis story meant the world was created in seven calendar days, and it was no good trying to weasel out of it by saying they represented geological epochs. In its own way, our outlook was as materialistic as the Communists we despised. The manna in the desert was bread like you buy in the supermarket, and the ark was a giant wooden boat that had every kind of animal inside, including freshwater fish who could not survive in seawater.

Despite a long tradition of allegorical and analogical interpretation that began with the Church Fathers and extended to Calvin, reading scripture symbolically was just plain wrong. That was trying to have it both ways and winding up with neither. Like Pastor Carpenter's joke about Christian Science, "no more Christian or Scientific than the Grape-Nuts in your cereal bowl has real grapes and nuts in it." From my description the people in our church may sound naive or oblivious, although the inconsistencies that seem painfully obvious in hindsight were no more glaring than those in the culture around us now, as invisible at the time as ours are to us. The congregation contained the usual spread of personalities. I recall many who were wise, warm, pious, and even holy, not to mention smart and funny. Others were obviously deeply damaged, but as Pastor Carpenter liked to say, the church should be a hospital for sinners, not a retirement home for saints.

If our internal splits ran deeper than those of our neighbors, that was partly because we took religion more seriously. "Heightening the contradictions," as Marxists were fond of saying in the books we did not read. We were a cultural backwater, at least three decades behind the larger society. And although we did not know it, our little congregation stood at the tail end of a series of tidal waves that had been hitting Christendom for centuries, washing away the unified religious universe of the Middle Ages.

Our own storm began in the nineteenth century with Darwin and the chip chip of geologists' hammers. An iconic poem from that period, Mathew Arnold's "Dover Beach," describes a melancholy withdrawing roar as the sea of faith that once encircled the Earth retreats "down the vast edges drear / And naked shingles of the world."[24] Supposedly written on his honeymoon, it calls on love to fill the void left behind—a tall order for any marriage. This enveloping sea of faith had receded to a distant memory by the time of my childhood, but for the faithful few Christendom was the mythic homeland mourned by exiles, our lost land of Israel.

Science had conquered the world, and like any occupied people, we assimilated its culture without realizing it, remaking religion in the image of the scientific method. Although we claimed that Christianity stood at the center of our world, I did not understand what a society organized around religion looked like until I spent a couple years in the Guatemalan highlands. Villages either were Catholic, with a heavy overlay of indigenous practices, or followed an ecstatic form of Evangelicalism. Everyone had a religion, whether they followed its precepts, and communal life in Catholic areas centered around religious festivals. People from villages we had never managed to interest in nutrition projects spent all night on their hands and knees covering the cobblestones with elaborate carpets of flower petals for statues of the saints to process over, one square per village in clashing patterns that stretched for blocks. The more zealous Protestants found such celebrations idolatrous, and tensions between the two groups occasionally erupted in machete fights.

Seeing firsthand how religion functions in a traditional culture put my own religious upbringing in a new light. Life in my family revolved around the church; however, membership was like being a Shriner, an activity we did in our spare time. For all our devotion, religion was an

---

[24] Matthew Arnold, "Dover Beach," https://www.poetryfoundation.org/poems/43588/dover-beach.

alternate reality that operated on a different set of principles than the rest of life, like something from one of the science fiction books I read as a boy. Living in the Guatemalan highlands, I understood for the first time the crucial difference between societies where religion is a matter of personal choice and those where it permeates all aspects of society, the glue that holds everything together.

As a minister's son coming of age at the dawn of twentieth century, Jung experienced the full impact of a society in transition between those two states of being. The culture around him was still officially Christian but religion was losing its grasp on the daily life of educated people. The big problem in my childhood church was how to square religion and science, spiritual experience and the empirical method. That issue would dominate much of Jung's adult life. The main challenge in his early years did not come from scientific empiricism; it came from the older tradition of rationalism and the struggle to make religion conform to the laws of reason.[25] Theologians of his father's generation had sacrificed mystery and metaphor to the spirit of the age, much as we did in a different way half a century later. Looking back on his religious education late in his life, Jung described waiting forlornly through a deadly dull catechism by his minister father, pinning his hopes on the splendid paradox of the Trinity and losing interest altogether when his father skipped over it entirely after confessing that he could not make heads or tails of the doctrine.[26]

Obviously, Jung's father was in no position to help his son understand the visionary experiences that began in his early childhood. There was little room for mystery in the Christianity of Jung's youth, as evidenced by his father's puzzlement over one of its most of central doctrines. The secular culture around them offered even less assistance in integrating these glimpses of a spiritual reality that left the youthful Jung shaken to the core. In the language of his later work, Jung's society lacked a mythic structure that could connect individuals with their inner depths through ritual and symbolic actions, the same mysterious force that led the Guatemalan villagers outside my window to cover the streets with mosaics of flower petals.

Such community rituals can seem exotic to an outsider, but they are the norm, the way most cultures have functioned for most of human

---

[25] C. G. Jung, *Memories, Dream, Reflections*, 73–74.
[26] Jung, 52–53

existence. The anthropological literature is filled with accounts of traditional cultures where religious observances interface seamlessly with the rhythm of daily life, guiding their members from planting to harvest, birth to death. A shared mythology ties together every detail of their lives. In one immigrant community where I worked the main question was where the guarding ancestors could live in an apartment without a central post. Sacred stories explain how the holy permeates every aspect of life, and rituals enable a community to participate in the life of the gods. Religion is not a matter of faith or a separate category of life but a daily activity involving everybody, like the cigarette-smoking men talking business on the church steps in Guatemala who somehow managed to cross themselves at all the right moments without missing a beat in the conversation.

The complexity and ambiguity of our own society makes it easy to romanticize traditional cultures, which are just as complicated and have their own dark sides. For many intellectuals of Jung's era, idealized accounts of Indigenous cultures offered an alluring counterpoint to the loss of religious faith in their own societies, the retreating roar of the sea of faith chronicled by Matthew Arnold. Instead of timeworn rituals involving the whole community, spirituality had become a private affair. Religious affiliation still provided a sense of meaning for many people, but its adherents risked the split existence of my childhood.

In his clinical work, Jung encouraged patients to reconnect with their own religious tradition if it still provided an adequate container for spiritual development.[27] Doing so often required a radical reworking of their childhood faith, expanding and personalizing what had previously been automatic. Patients lacking a meaningful connection to a religious tradition faced a far more arduous journey of personal integration that accomplished on an individual basis what shared rituals do in traditional societies, linking everyday life with depths of spiritual meaning across the lifespan.[28] What did not work, in Jung's opinion, was trying to deny the religious impulse that has shaped human culture, only to have it reemerge in fervent devotion to secular concerns like fitness or politics.[29] Equally

---

[27] Jung, 1935/43. "Introduction to the Religious and Psychological Problems of Alchemy," *Psychology and Alchemy*, CW 12, ¶17; Jung, 1935. "Principles of Practical Psychotherapy," *The Practice of Psychotherapy*, CW 16, ¶21.

[28] Jung, CW 16, ¶22.

[29] Jung, 1951/1968. *Aion*, CW 9ii, ¶170.

futile was his father's effort to continue affirming religious dogmas that no longer made sense to him.[30]

For Jung himself, there was no going back to the Christianity of his childhood, and he feared that without a religious structure he might be torn apart by the powerful spiritual forces he encountered, a fate described in his lectures on the philosopher Friedrich Nietzsche.[31] Like Mark, Jung was trying to work out his relationship to religious tradition in the light of new spiritual experiences. His search for spiritual analogues took him to the remote corners of Christian mysticism and other world religions. The approach he developed expanded the scope of psychology to include the realm of spiritual experience and patients' efforts to integrate religious experience in a personally meaningful way. In the process of his own inner work, he encountered an internal religious force that operated below the level of rational argument and scientific experimentation, a subjective reality too strong to be denied. After an initial period of solitary retreat, he spent the rest of his long career attempting to communicate this reality in terms that would be meaningful within contemporary society.[32]

A Letter to a Minister

In a letter written to a Protestant minister near the end his life,[33] Jung describes how the religious crisis he experienced as a child determined the course of his life's work. This brief missive, in which he reflects on the interplay between spirituality and psychology, conveys the flavor of Jung's complicated relationship with Christianity and summarizes the basic components of his approach. Because it offers a good springboard for diving into his system, I will examine it in some detail. First, a couple caveats are in order. The material that follows introduces some of Jung's more difficult concepts. It is intended as an overview, and the ideas it outlines will recur throughout our journey together. At this point, it is less important to grasp the details than to gain a general sense of how the pieces of his theory fit together. In addition, it touches on major points of tension between Jung's formulations and traditional Christian thought.

---

[30] Jung, *Memories, Dreams, Reflections*, 92–94.
[31] Jung, 1938/1940. "Psychology and Religion" (The Terry Lectures), *Psychology and Religion*, CW 11, ¶142.
[32] Jung, *Memories, Dreams, Reflections*, 220–222.
[33] Jung, *C. G. Jung Letters, 1951–1961*, 257–264.

The goal is not to discredit Jung, on the one hand, or to convince the reader of his ideas on the other, but to put the two perspectives in context and lay the groundwork for dialogue between them.

Jung's letter was written in response to a previous letter from a Pastor Bernet, who objected to the depiction of God in his 1952 monograph, *Answer to Job*.[34] I will have more to say about this controversial work later, in which Jung grappled with the Christian tradition and the problem of evil. Pastor Bernet was one of many Christians, including some of Jung's early Christian supporters, offended by its message. We do not have the minister's letter. It appears from Jung's reply that it questioned the latter's ability to address religious issues as a psychologist. In response, Jung describes his lifelong preoccupation with the continuity between psychology and spirituality, an interest he traces back to the religious conflicts of his childhood. Even then, he realized that his minister father was in the process of "cracking up before my eyes on the problem of faith."[35] For Jung, there was no denying the importance of either religion or psychology and the intimate relationship between them. As a university student, he rejected the prevailing scientific materialism, but he also found himself denied the "charisma of faith."[36] Inspired by the example of the Apostle Paul, he concluded that opening himself to religious truth necessitated following his own experience in order to "integrate my capacities headlong," despite the possibility of winding up in a "black hole."[37] What he took for religious realities might actually be projections of need, in keeping with Freud's concept of wish fulfillment, and the only way to decrease the risk was becoming aware of his own psychology.

Jung went on to describe how his therapeutic approach grew from this personal journey of discovery. His work with patients and his own inner life led him to posit a third basic motivator of human behavior, in addition to the sexual and aggressive drives identified by Freud.[38] Over time, this theoretical innovation would contribute to an irreparable breach between the former collaborators. Jung saw this third force as what has sometimes been called a *religious impulse*, an instinctual drive toward

---

[34] Jung, 1952. "Answer to Job," CW 11.
[35] Jung, *C. G. Jung Letters*, 257.
[36] Jung, 257.
[37] Jung, 258.
[38] Jung, *Memories, Dreams, Reflections*, 168.

meaning that found expression in religious imagery.[39] As Jung went on to describe in the letter, he discovered its influence was facilitated by deeply engaging the religious images that manifested in his internal awareness. This required accepting them without regard to their literal truth. Instead, these images were meaningful entities with a life of their own that he had not created himself. When approached in this way, his inner images offered a seemingly endless series of approximations for something mysterious and unnamable. Over time, they pointed toward an "empty center" of ultimate meaning that he somewhat confusingly dubbed the *Self*. In his letter to Pastor Bernet, Jung clarifies this apparent emptiness "does not mean 'absence' or 'vacancy' but something unknowable which is endowed with the highest intensity."[40] Elsewhere, he refers to it as the *archetype* or innate form of order itself, which organizes our ongoing experience in a meaningful way.[41]

Jung's Treatment of Symbols

For Jung, the images that present as living realities in inner life function as "archetypal symbols" of the indefinable Self.[42] This concept is a central aspect of his thought, albeit one that is hard to convey and frequently misunderstood. *Archetypal images* are perhaps best seen as mental representations that give form to recurrent patterns in human existence, like the ubiquitous frameworks of symbolic meaning associated with observing the stars or living with siblings.[43] At the microcosmic level, the underlying dynamics that define our experience are reflected in an endless flow of internal images that structure how we interpret our perceptions on a moment-by-moment basis. The archetypes they represent in symbolic form are emotionally charged patterns that span inner and outer life. These archetypal patterns find expression not only in dreams and collective cultural images but also in relationships with other people and the natural world. Their dual nature bridges the physical and the spiritual, to the extent these can be divided, so that symbolic images

---

[39] Jung, 1911–12/1952/1967. *Symbols of Transformation*, CW 5, ¶¶343, 344.

[40] Jung, *C. G. Jung Letters*, 258.

[41] Jung, 1934/1954. "Archetypes of the Collective Unconscious," *The Archetypes and the Collective Unconscious*, CW 9i, ¶66.

[42] Jung, *C. G. Jung Letters*, 258.

[43] Jung, 1936. "The Concept of the Collective Unconscious," CW 9i, ¶¶88, 89.

arising in awareness trigger physiological responses that ground them in embodied human life.[44]

It is important to keep in mind that archetypes are *hypothetical constructs,* not internal objects or ideas that can be defined conceptually. Like hidden magnets whose shape is guessed from the patterns they form in iron filings, their content is inferred from the images they produce. Jung's dedication to understanding archetypal images led him to seek cross-cultural parallels that would help amplify the symbols emerging in his own psyche and those of his patients. This ambitious enterprise, which has been questioned by critics who point to the subjective and culturally based nature of such interpretations, reflected Jung's belief that archetypal patterns manifested across multiple historical and cultural contexts. Although the details of their expression varied from person to person and society to society, he maintained that they organized our experience of the world in fundamentally similar ways that represented variations on a common theme.[45]

In the aggregate, these symbolic expressions constitute a cluster of related images that reflect essential elements of human experience.[46] Within a given culture, archetypal structures are systematically developed in myth and sacred ritual, the traditional domain of religion. On the level of the individual personality, they surface in fragmentary form in dreams and are enacted in human relationships, like the conflict between youthful innovation and guardians of the established order described earlier in relation to the *puer* dynamics operating in Mark's life. The powerful forces they unleash can either overwhelm or vivify an individual, depending on her or his ability to form a conscious and respectful relationship with them.

Jung tells Pastor Bernet he eventually concluded that the goal of the progressive approximations of the higher self he encountered in his inner life and that of his patients is the gradual "depotentiation of the ego" in favor of the ineffable reality toward which they point.[47] Opening oneself to this process allows deep levels of the personality to be expressed in a uniquely personal way, a process Jung called *individuation.*[48] To the extent

---

[44] Jung, ¶91.

[45] Jung, ¶¶92–93.

[46] Jung, ¶99

[47] Jung, *C. G. Jung Letters,* 258.

[48] Jung, *Psychological Types,* CW 6, ¶757.

he had a theology, a charge Jung took pains to deny, it centered around an idea that lies at the heart of systems as diverse as Ignatian spirituality and Lurianic Kabbalah, both of which emphasize God's presence in every moment and circumstance, leading us toward the best available possibility in the direction of wholeness. Jung tells Paster Bernet that over time this movement toward the Self would lead the ego to "dissolve as a reference point," although the process would remain incomplete since individuals retained awareness of relating to an otherness.[49]

God-images

Viewed from the perspective of development across time, archetypal symbols of the Self point toward greater integration and unity, representing both the means and goal of the life journey. In this journey toward integration and unity, the deepest levels of the undefinable reality associated with the Self are experienced through archetypal *God-images*.[50] Examples in the Christian tradition include the figure of Christ who bridges divine and human, spiritual and physical. Mary has a more ambiguous status as a God-image, as described in Chapter 4. An object of veneration throughout Christian history, she has been the subject of heroic theological efforts to prove she is not divine, or at least not quite. For Jung, her equivocal status points to Christianity's historical struggle to come to terms with the feminine.[51] Be that as it may, the meanings assigned to such profound religious symbols may change over time; what marks them as God-images is their capacity to represent the divine in a form accessible to limited mortal consciousness. In the Christian tradition, this ability to express the inexpressible can be compared with the creative Logos becoming visible through incarnation in human form. And just as the prologue of John's Gospel describes that Logos is the ordering principle of cosmic creation, Jung posits that the Self creates order and meaning on both the collective and individual levels.[52]

---

[49] Jung, *C. G. Jung Letters*, 259.
[50] Jung, *Aion* CW 9ii, ¶170.
[51] Jung, 1939/1954. "Psychological Commentaries on the Tibetan Book of the Great Liberation," CW 11, ¶627.
[52] Jung, "Introduction to the Religious and Psychological Problems of Alchemy," CW 12, ¶32.

Toward the end of the letter, Jung responds to Pastor Bernet's claim that he has reduced the living God to his theory of the Self, a frequent accusation by Christian critics. As elsewhere in his writings, Jung counters by asserting that he is only speaking about the God-image, not the deity itself, since it is beyond him to say anything about God. He then reverses the charge to accuse Pastor Bernet and other theologians of performing a sort of "word magic" in which naming God creates the illusion that they have defined the divine nature.[53] Jung complains that this removes the living archetype from its dynamic context in individual awareness and turns it into a safely predictable abstraction. Theologians pay lip service to God's ineffability, the fundamental unknowability that transcends all human conceptions, but they formulate doctrines that seek to codify God's nature, even stipulating what God will or will not do. In doing so, Jung charges, they forget that every conception of deity remains an anthropomorphism since the divine can only be experienced through human perception and is always expressed in images derived from everyday speech. He adds that his personal experience of the terrifying power of the Self makes him hesitant to address it familiarly as "Thou," although he recognizes it has this paradoxical quality.[54]

Jung's argument hinges on a critical distinction between images of divinity and the divine mystery itself. This point is lost on many Christian commentators and leads to fundamental misunderstandings of his system. Theologians distinguish between *cataphatic spirituality*, which emphasizes devotion to God through religious images, and *apophatic spirituality*, which stresses God's ultimate unknowability that transcends and negates every human image of divinity. On this *path of unknowing*, as it is sometimes called, every image of God must be relinquished in the face of a divine presence beyond all names, images, or conceptualizations. The very sacred images through which the believer comes to know God are relativized and finally surrendered, no matter how precious, as projections onto the divine nature are stripped away.

Like Pastor Bernet, most critics who accuse Jung of reducing God to psychology fail to take into the account the apophatic dimension of his theory of the Self, that unnamable reality to which God-images point. These images manifest within our psychology because that's our only

---

[53] Jung, *C. G. Jung Letters*, 262.
[54] Jung, 260.

window on the world, and they utilize the vocabulary of our personal symbol system because that's the only language we speak. However, for Jung, the Holy is a living reality that transcends the limits of psychological theory and the individual personality, just as it transcends the traditional religious images that give shape to the ineffable presence within a given culture.[55] Choosing an open-ended term such as "the Self" to designate this ultimate spiritual reality allowed him to avoid any fixed image of divinity. Like the unknown God of religious mysticism, it functions as a "borderline concept" for what is beyond conceptualization.

Similar distinctions between divine reality and human images of divinity are found across religious traditions. In the words of the Tao Te Ching, the Tao that can be spoken is not the eternal Tao. A similar insistence on the unrepresentable nature of the divine underlies prohibitions against images of God in Judaism and Islam. The same impulse inspired literal iconoclasm on the part of reformers in the Eastern church and the destruction of sacred images in Roman Catholic churches during the tumultuous early years of the Protestant Reformation. One of Jung's favorite Christian sources, the mystic and theologian Meister Eckhart, called on God "to make me free of God," a prayer that encapsulates the apophatic perspective.[56]

What Jung brings to this centuries-old discussion is a distinctly psychological view. Not only do universal human limitations shape our experience of inexpressible divinity, the Holy is always experienced by a given personality with a unique personal history. The simple fact that God is experienced through the structures of the personality means that psychology and spirituality cannot be separated. And since God's voice is always heard within an individual consciousness, its form is distinctive to each person.

Like Ignatius, Jung believed that the divine spoke through human faculties to lead us beyond them, and, also like Ignatius, he warned that careful discernment was needed to interpret its message. Where the two men differed is their starting point. Ignatius began with revealed religion and judged his experiences and insights against the doctrines of the Catholic Church. Jung started with his own internal experiences

---

[55] Jung, 1942/1958. "A Psychological Approach to the Dogma of the Trinity," CW 11, ¶232.
[56] Meister Eckhart, *The Essential Sermons, Commentaries, Treatises and Defense,* Sermon 52, 202.

and searched the vast storehouse of religious expressions for analogous images. This personalization of religious experience, in which the divine speaks within each personality in a unique way, lies at the heart of Jung's system. It prompted a mixed response from Christian contemporaries, who applauded his faith in God's intimate involvement with individuals in a secular age but worried that the contents of that encounter were no longer checked against the beliefs of an established church body.

Philosophical Underpinnings of Jung's Approach

Jung's approach to religious material needs to be understood in the context of the intellectual milieu that shaped his thought. He lived at a time when philosophy was still read by non-specialists and had a direct impact on the culture. It is possible to see philosophy's influence in his theory of personality development, which proceeds through a tension of opposites that gives rise to a mediating third, in accordance with the dialectical method associated with Hegel and his followers. Like many of his contemporaries, Jung was deeply influenced by German Romanticism[57] and the Kantian tradition,[58] two lines of thought that sometimes pulled him in different directions.

At the risk of oversimplification, looking at the intellectual trends of the late 1960s when Western culture got a crash course in Romanticism, an epoch that shaped Mark's worldview, gives us a rough idea of the former. Reacting against the rationalism and mechanization of modern life, its youthful adherents were drawn to nature and what they saw as the simpler life of traditional cultures. They valued feeling and direct experience over intellectual analysis and scientific experimentation, personal expression over societal norms. It is no accident that many were drawn to Jung. Like them, he stressed individual intuition, even at the expense of collective values. His emphasis on direct experience of the ineffable that bypasses logical thought is classically Romantic, as is his interest in the unconscious and nonrational ways of knowing associated with dreams and mythology.

His debt to Kantian thought is less obvious although equally fundamental. Immanuel Kant died almost a century before Jung's birth; however, his work helped set in motion a paradigm shift that Jung's culture

---

[57] Richard Tarnas, *The Passion of the Western Mind*, 384–387.
[58] Marilyn Nagy, *Philosophical Issues in the Psychology of C. G. Jung*, 49–104.

and our own are still struggling to absorb, not least in religious belief and practice. On a very basic level, Kant switched the focus of human inquiry from straightforward observation of an objective reality "out there" to include the perceptual categories of the perceiver, a profound shift Jung saw as foundational to his own world view. According to Jung, after Kant it was no longer possible to keep reason and empiricism separate from psychology—rarefied processes subject only to the laws of logic—so it was not just a matter of whether something had been seen or thought but who saw or thought it.[59] Reality does not come prepackaged but is constructed by the observer through organizing dimensions like time and space. Our reality is defined by our perceptual apparatus, and we cannot see or know what exists outside our filters, the hypothetical "thing in itself." As a biologist friend once quipped, if we had evolved from dogs, we would spend our weekends sniffing out rodents instead of birdwatching

And would our God, as the old adage says, bark and wag its tail? Such philosophical parlor games suddenly became uncomfortably real. In a quite literal way, Kant's work cut the solid ground from under his contemporaries and left them floating in space. Pointing out the subjective nature of perceived reality was one more blow to the established order in a society already buffeted by hurricanes of change. Like the parable of the blind men and the elephant, humans were not so much the measure of all things as the measurer of things they could not see. For educated people, this realization fostered a split awareness that continues to this day.

Just as the molecular physicist knows the chair behind her is mainly empty space but plops down anyway, the fact that the things we encounter are largely our creation is too disorienting to take in. What I smell may be my upper lip and what I see says as much about me as what's out there—this is the essence of Kant's so-called turn to the subject. The children's book *Charlotte's Web* offers a good illustration of this reversal in perspective.[60] As readers may recall, a compassionate spider tries to save a young pig from slaughter by weaving laudatory messages about him into her web. The ruse fools everyone except the farmer's wife. She remarks that the web is not so much evidence of an extraordinary pig as an extraordinary spider; her husband pooh-poohs the idea, pointing out that anyone can see it is just a common gray spider. From a philosophical perspective,

---

[59] Jung, 1938/1954. "Psychological Aspects of the Mother Archetype," CW 9i, ¶150.
[60] E. B. White, *Charlotte's Web*.

the farmer's wife is a good Kantian who looks beyond the message to the medium of communication.

Jung effected a similar reversal regarding religious experience. Instead of beginning with the doctrinal God of revealed religion, he worked backward from his own experience to understand the nature of the divine as it appeared in human awareness. In a radical turn to the subject, he used the emerging field of psychology to bridge the religious and scientific perspectives, the inner and outer worlds. In Kantian terms, this shifted the focus of religious inquiry from God-in-God self to how God manifests within awareness, a mixed experience that always contains an unknown quantity of human psychology. In the imagery of *Charlotte's Web*, Jung's letter to Pastor Bernet insists that God's message appears in the web of an individual personality and must be interpreted in that context, written by the larger personality that, like the plain gray spider, is more that it appears.

How much more is a question that led Jung to part ways with his former collaborator Freud and most other psychological theorists. His own internal experiences and those of his patients prompted him to expand his view of the personality beyond the individual perspective. Over time, he became convinced that it includes elements whose outer reaches are continuous with the presence of the Holy. The psychological experience of this inner guidance thus becomes indistinguishable from the religious experience of God.[61] This experiential approach to spiritual reality also had implications for Jung's view of divine nature, or at least what we can know of it.

The God of Our Experience

In the final analysis, knowledge of God derives from direct experience of the divine within a given individual's awareness, an experience partly shaped by accounts of similar encounters in sacred texts and rituals. Jung took pains to clarify that the sum of human experience of God does not necessarily reflect the fullness of God but rather the fullness of our collective knowledge to this point.[62] For Jung, religion is an ongoing process happening in each of us. Sacred truth is constantly being expressed

---

[61] Jung, 1955–56/1970. *Mysterium Coniunctionis*, CW 14, ¶778.
[62] Jung, 1938/1940. "Psychology and Religion" (The Terry Lectures), CW 8, ¶¶143–144.

in new and reconfigured images to fit the changing needs of individuals and cultures. In his own psychological material and that of his patients, he encountered many of the same religious images that run through mythic and religious systems across the world.[63] For Jung, this correspondence indicated that the divine is continually being born in individual awareness through the medium of imagery and sensation. The emergence of new God-images constitutes a source of ongoing revelation. Jung did not believe that humans had made up God, as some of his critics charged, but rather that humans see God within and by means of their own experience, in keeping with the core Christian belief that God assumes human form.[64]

This appeal to direct experience, which drew him to Romantic poets and mystics like Eckhart, is what keeps his approach from being yet another abstract analysis of the place of religion in modern society. It enabled him to steer a middle path between the dominant scientific paradigm and traditional religious faith. Internal spiritual experience falls outside the range of what the standard scientific method can measure and tends to be written off, and religious rituals are seen as pre-scientific attempts to control the environment. Reacting against what he referred to as the scientific materialism of his day, Jung developed a psychological empiricism that treats inner experiences as real entities that can be systematically observed.

Validation comes from three sources. One is evidence of positive psychological development in the life of the individual, as in the biblical dictum that "by their fruits you shall know them."[65] Another is what has been termed the *noetic* quality of the spiritual experiences themselves, an innate sense of their trueness, whereas the third involves the existence of similar images in other cultural contexts. Jung found that close attention to these inner experiences facilitates an unfolding sense of personal guidance.

Since this is specific to the individual and encompasses every aspect of life, as seen in the dreams that draw on the details of Mark's history, it avoids the split between everyday life and religious belief that I experienced in childhood. For Jung, psychology and religion point toward a single reality beyond definition. Each field has its own vocabulary, but

---

[63] Jung, "Archetypes of the Collective Unconscious," CW 9i, ¶¶ 5–8.
[64] Jung, 1937. "Psychological Factors Determining Human Behavior," CW 8, ¶233.
[65] Matthew 7:20.

the religious term "God" and the psychological term "the Self" both refer to something inexpressible.

Jung maintained that on a practical level this means that the experience of the Self as it manifests in our psychology cannot be distinguished from our equally undefinable experience of God's divine mystery.[66] As human beings, we encounter this presence in terms of personality, the "Thou" to which he refers in his letter. Since the experience always contains indeterminate amounts of our own personality, relationship with it proceeds through dialogue between the personal perspective and aspects of awareness that transcend the individual personality and find expression in dreams and reverie. Jung believed that prolonged interaction between these two viewpoints gives rise to a new perspective that encompasses both, by means of the so-called transcendent function.[67] This mysterious dynamic, which is central to his understanding of psychospiritual growth, manifests in guiding symbols that break down barriers and bridge divisions.[68] As this process unfolds, limited human concerns are relativized by an inner awareness that both includes and transcends the individual perspective, the same demotion of ego evident in Paul's proclamation that it is no longer I who live but "Christ who lives in me."[69]

Jung's depiction of spirituality as a living force in the psychology of contemporary individuals drew praise from members of the religious community, but many expressed concern when he extended his psychological analysis to topics like the doctrine of the Trinity and the Catholic mass.[70] Religious traditionalists were troubled by the implicit assumption that the experience of God recorded in scripture was shaped by the cultures and personalities who transmitted it. This is hardly a novel concept in theological circles. However, Jung's talk of an evolving God-image left many readers uncomfortable. In some ways, this idea parallels the theological concept of progressive revelation through which God's relationship to humanity unfolds across time. However, instead of coming at the process from the divine perspective revealed in scripture, Jung approached it from the human standpoint by tracking psychological

---

[66] Jung, *Mysterium Coniunctionis*, CW 14, ¶778.
[67] Jung, *Psychological Types*, CW 6, ¶828.
[68] Jung, 1917/1926/1943. "On the Psychology of the Unconscious," *Two Essays on Analytical Psychology*, CW 7, ¶121.
[69] Galatians 2:20. All biblical quotes are from the New Revised Standard Edition.
[70] Jung, "A Psychological Approach to the Dogma of the Trinity," CW 11; Jung, 1942/1954. "Transformation Symbolism in the Mass," CW 11.

developments in the religious mindset that gave rise to changes in the culture's images of God. Together with his willingness to apply methods used to study mythology from other cultures to the sacred texts of his own tradition, this shift in perspective stirred controversy.

Things came to a head with the publication of *Answer to Job*, which analyzed the divine personality depicted in the book of Job from a psychological perspective.[71] The picture of God emerging from this biblical narrative is unsettling for many modern readers, a deity who allows a series of misfortunes to descend on the righteous Job, including the death of his children, to win a bet with Satan. Jung unleashed a firestorm when he used the story to illustrate God's psychological growth across scripture. Here, as elsewhere, his distinction between God-images and the God of faith who transcends all images quickly got lost in the fray. The resulting conflict formed the backdrop for his exchange with Pastor Bernet and lay behind the minister's accusation that Jung had reduced God to a psychological principle.

In many ways, these issues were presaged by a childhood experience Jung recounts in his autobiography.[72] Gazing across the town square at the great cathedral of Basel with its newly refurbished roof, he pictured God sitting high above it in a golden throne suspended in the heavens. This irenic scene was shattered by an intrusive thought that seemed to threaten his very soul if he allowed it to reach awareness. For days, he resisted the offending image while his internal tension built to nearly unbearable levels. Finally, he could stand it no longer and allowed the visualization to run its course. As he watched, a great turd fell from the bottom of God's throne, shattering the roof and walls of the cathedral. To his surprise, the youthful Jung experienced a profound sense of relief. God had made him as he was, he realized, and he must allow God's voice to speak within him even if its message violated everything he knew of religious truth. Despite his initial relief, the experience left him ashamed and confused. For years, he struggled to understand its meaning.

For Jung's critics, the vignette offers a preview of his adult treatment of Christianity. His own conclusion was that what seemed to his childish self like an unpardonable sin against the Holy Spirit was prompted by the Holy Spirit. The incident, and Jung's startling interpretation, say much about

---

[71] Jung, *Answer to Job*, CW 11.
[72] Jung, *Memories, Dreams, Reflections*, 36–41.

his distinctive approach to religious material. For him, what transpired in his mind's eye was not just a puerile childish fantasy or an expression of childish anger against the authority of his minister father. Rather, it was a significant event whose meaning extended beyond strictly personal reactions. Whereas for Ignatius the first question would be whether the grotesque image was prompted by an evil spirit, as he eventually decided regarding his famous vision of the many-eyed serpent,[73] Jung saw it as a religious symbol that needed to be approached on its own terms. Viewed in this light, the defilement functioned like the Gospel story of Jesus cleansing the temple, an act of violent renewal that offended religious norms. In Jungian terms, distancing from the collective religious standpoint allowed him to experience the God of internal revelation, like Eckhart's prayer to God "to make him free from God."

If a symbol represents the best possible expression of something that cannot be formulated in words, why is this one so violent? Looking cross-culturally, there is a similar vehemence in the Zen Buddhist admonition to "kill the Buddha if you meet him on the road"[74] or the even more shocking declaration that "the Buddha is a shit-stick."[75] Here, the aim is to shatter every limiting image of divine reality by lowering the meditator's elevated gaze to the level of a communal toilet article, a radical reformulation of Ignatius's call to see God in all things. I have encountered similar images in the dreams of directees raised in highly religious settings, in contrast to the largely positive religious images more likely to emerge in dreams of directees from secular backgrounds.

Puzzling over this seeming paradox, I found myself reflecting on the very different paths taken by Ignatius and Jung. Both men were mystics who believed that God manifests in the imagination, and both emphasized direct experience of the Holy that extends to every facet of life, in contrast to the split existence of my childhood. Although both were products of Christian cultures, they differed sharply in their approach to institutional religion and its symbols. Prior to his conversion, Ignatius had

---

[73] Joseph Munitiz and Philip Endean, *Reminiscences or Autobiography of Ignatius Loyola*, 21. In the Ignatian literature, the reference is to ¶19.

[74] Koun Yamada, *Gateless Gate*, 17. The traditional title of this book is *Mumonkan*, a reference to the thirteenth-century monk who compiled the traditional Zen koans, Mumon Ekai. Zen Buddhists typically refer to the koan associated with the admonition to kill the Buddha as Case 1 and the one about a shit-stick as Case 21.

[75] Yamada, 209.

little real relationship with the religious rites and images that formed the cultural wallpaper of sixteenth-century Spain. When these came alive for him, the Church's complex symbolic system provided a helpful containing framework for his exploding inner life. By contrast, Jung, like Mark, came from a very religious household. Also like Mark, he felt imprisoned by his father's dogma and needed to burst free of it to engage with the strange religious symbolism flooding his awareness. In a sort of reverse iconoclasm, destroying the outward structures of his father's highly rationalistic faith allowed spontaneous religious images to arise. As you'll see in the pages ahead, Jung's relationship with institutional Christianity remained complicated throughout his life, at once intimate and prickly, and it is not always clear when his writings reflect his own messy process of coming to terms with his religious background.

Chapter 6
Up Pops the Devil

Time passed and Mark and I soon found ourselves nearing the end of our first year of journeying together. With my encouragement, Mark used the occasion to take stock of where he was in his spiritual life and journal about what had and hadn't changed. He summarized his thoughts in a long memo, which he emailed to me so we could discuss it when we next met.

In terms of daily practice, he still did an examination of consciousness most nights before going to sleep, reviewing the day, and scanning for God's presence and his response. He also continued to set aside a time of reflection in the morning prior to going to work. He would sit silently awhile before starting his reading, what he called "taking his internal temperature." "But no prayer!" he added in what had become a tongue-in-cheek routine between us, "or as I like to say, the 'p-word.'" Mark still read widely on spirituality, world religions, and Christian origins but his morning time was devoted to scripture and commentary, usually from the Gospels.

"My big challenge is seeing the Bible through fresh eyes," he told me. "Usually I already know what the passage means before I read it, the tired prefab interpretations I learned as a child, and am on to the next one before it even registers. Then I get frustrated at myself and the whole thing turns into a loop."

To short circuit this impasse, I encouraged him to run scriptural narratives like a movie clip—one way to describe Ignatian contemplation—and enter the scene from the perspective of one of the characters.

Mark was recording his dreams faithfully, sometimes illustrating particularly striking images, and he had become accustomed to using this technique with them, dialoguing with dream figures, and playing the scene forward to see where it took him. I suggested bringing the same question to scripture that he used with dreams: what is this saying to me personally that I do not already know?

Mark still had mixed feelings about Jennifer's church but attended regularly, although she sometimes asked if he could try to look a little less hostile during sermons or at least uncross his arms. He volunteered for the social justice committee and quickly grew impatient with the church's level of commitment. The chairwoman encouraged him to voice his concerns at the next meeting of the steering committee, where he spoke so forcefully that he expected them to kick him out. Instead, they asked him to join an oversight committee that reported to them monthly.

The invitation triggered a flood of reactions that Mark brought to direction. He had been feeling the need for some kind of spiritual ministry, although this was not what he had in mind, way too much like what he did for a living. He was not a big fan of committees anyhow and feared he would be locked into meaningless responsibilities that got in the way of real spiritual service. On the other hand, he felt stupid turning down the position after what he had told them. It would be like not putting his money where his mouth was. "But I just can't imagine myself sitting at the table with the board of elders," he told me. "They don't call them that in this church but it's what I picture from childhood, all those sour old men in their dark ties and starched white shirts with yellow sweat stains in the armpits." The committee needed an answer soon, and he agonized over the decision. "I'm definitely being called but I don't think it's to this, he said, "not that I have a clue what it is."

When I suggested bringing the question to his time of reflection, Mark shook his head. "That's what everybody says in AA, just pray over it, but the truth is God and I don't talk much; it's more of a hookup in the dark kind of thing."

Mark's preoccupation with discovering his spiritual calling was fed by growing dissatisfaction in his professional life. The advocacy part of the job still appealed to him, but he found the daily work tedious, his time taken up with difficult personalities and petty crises. "On paper I'm doing the Lord's work," he said, "serving the disenfranchised and all that. But it's hard to see God in it when I spend my time negotiating between rigid bureaucrats who won't take my calls and my clients' forehead-pounding lapses in judgment."

The religious quandaries he brought to our first session still troubled him. What did it mean for him to have a personal relationship with God?

How could he read scripture as timeless truth given what he knew about its composite layers and cultural overlay? What did the scattered moments of transcendence mean for his spiritual life and why were they so fleeting? Reflecting on the last question during our session, he decided this sharp distinction between transcendence and banality was not entirely true to his experience, or at least not as true as it had been in the past.

"There's to be more land between the islands," he told me, referring back to our initial metaphor of his spiritual life as a series of God-moments jutting like volcanoes from a sea of meaninglessness. "I may not know who or what God is but there's definitely more continuity in the relationship, even if most of it's still below high-tide line. My homecoming moments still arrive on their own schedule—during communion, driving to work, or for no good reason—but I'm starting to relax more in the meantime."

"I read this Sufi poem about chasing God like a caravan that's always just ahead of you, the ashes from its campfire still warm to the touch and you can see it silhouetted on the far horizon. I know from experience God will be back again, but part of me doesn't believe it, like a woman I knew who grew up in the refugee camps and went on to become a lawyer but always kept a can of tuna in her purse. Actually, that's being kind, I think I'm probably more like a kid I overheard when Jennifer and I went whale watching. The pod let us track them for the better part of an hour, and they hadn't been gone five minutes before he started tugging his dad's sweater asking, so when's the next show?"

Mark mentioned in passing that his verbal outbursts at work had decreased, although he still occasionally lost it with random strangers in parking lots and theater lines. When I probed this further, it soon became obvious that he had been minimizing the scope and intensity of the problem. Mark was clearly reluctant to discuss it, ashamed of his volatility yet helpless in its grasp. "I'm too old for this stuff," he told me, eyes on the floor. "It's getting to be embarrassing. Not to mention a potentially stupid way to die now everybody's packing. Things were a lot easier when I knew I was right. Now I feel totally justified in the moment and totally embarrassed afterward, like getting caught cheating on a spelling test."

Even as Mark's work relationships improved, conflicts in his marriage were increasing. His reactivity was a factor. He could not tell if he had become more critical or his wife had grown less tolerant of his behavior. Either way, both partners seemed to be in a period of transition and the tensions between them had mounted. "It's usually over such stupid stuff too," he continued. "So why can't I be more Zen about it? I finish my morning reading feeling generous then all my good intentions evaporate the minute I walk back into the kitchen and she's not being friendly enough. I keep waiting to be more spiritually evolved but that doesn't to be happening any time soon. Right now, I'd settle for just being a reasonable person. Otherwise what's the point of sobriety and all this prayer and meditation, as Jennifer is too polite to point out?"

One night, he fell asleep ruminating over his most recent blowup and had the following dream.

> *I am repairing the kitchen faucet to keep it from leaking. When I take apart the spout, it contains two intricate and interlocking pieces of reddish-brown plastic. I hurriedly separate the inner one, then worry whether I'll remember how to fit it back. It's a figure of Satan done in soft plastic, reminiscent of cheap toy soldiers or the action figures that children play with. I show someone, perhaps my wife or brother, as though to indicate that he is found everywhere.*

Although his attitude in the dream was one of detached bemusement, Mark felt deeply disturbed on waking. Satan had loomed large in his childhood world, and his appearance here left Mark uneasy, as though he had done something wrong. That may be why he had not done much with the dream when we met, apart from sketching the Satan figure, which he described as all head and torso with an unformed lower half. He puzzled over this odd shape, and I encouraged him to put off analysis for the moment and simply observe what the images brought up for him. His mind went back to a recent blowup when he had become frustrated while repairing the plumbing in his old house, in which he threw tools around and yelled at Jennifer when she tried to help, and he ruefully identified the leak with his seemingly unstoppable outbursts of anger. He began speculating about the pattern's psychological roots, and I again recommended that he stick with the images.

As usual, his initial associations were somewhat heady. He described the kitchen as the heart of domestic life, a shared common space for cooking and eating, whereas the sink was where cleanup happened. The phrase "everything but the kitchen sink" came to mind, suggesting a hodgepodge of everyday stuff. After a few minutes, I suggested that he might want to return to the recent blowup prompted by the couple's chronic plumbing problems since this seemed to bring up a lot of feelings. Instead, he listed a string of associations to water, another image he found compelling and had googled in the waiting room.

"Let's see," he began reading off his phone, "it's the primal substance necessary for life. In the biblical model of the universe, the Earth lies sandwiched between two vast expanses of water that God keeps in check, the reason it wells up from the depths and falls from the heavens. Lots of Jesus's teachings and miracles revolve around water, of course, from the living water he alone dispenses to the dangerous waves he calms. It can be destructive if it isn't contained and directed, which is what the faucet's supposed to do. That's why you need to fix little leaks; they lead to waste and have the potential to escalate. So I guess you could say that water is the all-pervading reality we depend on, life-giving and dangerous," he summarized and then added in a thoughtful voice, "Like God I suppose. In the dream, the faucet's supposed to contain and direct the flow of this primal substance, but there's something wrong with the seal that keeps it from running out all over the place." Here Mark paused, looking chagrined as the phrase sank in.

I pointed out that this dream seemed related to the earlier ditch dream, as though the water there had moved into his house, and something was interfering with its flow. He had not made the connection and reflected on it a moment before moving to the Satan figure. He associated its reddish-brown color with blood, fire, earth, and rust. The dream compared it to a toy soldier or an action figure, and to Mark this suggested a boy playing at being heroic, an attitude appropriate to a child but childish in an adult. "It may look like a kid's plaything but looks can be deceiving," he decided. "Just like little leaks can do serious structural damage or anger that starts small can spiral out of control."

Returning to the drawing in his journal, he was again struck by the contrast between the figure's top half, with its well-defined head and swelled chest, and the undefined lower half. The puffed chest and enlarged head reminded him of Milton's Satan, a creature defined by intellect and pride. This literary association was personally meaningful since he recalled arguing Satan's side in class discussions when he read *Paradise Lost* in college and feeling stupid when the professor inquired with a knowing smile if, by chance, he had had a religious upbringing.[76]

---

[76] John Milton, *Paradise Lost.*

After studying the drawing, Mark commented that the figure's well-defined upper half and shapeless bottom mirrored the contrast between the figure and the amorphous piece of plastic he separated it from. "That part reminds me of the leftover pieces when I put together plastic models as a kid," he continued. "The blobby strips of plastic that held the actual pieces. Unformed, like the bottom half of the Satan figure." He held up the drawing and pointed with his pen. "That's where the lower instincts are," he smiled, "at least geographically. The mammal bits you can't get rid of, no matter what your Sunday School teacher says, sex and greed and all that good stuff. So I guess you could say there's a leak in the fit between my instinctive side and whatever the Satan figure represents."

Although this rather abstract interpretation appealed to him intellectually, it left him cold. For my part, I could not help wondering if the unformed and underdeveloped parts of him might not be wider in scope and more varied than he envisioned.

We were nearing the end of hour, and I suggested that instead of trying to pin down the precise meaning of the dream he simply sit with it over the coming week. He did this and shared some of his reactions the next time we met. The image of Satan as an action figure had been especially compelling, and he found himself musing what its superpowers might be. The exaggerated head prompted him to reflect on the ambivalent role intellect played in his own spiritual life. His analytic abilities had been helpful in separating from the immature faith of his childhood yet could block his openness to God when he became overly focused on theological questions. The phrase "swelled head" came to mind, and he remembered times when he had been particularly full of himself, sure he was right and others just too stupid to see it.

Besides pride, the figure's puffed chest suggested ambition. Looking back over his life, he could identify a driven quality dating back to childhood. His wife called him a man on a mission, sometimes affectionately and sometimes in exasperation. This trait was likewise ambivalent since it propelled him forward in positive ways but left him forever dissatisfied with where he was. "It's happening now with the whole question of calling," he told me. "Focusing on the future instead of where I am now. Second-guessing God's plan, like Milton's Satan who thought he had a better idea."

This way of looking at the dream felt more alive to him, yet he could not shake the feeling he was missing something obvious that hung just out of reach. I encouraged him to move back into the uneasy mix of emotions stirred up by the dream. When he placed himself in the scene, what came up first was the jolt of anxiety when he removed the plastic figure. Mark found it odd that his main reaction to encountering Satan was to worry whether he could fit the figure back in place once he took it out. He began speculating about possible reasons for this, and I steered him back to the feeling of anxiety. As often happens, it manifested in physical sensation, a visceral sense of dread centered in his chest. This felt very familiar, and he had a mental picture of himself as a teenager listening to an altar call in his boyhood church, torn between intellectual doubt and the desire to go forward to be prayed over. To his shock, the memory was immediately accompanied by the proud and contemptuous phrase that defines Satan in Milton's epic, "better to reign in hell than serve in heaven."

The intensity of this reaction left him shaken. Its tone of blasphemous defiance also felt familiar. Sitting with this feeling, he found himself bouncing between two images. "One minute I'm this fifties-style juvenile delinquent with a pack of Lucky Strikes rolled up in my sleeve," he told me. "Probably named Ace or something, and the next I'm a little kid scared I've committed the unforgivable sin. The same split I had as a teenager, part of me rolling my eyes and another part terrified of going to hell."

The image of Ace stayed with him through the coming week, and over the next few days he became aware of a similar adolescent quality in his current life that was out of synch with his adult self. He noticed it first during interactions with the marginalized clients he represented. "Here I am 'The Man' personified and I'm trying to impress former gangbangers with how bad I am," he told me in our next session. "Talk about a rebel without a clue. I've spent my whole life pretending, like a boy playing pirate and half believing it myself. It's the same dynamic that comes up in relation to authority, whether we're talking about my supervisor at work or my reluctance to take a position of authority in the church."

Over time, Mark's reflections on the pattern deepened to encompass similar reactions in his relationship with God. As near as he could figure, this reflexive resistance was rooted in a childhood view of God the Father as an authority who demanded obeisance and submission, a glowering figure that fused with his minister father and made it almost impossible to experience God relationally.

Mark had moved on to other things by our next session. The dream came up near the end of the hour, however. Despite all his work with it, he still did not understand the dreamer's anxiety about removing the Satan figure that interfered with the flow of life-giving water. "Removing barriers should be a good thing," he told me in a puzzled tone. "After all, the whole point of spiritual life is getting pride and ambition out of the way so God's goodness can flow through our God-given instincts."

Striking a familiar note, I encouraged him to sit with this paradox and see what developed instead of pushing for resolution. Only years later did Mark realize that the dream had touched on many of the themes that would recur throughout our work together. With the perspective of hindsight, he could see that the unwinnable tug-of-war between the defiant teenager and the scared Sunday School boy was a function of the rigid categories he had grown up with and still carried within him. "It's as if you lay a cookie cutter over life and whatever doesn't fit inside doesn't exist," he explained, "like the leftover pieces of the model. God can't accept them and neither can I. Everything squeezed to one side or the other, and you gotta figure out which is which. Same thing I did as a Marxist, a true believer in every sense of the word."

Mark also came to realize that a similar need for clarity drove the quest for theological certainty that dominated his spiritual life. "Source criticism and the historical/critical method are their own kind of fundamentalist literalism," he told me, "Or at least they are for me. There's a split between my skeptic's brain and my Evangelical heart and what satisfies one makes the other one snort or shake its head sadly. Poor old Paul would sympathize. The only way out of my childhood box was jumping into a whole new identity, but that just made the old one go underground. I know self-creation is what adolescence is all about, but mine lasted decades longer than most. You shoulda seen me reading Nietzsche, along with every other recovering fundamentalist in my dorm, scripted as hell and all thinking we got there first, like Columbus discovering America."

As Mark's internal divisions gradually eased, so did the splits in his outer identity, until the "bad boy" stance that had enabled him to resist the forced conformity of childhood began to seem like a relic of a bygone era. All this happened gradually, and for now he was stuck with the competing crosscurrents, swimming his hardest and caught in the undertow.

The complicated tangle of internal pulls and pushes spotlighted by the dream illustrates how the psychological and spiritual spheres intersect, so what appears as a spiritual problem leads into personal psychology and vice versa. The reflexive pushback that began in adolescence was causing

Mark problems as an adult, both at work and in his marriage. It also interfered with ministry in his faith community and made it difficult for him to develop a personal relationship with God. As the dream makes clear, dismantling his protective anger felt scary. It seemed as though letting down his guard would leave him powerless in the face of coercion, the vulnerable child he had once been. That had been long ago, but the threat felt painfully imminent the moment he sensed someone was trying to pressure him, including the picture of God he carried within him. By the same token, surrendering his outsider status so he could bring himself forward in his faith community stirred up fears of rejection and retaliation. Like the alienated freshman reading Nietzsche, his separateness was bound up with feeling somehow special and the secret fear that he wasn't. This sense of mission had carried him through difficult times but left him intolerant of flaws in himself and others. And when a recalcitrant water pipe challenged his competence, he responded with floods of anger.

The plastic figure, with its puffed chest and unformed lower half, captures this brittle sense of entitlement. Mark did not fully understand the image at the time; it worked on an interior level anyway, giving form to the new developments stirring in his inner life and helping drive them forward. Dreams tend to frame things in comic book terms, and this one drew on his deepest childhood fears to present the most shocking image possible.

Here Satan embodies the exaggerated sense of his own badness that powered Mark's teenage rejection of the frightened and compliant piety of his childhood. Both were extremes, like two kids scooting farther and farther out on a teeter-totter, each balancing the other and getting more and more polarized.

As Mark described this inner conflict, I found myself thinking of Jung's *principle of psychic compensation,* in which the psyche maintains balance by bringing up a countervailing image.[77] If Mark was not a sacrificial lamb, he must be the prince of darkness, a tragic doomed hero like Milton's Satan. Dreams have an uncanny habit of putting their thumb on the sore spot, and the rebellious pose that drove him to identify with gangsters now seemed ridiculous. In fact, everything was beginning to look different in the new light dawning in his internal world. In place of his adolescent image of a grand and tragic embodiment of evil, his personal

---

[77] C. G. Jung, 1921/1971. *Psychological Types,* CW 6, ¶693.

demons were reduced to a child's action figure, his satanic badness shrunk to the level of a dripping faucet. And as the dreamer informs his wife or brother at the end of the dream, there was no escaping this banal leakage, something to be lived with rather than exorcised. This humbling demotion was elaborated further in a dream that came a few weeks after the plumbing dream and took on new meanings over time.

> *A man gives me a test of my understanding, clearly expecting me to succeed. He shows me two pieces of toast with mold on them, although it is less or even absent on one. He scrapes the darker one, which thins and spreads the mold. The question seems complicated to me, and I hesitate while he tries to give me hints. Later, I realize that scraping it off will only activate spores and spread it. This seems like a comment on trying to eliminate instinct.*

This dream is less personal than the previous one. Like something out of a fairy tale, it presents an archetypal situation with few direct links to Mark's personal history. Its format follows the classic pattern of spiritual tests in mythologies across the world. An anonymous man who appears to be a spiritual teacher presents him with a choice. In contrast to Mark's usual picture of authority figures, this one seems positive and supportive, expecting him to succeed and even giving hints when he hesitates. The exact nature of the question he must answer remains unclear; it has something to do with the right way to deal with ordinary imperfections and frustrations, here represented by the prosaic image of moldy bread.

Taken together, the two dreams illustrate the ongoing dialogue that emerges when individuals begin paying attention to their dreams, one image following another in conversation with the conscious perspective. As though someone was listening in on our sessions, the second dream incorporates Mark's reflections on the first one and provides its own commentary on his relationship with instinct and the leakiness of life. The setting is similar. He's still in the kitchen, and bread, like water, is a primal source of nourishment. Also like water, it is rich in scriptural connotations, from the seeds cast by the sower to Christ's body broken for the believer, but unlike water it is a human invention, "the work of human hands" as the Communion liturgy points out.

Toast is a rather cozy and homey image, although "being toast" carries connotations of something doomed or past its time. The two pieces of bread are differentiated by the amount of mold on them. Mold indicates decay but is also an aspect of nature with a life of its own, a necessary part of the life cycle that helps break down old structures. Something new is growing out of the old bread, however inconvenient this may be for the dreamer. Both pieces of toast are moldy, but one is less so, with an added suggestion that the second may lack mold altogether. (Here the dream contradicts itself to have it both ways, in keeping with a common dream pattern.)

One piece appears darker though it is unclear whether this is the moldier one. The man enacts the question by scraping it, which thins and spreads the mold. His action poses a sort of Zen koan that the dreamer must answer. Even with help, Mark cannot formulate a response in the moment. Later he sees that scraping mold only serves to activate or spread it. The dream is also in dialogue with itself and ends with an unusually direct commentary when the dreamer concludes that the test has something to do with trying to eliminate instinct, leading Mark to entitle the dream, "Learning to Live with Mold."

Despite its philosophical overtones, it is important not to reduce the dream to abstract principles. Like the Zen koan it resembles, the point is not conceptual understanding but inner transformation. It extends the conversation opened in the first dream by Mark's discovery that the human flaws he sees as satanic are everywhere. In his daily life, these surfaced in the struggle to manage his anger without sending it underground. "Trying not to get mad is like holding in a burp," he told me, "The harder you push it down the more it pushes back. I know from the program that the only way to deal with things you can't force is to relax your grip, admitting powerlessness and turning it over in twelve-step terms. And any good sponsor will tell you that's always humbling for the ego who wants to be in control. Not just control but total control," he added on reflection, "determined to rule the roost. Which never works, of course. As a grade school kid terrified of going to hell, I knew I'd be safe if I could just be good enough, but I kept falling down on the job. Like the verse in Romans where Paul talks about not doing the good he wants to do and watching himself do the evil he doesn't want. Except it can't be my fault, that's unbearable, so I wind up getting mad at the people who made me do it, the classic abusers' rationalization."

Listening to Mark, I was reminded of Jung's remark that *"the experience of the Self is always a defeat for the ego."*[78] In Jungian language, confronting shadow catalyzes the very dilemma Paul describes so well. On the one hand, we need to resist evil. On the other, this intensifies the conflict since our allegiance is divided and resistance is futile. By pointing out that Mark's efforts to be perfect turned him into a monster, or at least a tantruming child, the first dream grounds this paradox in the images and situations of his daily life. Removing the Satan figure that blocks the flow of life-giving water not only raises his anxiety but also reveals it to be a badly made child's action figure, a half-formed embodiment of brittle pride and intellect. Mark knew this defiant stance well, and it always reminded him of the classic line from the film *Rebel Without a Cause,* in which a teenage hood is asked what he's rebelling against and replies, "Whadda ya got?"[79]

The plastic Satan is a complex image, blending personal history and deep symbolic resonances. On a psychological level, the toy figure captures the developmental arrest that kept Mark locked in old attitudes and behaviors. However, its potent religious symbolism also points to a spiritual dimension. Predictably, reengagement with his childhood faith reopened spiritual conflicts Mark hadn't been able to resolve at the time. The awakening instincts and need for independence that came with adolescence did not fit within the limits of his childhood religion, in which Jesus's admonition to become as a little child meant never graduating from Sunday School. In the binary categories of his youth, establishing his own identity required going to the dark side, the doomed dark angel of Milton's epic who later generations would see as a symbol of individuation.

Mark's teenage declaration of independence had come at a price and reinitiating negotiations was scary, as his anxiety in the first dream demonstrates. If he once thought and reasoned as a child, he now was called to a more mature faith. This new outlook is the subject of the second dream, which pushes him toward a less binary perspective. The identity he had adopted in adolescence not only interferes with the flow of life-giving water but also, in the mixed metaphors of dream logic, leaks out in childish displays of anger.

---

[78] Jung, 1955-56/1970. *Mysterium Coniuntionis,* CW 14, ¶778, italics in the original.
[79] *Rebel Without a Cause.* 1955. Screenplay by Stewart Stern and Irving Shulman. Directed by Nicholas Ray.

Like a how-to video, the first dream begins by separating this distorted legacy from otherwise neutral instincts. No sooner is it removed from the pipeline than the dreamer discovers the figure he has painstakingly extricated is everywhere. There is no eliminating mold and the effort only spreads its spores. Like the old beer commercial about the taste being in the water, contamination is omnipresent, encoded in the very instincts that give rise to life.

Reflecting on this disquieting image, Mark realized that even his desire for ministry was tainted by spiritual grandiosity and entitlement. Efforts at self-mastery quickly became an exercise in childish heroics, invoking the very demons he sought to exorcise. In the pivotal passage from Romans he referenced, Paul goes on to stress that we cannot rely on our own resources to escape the trap. This helplessness does not let us off the hook, apparently, since his letters spend much of their time admonishing the fledgling churches to try harder. The same paradox shows up in the AA philosophy Mark liked to quote, in which admitting powerless is the first step in a lifelong program demanding rigorous work. As usual, the Gospels express the matter in a story. In their encounter in the wilderness, Jesus vanquished Satan by resisting multiple temptations to abuse his power. Having finished every test, we are told, the devil departed from him until an opportune time, a dynamic psychologists know all too well.

Chapter 7

But It Feels So True: Complexes, Projections, and Vampires

Jung's name comes up regularly in the spiritual direction literature. He's a favorite for epigraphs, those gnomic quotes at the beginning of chapters, and a good source of punchy soundbites to bolster an argument. He gets kudos for insisting on spirituality's role in psychology, although that's usually where the conversation ends. A few religious writers explore spiritual aspects of his thought in detail,[80] but most references to him are superficial, a tip of the hat in passing.

What's almost entirely missing, oddly enough, are the psychological dimensions of his work. This is unfortunate since psychology was not only his area of expertise—he was a psychologist, after all—but also his vantage point on spirituality. Psychology grounds his work in practical life and keeps it from being just another interesting take on post-religious spirituality.

For Jung, psychology and spirituality were inseparable, two ways of looking at the same person. Our being is rooted in spiritual depths, and our relationship with God has continuity with our human relationships because we bring the same relational templates to both, for better and for worse.[81] In this chapter, I will examine the theoretical and clinical underpinnings of his views regarding this connection. Jung's ideas grew from work with specific individuals and his writings are studded with clinical examples that provide the foundation for his theoretical conclusions.

---

[80] Wallace Clift, *Jung and Christianity*; John P. Dourley, *Paul Tillich, Jung and the Recovery of Religion.*

[81] C. G. Jung, 1938/1940. "Psychology and Religion" (The Terry Lectures), *Psychology and Religion: West and East*, CW 11, ¶¶142–144.

In keeping with this approach, the previous chapter utilized dream material to demonstrate how psychological and spiritual dimensions of personal history interwove in Mark's inner life. Here I will examine the same material from a more theoretical perspective, framing my discussion within the larger context of Jungian theory. In terms of the journey metaphor put forward in the introduction, this is a section of trail where the theoretical and practical paths converge. At the end of the chapter, I will apply these ideas to new dream material to demonstrate how Jungian concepts can help illuminate recurrent patterns in spiritual life and human relationships.

Psychological Triggers and Spiritual Growth

From the perspective of traditional spirituality, what I am calling the interaction between psychology and spirituality is simply how spiritual reality manifests in an embodied life, with all its individual quirks and human vulnerabilities. The painful spots where psychology focuses are crucial to spiritual growth because nothing highlights spiritual impediments like distorted responses to triggering situations. In the imagery of the previous chapter, scar tissue blocks the life-giving flow. At the same time, this is the location where healing happens, the crack where spirit can seep through, a paradox at the heart of Jung's vision and the biblical idea that God is made manifest in our weakness.

Most of these tender places stem from early formative experiences, although overwhelming situations throughout the lifespan can intensify their impact and create new wounds. Some simply reflect a childish attitude that never grew up, like the man who expects women to mother him. This dynamic operated in Mark's relationships, but I am going to focus on another type of distorted pattern that had a dramatic impact on his life, those with traumatic situations at their base. These come about when problems and conflicts in the family and larger community, together with the child's sensitivities and the limitations of caregivers, expose children to intense emotions they cannot metabolize and the adults in their life cannot contain.[82]

Children are wonderfully creative in crafting the best available solution for dealing with overwhelming situations, based on the coping

---

[82] Jung, 1921/1971. *Psychological Types*, CW 6, ¶¶926–927.

strategies and worldview they observe in those around them. In later life, these ingrained reactions arise automatically in response to stressful events. Unfortunately, such "knee-jerk" responses lack specificity and are often a poor fit for the new situation. In terms of biblical imagery, they are a place of bondage, where compulsive patterns bind us with invisible shackles we cannot unlock on our own.

Tied Up in Knots: Complexes

In Jungian theory, the complicated mix of internal and external reactions associated with these knotted spots constitutes a *complex,* an emotionally based response set that shapes our stance toward the outer world and inner reality.[83] I find it useful to picture a complex as a piece of personality with a mind of its own, which makes itself felt in automatic reactions that leave us wondering, "Where the hell did that come from?"

In Jungian language, a *complex* is a constellation of images with an archetypal core that is organized around a strong emotional response that manifests in the body,[84] as evidenced by their early association with measurement of galvanic skin response.[85] (As readers may recall, *archetypes* reflect universal patterns of key human experiences, like religious awe or sibling rivalry, and perhaps even the structure of the cosmos itself, at least as it appears from a human perspective.[86]) An example from the previous chapter may give a feel for what Jungians mean by a *complexed reaction,* a concept central to Jung's understanding of the personality and his approach to healing.[87] Situations in which Mark perceived a threat to his competence or felt coerced by others reactivated early experiences of powerlessness, and he would respond with adolescent defensiveness out of keeping with his current life phase. His plumbing dream personified this reactive pattern as Satan, using archetypal imagery that resonated with his personal and religious history. When the teenaged Mark rejected the role of suffering victim that led him to identify with Jesus in childhood, he

---

[83] Jung, CW 6, ¶¶469–470.

[84] Andrew Samuels, Bani Shorter, and Fred Plaut, *A Critical Dictionary of Jungian Analysis.*

[85] Jung, 1934. "A Review of the Complex Theory," *The Structure and Dynamics of the Psyche,* CW 8, ¶¶197–198.

[86] Jung, 1934/1954. "Archetypes of the Collective Unconscious," *The Archetypes and the Collective Unconscious,* CW 9i, ¶¶80–82; Jung, 1951/1968. *Aion,* CW 9ii, ¶¶386–389, ¶¶394–395.

[87] Jung, "A Review of the Complex Theory," CW 8, ¶¶201, 202.

swung to the opposite pole, a stance the dream identifies with Satan. This dark identity, which he tried to live out as an angry adolescent, still lurked just beneath the surface. One of the roles attributed to Satan in early Judaism was that of adversary, and the adversarial mindset Mark adopted in adolescence helped him regain a sense of agency. Unfortunately, the prickly alienation that enabled him to feel safe often played havoc in his adult relationships and made it hard for him to experience God in nurturing ways.

Like many young people, Mark organized his teenage identity around an exaggerated sense of his own badness. In the cartoon world of dreamland, this distorted self-image is depicted as a demonic action figure. Like all dream symbols, the plastic Satan operated on multiple levels, the kind of evocative image you'd expect from a poet or visionary. It captured the contradictions of Mark's childhood as he struggled to understand abuse by his minister father within the symbolic framework available to him. His childhood identification with the divine son tortured by the Father God gave rise to a world view organized around righteous suffering in the outer world and covert inner defiance.

These inner and outer attitudes switched places in adolescence, and the dream figure juxtaposed his early piety with the adolescent pushback that prompted him to identify with demonic forces. Mark's conflicted reaction to the dream during our session echoed this split. On an intellectual level, he associated the dark figure with the Romantic poets' vision of Satan as a grand tragic hero who resists authority and asserts his individuality in the face of overweening power.[88] This intellectual view of Satan as a symbol of individuation was contradicted on an emotional level by a sort of superstitious guilt over dreaming about the devil in the first place.

In this way, the dream image went to the heart of his religious conflict and the tangled feelings of fear, awe, guilt, anger, and resentment that he transferred from his human father to his relationship with Christianity and its patriarchal God-image. Mark's formative experiences of male authority, and the meanings those held for him as a child, were internalized in emotionally charged reactions and images. When interactions with people in his present world touched this node of memories, feelings, and

---

[88] William Blake, "Milton, A Poem in 2 Books," *The Complete Poems and Prose of William Blake*; Shelley, *Prometheus Unbound*.

attributions, a spring-loaded response was triggered. This intense reaction, which sometimes blindsided him, illustrates how complexes operate, a sort of three-way bridge between personal psychology, internal symbolic reality, and outer events and relationships.

In my experience, complexes, like archetypes, are bipolar in nature and contain both sides of a conflict. When a complex gets triggered, middle ground disappears and the world is perceived in terms of polarized pairs—martyr and inquisitor, ascetic and libertine. Because complexes encompass both sides of the dyad, they contain opposing forces. Usually one is lived out and other goes underground, which explains why people sometimes switch abruptly from one extreme to the other, like the story of Paul's encounter on the road to Damascus that changed his religious orientation and the course of history.[89] Although the unlived identity remains largely hidden from the world, both show up in dreams and internal dialogues.

The two characters in Mark's internal drama were an oppressive authority and a defiant rebel. Earlier, I described this pair in terms of the puer/senex split that comes up frequently in mythology and plays out in personal relationships and the larger culture.[90] On an archetypal level, the *puer aeternus* or *eternal youth* channels creativity and imagination but can be flighty and ungrounded. As the voice of established authority, the *senex* embodies rooted stability that can ossify into rigidity. Taken together, the two impulses balance each other in society and the personality, an ongoing struggle playfully depicted by battling dyads like Peter Pan and Captain Hook. However, this dynamic tension can easily degenerate into destructive conflict on either the individual or collective level. On an individual level, complexed identification with either the puer or senex can ruin relationships and block growth. On the level of society, the eternal clash between idealists demanding change, often young people, and the massed forces of the status quo has been enacted time and again throughout human history, sometimes peacefully, sometimes in murderous tragedies like Tiananmen Square.

In Mark's case the tyrannical tormentor and his misunderstood victim coexisted as two aspects of his personality. On an internal level,

---

[89] Jung, 1926. "Spirit and Life," *The Structure and Dynamics of the Psyche*, CW 8, ¶¶582–584.
[90] Marie-Louise Von Franz, *The Problem of the Puer Aeternus;* Samuels, Shorter, Plaut, *A Critical Dictionary of Jungian Analysis*, 137.

the tyrant manifested in a self-critical drive for perfection, the victim side in a pervasive vision of himself as perennially wronged. When he projected these conflicting forces onto people and situations in his life, Mark's stance toward them became demanding or victimized, sometimes both simultaneously.

I Know You: Projection

It is worth pausing a minute over the concept of projection. Although projection gets a bad rap in psychological circles, the process of projection is inevitable and not necessarily problematic. We all project our experience onto other people. After all, assuming their feelings and perceptions are like ours is what allows us to communicate in the first place. By the same token, we sometimes view those we meet in terms of previous relationships, in effect projecting our past onto them. Otherwise, we would be starting from scratch every time we encounter someone new. This shortcut is a crucial component of child development that allows infants to make sense of their environment by formulating general rules that get tweaked and updated as they go along. If the child is lucky, the relational templates she takes from her family are sufficiently like how most people operate so she can apply them automatically with minimal glitches.

Things break down, however, when it comes to complexes. Not only are the relational models forged in trauma a poor match for everyday interactions, but they also have a nasty habit of reshaping every encounter in their image, like the old joke about a hammer seeing everything as a nail. Complexes have a hair trigger and perceive threats and parents everywhere. Once triggered, a scripted response unfolds that keeps us locked in old reactions, responding to those around us in terms of past relationships and re-creating the same mess all over again.[91]

As with the concept of projection, pathology is a matter of degree since complexes are only a more extreme form of the inevitable tendency to develop default responses in relationships, familiar patterns repeated in new settings. The challenge is not so much integrating all these internal states as learning to stand in the spaces between them. Jung was less concerned with finding the "true self" than forming a relationship with the various expressions of self from an enlarged perspective permeable

---

[91] Jung, "A Review of the Complex Theory," CW 8, ¶198.

to a deeper reality.[92] As you'll see in later chapters, connecting with this spiritual core was a primary focus for Jung, perhaps *the* primary focus, an aspect of his theory where the romantic trumped the Kantian.[93]

Complexes in Jung's Psychological Model

Having described the role that complexes play in relationships, I will now turn to the big picture and their place in Jung's overall psychological model. I will begin with two overarching concepts that are foundational to his theory of complexes and his entire system of thought. The first is the principle of psychological compensation, a dynamic force that drives growth and change within Jung's system, whereas the second involves the compound nature of the personality.

Balancing on a Seesaw: Psychological Compensation

Turning first to psychological compensation, Jung saw the personality as a self-regulating system that aims at *homeostasis,* another key concept in his model.[94] This perspective is shared by most branches of psychology, not to mention human biology, but it takes a distinctive form in his approach to healing. The larger personality—a unity that includes both conscious and unconscious contents as well as the spiritual and physiological strata at the core of the individual human being—strives toward wholeness.[95] Across time, its movement appears deliberate and goal-oriented, *teleological* in the language of philosophy, both moment-to-moment and over the lifetime of an individual.

Whenever the conscious attitude gets too one-sided, the unconscious compensates by bringing up what's missing.[96] Inconvenient and omitted truths bubble up in various ways. They can burst to the surface in involuntary reactions, like the little boy who could not help blurting out that the emperor was naked. They also have an eerie way of popping up in the outer world when the very situation we are trying to avoid confronts

---

[92] Jung, 1928. "The Relations between the Ego and the Unconscious," *Two Essays on Analytical Psychology,* CW 7, ¶¶312–313.

[93] Jung, 1911–12/1952/1967. *Symbols of Transformation,* CW 5, ¶¶343, 344.

[94] Jung, 1934. "The Practical Use of Dream Analysis," *The Practice of Psychotherapy,* CW 16, ¶¶330, 331.

[95] Jung, 1939. "Conscious, Unconscious, and Individuation," CW 9i, ¶¶490, 491.

[96] Jung, *Psychological Types,* CW 6, ¶843.

us around every corner until we finally deal with it, the dynamic behind the spiritual maxim about life being the teacher.

In Christian thought, the principle of compensation is writ large in the Beatitudes with their assurance that the last shall be first and those who laugh will weep while those who mourn will be comforted. In a similar vein, Ignatius describes oscillating states of desolation and consolation and advises directees to balance each one by reflecting on the other's inevitable return.[97] The principle of psychological compensation also underlies Jung's theory of personality types. In this model, a person's primary way of approaching life starts growing stale by middle age and parts of the personality that haven't yet been developed begin coming alive.[98] The engineer is suddenly obsessed with writing haiku, and the poet finds building a pergola strangely satisfying, despite her initial clumsiness with power tools. In Jungian terms, Mark was a thinking type, so it was no surprise that his religious renewal took the form of explosions of emotion that left him baffled.

In his work with patients, Jung found that dreams and waking fantasies helped supply what was missing from the conscious standpoint and engaging with them sped the growth process.[99] Approached in a conscious way, complexes offer a natural conduit for connection with the deeper self. In Mark's case, the powerful dream images associated with complexes grabbed his attention and forced a shift in perspective. However strange in appearance, these spontaneous symbols were the best possible representation of something not yet known, the inchoate solution he was groping toward.

Mark's dreams are typical in their blend of personal associations and collective symbols, including religious ones, which they mix and match promiscuously while reworking them in creative ways. This diversity creates a dialogue within the symbol itself, as witnessed by how the Satan dream picks a shocking image to characterize Mark's stance toward the world and then slyly undercuts it by turning the demonic figure into a child's plaything. Complexes may show up in dreams as massive forces that inundate the dreamer, so fear becomes a tsunami and road rage a

---

[97] Joseph Munitiz and Philip Endean, Spiritual Exercises of Ignatius of Loyola in *Saint Ignatius of Loyola Personal Writings*, 359, ¶323.
[98] Jung, *C. G. Jung Speaking*, 446–447.
[99] Jung, 1935/1953. "Psychological Commentaries on the Tibetan Book of the Dead," CW 11, ¶779.

zombie invasion. In the outer world, the dreamer may find herself acting in uncharacteristic ways that shock the conscious perspective. These can be operatic in scope, murderous rage, passionate sex with forbidden people in public places, or excruciating guilt over a minor social lie. On the other hand, shock value may derive from underreaction, like a woman who dreamed of a Sunday dinner with her family where the platter that at first glance appeared to hold corn-on-the-cob was full of giant penises, which everyone shucked and chewed calmly, a perfect picture of unacknowledged sexual abuse in the family.

All These Voices in My Head: The Personality's Compound Nature

The second core principle underlying this discussion is the compound nature of the personality. In contrast to psychological models in which a cohesive ego regulates biological instincts and interpersonal interactions, for Jung the personality operates more like a fractious committee than a stratified bureaucracy.[100] Because different parts of the personality are competing for airtime, it speaks with many voices. This splintered depiction of the psyche mirrors the Pauline description of the split self I referenced earlier, in which we do what we would not do, not to mention those mornings when we wake up wondering who got us into this mess. At such times, our internal organization feels like a town-hall meeting with an open microphone or perhaps a seesawing democracy where the current government is always having to keep commitments made by the previous administration.

In psychological parlance, Jung's model emphasizes dissociation over repression.[101] Rather than a tightly organized hierarchy, the personality is seen as a loose association of personal and collective elements that fractures at the edges. To extend my political metaphor, the personality has a weak central government and what falls into the unconscious is not so much *suppressed* by a central power as *under the control of a semi-autonomous regional authority.*[102]

---

[100] Jung, 1945/1948. "The Phenomenology of the Spirit in Fairy Tales," CW 9i, ¶¶406–407.
[101] Jung, *Psychological Types,* CW 6, ¶344.
[102] Jung, CW 6, ¶923.

This image of regional semi-autonomy resonates with Jung's view of complexes as mini personalities, by which he meant that they not only operate outside our conscious control but also tend to assume the tone of a personality.[103] Jungians take advantage of this personifying tendency when they encourage clients to establish communication with complexes in order to bring them closer to awareness and diminish their power to rule from below. Many people find it useful to give the complex a name or even open a dialogue with it. Despite feeling self-conscious, Mark took this approach when he chose to engage the driven part of his personality unable to tolerate imperfections in himself and others. He called it The Drill Sergeant and began recognizing when it popped up in his thinking, allowing it to have its say without taking its pronouncements as marching orders.

In discussing the inner workings of complexes and how they function in the personality, I am talking about a theoretical construct used to explain behavior, not some kind of internal entity. Like the equally hypothetical model of the archetype, complexes span instinct and image, body, and psyche. This breadth is not so much a function of their flexibility as the rigidity of our theoretical models, which divide an organic process into disparate parts. Seen in this way, Mark's relationship to authority represented a complicated interplay of multiple elements. A skewed perception of outer events interacted with hardwired primate dominance behaviors to trigger negative attributions that drew on personal history, accumulated human experience, and expectations derived from his family and culture.

This cultural dimension is often overlooked in psychology, which tends to focus heavily on family dynamics.[104] Most of the time culture remains unconscious. We are so deeply embedded in culture that we do not even see it until we bump up against someone with different cultural assumptions or become aware of conflicting cultural values within ourselves. I sometimes encounter this kind of split when working with first-generation students from more collectively oriented societies. A typical flashpoint involves family pressure to study medicine or engineering when the young person feels called to art or literature. The resulting conflict enacts the puer/senex drama I described earlier and forces students to

---

[103] Jung, CW 7, ¶¶312, 313.
[104] Jung, *Symbols of Transformation*, CW 5, ¶45.

reexamine their parents' values and their own. Whatever vocation they eventually choose, the process highlights internal divisions in the young people themselves that can leave them feeling caught between their traditional culture and the individualist society in which they've been raised. Although Mark was not an immigrant, he experienced a similar disconnect between his family's religious values and those of the culture around him, tensions that surfaced in the complex Satan figure and his equally complicated response to it.

The dream image, and his reactions to it, reflected splits in Mark's view of his family and religious background that dated back to childhood. Like all children, he had a mixed experience of his parents and other important adults in his life. In the overarching system of religious meaning that defined his childhood, both positive and negative aspects of these early defining relationships intertwined with his view of God. On the one hand, Jesus was a comforting companion and the church a place of order and security. As often happens, negative elements in his experience of paternal authority wound up projected onto the Father God. The fact his own father literally spoke for God from the pulpit on Sunday mornings cemented the fusion in his mind.

And although there were also positive aspects of their relationship, its worst moments organized themselves around what Jungians would call the *archetype of the devouring father*.[105] A common mythological image for this toxic generational conflict is *Chronos* (Roman name *Saturn*) devouring his newborn children. A similarly violent determination to prevent new possibilities from coming into the world enters the Gospel narrative with Herod's Slaughter of the Innocents. On an unconscious level, Mark extended this deadly dynamic to Jesus's relationship with the Father who sacrificed him. It is an idea that has surfaced repeatedly over the ages, usually in heresies that vilify the paternal God, and it points to the universal human tendency to literalize symbols, turning metaphor into a family drama.

The ugly parts of Mark's early experience of authority that I grouped under the negative senex pulled for equally strong puer defiance on his part. This remained an underground movement in childhood; it roared into open civil war during adolescence, a generalized rebellion that lasted well into adulthood. Like all psychological adaptations, it solved

---

[105] Jung, CW 5, ¶548.

a problem but came at a price. By midlife, the alienation that had helped Mark define himself in adolescence blocked access to his own emerging adult authority.

Complexes generally have an exaggerated quality and this one bordered on melodrama. The dream sees things more objectively and undermines its hyperbolic quality by turning the Prince of Darkness into a child's action figure. The complex's overblown tone makes perfect sense given the fact that Mark's defiant stance sprang to life in adolescence, a life stage synonymous with drama. Teenagers are famous for thinking it is all about them. But however much it may annoy their elders, their self-focus and exaggerated sense of their importance in the world serve an important developmental function in helping them claim a separate identity. The myth of Icarus offers an archetypal image of this useful although dangerous adolescent grandiosity, the classic puer determined to soar above his father, a cocky young man who thought the rules did not apply to him. In the sober light of day, seeing yourself as a tragic doomed hero is a bit much. Mark would have been the first to deny he was a mythic figure, his daily frustrations the stuff of Greek tragedy. Yet in reflecting on the dream image, he realized this was precisely the viewpoint that dominated his internal fantasies and elbowed to the surface when he felt threatened.

Mark's adolescent identification with the dark side was hardly unique. Images of darkness pervade youth culture, something canny marketers use to their advantage, from black nail polish to the satanic imagery of countless mediocre metal bands. On a societal level, marginalized communities get hit with similar projections, casting them in the role of perpetual adolescents. Mark's radical politics did not inoculate him from these kinds of unconscious projections. There is nothing more clichéd than a middle-class teenager boasting in pseudo-ghettoese about keeping it real. Mark knew this and his embarrassment over the absurdity of trying to impress former gangbangers by talking tough showed he was beginning to distance himself from the complex.

From a Christian perspective, the defining characteristic of the Satan narrative is the sin of pride, a religious concept that parallels the psychological notion of ego inflation. Lucifer's refusal to acknowledge God and his contempt for mere mortals conveys the same exaggerated self-importance as the Icarus myth. As I have pointed out, adolescent grandiosity is a necessary part of psychological development, the rocket fuel that enables teenagers to break free of the gravitational pull of childhood. Its persistence into midlife, however, represents a developmental arrest that keeps the person stuck. In Mark's case, the problem was exacerbated by early substance abuse, which interferes with normal psychological growth. Few people experience a totally smooth developmental progression. If all goes well, adolescent grandiosity gradually morphs into the heroic stance of early adulthood as young people struggle to establish their place in the outer world and intimate relationships. It is the hero's journey chronicled in myths around the world, not to mention countless blogs and movies.

According to Jung, a major task in the second half of life is to surrender this heroic stance in turn, as maturing adults gain a more realistic sense of their true place in the grand scheme of things.[106] Its relinquishment involves real sacrifice and spiritual teachers from every tradition are quick to point out that the ego does not surrender territory without a fight. In Milton's epic, Satan declares that "it is better to reign in Hell, than to serve in Heaven" and anyone who's spent time around addicts has watched this choice play out in brutally literal terms.[107] Accepting limitations feels like death and the brittle grandiosity that drugs facilitate is so addictive many would rather die than kick the habit.

The twelve-step model that saved Mark's life begins with admitting powerlessness and recognizing a higher power. Like many recovering addicts, he found sobriety only intensified the level of internal conflict, which also spilled out into his relationships. Not only had he lost his default way of soothing himself, but also the step work he completed with his sponsor challenged the repertoire of easy rationalizations that allowed him to avoid dealing with difficult emotions. Chief among these was the cheap cynicism that goes hand-in-hand with addiction. Mark called it his *futility alibi,* an all-purpose sense of pointlessness that excused him from fully engaging his life. Ever the intellectual, he associated it with the myth of Sisyphus he first encountered when reading Camus as a teenager,[108] the story of a man sentenced by the gods to endlessly push a boulder up a mountainside only to watch it roll back down. The game is rigged and wise guys don't play. Reflecting on his reluctance to take a position of authority in his faith community, Mark realized that he was reenacting

---

[106] Jung, 1931. "The Aims of Psychotherapy," CW 16, ¶75.
[107] John Milton, *Paradise Lost,* Book I, line 263.
[108] Albert Camus, *The Myth of Sisyphus.*

an old pattern. The logic was classic puer, since immersing himself in institutions with all their boring inertia and failings would compromise his sacred individuality.

On a psychological level, keeping himself above the fray allowed him to dodge facing his limitations, the unthinkable possibility that his best efforts might be less than meteoric. Confronting this depressing prospect had been a major focus of therapy in his early forties when it became increasingly clear that his adolescent dreams of glory were not going to materialize. As the reality of his ordinariness settled in, Mark was besieged by thoughts of hanging himself. At such times he felt like a total failure, unworthy to live—"a waste of carbon," as he told me with a self-mocking eye roll. It was as though the opposite sides of the complex were acting in concert, the uncompromising idealist conspiring with the punitive perfectionist to condemn him to a convict's death.

Jungians talk about *negative grandiosity*, the exaggerated self-importance that leads people to believe they are the worst human who has ever lived, a dynamic referred to in AA as being an egomaniac with an inferiority complex. Mark's determination to preserve his specialness, even at the expense of life, offers a case in point. In the imagery of the plumbing dream, satanic pride was dying to preserve its dominance, choosing rule in hell over submission in heaven. Therapy and step work helped Mark gain insight into this lethal pattern, including his terror of being just another guy, and better manage painful feelings without acting them out or using substances. Like a banned rebel group, the complex went underground and continued to agitate in subterranean ways, a low-level guerrilla war that flared up with supervisors and in relation to his own authority.

The Bigger Picture of Psychological Wounding and Spiritual Transformation

Let's step back a moment to look at the big picture. I have concentrated on a single complex, one of many interweaving threads in the larger tapestry of Mark's inner life. This particular dynamic surfaced frequently in his dreams during our early work together and played an outsized role in his interactions with others and in his spiritual life, where it shadowed his relationship with God and his faith community. Given this wide reach, it offers a good illustration of how spiritual and psychological dimensions of the personality interpenetrate in outer life experiences, developmental challenges, and internal guiding images.

Jung believed that the gritty details of psychological wounding and the complexes it creates are the grist of spiritual transformation, a core aspect of his thought that tends to get shorted in the spiritual direction literature.[109] Tracking Mark's complexed relationship to authority reveals the specific ways in which his personal psychology impacted his spiritual life and his relationship with God. Future chapters will explore ways in which prayerful dialogue between the psychological and spiritual dimensions facilitated healing on both levels.

Here a caveat is needed. Throughout the book I have stressed the ultimate lack of separation between psychology and spirituality. Although it is convenient to talk about dialogue between the psychological and spiritual domains, doing so dichotomizes what is fundamentally a unitary whole. Unfortunately, this kind of holistic perspective is hard to maintain in an intellectual environment where we know so much about so many things and every topic is its own field of study with multiple subdisciplines. By contrast, descriptions of the soul's journey to God in classic spiritual texts written centuries ago assume a holistic worldview, in part because psychology had not yet been recognized as a separate category and was seen in terms of God-given faculties like will and memory that needed to be returned to their creator.

Although psychology in the modern sense did not exist until the current era, spiritual guides throughout the ages have shown considerable psychological acumen in chronicling how spirituality unfolds in individual human lives, with all their knots and soft spots, often adapting their advice for various personality types and identifying the subtle resistances associated with each. In keeping with our more splintered worldview, psychological theorists tend to treat personality as an emergent process arising from the interaction of various factors. For the most part, spirituality either does not make the list of factors or gets thrown in as an afterthought, like a nod to diversity in a grant proposal.

Given their many differences, it is easy to forget that psychological and spiritual models share the same basic aim of enabling individuals to lead more fulfilling lives. Both see growth toward this goal as a developmental process and both are ultimately practical in orientation.

---

[109] Jung, 1951. "Fundamental Questions of Psychotherapy," CW 16, ¶¶249, 250.

Classic spiritual texts may lack a psychological dimension consistent with our current self-understanding, but they demonstrate an abiding concern with helping believers flourish on all levels of the personality. The reverse deficit exists in psychology, which lacks a viable model of spirituality's role in facilitating personal growth. To the extent the two fields take up the challenge of integration, both are groping toward a unified vision that encompasses the whole person. Jung's preliminary foray into this territory established parameters for such a synthesis. More thoroughgoing efforts to build on his intuitions will require a radical revaluation of the meaning of both psychology and spirituality.

The Vampire in the Details

My attempt to place psychology and spirituality in a larger theoretical framework has led far away from the messy reality of how complexes manifest in a given human life. Before closing, it may be helpful to climb back down the ladder of abstraction and observe how the process plays out in a concrete life circumstance. As before, the point of entry will be through dream material.

Earlier in the chapter, I described the personality as a loose confederation of impulses and perspectives overseen by a weak governing body. If the conscious viewpoint is the central government in this analogy, sleep is a border state where its authority is especially weak. This diminished influence allows aspects of the personality ordinarily excluded from consideration to have their time in the sun. Dreams depicting complexes are particularly important since they spotlight unconscious patterns that impact life in otherwise unseen ways.[110] Complexes derive their power from their pivotal role as the point of contact between inner life and outer situations, the place where the psychological rubber meets the road. They typically manifest in relationships, especially when current interactions evoke previous experiences and stir up strong emotions. The example I will explore was no exception.

A series of events in Mark's family of origin thrust him back into the original tangle of childhood relationships. That emotionally loaded situation and his reaction to it evoked a dream that illustrates the rich

---

[110] Jung, "Psychology and Religion" (The Terry Lectures), CW 11, ¶37; Jung, 1940/1950. "Concerning Rebirth," CW 9i, ¶203.

interplay of personal details and mythic representations inherent in the symbolization process. Being back with his family spotlighted pervasive patterns that had given rise to complexes that continued to distort his current relationships. I have edited the dream slightly to protect his privacy, omitting specific references to the personalities involved. This is unfortunate since the devil is in the details when it comes to dreams and complexes. Part of what made this dream so powerful for Mark was the incisive way it connected old family dynamics to current patterns in his life and his treatment of those around him. Here again, I have had to sacrifice specificity for confidentiality, blurring somewhat the clarity of the conclusions he reached. Although details of the interactions mentioned in the dream would take me too far into his personal material, I believe you can still get a general sense of the underlying dynamics and the complexes they triggered, which shadowed his present relationships with himself, others, and God.

> I'm driving with my brother and others down to the river on the farm. We're in a sedan, perhaps a Saturn, and he's driving. Various family members are there. Looking up at a tall pine, we see two large shapes hanging far up. Then I see they are wrapped, like flies in a spider web. Suddenly, I realize they look like giant bats hanging upside down and I remember that I saw giant bat-like creatures there earlier and should have warned the others. A man, perhaps my brother, shines a flashlight at them and we turn around hurriedly. They swoop down from the tree in the dark with human faces. I am running. Then I find myself eating a freshly killed corpse. I realize it is one of the people with us and I have been transformed by the attack into a sort of vampire. I back off, thinking it isn't right to eat your friends.

Like the earlier irrigation ditch dream, the setting is the family farm. This was where family members reconvened in the current crisis and the scene juxtaposed past and present. Predictably, coming together as adults resurrected childhood roles and power relationships, which did not always sit easily with the siblings' grownup identities. I haven't talked about the way complexes can be shared across a family, either jointly or in complementary ways that trigger each other, but all these potent dynamics were operating. Mark saw them more clearly than ever before; that did not keep him from getting caught up in living out unconscious patterns, what psychologists call an *enactment*.

In the imagery of the dream, his conscious self was not in the driver's seat. The car that carries the family is a Saturn, a typical dreamworld fusion of actual brand names and mythic references. This allusion drove Mark to the internet. He was leaning on Guru Google less these days but still appealed to its authority when he felt insecure. According to his research, Saturn was a harvest god with an especially complicated mythology whose dark senex side emerged in stories of devouring his children. Because cars are the way people in our culture navigate the world, the family appears to be operating under the auspices of Saturn at the beginning of the narrative.

Having set the scene, the action gets rolling when they spot a tall pine containing two hanging shapes. This detail is important. There were no pines on the actual farm and its inclusion sets up a dialogue between the literal situation and mythological imagery. The pine tree is a particularly evocative symbol. As an evergreen, it carries the promise of eternal life and renewal in the depths of winter, leading to its association with Christmas and the birth of the divine child. It is also linked to Attis, the doomed young consort of his mother/lover who castrated himself and died beneath a pine tree, another of Mark's references from the internet. Religious rituals involving puer figures who die in the flower of youth tend to be associated with agricultural societies and are often interpreted in terms of the planting cycle, in which seeds fall to the earth and rise again in new growth. However, this is also perennial theme in literature and pop culture; every generation romanticizes its crop of young men and women who "live fast, die young, and leave a pretty corpse," in the words of an old biker cliche Mark quoted in his journal.

His personal associations were equally cerebral but led straight to the family dynamics resurrected by the reunion. One involved a medieval woodcut of Jesus hanging on the tree where Adam fell from grace. The other was the early Germanic custom of sacrificing prisoners to Wotan by hanging them on a living tree, in commemoration of the father god's willing self-sacrifice when he hung on the world tree to gain power and wisdom. Mark could not help noticing similarities to the Crucifixion, a parallel that facilitated Germanic tribes' conversion to Christianity, and his understanding of the dream took off from there. I will not go into all the details. Basically it revolved around the idea of gaining power through suffering. This is by no means the only possible interpretation, and I floated a couple other options, which he examined politely before discarding. In the end, his experience of an inner "click" was what mattered, although sometimes additional meanings emerge with time so that people look back at an old dream and wonder "when did they stick that in there?"

Partly due to our work together, Mark arrived at the family gathering with heightened self-awareness. Watching himself interact with family members, he soon realized that suffering had been a source of power over others in his childhood, a universally cashable currency like cigarettes in prison. The pattern was still going strong between them, a band of Christian martyrs whether they practiced their childhood religion, and the shared complex led to cutthroat competition for the role of most wounded. Since the one with the biggest booboos could make demands on the others, the question quickly became who had been hurt worse. In different ways, both parents had modeled this attitude in their long battle for the moral high ground. Like many abusive men, Mark's father felt perpetually aggrieved and complained loudly. His mother had been brave, wronged, and stoic. This silent suffering lent extra power to her victimization and her claims on others, while exempting her from taking responsibility for the mess in the family.

Her marital role was passed on to her children, a dynamic Mark characterized as "topping from below," a phrase borrowed from the sadomasochistic community. The dream employs a different image, that of a vampire, the victim who becomes a predator and sucks the life out of others. Reflecting on the dream during a quiet moment at the farm, Mark realized that he played out both sides of the parental dynamic in his interactions with others, sometimes simultaneously, including his father's role of justified aggressor. This insight was prompted by an exchange in which he berated other family members and then excused himself by invoking his global sense of victimization. The progression of images in the dream closely paralleled the actual incident, in which he took out his perceived hurt on someone weaker than himself, a pattern he characterized as "shit runs downhill" and identified as another family value. The morphing figures in the tree capture this shift from passive prey to predator, trapped flies to attacking vampires. Mark's internal dialogue within the dream, in which he sees the trap too late to avoid it, also corresponded to day-world events. He had grown increasingly aware of old family patterns in the weeks leading up to the reunion, determined not to perpetuate the cycle when they met. As in the dream, he arrived intending to warn the others but soon found himself caught up in the shared complex.

The part of him that was able to step back and look at the family dynamic is personified in the dream by the sibling who shines a light on the problem. As often happens, this brother's personality and role in the family offered a good hook on which to hang the projection, a natural mediator liked by everyone. The act of focusing attention on the complex gives it a human face but also sets the unconscious juggernaut in motion. Despite Mark's good intentions, its descent overwhelms him. After a blank period of fear and flight, he comes to his senses while acting out the pattern, like Peter's moment of clarity when the cock crows and he realizes Jesus's prediction about denying him thrice has been fulfilled. In the dream, Mark realizes that he's missing a chunk of time, like waking from an alcoholic blackout. It is clear that he's lost consciousness or, in the language of psychology, been overcome by an unconscious complex.

When Mark comes to his senses, he discovers he has become a cannibal. In fact, at that very moment he is busy gnawing the corpse of a dead family member. The part in the dream where he tells himself that he really shouldn't eat his friends referred to something Jennifer used to tell her nephew when he was small and she had to remind him, "We don't hit our friends," a saying from his daycare that became a running joke in the marriage. Viewed in this light, the admonition sounds like a line from an especially dark comedy, a perverse variation on the basic socialization that's supposed to happen in toddlerhood. Realizing what he's doing, the dreamer backs off immediately. This backward movement represents conversion, literally the act of turning again in New Testament Greek.

Inner conversion calls for new behavior, and in his waking life Mark violated the family ethos by making a public apology to his siblings that named his behavior, despite the general discomfort and quick reassurances this aroused. Accepting personal responsibility opens the door for change, in contrast to simply repeating the same old pattern. As it happened, these two options had been graphically illustrated in the scripture reading from his morning reflection. Matthew's account of Jesus's betrayal and trial juxtaposes Peter's humble willingness to repent and accept forgiveness with Judas's grim determination to salvage his pride by acting as his own judge and executioner. Even in despair, this shameful death by his own hand preserves his arrogant alienation. Reading the passage, Mark realized with a sickening shock that Judas's suicide mirrored his own preoccupation with hanging himself, a parallel that took his breath away.

Symbols resonate on many levels, managing to have it several ways at once. Reflecting further on the dream, Mark could not help noticing Eucharistic overtones in the reference to eating your friends. The phrase reminded him of the passage in John's Gospel where Jesus tells the disciples they are no longer servants but friends and enacts the servant role himself by washing their feet. This attitude of openhearted humility, even toward those who would soon betray him, contradicted the darker aspects of Mark's childhood identification with the crucified Jesus. In his version, represented by the hanging figures at the beginning of the dream, suffering becomes a source of power over others. The pattern was hardly unique to Mark's family since it lies near the heart of the Christian shadow. From the first, martyrdom has been an ambivalent force in Christianity whose dark side emerges in self-satisfaction and moral superiority, along with a secret desire for revenge that came to the fore in pogroms and apocalyptic writings. The family dynamic of martyred resentment and entitlement Mark observed during their reunion embodied this complex, a shadow theology in which injured righteousness makes moral demands on others while justifying violence and exacting retribution.

Jesus's actual message requires relinquishing power, just as he surrendered all claims against others by begging God to forgive his tormentors. It is not right to eat your friend, the dream reminds us, but in Jesus's case your friends can eat you. From a Jungian standpoint, Christ transforms the world by taking on its shadow and absorbing its violence without retaliation. Eating his flesh allows us to assimilate him within us. In small ways we can even participate in the act of redemption, providing we remember that we are not actually Christ and the world does not revolve around us. Claiming our shadow lightens a tiny piece of the surrounding darkness, just as becoming conscious of a complex lessens its impact on ourselves and those around us.

The preceding paragraph takes us beyond Mark's reflections on the dream and brings me back to the question raised at the start of the chapter regarding the intersection between psychology and spirituality from a Jungian standpoint. I have examined the issue from several angles, both theoretically and through practical application. The next two chapters will focus on dark aspects of the personality that I have referred to as the *shadow,* a term coined by Jung. The topic of darkness is a major concern for Christianity, like every spiritual system, and it will resurface repeatedly as I explore new dimensions of the relationship between psychology and spirituality.

Chapter 8
Wrestling in the Dark

About three years into our work together, Mark hit what he described as a rough patch in his life, although the phrase does not do justice to the loss and turmoil he experienced. His father died after a long illness. Tensions in his marriage increased, with growing distance and periodic flare-ups that lasted for days. He clashed with his long-term AA sponsor and broke off the relationship. His position at work was restructured in ways that made it less satisfying and decreased his autonomy, bringing him into conflict with a new supervisor. He felt trapped in his job but worried about being fired. The upheaval at work intensified his desire for vocational change. Despite a vague sense of calling, however, his efforts to transition toward something more in line with his spiritual interests never seemed to lead anywhere. He wound up taking the leadership position in his faith community, after much deliberation. Now the church was undergoing its own period of transition, and he found himself at loggerheads with more conservative board members. Given his history of impulsive exits, Mark had promised himself he would finish his term regardless of what happened. He stuck it out gamely but was glad to see the time end and declined reappointment. A new minister had come on board with a more extroverted style of worship that left him feeling empty. Jennifer shared his dissatisfaction, and they tried various other churches before settling on a new congregation. It had many pluses, including a good youth program for her niece and nephew, but Mark did not feel fully at home there either. To complete what he jokingly dubbed his midlife trifecta, he developed several health issues that he disdainfully referred to as "old man diseases," including prostate problems and elevations in blood pressure and cholesterol he made sporadic efforts to control.

Despite Mark's tendency toward drama, his account of these difficulties was surprisingly low-key. His tone ranged from sardonic to matter of fact, with a cynical undercurrent I could not quite put my finger on. He smiled knowingly when I mentioned it, acknowledging what he called his "so whadda ya expect? schtick." He had a sharp wit and, like many men, covered emotion with humor. This played well in twelve-step meetings, where he got big laughs by turning his struggles into dark comedy; it was clear from his journal entries that was not the whole story, however.

In response to gentle probing, he disclosed moments of acute despair and recurrent thoughts of suicide, which had intensified over the last few months. "I'm not actually going to do it," he assured me. "It's just this B-movie thing my brain does. The images get stupid after a while. I pass a rafter and think yep, just the right height, I see a rope and imagine how soft it would feel around my neck."

His dreams were chaotic. In one, *he wandered an empty underworld armed with an ancient blunderbuss that might not even work.* Mark had to look up *blunderbuss*, a short muzzle-loading firearm used for close combat and wondered where on earth he had heard the term, which also refers to a blundering person or something done in a heavy-handed way. There were lots of underworld dreams now, mirroring his darkening mood. He recounted an especially memorable one in which, *he was in a group of people flailing desperately across a dark underground lake viscous as Jell-O. Their captors jeered as ghosts and bears moved through the darkness, consuming people at random. Following a faraway light, they came to a barred window that blocked their exit onto an urban street where everyone ignored their cries. Pressing himself despairingly against the grate, he looked up to see the words "Hear oh Israel, the Lord thy God is one" scrawled like graffiti on the wall above.*

The phrase sounded familiar, and, sure enough, Guru Google identified it as The Shema, the central Jewish prayer repeated morning and night. Clearly there was a message for him here, but he puzzled over its relevance to his current life situation. The classic declaration of monotheistic faith did not seem especially related to the mundane difficulties he was experiencing. Neither of us had any further insights, and he was forced to leave the question dangling, which frustrated him.

We had begun meeting more frequently, and the tone of the sessions changed. There was less talk of theological quandaries and more time spent in silence. A heaviness settled over the room as he engaged his inner tumult and discouragement. At the same time, his spiritual life seemed to have a more grounded quality than before, although he was ambivalent about the change. "I've been approaching spirituality like an extreme sport," he confided during one of our sessions, "something to master like skiing black diamonds, but lately it's just putting one foot in front of the other and living like a grownup, what we call doing life in the program."

He seldom teared up in church anymore and rarely felt overcome by beauty on his way to work. As the intensity of his religious experiences faded, Mark found himself missing the comfortable sense of God's presence he had experienced as a child. Despite misgivings, he followed my suggestion to voice his feelings about this absence during his daily time of reflection. "You do get the irony, right?" he said next time we met. "Complaining to God about not being there, but I have to admit there's something comforting about having the conversation." He was spending more time in the Hebrew scriptures and found himself drawn to the darker Psalms, even writing a couple himself with my encouragement. His morning devotions had shifted away from reading, apart from a brief passage of scripture, and even that sometimes seemed pointless. Still, he missed the time keenly if something interfered. On clear mornings, he sat in silence as the yard gradually lightened around him, listening to the birds, and feeling a sense of respite. He described a similar experience during worship. His new church incorporated more ritual and he looked forward to the monthly communion services, where he found the shared silence oddly rich.

Two developments in his life turned what was already a difficult time into a period of personal crisis. The first came one hot afternoon when he was stuck making yet more plumbing repairs on his old house. Midway through the job, he realized he had bought the wrong part and went back to the hardware store to replace it. It was Saturday afternoon, and the place was jammed. He was almost to the counter when a child edged in line ahead of him. He said nothing, figuring she was headed to the candy display, but soon a man with a full basket squeezed past to join to his daughter. Mark objected and the man ignored him, waiting until they reached the check-out stand to mock his anger publicly. Furious, Mark promised him they'd meet outside. Tossing his purchase in the truck, he retrieved a club from under the seat and went looking for him. A clerk from the store saw him walking across the parking lot and tried to intervene. Mark brushed her off, but the young woman's expression jarred him into awareness.

"I realized I looked like a crazy person," he told me in an embarrassed voice, "some pathetic old guy making an ass of himself. I knew I was being stupid but just kept walking, like something out of a dream. There was no good ending to this story, and I knew it. In a world of guns, a sawed-off baseball bat is too much or too little. Either a middle-aged professional makes the paper for aggravated assault or the jerk winds up shooting me, and I die on the pavement of a box store parking lot. Over nothing too, just stupid testosterone posturing." Fortunately, the man had vanished by the time Mark reached the front of the store. He crossed back to his pickup and drove away, feeling shaken and ashamed.

Even though nothing happened, this turned out to be a watershed event whose meaning grew with time until it became a defining narrative in our work together. In that respect, it resembled Augustine's story of the stolen pears, an act of adolescent vandalism that became for him a symbol of gratuitous evil.[111] Although Mark had alluded to similar incidents in the past, I had never understood before just how out of control things got. This one had fizzled; others had ended in violent physical confrontations that did not fit my image of him as a rumpled hippie activist. I have known my share of tough guys and Mark just did not seem the type. He had mentioned a couple of alcohol-related citations during his drinking years, but most of these confrontations had occurred during sobriety. He spent the bulk of the session on this one. Though the next time we met, he passed over it with a wry aside, looking momentarily irritated when I doubled back to inquire further into his experience at the time.

"It's really hard to describe what happens in those moments," he said after a thoughtful pause, shifting in his chair and looking away. "It's like there's no space left and no room to maneuver. I can't let anyone humiliate me or I'll die, like the scene in *Gone with the Wind* where Scarlet swears she'll never be hungry again."[112]

"Why did I have a club in the truck in the first place?" he wondered aloud. "Like some kind of damn caveman. This crap's been happening since I was a teenager, but at this point in my life it's completely incongruous with who I am, this supposedly spiritual guy. I've had so many chances in life, second, third, and fourth chances while kids in the families I work

---

[111] Augustine, *Confessions,* 41–42, Book 2, section 9.
[112] *Gone with the Wind,* 1939, screenplay by Sidney Howard, based upon Margaret Mitchell, *Gone with the Wind* (New York: Macmillion, 1936), directed by Victor Fleming.

with are lucky if they have one. That should be a deterrent, knowing I'm taking advantage of my demographic, but all it does is increase my self-hatred when I mess up. I've been lucky so far but it can't last forever. I know all that intellectually, but nothing seems to matter in the moment."

"It happened a lot right after I got sober, and my first therapist said it was probably some kind of counterphobic reaction, like a rescue dog we got from the shelter who the vet thought had probably been used to train fighting dogs. Sweetest disposition in the world until you passed some giant pit bull with a spiked collar and then you couldn't hold her back. All I know is I disappear into this Incredible Hulk thing, and when I come to my senses everything feels unreal. Like sobering up from a binge and going out in the driveway to check the car, wondering where you've been and what you've done. I once read a gnostic text that described coming into higher awareness as waking from a dream and looking down at your hands, surprised to find blood on them. I know it's only supposed to be a metaphor, but the image always stuck with me."

I said I understood, and he gave me a searching look before relaxing visibly.

The theme of rage dominated our next few sessions. He was seeing the pattern in a different light, which seemed somehow related to his father's recent death, although he could not pinpoint how. "I'm glad we're talking about it," he told me, "Much as I hate to. I never used to think about my meltdowns much afterwards, just thanked my lucky stars and swore I had never do it again. Knowing inside I would, of course, like a Baptist kid telling himself he won't masturbate again."

This lack of reflection seemed strange, given Mark's introspective disposition, and I suggested he might want to journal about it. Over the next couple weeks, he gradually realized that despite his shame he had always taken a perverse pride in his crazy anger. "Getting in fights wasn't even the worse of it," Mark decided as he gradually took in how much harm his anger caused across his relationships. He had always taken comfort in the fact he was not physically abusive like his father, as though that somehow exonerated him, but now he could see just how destructive his verbal attacks had been. It was a crushing vision made worse by the memory of all the ways he had tried to justify his behavior by blaming those around him, the classic abuser's reversal. The disconnect between this complexed pattern and what he called his "do-gooder" adult identity felt especially bizarre and painful. One dream captured this discrepancy.

I'm walking down dark streets at night, including a sort of indoor market like the one I visited in Managua. I'm aware of the danger but go on, eventually jumped by a large man. I wrestle him to the ground and press his temple, inflicting some kind of brain damage to disable him. Later, I wind up caring for him as a disabled street person at a Unitarian church where I help with some kind of evaluation. I'm aware of the irony but say nothing, acting innocent.

Like many dreams during this period, this one took place at night. The setting was a dim underground world where tangled paths twisted like a labyrinth. I encouraged Mark to enter back into the dream, which quickly became vivid for him. *The air was stifling, and the heat increased as he worked his way downward. He met no one and the silence became oppressive. All the stores were shuttered, but he could smell spoiling meat hanging in the butcher shops. He wanted to turn around but felt compelled to continue, even though everything was closed and there was nothing to buy. The ominous feeling grew as he walked.*

"That lurking sense of menace is totally familiar," Mark told me when he returned his focus to the room, "this vague dread hanging at the edge of my awareness." Also familiar was the way he kept walking into danger, just as he had watched himself march across the parking lot knowing it was a bad idea. Reflecting on the dream, Mark was struck by how the anticipated attack comes as a relief, a reaction that reminded me of abused children I worked with in shelter care who talked about provoking their abusers just to get the waiting over.

The man who attacked him from behind seemed impossibly large, like Mark's earlier description about turning into the Incredible Hulk when seized by anger. He puzzled over pressing his thumb against the man's temple to cause brain damage, which seemed anatomically unlikely. Although he could not connect the dots logically, on an intuitive level he believed the image had something to do with living in his head and losing his head when he got angry.

I encouraged him to worry less about analyzing his associations and connect with the feeling of the dream. Immediately, he felt a sharp sense of exultation over his victory, reminding him of a story about Billy the Kid getting the jump on an abusive jailor and breaking the man's rifle after shooting him, saying now you won't chase me with that big old gun.

Looking for breaks in the flow of a dream is always useful because they often signal a shift in perspective. Here a time jump marked by the word *later* bridged into Mark's current life as an advocate for marginalized clients. He had no particular associations to the Unitarian church, apart from a vague impression of earnest do-gooders and his childhood pastor's jibe about Unitarians believing in at most one god. I pointed out similarities to the Shema in his earlier dream and the assertion that God is one. He agreed there seemed to be a relationship but expressed his usual frustration over its vagueness, yet another example of fuzzy dream logic that seemed to be heading somewhere though it never quite arrived.

But the message was unmistakable in the second part of the dream where his caregiving role had direct parallels to his day-world occupation. The Mark in the dream tries to keep the relationship strictly professional when evaluating the poor man's disability, as though he has nothing to do with it. Dreams often present a situation without drawing conclusions; this one appeared to have a definite opinion about his failure to take responsibility. Like the earlier vampire dream, the victim had morphed into a predator. He had become the monster he feared, like the old joke about the man who conquers a snake and slithers away.

It is often useful to name characters in dreams—pious me, accommodating me, snide salesgirl, or sarcastic bus driver—and he called this one Slippery Mark. "It's a part of me I don't much like to think about," he admitted, "and being in a position of responsibility only makes it worse. A trusted helper who preys on the vulnerable, like the lingering suspicion that Jack the Ripper was a respectable surgeon by day or the standard horror movie trope of the heroine finally reaching safety only to discover her rescuer is actually one of them." The incongruity between his two roles in the dream harkened back to Mark's epiphany in the parking lot when he pictured news reports about a respected community advocate getting charged with manslaughter or dying in a street fight.

The incident in the parking lot, which disclosed new dimensions as he worked with the dream, shook his faith in the righteousness of his anger. He found himself uncertain in work situations where he had always seen himself as the courageous defender of the weak. The issue of justified anger struck even closer to home in the second development that upended his life, a crisis in his marriage.

The couple had become increasingly estranged as both underwent periods of professional and personal turmoil. Interactions between them often ended in mutual frustration and gradually they had begun living around each other, maintaining cold civility with little real engagement. He felt abandoned by Jennifer and blamed their distance on her inability to process conflict. From time to time, his simmering resentment over feeling emotionally unmet erupted in verbal explosions that only made her withdraw further. After one such outburst, she told him she could no longer live with the situation and had consulted a lawyer about divorce. I had seen Mark tearful before, but this time he cried through much of our next session. I asked if he was feeling suicidal, given his history, and he gave me a wan smile, the only inkling of his usual wry demeanor. "Nope," he shook his head, "no time for that now. Things are way too serious for drama."

Although Jennifer offered to get her own place, he encouraged her to stay in the house while she decided whether to reenter couple's therapy or go ahead with divorce. Tension between them lessened when they moved into separate bedrooms, and their exchanges took on an air of respectful formality. Over the ensuing months, he responded to his unsettled situation with an emotional balance that surprised me. Him too, apparently. "The old Mark would have pressed for an answer and stormed out feeling wronged," he told me, "Then promptly regretted it and apologized profusely, getting mad all over again if she didn't jump to make up. Like I said, we can't afford that kind of drama now. Jennifer has a right to her own space while she figures things out and I need to live with the uncertainty."

At some deep level, he trusted his wife and agreed their current relationship was untenable. He credited this strange ability to hold the tension without acting out to an unexpected deepening in his spiritual life. "It feels like something new is growing in there," he confided in me. "I can't see it but know it's there. I remember watching my grandmother candle eggs to check for embryos—except it wasn't actually a candle but more like a Christmas bulb, which always confused me as a child. Most of the eggs were empty but every once in a while, you'd hold one up and there'd be a whole world in there, red against the light, with a tiny chick curled up inside to put in the incubator. That's what it feels like sometimes, like I'm in some kind of incubator, the only upside of all this mess."

Mark slept badly most nights and frequently found himself lying in bed replaying scenes from the marriage. "It's like watching old movie clips," he decided, "seeing times when I was so sure of myself in a whole new light." Often, he wound up getting out of bed and sitting in the dark yard listening to the night sounds around him. To Mark's surprise, his childhood relationship with Jesus had resurfaced. He found himself conversing companionably as they sat together in the darkness, feeling like a kid again. "It's weird," he told me, "A totally split experience. On one level it makes total sense and on another it's total bullshit. I mean, what's a dead Palestinian guy got to do with my marital problems? Basically, it works as long as I don't think about it, like I'm seeing him out of the corner of my eye, but he disappears the minute I look at him directly."

One night he had two dreams that he brought to our next session:

Jennifer is clearing a clogged toilet bowl with a long scoop like dog owners use to throw balls. She puts shit in one bucket and objects to keep in another, including an 8-ball. I say I will rinse them. My tone is defensive as it's my toilet.

I'm wiping myself but can't seem to get clean, flushing gobs of toilet paper down the toilet. Jennifer is beside me but turned the other way, as though we're sitting in bed. I'm embarrassed and being as discreet as possible. She seems half aware of what I'm doing.

The two dreams felt like variations on a common theme, and we worked on them together. What grabbed Mark's attention in the first one was the mundane image of a clogged toilet, a common occurrence in their old house with its struggling pipes. Apparently, there was a blockage, and sewage was mounting with no way to flush. Worse yet, someone had to sort through the soupy glop to see what could be salvaged. "Looks like I've got to confront my shit," Mark said with a rueful smile, "just in case I didn't know."

In waking life, he was usually the one to deal with plugged toilets. Here the job fell to Jennifer. Reflecting further on the dream, it occurred to Mark that her involvement in the plumbing problem linked their domestic situation with his encounter at the hardware store, which happened in the middle of replacing the toilet. When he placed himself back in the dream, it seemed bad enough needing her help to sort through the mess and the fact it was his crap felt doubly humiliating, triggering immediate internal defensiveness. Mark hurried over this part of the dream to focus on the tool she brought to the job. "It's basically a primitive throwing stick like you see in museums," he explained, "a prehistoric hunting implement that predates the bow. Dog owners use them to keep their hands from getting covered in drool when they play fetch," he mimed the motion. "The same reason Jennifer does here. Using it to fish around in the toilet allows her maintain distance in the midst of all the crap. That's what I'm doing differently this time, or trying to anyway, maintain a little distance. Looking squarely at what's there without getting swept away or at least keeping one toe out of the water, like you say. Jennifer's always been better at that than me but I'm learning. I have to."

Mark's other associations were less safely remote. "Jennifer used to call me a hyper puppy when we were first dating," he remembered, "mostly affectionately, or at least I like to think so. I've always been a little hyper and impulsive, but the other side of puppyhood is how I wind up demanding attention. I've always told myself that connecting with people is paramount for me, as though that proves how altruistic I am. The truth is, she's right when she complains that it's feast or famine with me and the contact is pretty much on my terms. I seek her out when I need her and ignore her when I don't, especially if she's feeling down or has her own stuff going on."

"In some ways, her attention has been far too important to me over the years, like a puppy who stares at you while you eat and jumps on you the minute you get up. I don't much like the comparison but it's right on, the way puppies can't just hang out quietly and let you be. And if she's not up for playing ball right then, I go out in the garage and 'pout.' That's her word, of course, and I hate when she says it, but I have to admit it's accurate, more of my shit she winds up sorting through. Classic male behavior, that's the embarrassing part, depending on women to regulate our emotions for us. I pride myself on being liberated but looking back over the years I can see all the ways I've expected women to take care of me. That's part of what the midnight movie clips are about. Clear back to middle school when I'd get high and space out in class, then borrow some nice codependent girl's notes when it came time for the test. Probably even before that, all the way back to nursery school and dear old mom."

Listening to Mark, I found myself curious about Jennifer. Marriage is like a complex chemical reaction, and seeing her through his eyes, I could only speculate about her side of the equation. I suspected the figure in the dream had less to do with the actual woman than what he had found in her and internalized, an "inner Jennifer" to match his "inner Evangelical."

It probably had elements of both, the person out there and the one inside Mark, what Jung called the *objective*[113] and *subjective*[114] aspects of a dream image of someone in the dreamer's life.

Mark interrupted my musings. The idea of sorting through the crap to see what could be salvaged rang true, but the image of the 8-ball stumped and bothered him. His first association was the street name for an eighth ounce of cocaine but that did not seem especially relevant. Others had to do with shooting pool. "The 8-ball's the goal of the game but a dangerous one," he ventured uncertainly. "Sudden death if you knock it in by accident or scratch on the last shot. Choking on the eight has always been my personal specialty. It's also a very masculine image, and I suppose you could get sexual about it. An 8-ball has a pretty dark connotation in pop culture; besides the color I mean. Like being behind the 8-ball or the depictions you see in truck decals and street art. So I guess there's something in this mess that's powerful but dangerous, whatever that means." Mark paused, clearly frustrated.

I worried he would keep hammering on the image until he flattened it into a concept rather than allowing the dream to speak in its own language and letting the symbols work on him. Instead he shrugged and skipped ahead to the next dream, looking impatient when I encouraged him to connect with the emotions in this one before moving on. "I guess embarrassed and defensive pretty much sums it up," he said after a moment's refection, "like when Jennifer comes home and does the dishes I've been meaning to do all day and I struggle not to let my embarrassment make me defensive and blaming."

These same emotions carried over into the second dream. Mark often complained about the obscurity of dream images, but this one seemed uncomfortably obvious. What stood out immediately was the idea of not being able to get clean no matter how much he wiped himself. "My dad would have loved that one," he smiled, "total depravity and all our righteousness as filthy rags etc. Except here it doesn't feel like any big deal, just the way things are. A natural bodily function and all that, even if the context is awkward since we're in bed together, or at least sort of. The hard part is not getting defensive over not being perfect, just like real life. Being

---

[113] C. G. Jung, 1921/1971. *Psychological Types,* CW 6, ¶779.
[114] Jung, CW 6, ¶812.

seen warts and all feels so vulnerable, like the whole macho thing about not showing your ass."

Mark was speaking more quickly now, the words pouring out in a torrent. "Always needing to justify myself is a big one with me, like if I'm not perfect I don't deserve to live. I think Jennifer is probably more realistic and forgiving of human imperfection than I am. Actually, I know for a fact she is. That fits how she acts in the dream, tactfully looking the other way so she doesn't shame me, she has that kind of generosity. Me being half aware fits too, although I'm always accusing her of not being as quote psychologically minded as me. She knows what's going on but doesn't need to examine it under a microscope, unlike some people I could name. On the plus side, the dream shows I'm finally beginning to take responsibility for managing my own shit and being discreet for once, instead of waving my arms around and making a bigger mess. Hopefully it's not too late and if it is, well it's what I needed to do anyway." This note of sober optimism was reflected in a dream that came the night after our meeting, almost like a commentary on the proceedings.

We're in some kind of barracks like a prison camp as a terrible storm is falling. Soldiers fire automatics outside the cabins to keep us from fleeing. It's raining inside as well, although not as badly. On inspection, the droplets turn out to be pale insects like white larvae with tiny leg buds.

We explored this dream the next time Mark came in. Like his domestic situation, at first glance everything seems bleak. Dreams tend to put things in dramatic terms, and the setting captures his feeling of danger and alarm. As in the earlier Shema dream, he's being held captive along with unnamed others. A terrible storm has hit, as indeed it had, and there is no denying the peril. There is also no escape and, just to make sure, soldiers guard the exits.

Being a Jungian, my mind went to the alchemical idea of sealing the container, an image Jung applied to the psychological endeavor.[115] In this archaic mix of chemistry and spirituality, in which he saw a precursor to

---

[115] Jung, 1936. "Individual Dream Symbolism in Relation to Alchemy," *Psychology and Alchemy*, CW 12, ¶¶186, 187.

his model of psychospiritual transformation,[116] intense heat and pressure was thought to produce gold from unpleasant substances that included human excretion.[117] This painstaking undertaking depended in part on the inner state of the alchemist, whose own spiritual transformation mirrored the transmutation of gross matter into the philosopher's stone, a magical substance able to transform base metals.[118] The procedure always took place in a sealed container, for Jung a symbol of the dedicated inward focus that facilitates transformation.[119]

In Mark's case, the prayerful concentration he brought to his marital crisis allowed him to stay in the situation and bear the heat needed to transform the patterns that imprisoned him, without melting down or blowing out. The communal nature of the barracks suggests this is not a strictly individual problem but a group issue with larger social ramifications, in keeping with his description of typical male patterns of relating to women. Although rain penetrates the cabin, staying inside the claustrophobic enclosure provides him a certain amount of shelter. Images of life-giving rain permeate sacred writings across religious traditions; like the ambivalent 8-ball, it can be dangerous as well, as witnessed by the Noah story. At the end of the dream, Mark inspects the droplets and discovers they are live insects. He found this image disgusting at first but then realized on reflection that it indicated potential for growth. "It's got legs," he decided, "or at least limb buds, but it's still pretty vulnerable and needs time to hatch. Maybe even sprout wings, worms to butterflies and all that."

I kept my alchemical associations to myself, knowing they would steer us down an intellectual rabbit hole. However, Mark's emotional experience over the next few months resonated with Jung's image of making gold from dung through humble introspection during difficult situations, an idea that parallels Ignatius's injunction to find God in all circumstances. As the session drew to a close, Mark had no tangible reason for optimism, yet he felt comforted by the dream and oddly confident in the direction he was taking, wherever it led. It was apparent to me that he was addressing not only his relationship with Jennifer, both past and present, but also his relationships with women and the parts of himself he expected them to

---

[116] Jung, *Memories, Dreams, Reflections*, 205.
[117] Jung, 1937. "Religious Ideas in Alchemy," CW 12, ¶¶342, 343; ¶¶420, 421.
[118] Jung, CW 12, ¶¶423, 424.
[119] Jung, "Individual Dream Symbolism in Relation to Alchemy," CW 12, ¶¶186, 187.

carry. This latter point touches on a complicated issue I will return to in a future chapter. For the moment, it is enough to say that dream images of intimate others operate on multiple levels. Like all symbols, they both embody the thing itself and point beyond it, just as the Jennifer in the dream is associated with budding capacities within Mark as well as the flesh-and-blood person whose presence facilitated their unfolding.

Chapter 9
The Me I Do Not Want to Be: Jung's Concept of the Shadow

As I listened to Mark's violent response to feeling humiliated, my mind went back to an incident that happened when I was a teenager. Like countless other adolescents from strict religious backgrounds, I spent those years busily doing the things I had been told not to. It is a time-honored tradition in fundamentalist circles, declaring your independence by becoming your evil twin, a sort of inverse identity like a photographic negative. Not surprisingly, it did not work. Despite my best efforts, I remained a nice Christian boy at heart, and my stabs at badness paled in comparison to my new companions, who were not fooled for a minute.

Chief among these was a man in his late twenties who I idolized for his hard living. I was too young to go to the bars, and he was out drinking with some people I did not know when he left his sunglasses on the table. He returned for them a few minutes later, and everyone denied seeing them, including the smirking man who held them in his hand. A fight ensued and my friend wound up being charged with second-degree murder. I was aghast at the news but did my best to hide the fact, outwardly admiring his refusal to take crap off anybody and inwardly admiring myself for knowing him. My friends and I dissected the incident endlessly over beer and pot. Everyone agreed he could not let the insult pass. "It bites losing your freedom over a pair of shades, but he didn't have a choice, man," ran the consensus.

Although our ages ranged from late teens to early forties, our response strikes me now as a very adolescent perspective. In language that I will explain later in the chapter, we were identifying with the *collective shadow*. In my case, this allowed me to avoid my *real shadow,* the part of myself I could not acknowledge, a scared boy in way over his head and refusing to admit it, much as everything my friend could not let himself feel remained frozen in the teardrop tattooed on his cheek.

Things looked very different by my late thirties. I had grown up considerably by then and was providing psychological services at a grade school in a low-income district. Tragedy struck shortly after the Christmas break when the parents of one of my students went out for an evening at a neighborhood tavern. The place was crowded and service slow. They left their booth to go up to the counter for more drinks, and when they returned another group had moved their things and taken over the table. The interlopers refused to move, and after a brief argument, the couple stormed out. The husband returned a few minutes later with a handgun and shot everyone at the table. Two died, including the mother of one of their daughter's classmates.

In an effort to bring healing to the traumatized community, a meeting was scheduled at the school, and I was asked to help facilitate. My anxiety mounted as I watched the families stream in, filling the auditorium. I knew the man accused of the murders and I liked him. He was a loving father concerned about his children. I had kids myself by then and could not imagine what I could possibly say that would be remotely helpful. A sociologist might point to marginalization that renders any sign of disrespect unbearable, a psychologist to early experiences of trauma and powerlessness, but neither explanation seemed much help when I looked into the stricken faces of the children in the audience. Things were little different for their parents, who stared back at me with the same mix of shock, fear, and anger. This was our second tragedy of the year, after kids playing in a closet found a shotgun that went off, killing a toddler. In a strange way, the situations felt oddly similar, as though we were all impulsive children playing with forces we did not understand, especially when I thought back on my own worst moments.

The principal made some opening remarks and a staff member got up to speak. I had done a lot of group work by then and could tell we were losing the crowd. Once people started voicing their concerns, the audience split along the usual fault lines, not just ethnicity, which was mostly Latino and Southeast Asian with a mix of nationalities including Hmong and Cambodian, but also subtler divisions like what region they came from or how long they'd been in the country. The mood grew increasingly tense, with an ugly undertone of mutual blame, when a recent arrival from the refugee camps in Thailand declared that the killer had been taken over by an evil spirit. There were general murmurs, and the room went silent while the community facilitators looked to me, the supposed expert.

I sat there stupidly, not sure how to respond, and a shaman in the audience came to my rescue, explaining through interpreters that there were three kinds of spirits: good, bad, and wild. As near as I could understand, the latter were like tigers, morally neutral but deadly if you crossed their path. Something shifted in the air as he spoke, one of those intangible tipping points that happens in groups. I could feel tension ebbing from the room. A woman stood up next and said something I could not hear about *la comunidad y los ninos preciosos*. Only about a quarter of the audience were Hmong and not all these followed the old ways; however, the shaman's remarks had struck a chord that resonated throughout room. It did not seem to matter that the victims and the perpetrator were from entirely different cultures. I was too, for that matter, but the explanation made as much sense as anything in accounting for the demonic force unleashed in the bar that night.

Shifting Shadows

In Jung's terminology, those dark and powerful forces constitute the *shadow*, the topic of the current chapter. It is the only Jungian concept that has passed into general usage and the easiest to grasp. We all know there are parts of us and those we love that simply do not fit, that do and say things we would never do or say and yet we did. These two incidents illustrate more dramatic expressions of shadow and the importance of a person's stance toward it as well as the interplay of individual and collective dimensions that makes the shadow so powerful.

One reason the concept has proved so popular is the vividness of the image. If you picture consciousness as an illuminating light, aspects of yourself that you are unaware of are cast in shadow, including the parts you cannot bear to look at. And you really do not see them, that is the eerie part, like objects in the blind spot of a car. They are notoriously hard to pin down and, like literal shadows, their appearance is a matter of perspective—what you see depends on where you are standing. Shadow becomes most visible when an inner attitude collides with external circumstances, like leaving sunglasses behind or happening to sit at someone else's table.

Shadow can assume many forms and how it manifests partly depends on our attitude toward it. This can change over time, like my very different reactions to equally pointless murders as I matured. Since none of us can see our own shadow, misunderstandings often feel like somebody else's fault, a tragicomic charade that plays out endlessly in groups, companies, and families.[120] Learning to own your shadow is the work of a lifetime since it requires taking responsibility for something you can only perceive obliquely. If you are lucky, a friend or spouse points it out; on the level of society, however, we are all in the dark, the blind blaming the blind. Obvious howlers become visible only in hindsight, like the founding fathers eulogizing the rights of man while excluding women, enslaved people, and laborers, not to mention the original inhabitants of the land. In practice, most discussions of shadow are not referring to these cultural blind spots but personal imperfections, the ugly remark that pops out like a burp, the embarrassing or reprehensible aspects of the personality we downplay, deny, or project onto someone else.

Perhaps the most well-known literary treatment of this propensity to split off unpleasant parts of the personality is Robert Louis Stevenson's classic, *The Strange Case of Dr. Jekyll and Mr. Hyde*.[121] The book describes a respectable Victorian physician, prone to unnamed secret vices in his youth, who develops a potion that transforms him into his opposite, a violent cad named Mr. Hyde who tramples children in the street. In Jungian terms, Hyde represents shadow and Dr. Jekyll persona, the public face we turn to the world. Over the course of the story, the doctor gradually loses control over his unsavory counterpart, who begins possessing him whether or not he drinks the proverbial Kool-Aid. Their eventual merger points to an underlying identity, two sides of the same personality, as well as the ultimate futility of trying to repress shadow. Because one way or another, it always worms its way to the surface.

Groups or individuals who identify with the shadow may live it out directly and even turn it into a uniform, like the skulls and devil heads favored by outlaw motorcycle gangs and paramilitary organizations. When the shadow is partially disowned, it is often denounced in public and lived out furtively, like the minister who rails against homosexuality and gets caught soliciting sex in an airport bathroom or the politician whose outrage over sexual harassment does not extend to his office staff. Shadow that is completely denied usually winds up projected onto

---

[120] C. G. Jung, 1951/1968. *Aion*, CW 9ii, ¶16.
[121] Robert Louis Stevenson, *The Strange Case of Dr. Jekyll and Mr. Hyde*.

someone else.[122] This can be catastrophic if others are seen as the source of the evil that a person cannot own and must eliminate, even if that means taking them with it.

As in Stevenson's novella, the shadow often involves instinctual forces like sex or aggression. However, it can encompass any part of the personality that does not get lived out and integrated. Jungians talk about the "bright shadow" of individuals who embody their dark side in daily life.[123] I sometimes encountered this during psychological evaluations of career criminals who waxed sickly sweet and relatively sincere about being a good boy and making their sainted mothers proud, at least until it got to the details of behavioral change. Surprisingly, every once in a while one would actually switch sides and start living out positive parts of themselves that had previously been buried, usually after some sort of conversion experience.

On the level of society, the collective darkness we deny in ourselves tends to get projected onto people or groups seen as "other" to ourselves. This phenomenon is often referred to as *scapegoating,* an image derived from a widely dispersed religious ritual in which an animal is loaded with the group's guilt and driven into the wilderness.[124] People targeted for scapegoating are typically excluded, whether socially or geographically, as in racial segregation or the expulsion of Jews from Spain. Other recipients of projected shadow are rubbed out like so much dirt, the image behind "ethnic cleansing." Sadly, religious ideology often plays an active role in the process, whether by demonizing instinctual aspects of our shared humanity or enlisting believers in various kinds of holy war.

Whatever Possessed Me: Spirits and Complexes

Coming from a prescientific culture, the biblical perspective is closer to the shaman's model of demonic possession than our current psychological orientation. Both approaches have their merits. It is hard to know exactly what is meant by spirits in the contemporary cultural context, whether those the shaman mentioned, or the ones Jesus exorcizes in the Gospels. Jung refers to them as *autonomous complexes,*[125] an idea

---

[122] Jung, *Aion,* CW 9ii, ¶16.
[123] Jung, CW 9ii, ¶13.
[124] Sylvia Perera, *The Scapegoat Complex: Towards a Mythology of Shadow and Guilt.*
[125] Jung, 1921/1971. *Psychological Types,* CW 6, ¶923.

with its own complications, and at one point compares them to the medieval concept of demons.[126] On the other hand, talk of bad parenting or social marginalization seems anemic in the face of our capacity for cruelty, whether the murders in the tavern or the killing fields that drove many of the families in the audience to an urban ghetto.

Writing at the cusp of the Renaissance, Ignatius bridged these two world views by tracking the influence of good and bad spirits through their impact on emotional experience.[127] Coming at the issue from a psychological perspective five hundred years later, Jung's transpersonal model offers a similarly nuanced analysis of the complicated interaction between individual personality and the unseen forces that extend beyond it. Like Ignatius, he paid particular attention to feeling aspects of the process, as witnessed by his concept of complexes organized around an emotional response,[128] a quality that also applies to archetypes.[129] Also like Ignatius, he was preoccupied with finding the best way of relating to these larger forces, which have the potential to overwhelm the personality. He described in detail how vulnerabilities based in individual psychology can open the floodgates to powerful unconscious forces.[130] Put another way, personal shadow that goes unrecognized provides a portal for the collective shadow, a dynamic noted at the Nuremberg trials and subsequent inquests into genocide, when fear, greed, or ambition lead otherwise ordinary people to do the unthinkable. Ignatius makes a similar point when he compares the spiritual enemy to a military commander who sizes up defenses in order to attack at the weakest point,[131] appearing to the pious as an angel of light in order to play on higher-order vices like spiritual pride.[132]

Chapter 7 described how emotional responses get supercharged when a complex is activated. By way of quick review, a *complex* is a constellation of images and meanings with an archetypal core that is organized around

---

[126] Jung, CW 6, ¶175

[127] Joseph Munitiz and Philip Endean, Spiritual Exercises of Ignatius of Loyola in *Saint Ignatius of Loyola Personal Writings*, 348–353, ¶¶313–336.

[128] Jung, CW 6, ¶924.

[129] Jung, 1961. "Symbols and the Interpretation of Dreams," *The Symbolic Life*, CW 18, ¶589.

[130] Jung, 1936. "Psychology and National Problems," CW 18, ¶¶1311–1330.

[131] Munitiz and Endean, Spiritual Exercises, 351, ¶327.

[132] Munitiz and Endean, Spiritual Exercises, 352, ¶331.

a powerful emotion.[133] It spans three interrelated domains: personal psychology, outer events and relationships, and a system of internal symbolic meaning that draws on past experiences and the surrounding culture. All three likely came together that fateful night in the tavern, a perfect storm of primal impulses, personal and family history, and a model of masculinity that could not let disrespect go unavenged. The complexity of this real-time interaction between individual psychology, societal forces, and unfolding external events helps explain why therapists fail so miserably when asked to predict what patients will do outside their offices.

Jung's emphasis on archetypal forces adds yet another dimension to this complicated interplay of outer events and inner responses. Like the primate responses encoded in our biological makeup, he saw *archetypes* as recurrent patterns in human experience that carry a power that can overwhelm individual decision making.[134] Similar to the shaman's wild spirits, they are morally neutral, and their impact can be either positive or negative, depending on how they are channeled. One indication of their presence is an uncanny ability to grip individuals with a sort of religious intensity.[135] Those affected may not be religious in the traditional sense, but there is definitely a reverential tone in the way people and groups who are seized by a complex talk about their beliefs. From diet to politics, these truths become self-evident and cannot be questioned. Whether they were justified in religious or secular terms, the worst events in human history have been driven by a sort of holy fervor. Once a complex gets catalyzed it can possess an entire society, animate a coterie of zealots, or conjure up an internet army who have never met directly. The full range of human capabilities and emotions is invoked and highjacked. A quick look at the rhetoric of extremist groups reveals that most are driven as much by love as hatred, whether for a hypothetical "white race" or the idealized rural proletariat that Pol Pot dreamed up in Paris cafes, a cracked vision whose shattered survivors struggled to make sense of yet more senseless death.

I have given a general sense of what Jung meant by shadow along with some examples. Before exploring the topic in more depth, I need to

---

[133] Andrew Samuels, Bani Shorter, and Fred Plaut, *A Critical Dictionary of Jungian Analysis*, 34.
[134] Jung, 1936. "The Concept of the Collective Unconscious," *The Archetypes and the Collective Unconscious*, CW 9i, ¶¶98, 99.
[135] Jung, CW 9i, ¶99.

address a couple overarching issues. First, technically speaking, there is no such thing as shadow. Like ego or Self, the term is a metaphoric way of talking about a particular class of psychological phenomena, whether experienced in ourselves, someone else, or the field between us. This brings me to the second point. Psychological concepts are notoriously squishy, and the shadow is especially nebulous and hard to get hold of. This amorphous quality makes sense in an imagistic way given the fact that literal shadows have no set form yet take the shape of whatever blocks the light, an almost infinite number of permutations. To extend the metaphor, my best shot at conveying the shadow is not a list of general characteristics but specific examples that give readers a feel for the concept so they can apply it for themselves.

Returning to the model of a psychological case study mentioned in Chapter 1, the introduction to the book, the goal is not to be comprehensive but illustrative in conveying how shadow manifests in an individual life, in this case Mark's. This sort of detailed exploration of the interface between his inner and outer worlds has the advantage of moving the discussion outside the realm of abstraction but also has serious limitations. Where Mark reacted to feeling diminished with violent assertions of specialness, another person might respond with deference or earnest appeals to reason. His was only one of many paths through the vast underworld of shadow and I will only be looking at one aspect of his experience. Obviously, it shouldn't be taken as universal, let alone normative, although I will do my best to highlight some general themes and patterns that resonate throughout the culture.

Types of Shadow

There are many ways to talk about the shadow. For purposes of this discussion, I would like to divide it into four broad categories: personal, relational, collective, and archetypal. Although this chapter will concentrate mainly on the first two, I will begin by touching briefly on the collective and archetypal shadow. Both will be addressed in more detail in later chapters when I consider them in the context of Jung's religious model and the encounter with the "other."

Turning first to *collective shadow*, I spoke earlier about scapegoating and the negative projections directed at those seen as inferior or threatening. When shadow involves instinctive impulses that are at odds with our elevated picture of ourselves, these primal energies become a weapon turned against whoever seems to embody them, typically a person or group we do not know well and can see however we want.[136] The remote target may be a stranger, in the case of road rage, a media figure, or someone at the periphery of our social world, like the coworker I think is out to get me. Collective shadow encompasses the shared blind spots and areas of darkness within a group or society.[137] The negative qualities people deny in themselves are projected onto members of another group seen as violent, rapacious, lazy, or otherwise flawed, an attribution based on ethnicity, religion, culture, immigration status, or some other identifiable characteristic.

Archetypal shadow, by contrast, reflects a fundamental tension within the concept of shadow itself. A plethora of popular books urge us to befriend and claim our shadow. This advice begs a fundamental question, however: are we talking about garden variety nastiness or something truly monstrous? Expressing our feelings may or may not be a good thing, depending on whether it means a timid person learning to voice her needs or a teenager acting on the desire to rape a child. In the case of genocide and serial killers, shadow seems to have moved into another dimension, a qualitative difference that makes it difficult to know if we are talking about the same thing.[138]

Mark's uneasiness regarding the Satan dream reflected this dilemma. The dream's actual message had to do with his exaggerated sense of badness, which it caricatured as the devil incarnate in a plastic action figure, but he worried that simply connecting with the image would open him to real demonic forces. Jungians address this issue by differentiating between the personal shadow that needs to be integrated and the archetypal shadow that manifests in absolute evil, which cannot be absorbed into the personality but only resisted to the best of one's ability.[139] The Lord's Prayer expresses a similar recognition of human limitations in regard to shadow with its humble request not to be led into temptation but instead delivered from evil.

On a note of caution, broad categories like archetypal or collective shadow offer a useful way to approach the topic, however, they need to

---

[136] Jung, *Aion*, CW 9ii, ¶¶16, 17.
[137] Jung, "Symbols and the Interpretation of Dreams," CW 18, ¶¶560–563.
[138] Jung, 1946. "The Psychology of the Transference," *The Practice of Psychotherapy*, CW 16, ¶452.
[139] Jung, CW 16, ¶452; Jung, *Aion*, CW 9ii, ¶19.

be taken with a grain of salt. There are no sharp divisions in the land of shadows and each blurs into its neighbor. It is easy to see this smudging of boundaries in the case of genocide. Once the process gets rolling, collective shadow projections that lie simmering below the surface of the society take on an archetypal, even demonic, dimension of evil. Personal and relational shadows get fed into the larger pattern, as greed for others' possessions and the desire to avenge old vendettas turns neighbor against neighbor. In a massive amplification of what happens on an individual level when a complex is catalyzed, the entire society becomes possessed as commonplace shadow takes on apocalyptic proportions. A less dramatic mingling of the individual and collective levels occurs in what have been called *micro-aggressions,* when seemingly minor acts by ordinary people during everyday interactions reinforce oppressive societal patterns that carry within them a potent core of shadow projection.

Not surprisingly, there is a similarly blurry boundary between *personal* and *relational shadow,* the complexed patterns that arise in relationships. Distinguishing between them is a matter of degree since all shadow has a relational component. This was obvious in the case of Mark's marital problems, yet relational shadow also underlay his encounter at the hardware store when a minor interaction triggered an intense internal response rooted in early relationships. At first glance, the merciless self-judgment he visited on himself while tossing sleeplessly in his solitary room appears to be entirely self-generated, even solipsistic. However, closer examination reveals that it too arose in the context of relationship, this time with the internal jury he brought from childhood. I will say more about these interactions with inner and outer people in relation to the complicated interplay between personal and relational shadow.

I noted at the start of the chapter that *personal shadow* involves the parts of ourselves we cannot bear to acknowledge and so deny or project onto those around us. These can be instinctive impulses that violate self-image, in keeping with shaman's model of wild spirits, or normal limitations and failings that feel unbearable. An individual's relationship with them is rooted in personal history and depends to a large degree on what was judged unacceptable in that particular person's background. Often these parallel traditional lists of faults like the seven deadly sins of pride, greed, lust, wrath, gluttony, envy, and sloth, to which might be added modern sins like mediocrity or intolerance.

Shadow also may involve sins against the self that lead people to focus on others at the expense of themselves. Women I see in my therapy practice often complain about unspoken pressures toward this kind of deference, which contradict more overt societal messages about self-assertion and leave them feeling perennially judged. In intimate relationships, this can lead to a power imbalance that one woman described as two against zero, since both are focused on the needs of one partner. Much has been written about ways in which institutional Christianity's emphasis on self-sacrifice has perpetuated social inequality and weaponized a religious ideal in the interest of the status quo. Here, as elsewhere, there is a convergence of collective and personal shadow. Because most couples struggle with power issues in one way or another, this is another place where personal shadow intermingles with relational shadow, as seen in Mark's struggle to come to terms with the shifting balance of power in his marriage.

Weighed and Found Wanting

At this point, it may be helpful to offer specific examples of the topics discussed so far. Mark's dream about the underground market offers a good illustration of the personal level of shadow, especially in the context of the confrontation at the hardware store that preceded it. Descent into a labyrinth is a recurrent motif in mythology and literature, often associated with confronting the murky depths of the personality. From this perspective, the assailant he encounters there represents a dark aspect of himself. It seizes him from behind, the side he cannot see, just as a literal shadow streams behind him when facing the light. Like many dream images, it provides an individualized portrait of an aspect of his personality, in this case shadow material triggered by a sense of threat that is expressed in images taken from his personal history.

During our session, he associated the man who ambushed him with times he found himself seized by sudden anger, in keeping with Jung's idea that dream figures personify a cutoff aspect of the dreamer.[140] The threatening stranger embodies both his deeply rooted expectation of attack by others and the violent overreaction this fear catalyzed in him, a response he compared to the counterphobic reaction of a family pet

---

[140] Jung, 1938/1940. "Psychology and Religion" (The Terry Lectures), *Psychology and Religion: West and East,* CW 11, ¶¶37–39.

previously used to train fighting dogs. It is an old cliché that we become what we hate. The abused child grows up to be an abuser, and people who feel physically threatened often turn to preemptive violence, a dynamic at the heart of gang life. On a societal level, this same pattern plays out all over the world. The traditional psychological term for this violent chain reaction is *identification with the aggressor,* an unconscious process that enables us to overcome our terror by mimicking the scary behavior that makes us feel powerless.[141]

When Mark felt threatened by others he channeled his abusive father, a reenactment that allowed him to regain a sense of personal power by directing at others the kind of escalation that terrified him as a child. The picture gets more complicated when considering how this process played out on an internal level. A hallmark of Mark's early life was feeling judged and insufficient, "weighed and found wanting" in the biblical language of his youth. As often happens with children who bear the brunt of negative parental projections, what rescued him from feeling completely crushed was a secret sense of his specialness. This buoying belief echoes the fairytale motif of the prince in disguise, a universal motif recently reworked in the popular *Harry Potter* series.

At a core level, Mark felt as though his very survival depended on a secret identity that enabled him to preserve a sense of self in the face of attack. Throughout childhood, this feeling of specialness was reinforced by a secret alliance with his mother, whose own sense of importance partly rested on having an extraordinary child. Mark's native intelligence provided a handy hook for the projection yet, like all exaggerations, it remained brittle and vulnerable to puncture. In my work as a psychologist, I am often reminded just how fragile this sustaining sense of specialness can be. "If you ain't first you ain't shit," a college athlete once told me, "And any fool in the stands can see the stats." A minor recording star voiced the same lament in different words when she told me, "Your first record competes with everybody else. After that you're in competition with yourself and that's a game you're bound to lose eventually."

The brighter the light, the darker the shadow it casts. Like the young track star in my office, what scared Mark most was the prospect of being ordinary, giving his all and just being average. A therapist colleague of mine who sees young researchers and grad students from a nearby

---

[141] Sandor Ferenczi, "Confusion of Tongues."

university calls this the Nobel Prize syndrome. All of them have spent their lives at the head of the class, being told since they were small that they could grow up to be anything. Who knows, a parent or teacher might say, someday you could even win a Nobel Prize. This magic bundle of abilities and expectations becomes the core of their identity, especially if other parts feel shaky, and the burden grows heavier as the years drift by and successes roll in. If they do not preempt the possibility of failure by dropping out the race, like Mark did as a teenager, their career eventually lands them into the company of peers. There, for the first time in their lives, they find themselves in the middle of the herd and the experience can be devastating. For Mark, the mere possibility of being less than stellar nearly killed him. When he could not suppress evidence of ordinariness in the outer world, the only way to save his inner specialness was to attack himself. Like a defeated army searching out traitors, the reason for failure had to be ferreted out and punished. If he could not blame others, then clearly *he* had not been trying hard enough.

This type of internal conflict usually intensifies with age, as the odds of brilliant success grow progressively dimmer and being a legend in one's own mind begins to wear thin. Mark could not tolerate his dismissive treatment at the hardware store because it validated his worst fear. He reacted explosively when he felt diminished by others, but his attacks on himself were equally violent, like a revolutionary government that runs out of external enemies and begins executing its own. Psychologists joke about the *Iron Rule,* whereby we do unto others what was done to us. This usually works both ways, since at some level we treat ourselves the same way we treat others. Mark's eruption in the parking lot mirrored the murderous violence he turned against himself and the sentence for failure was death by hanging, a particularly degrading form of punishment. Like the classic quote from the Vietnam War about blowing up a village to save it, there was real danger he would preserve his specialness at the cost of his life. "I get the irony," he told me a few years into our work together, "the punitive God I grew up with has nothing on me when it comes to smiting and vengeance."

When I work with someone over a period of time, we begin developing a language of our own so that a story, a dream, or a gesture takes on a world of shared meaning. Mark's encounter at the hardware store had this quality, a compressed way of referencing what happened when these complexes got triggered. The phrase "a hero in my own mind" began playing a similar role in our conversations, a shorthand way to talk about his dreams of glory and the specter of insignificance he tried to exorcise by attacking his attackers or failings in himself.

Self-overcoming is glamorized in our society, like the bodybuilders' maxim that pain is only weakness leaving your body. The Jungian writer Marian Woodman describes eating disorders as an addiction to perfection, the obsession that drives a teenager to starve herself to death in an effort to eliminate an infinitesimal ripple of belly fat.[142] Christianity has its own dark history of self-overcoming, a gnostic longing for transcendence that comprises the shadow side of imitating Christ. In Christian circles, the psychological need for specialness can disguise itself as a religious injunction to be perfect. Ignatius documented his struggle with scrupulosity in some detail, and today his fear of sinning by inadvertently stepping on crossed twigs in the shape of a crucifix might well be classed as OCD.[143] Mark's addiction to perfection had its roots in his religious upbringing, although at this point his spiritual practice did not so much feed the complex as provide respite from it. The relief, however, did not always carry over into daily life.

Mark had long ago abandoned the religious strictures of childhood, but his adult identity as an advocate for the downtrodden brought its own moral imperative. It sometimes made him judgmental and defensive, like the old joke that hell hath no fury like a progressive accused of racism. The righteous zeal he brought to his work gave rise to what he came to call his "do-gooder" shadow, the take-no-prisoners attitude evident in the dream about the underground market. Although indulgent to a fault with his indigent and adjudicated clients, he could be harsh and explosive with colleagues or bureaucrats he found insufficiently compassionate. Outside work, this sense of rectitude gave rise to free-floating entitlement, a sort of moral slush fund he could draw on at will. He drove himself to exhaustion and expected others to make allowances for him, not just his wife but also anyone who crossed his path after a long day at the office. Shadow is the part of ourselves we do not want to look at and Mark's dirty secret was that he was not actually any more moral than the next guy and not above cashing in on his virtuous vocation to avoid taking responsibility for his faults. The dream burlesques this hypocrisy when he solicitously cares

---

[142] Marion Woodman, *Addiction to Perfection*.
[143] Munitiz and Endean, *Spiritual Exercises*, 355, ¶¶346–348.

for the poor brain-damaged man who shows up at his office while never acknowledging that he inflicted the injury in the first place.

Not surprisingly, these same patterns emerged on the level of *relational shadow*, the complexed patterns that emerge in relationships. To the extent his identity was entangled with Jennifer's, her flaws felt as unbearable as his own. The things she did or did not do reflected on him, and her imperfections felt like a personal affront. Even more unbearable were the times she did not protect him from experiencing his own flaws and unbearable feelings. Like many men, he expected her to anticipate his needs because having to ask made him feel vulnerable. Although I never met Jennifer, it appeared to me that she had bought into his demand for mirroring earlier in their relationship, perhaps because it was easier than taking responsibility for her own needs. But based on Mark's description, she seemed to be undergoing her own psychological development and this was destabilizing the old pattern. Sometimes I half-jokingly warn heterosexual couples entering joint treatment that the end result of most marital therapy is men becoming less self-centered and women more so. Something of the sort seemed to be happening for them, probably prompted by growing independence on Jennifer's part. Her changes forced Mark to change in turn, and both were experiencing intense growing pains. And while this was a good thing from the perspective of individual development, it placed the relationship in jeopardy with no guarantee of survival.

I am only looking at Mark's side of the story, but it is safe to assume that Jennifer had her own issues that contributed to what went on between them. Even leaving these aside, my brief account gives a sense of the complexity of relational shadow, the shared matrix of complexes and shadow material that emerges in the context of intimate relationships, whether with siblings, parents, close friends, and (especially) partners.[144] It is always bound up with individual shadow since default reactions that come up in close relationships are closely tied to personal history and formative relationships, especially those experienced in the family of origin.

As I mentioned earlier, projection is inevitable and not a problem in itself, but distorted projections cause no end of difficulties. These are

---

[144] Jung, 1917/1926/1943. "On the Psychology of the Unconscious," *Two Essays on Analytical Psychology,* CW 7, ¶152.

especially likely when the recipients are either far away or very close to us. With people at a distance, there is little to go on and no way to correct distortions, whether positive or negative. With someone close, it is hard to separate our own needs and wishes from the actual person, especially when a complex is constellated. Partnered relationships are prone to a particularly intense and tangled mix of idealization and devaluation, light and shadow. We do not need Othello to tell us how quickly love can turn to hate, all we have to do is watch the news. As relationships deepen over time, the level of complexity grows exponentially, a dynamic interplay of past and present, joys and resentments, shared understandings, and irresolvable impasses. The inner children come out to play or cry for comfort as patterns from early life get reactivated, what happened back then and our interpretation of it, the core interpersonal programming we bring to significant relationships.

Nothing yanks the covers off illusions of perfection like sharing a bathroom, and Mark's toilet dreams offer vivid images of this awkward intimacy. In the first, his wife is having to deal with his shit. This is inevitable in a relationship and, as in waking life, the Mark in the dream struggles with defensiveness. In their day-world relationship, Jennifer had grown tired of taking his shit and having to sort through his crap for him. Psychologically speaking, she was no longer willing to absorb his shadow projections. Like many men, he looked to the woman in his life to pick up the emotional slack so he did not have to deal with his uncomfortable feelings. And like an accountant keeping double books, he excused his tantrums while blaming her for not being sufficiently attuned to his volatile emotions. When she stopped soothing his ego by reassuring him after he acted like a spoiled child, the whole game was exposed, and his shit laid out for all to see. In the second dream, he's taken over the job of dealing with his crap and must grapple with the humiliation of knowing that she is witnessing his struggle to clean himself. Jennifer sits beside him but he's on his own. Her gaze is averted in a gesture he interpreted as tact; it also could point to her growing sense of self apart from the relationship.

Although their marital crisis actually reflected personal development on both their parts, it did not feel that way to him at the time. It is a measure of Mark's psychological growth that he chose to tolerate this painful and humbling experience without blowing up or blowing out of the marriage, a newfound strength he attributed to his deepening relationship with God. Doing so required acknowledging his faults, both to himself and others.

In psychological parlance, his ability to project his shadow outside himself was being hammered from all sides. He was getting too old to play the role of angry young man and tensions were mounting—at work, at home, and even in his church. On an internal level, he could no longer justify acting like a teenager whenever he got frustrated, the change in perspective that prompted his epiphany in the parking lot with its painful vision of his ridiculousness. In a kind of feedback loop, working with the dreams helped Mark to become aware of these developmental pressures while the increased awareness they fostered helped illuminate the dreams' meaning at this juncture in his life. Future chapters will examine how dream images of partners also can reflect aspects of the dreamer's own personality that need to be recognized, but right then Mark's entire attention was focused on the literal level of the dreams and his part in the patterns that threatened the relationship.

Old Shadows Never Die

Having laid out some of these patterns in general terms, I want to ground the discussion in a later dream that provides an unusually comprehensive exposition of shadow material and the ways it functions in relationships. It came after Mark had been grappling with these issues for several months and demonstrates how his deepening self-understanding was altering the emotional complexity of his dreams. Although lengthy, it is worth quoting in totality as it summarizes many of the themes I have been discussing. Mark titled it "Old Shadows Never Die," after considering the more descriptive "Nailed Him!" Both names give a sense of his hard-won progress in owning his shadow.

I'm standing in line in front of a small booth or kiosk, like a phone booth. There's a television screen in the booth and I'm ordering up a video on my cell phone that will be shown on it. This takes a long time, and I have the guilty sense that I should have done it somewhere else. A group of young women are waiting impatiently for the booth; they look like sorority sisters. The movie has to do with demonic possession, perhaps a documentary, and I become mildly possessed watching it. This is communicated to the young woman behind me when she looks up angrily and both our eyes gleam a livid green. Then I'm walking and notice a white substance on the screen of my cell phone. It looks like gum, and I begin wiping it off before realizing that it's coming from inside the phone, a sort of white froth. It has to do with ordering the movie on possession. I hurry home to talk to Jennifer about ordering new phones. We're living in a two-story house by the beach, and I climb up an outside stair facing away from the water. I hear her yelling and the sound of a mouse squeaking. It looks like she's driving a huge rat off the side of the porch. As I watch, it becomes a decrepit old stag with a huge rack of antlers. These look cracked and withered, as though they've sat out in the elements for a long time. It scurries down the side of the building on its hind legs, like a person with withered front legs. Jennifer shows me it has knocked loose a piece of the banister on its way down. As we talk, I see it climb back up on the roof above us and begin tearing off boards. I yell at it, and it turns into a cocky young man like a muscular construction worker. He glares at me contemptuously, passing a claw hammer back and forth between his hands in a threatening manner. I move out onto the stairs, yelling to Jennifer to move under the stairway in case he throws it. She hesitates and I repeat the demand with growing urgency until she does. I wrench off a two-by-four to confront him. By this time, he is hanging upside-down and coming out of the ceiling above me, as though squeezing out of a light fixture. I stretch up off the stairs to swing at him with the board, I miss but a jutting nail gashes his cheek. He becomes an old man. He begins moving back into the opening as I jab at him, then roars at me as he morphs into a grotesque figure like a demonic Muppet or an illustration from Where the Wild Things Are. I'm not sure if he'll be back and wish I had been able to reach and destroy him.

The dream proved pivotal in Mark's life, an example of what Jung referred to as "big dreams."[145] The narrative is crammed with details that held private meaning for him or, as he put it, "nailed" him. Detailed examination would draw us too deeply into his private material, so I will content myself with a few high points, incorporating enough of his personal associations to flesh out the meaning of the images.

The opening sequence involving a video and impatient sorority sisters offers a graphic depiction of what it is like to be seized by a complex

---

[145] Jung, 1928. "The Relations between the Ego and the Unconscious." CW 7, ¶276.

and then transfer the problem to others through shadow projection. Dreams love puns, both visual and linguistic, and over the years I have listened to many that frame psychological projection in terms of movies and television screens, whereas references to a television remote control bring up an entirely different set of puns. Downloading an online movie onto a personal phone is an apt image for internalizing a complex that has a collective component, in this case, the sense of entitlement he attributed to sorority sisters. Mark's associations added a personal twist.

The scene where he hogs the movie kiosk referenced a recent incident when he was gathering material for a client at the county courthouse. Instead of lugging the stack of bound documents to a copy room as a nearby sign indicated, he created a long line by monopolizing the single Xerox machine in the lobby. When confronted, he played dumb while justifying himself internally with the righteousness of his advocacy work. In our session, he linked this "innocent" passive-aggressive behavior with sorority sisters, based on B-movie stereotypes, and associated the green hue of their shared possession with the old cliche about being "green with envy." Although this may sound like a stretch, it fit his personal psychology and his negative projections regarding the competence of sorority sisters, since entitlement usually compensates an underlying sense of insufficiency.

The topic of the movie, demonic possession, offers a good metaphor for being taken over by a complex and the contagious quality of shadow projections. The movie is a documentary, in keeping with Mark's intellectualized approach to the world. At times this capacity for thoughtful overview provided a useful perspective on himself but here cerebral detachment is not enough to prevent contagion. We only know in hindsight when we've been seized by a complex, and it is not until the dreamer steps back from the situation that he discovers he's been possessed. Psychologically speaking, this realization reflected Mark's growing ability to gain sufficient distance from his complexes to begin taking responsibility for his shadowy behavior.

His phone has been taken over by something like a computer virus, and in good horror movie fashion, it foams at the mouth. As in the earlier toilet dream, he tries to clean it up himself and finds he cannot do it alone. What's been tainted is his means of communication, and his first thought at this point in his life is how it will affect his marriage. Apparently, the couple needs to change their shared cell-phone plan, and he hurries home to start the process, climbing the stairs to the raised deck of a fictitious house. References to second stories abound in dreams, usually connoting either elevation that offers perspective or the latter part of a process, like the second half of life when this capacity often develops. In contrast to most beachfront houses, the outdoor deck where he meets his wife faces away from the ocean, a nearly universal image of the collective unconscious; instead it is turned inward toward the intimate space of their private backyard.

He arrives to find Jennifer is driving out a rat, much as she did when she stopped absorbing his negative projections and accommodating his tantrums. I cannot imagine a better symbol for shadow. Many idioms convey rats' sneakiness and malice, like ratting out a friend or smelling a rat when something nefarious is going on under the surface. This one starts out as an innocent-looking mouse but quickly grows in size, as though its full magnitude only becomes apparent when he turns his attention toward it. It morphs first into a giant rat and then a decrepit old stag. In popular culture, stags are associated with isolated maleness, like stag movies or going stag. The withered antlers suggest an outgrown competitive attitude, which needed to be shed as Mark entered a new life stage. At first the stag seems content to go quietly, shuffling down the side of the building like a tired old man, although it does manage to damage the protective banister in the process.

Getting rid of shadow is never that easy, however. I noted earlier that the Gospel account of Jesus's temptation in the desert ends when the devil goes away "until an opportune time,"[146] and, true to form, this incarnation of shadow makes a comeback. Its next incarnation is fully human and hit closer to home. Mark had worked construction as a young man, the only time his father approved of his career choices, and he used to joke about doing the hammer toss during mock confrontations with coworkers. This was the cocky adolescent stance he fell back on when threatened, now wildly out of synch with his life, and the scene echoes his recent confrontation at the box store right down to the wooden club wielded by the Mark in the dream.

By this time, the dream ego is also in full macho mode and squares off with the threatening presence. The two antagonists are bonded in mutual possession, like the earlier exchange with the sorority sister, and between

---

[146] Luke 4:12.

them they are tearing the house apart. The intensity and archetypal tone of the dream imagery ratchets up further as the shapeshifting shadow goes from animal to human to monster. The upside-down figure hanging from the ceiling harkens back to the vampire bat in his earlier dream, which also dealt with shadow material and possession by a complex. This time an odd detail complicates the picture. In that dream, shining a flashlight up into a tree set the action in motion by illuminating the complex. Here the shadow is depicted squeezing out of a light fixture, as though somehow coming from the light itself. This is literally true, of course, since light creates shadow. As often happens, Mark's reflections on the image split into two contrasting meanings. He associated darkness emanating from the light with the brittle perfectionism that sometimes made him unbearable to those around him. However, the image also points to positive aspects of his shadowy relationship with aggression, including the impulse to protect himself and those he loved, which got diverted into destructive aggression when he felt helpless and frightened.

The two-by-four he swings in the dream took Mark back to the persona he adopted as a young man working construction. People sometimes compare an event that stops them in their tracks, like the incident at the hardware store, to getting hit with a two-by-four. But the image has many layers. On one level, it turns something meant for constructive purposes into a weapon, like his ready recourse to verbal aggression and physical violence when he felt threatened. On another, it allows him to finish the job begun by Jennifer when she confronted the complex and began driving out the rat. In contrast to the sneering construction worker, protecting his home and family offers a positive—if somewhat hackneyed—image of male assertion, just as manual labor gave Mark a positive sense of agency and male identity during a difficult period when he was first struggling to get clean.

I noted earlier that collective shadow sometimes manifests in archetypal evil, which must be resisted to the best of our ability. Things are more ambiguous on the level of personal shadow, which often contains a positive core that needs to be assimilated. The dream offers a prime example when Mark's blind swing at the monstrous figure unmasks the shadowy complexes surrounding power and perfection that stood between him and those around him. Although his blow misses, the creature retreats when a protruding nail grazes its cheek. Mark associated this image with the movie *300*, in which a Spartan commander's dying spear toss strips away the grandiose pretensions of the Persian god-king when it grazes his face and shows him to be mortal.[147] As in the movie, the injury has a deflating effect, reducing the tyrant to human size and revealing his vulnerability, just another guy who bleeds when cut.

Mark's marital crisis, along with mounting interpersonal problems at work and the growing self-awareness that sparked his epiphany in the parking lot, led to a similar unmasking. It turned out he was not so special after all. The only way forward was to accept his vulnerability and look under his defensive anger to the frightened child hiding beneath. Age often helps catalyze this kind of sea change as late middle age forces individuals to come to terms with mortal limits. In the dream, the tide turns when the figure is confronted and transforms into an old man who recedes into the woodwork. But things are never final when it comes to shadow. Just as the soundtrack swells and the credits start scrolling, the creature comes roaring back.

The dream began with a documentary on demonic possession and its final image is a monster, albeit a more approachable one. Having faced down a demon, the dreamer now finds himself in the realm of wild spirits that need to be respected but also have their useful side. This time the images are drawn from childhood. The first is the manic drummer from the Muppet rock band, a ball of shaggy energy named "Animal." The second is the children's classic, *Where the Wild Things Are,* in which a boy must come to terms with his wild impulses in order to rejoin the family,[148] the same lesson Mark was having to learn in late middle age. Ironically, his regret at the end of the dream that he did not completely destroy the monster points to a subtle resurgence of the old complex, the lust for transcendence I referred to as Mark's Christian shadow.

Darkness cannot be stamped out, and the history of Christianity, like all religions, offers sobering evidence of what happens when shadow is driven underground. Like the old tale about oyster fishermen who tried to get rid of starfish by cutting them in pieces and ended up multiplying them in the process, when it comes to the shadow we cannot hope for victory, only detente. The crucial thing is knowing what's there, as Jesus intimates in the parable of the unjust servant and his admonition that we must be wise as serpents if we want to be harmless as doves.

---

[147] *300*, 2006, screenplay by Zack Snyder, directed by Zack Snyder.
[148] Maurice Sendak, *Where the Wild Things Are.*

Shadow and Evil

This ambiguous relationship between light and darkness touches on a final issue that needs to be addressed before closing. Earlier I differentiated between *personal* or *relative* shadow and the *archetypal* or *absolute* shadow. The first involves ordinary but unvirtuous human drives and impulses that need to be claimed and integrated into the personality. By contrast, archetypal shadow threatens to overwhelm the personality. Jung believed it could not be integrated but only resisted. In terms of the shaman's three categories of spirits—good, bad, and wild—if the neutral forces within the personality can be classed with wild spirits, then absolute shadow would fall in the realm of evil spirits.

Working from a very different cosmology, Ignatius maintained that evil spirits act at the behest of the spiritual enemy to lure believers away from God, and their influence on the personality can be tracked through emotions and fantasies.[149] By Jung's time, the idea of evil spirits no longer resonated on a cultural level. Although theologians might espouse in a theoretical way the existence of dark spiritual forces operating in the world, few saw monitoring their presence as a central concern of religious practice. This shift gave rise to a troubling question in the culture, the same one that came up in the meeting in the auditorium. How do we account for the presence of evil in a post-religious age?

Psychology and sociology have ready explanations for garden-variety evil like the shooting in the bar, whether or not we find them completely convincing. Things get murkier when it comes unfathomable horrors like the genocide that had driven many of those in the audience from their homelands. The biographies of major tyrants in the twentieth century are oddly unsatisfying on this score, and I am always left wondering how these banal men with the usual messy childhoods wound up murdering millions.

The question of evil preoccupied Jung during the latter part of his career as his quest to account for the spiritual forces operating in the lives of his patients and the larger culture drew him into traditionally theological territory. His point of entry was the so-called theodicy problem endemic

---

[149] Munitiz and Endean, *Spiritual Exercises,* 348–353, ¶¶313–336.

to monotheistic religions: if the creator God is all good, all knowing, and all powerful, why is there evil in the world?[150]

Christianity has grappled with this conundrum throughout its history, and a broad range of solutions have been proposed. Early Christian writers invoked the Eden story to explain God's permissive will in granting Satan partial power over the Earth. In the modern era, some theologians have responded to the problem by asserting that God is beyond our limited moral judgments. Others appeal to our God-given freedom to make wrong choices or point out that evil is not a created "thing" but an emergent property in human relationships. A major strain in Christian thought views evil as *spoiled good,* a doctrine cleverly illustrated by the Catholic writer J. R. R. Tolkien when he described the evil orcs as inferior copies of the good elves in his trilogy *Lord of the Rings.*[151]

It was this optimistic view that Jung attacked, in part, because it permeated the Christian milieu of his time. He argued that evil is quite real[152] and must originate in God, who is the source of all and contains all opposites,[153] adding the usual Kantian caveat that he could only speak to our experience of God and not God in Godself.[154] The argument reflects his core belief that *wholeness,* rather than *goodness,* is the goal of psychological development. In Jungian terms, a full account of human reality must include the shadow, which derives from the Self and the God-image it contains. From this perspective, a religion that only values good and views evil as unreal, forces its adherents to deny a part of themselves and drives evil into the unconscious, where it can reign unseen and unchecked.[155]

Jung's 1952 monograph *Answer to Job* explored the ambivalent nature of the divine in the context of the biblical account of Job, in which Yahweh destroys the life of an innocent man in order to win a bet with Satan.[156] In contrast to previous works, the writing was polemic, at times sarcastic. According to Jung, he deliberately chose this tone to avoid giving the impression he was announcing an eternal truth. In his introduction to the

---

[150] Jung, *Memories, Dreams, Reflections,* 55–59.
[151] J. R. R. Tolkien, *Lord of the Rings.*
[152] Jung, 1956–57. "Jung and Religious Belief," CW 18, ¶1592.
[153] Jung, CW 18, ¶1593; Jung, 1952. "Answer to Job," CW 11, ¶574.
[154] Jung, CW 18, ¶1595
[155] Jung, CW 18, ¶1594.
[156] Jung, "Answer to Job," CW 11.

book, he characterized it as a highly subjective response to his experience of God, a personal reaction that gave voice to "the shattering emotion which the unvarnished spectacle of divine savagery and ruthlessness produces in us."[157]

There is no denying the Job story has disturbing implications for the nature of God if taken at face value, and a myriad of interpretations have been advanced over the centuries. In Jung's psychological approach, the infinitely powerful and largely unconscious Yahweh gains self-awareness from his encounter with a finite human being who confronts his actions,[158] whereas Job himself learns the limits of human understanding.[159] In Jungian terms, Job represents the ego and Yahweh the boundless unconscious, which, by definition, is unaware of itself.[160] From this perspective, the biblical account can be seen as a mythic formulation of the process of psychological maturation, in which the ego's encounter with the unconscious leads to increased awareness and changes the face the unconscious turns toward it.

Theological critics maintained that whatever the book's psychological value, it could not be taken seriously as a theological model. Not surprisingly, its publication alienated many of Jung's religious contemporaries, including his most serious Christian collaborator, the Catholic theologian Victor White. Their correspondence makes painful reading as it became increasingly apparent to both that they were working from radically different models of religious truth, talking past each other despite good intentions on both sides.[161]

So what does this mean for contemporary efforts to approach Jung from a Christian perspective? Christian writers sympathetic to Jung tend to gloss over the controversy but, like shadow, it must be faced. I will explore the subject more fully in subsequent chapters. For now I will address a couple key points directly relevant to Jung's concept of the shadow and the problem of evil.

Coming at spiritual development from a psychological perspective, *Answer to Job* emphasizes individual experience over the revealed truth favored by theology. Whereas theology typically takes as its starting point

---

[157] Jung, CW 11, ¶366.
[158] Jung, CW 11, ¶575.
[159] Jung, CW 11, ¶¶588, 589.
[160] Jung, CW 11, ¶579.
[161] Ann Lammers, *In God's Shadow: The Correspondence of Victor White and C. G. Jung.*

principles derived from scripture and religious tradition, Jung begins by asking what human experience reveals about the divine, although sacred texts and myths can help inform our understanding. Viewing God through this psychological lens highlights contradictions in the anthropomorphic model of divinity, even though Jung himself recognized this is the only possible way to conceptualize what is beyond human comprehension.[162] In many ways, the book can be seen as a variation on his youthful vision of a heavenly turd shattering the Basil cathedral, another attempt to free himself from an imprisoning God-image. As with that initial rejection of the optimistic and rationalistic theology of his childhood, Jung reacted violently to what he saw as a naive and destructive effort to deny the reality of evil, an idea rendered absurd by events of the twentieth century.[163]

What about good spirits, the final category in the shaman's cosmology? The violence of Jung's language makes it easy to miss the deeply religious sensibility underlying the book. In his reading of the biblical story, Job's appeal for justice seeks help from God against God, or perhaps a God-image, and encounters a secret ally within the divine nature.[164] Like the hidden God of the alchemists imprisoned in matter, his appeal points toward an unknown God beneath the God-image that Jung attacked. But what kind of God?

In an interview recorded late in his life, Jung attributed a patient's cure to God's grace and called guiding dreams gifts from God, which he went on to define as the most comprehensible name for people of our time to designate the Power beyond us.[165] Such statements did little to mollify his Christian interlocutors, although some still saw value in specific aspects of his approach, just as Freudian and Marxist tools of analysis may be employed without necessarily accepting their conclusions. I will return to these issues in later chapters, without hoping to resolve them.

In the meantime, the next two chapters will address a core Jungian principle that gives rise to a different kind of controversy as I take a closer look at how significant others are incorporated into our inner world and impact subsequent relationships. As usual, I will begin by examining the processes unfolding in Mark's life.

---

[162] Jung, CW 11, ¶574.
[163] Jung, "Jung and Religious Belief," CW 18, 1593.
[164] Jung, CW 11, ¶567.
[165] Jung, C. G. Jung Speaking, 375.

Chapter 10
In the Night Kitchen

"Just living the dream," Mark quipped glumly one afternoon in late fall, then grinned crookedly with a flash of his old sardonic self. The challenges in his life continued to ramp up. Budget cuts led to yet more streamlining at the agency where he worked. He had to account for every minute now, something he bristled at, and productivity demands increased by the month. Yet another messy legal issue involving the old family farm drew him back into his family of origin. Jennifer requested a formal separation and moved out of the house while they tried to work things out in therapy. He surprised them both with the openhearted way he encouraged her to take all the space she needed. "I know it sounds like clapping for Tinkerbell," he told me, "But I really do want whatever's best for her and even have a kind of peace with it."

Nevertheless, the accumulated stresses were taking a toll on him. He slept badly and was eating poorly, with frequent late-night runs for fast food. Early one morning, he wound up in the emergency room for what he thought might be an ulcer, only to discover that he had actually suffered a mild heart attack. His doctor put him on medication for blood pressure and high cholesterol and enrolled him in a class on cardiac fitness. Mark dropped out after the second meeting and took things into his own hands by starting a rigorous exercise regimen and switching to a plant-based diet. True to form, he embraced these lifestyle changes with the zealousness of new convert. The painful nighttime memories continued, stronger than ever, not just about actions he regretted but times he had been clueless and played the fool. His insomnia worsened and he had trouble concentrating at work. He went off verbally on a colleague and called back immediately to apologize.

"Not something I have much practice with, and I don't know who was more uncomfortable," he said with a sour smile. "If nothing else avoiding that awkward conversation should help me bite my tongue next time. Never mind that taking responsibility is what the steps have been telling me to do for years, one more thing to journal about for my sponsor."

Projects fell behind and his supervisor called him in for a performance review. He anticipated the worst yet left the meeting feeling touched by the genuine concern he received from her and his other coworkers. Mark puzzled over this unexpected kindness, and I wondered aloud whether it might have something to do with the softer demeanor I had noticed during our times together.

He sat with this a moment before replying. "I know it sounds melodramatic, but I feel like a dam burst somewhere upriver and suddenly there's all this water rushing down the canyon." He paused, groping for words. "I mean, last week I got tearful over a damn cell-plan commercial. You know, the one where the soldier calls home from Afghanistan to wish her daughter Happy Birthday, never mind the political subtext. Things are definitely pretty awful at the moment, but I'm noticing bits of beauty I never saw before. Little things you wouldn't expect, leaves silhouetted on a dusty windowpane or a swarm of midges dancing in the sunlight."

To Mark's surprise, short bursts of prayer had begun bubbling up spontaneously during the day, sometimes gratitude, sometimes pleas for help. It seemed to happen of its own volition and made him uneasy at first, as if he were being drawn back into his Evangelical childhood. Usually they just hung in air, a one-sided conversation that nevertheless seemed oddly relieving, though every now and then he felt an emotional warmth that startled him. "Like a loving parent," he told me, "The usual metaphors. My grandfather, actually, sitting on the porch together with the sun going down over the pasture. Not talking, just sharing his space, and feeling safe."

Mark still struggled with anger. Once he found himself on the brink of another physical confrontation, this time over a parking place, and broke off abruptly. "I felt stupid and told him look, I'm having a bad day, and walked away quick before he said something to piss me off."

During our sessions, we explored ways to support himself emotionally during this difficult period. He signed up for a weekend Centering Prayer retreat and joined an ongoing group at his church after he got back. Soon he was centering most mornings and the experience left him rueful. "There's five different movies playing at once," he told me, "A veritable cineplex. The most random stuff too. I want to blame it on Centering

Prayer, but I'm pretty sure the chaos has been there all along, so much for equanimity and being spiritually evolved." Even when the minutes dragged and he got up from the chair feeling like a complete failure, the time still felt like a respite. "I keep reminding myself what they said in the workshop," he continued. "Every time I come back to my sacred word it's a tiny awakening, like realizing you've nodded off and steering back onto the highway."

In addition to his usual 12-Step meeting, he joined a men's group at his church. "Now that's something I never saw myself doing," he told me, "Sitting in a circle in the church basement spilling my guts to a bunch of dudes. Liberated guy or not, there's so much wrong with that picture, beginning with the circle and the church basement. Granted, it's the same room as my noon meeting, but this one's got crosstalk and the damn choir director leading it."

Although Mark liked some of the men better than others, he welcomed the chance to be heard without advice or judgment. "Turns out I'm still not comfortable discussing my feelings with men," he said. "Go figure. I struggled with that a lot when I first got sober, the usual clichés about competition and vulnerability. I support the concept of men's groups on principle, of course, but always told myself I just wasn't a joiner, the usual crap. Not into drums and getting smudged with eagle feathers, all that self-conscious male camaraderie, which doesn't actually happen there by the way. I had a million good reasons, but it's just like AA. There's always stuff you can pick on, platitudes and alarming politics, but in the end it's just an alibi, another way to be different and 'terminally unique,' as we say in the program."

In addition to joint counseling sessions, their couple's therapist scheduled individual meetings with Mark to explore the patterns he brought to the relationship. He journaled about these during his morning devotions, an activity he described as sweeping his side of the street, and sometimes reflected on them in our sessions. The marital separation brought home to him just how much he relied on Jennifer to smooth out his feelings. "Expecting her to carry my emotional water for me and didn't even know it," he said. "Probably because my neediness mostly comes out in anger when she didn't listen exactly the way I wanted her to. Excuse me, that's needfulness, according to the therapist. I used to tell myself she wasn't available but everyone always joked about us being joined at the hip. Like Plato's missing halves, I'd say when I was being sentimental, as if that was a good thing. In his toast at our wedding, my best man called us a Mobius strip."

I looked puzzled and Mark explained. "You know, you used to see pictures of them on posters in the seventies, a strip of paper twisted into an infinity sign that looks 3D but really just has one surface," he traced the shape in air. "Glued together and all tangled up. Jennifer's definitely got her part in all this but that's her business; she's working on it in her individual therapy, and we're trying to sort out what's whose in the couples' sessions. I can see now that I was coasting on her energy, like race drivers drafting the car ahead of them, and never even noticed until she decided not to play anymore, to mix metaphors. She talks about having to figure out who she is apart from me, and I need to do the same thing, whether we get back together or not. 'One day at a time' and 'more will be revealed,' as they say in the rooms."

Mark always dreamed prolifically; now they came in torrents, filling the pages of his notebook. Dreams at the beginning of therapy are often fairly straightforward and easy to interpret, which makes the therapist look smart. They tend to get more convoluted as time goes by, the difference between flying over a city and working your way through its tangled alleyways. Mark's dreams at this point in our work together were no exception. They included elaborate productions with large casts of characters and plots lines that spanned multiple episodes, looping narratives that he called "miniseries." Women figured prominently, not just Jennifer but a parade of unknown female figures ranging from nurturing to sinister.

The images spilled over into waking life, and he found himself returning to them during the day, losing himself in vivid daydreams. He sometimes felt as though he had fallen down the proverbial rabbit hole, stumbling into a surreal world where inner life began to eclipse the outer. This kind of flooding is common during times of transition, not that this makes it any less overwhelming. I encouraged Mark to open a dialogue with some of the more vivid figures, one technique of active imagination. Like returning to his sacred word, these conversations made him feel less inundated even when they went south. In Jungian terms, this method enabled him to maintain his own vantage point when approaching archetypal forces so he wouldn't be swallowed by them.

The patterns that emerged as Mark began engaging these figures surfaced not only in his relationship with Jennifer but also with others, including the relationship with God. Some of the more straightforward dreams mirrored his unsettled situation so directly that he wondered what the point was. As a general rule, dreams compensate the conscious attitude by bringing up what's missing. Sometimes that just means spotlighting something the person already knows yet is not giving enough attention. In one such dream from Mark's journal, *he moved in with a disturbed woman from his caseload who took him to look at rings, which didn't fit, and used wallets, none of which were his.* "So I can't find where to put my ID and the rings, well that's obvious," he smiled, "straight out of a bad country song." A second dream kept him awake for hours.

> *I'm living with Jennifer and a female friend of ours, nobody I know. It seems we're young, perhaps in our twenties. The woman says she and Jennifer will become a couple. Jennifer says nothing to contradict this, remaining quiet. I'm sad and hurt, feeling the woman's strong desire will make it true.*

Despite a flash of what he described as paranoid jealousy, Mark opted against a literal interpretation. Nobody in the outer world fit the bill and the most likely explanation involved ways Jennifer was reconnecting with the sense of self she had lost when they got together in their twenties. "We met and sort of fused," he said, "which mostly meant having things my way." Listening to him reflect on the dream, I wondered whether it also might point to emerging parts of himself that he had expected her to carry for him, including the more emotionally open stance people around him were noticing. Another dream a few nights later seemed to confirm this interpretation.

> *I'm fleeing in fear, pursued by someone. They catch me outside the walls of the city as I run into the night, terrified. It's a blond girl of perhaps eight, ghostly and superhuman in her powers. She flies through the air and overwhelms me, encircling me as though she will take me over. I scream out, "Who are you?" And she says, "Me, I'm me." It sounds like she's saying she is me.*

He associated the eight-year-old with the daughter of a client, a parentified girl whose homeless mother was on his caseload. "I remember the type from grade school," he made a wry face, "the senior litigator of the

foursquare court. Always right and determined to have the last word."
Much as he hated to admit it, the lawyerly girl offered a good picture of
his argumentative self. Sitting with the image, he felt a sudden surge of
empathy for his client's sometimes obnoxious daughter, an overwhelmed
child struggling to impose rules on an out-of-control world.

Another dream moved the pattern into his marriage.

*A dishwasher in the living room is spraying onto the hardwood
floor, and I try desperately to plug the leaks with my hands and
bare feet, screaming at Jennifer to turn off the water. She calls
back calmly from the other room to say she doesn't have access
to the shutoff valve, and I can either turn it off myself or carry
the dishwasher outside. The water stops eventually, perhaps with
the help of another man, and she remains blasé while I fume
internally, half-wishing the problem hadn't been resolved so I
could point out how wrong she was.*

This dream, which summarized the dynamics between them in almost
clinical terms, was followed by a deeply disturbing dream he brought to
our next session. It is too long to quote in full so I will summarize the first
portion. In the opening sequence, he interrupts an Evangelical church
service by mocking the minister and storming out dramatically. Then the
scene changes and he's serving as a revolutionary guard for some kind of
development project. A convoluted chain of events unfolds during which
he seeks out secret supervision from a fundamentalist uncle. The dream
culminates in a series of graphic images.

*… People come and go out the back door, plotting. I'm relaxing
in the dark hallway that I'm supposed to be guarding with my
shoes off and then put them back on, reminding myself of the
importance of my job. A woman comes in claiming to be with us
and identifies herself as Dr. Rambo. She's blond and in her early
forties, dressed in hippie professional attire, attractive with a flat
chest and distinctive features. I question her in a church kitchen
and realize she's an imposter, probably a professional spy. I have a
small automatic and tell her to keep her distance. She advances on
me in an ostensibly friendly way as she explains herself. I wind up
shooting her in fear when she continues to come at me. No wound*

appears but she seems to be hurt while continuing to talk. This goes on for a while as she moves into the other room and comes back again, walking toward me. She lies on the floor with a door over her and I lie beside her, as though comforting her. I shoot her several more times in the course of these exchanges. She tells me in a provocative way to just get a knife and behead her. I find a small steak knife in the kitchen and put it in my back pocket. As I turn, she suddenly runs at me, now a headless and mutilated corpse the size of a child. I'm terrified. She disappears in the other room and reappears just as Jennifer comes in. I try to warn Jennifer but am speechless with fright as the shrunken woman, now a child, comes toward her. She has put her head back on her neck, a little crookedly. Jennifer smiles as she advances toward her. The child says, "Hold baby's head," and throws it at her. I wake up screaming.

The images in the dream referenced different parts of Mark's life, sometimes several at once, and new meanings kept opening the longer he sat with it. This was not easy, given his raw emotional state. He was particularly struck by his attitude in the dream, an ambivalent push/pull that swung between extremes. The Mark in the dream seems unable to make up his mind, storming out of a church service dramatically and then secretly seeking guidance from his Evangelical uncle. "Like that line in Ash Wednesday about the 'children who at the gate / who will not go away and cannot pray,'"[166] he decided. "Sorry I'm intellectualizing again."

In an "automatic" response, he shoots the woman in panic as she comes toward him smiling, then lies down to comfort her and winds up shooting her several more times. "Classic approach/avoidance attachment style," he said and caught himself again, "well that's what Guru Google says, not that I have the faintest idea what it means."

Going over the dream with Mark, what stood out for me was the way its imagery linked patterns in his intimate relationships to his spiritual life, a parallel most apparent in the omitted part of the dream where he storms out of a church service and then consults secretly with the preacher. I pointed out that our recent sessions had zigzagged between the two, his troubled marriage and a prayer life where he longed for connection but

---

[166] T. S. Eliot, "Ash Wednesday," *Collected Poems,* p. 93.

could not feel it on a personal level, adding this seemed to be changing based on what he had said about the memory of his grandfather.

"Um, not so much," he corrected me, "that was kind of a one off. I think I was probably giving you the holy bits like a good directee. Things aren't like that most of the time." He paused. "I don't want to exaggerate the other way either; it's more accurate to say they're a mix. All over the place with lots of stuff that's hard to classify. Sometimes close and mostly faraway, watching myself from outside like a character in a movie. The faraway part isn't me aching for God like that Sufi poem I quoted about chasing the beloved's caravan across the desert and watching it disappear over the horizon, but more like times when the whole idea of God seems stupid. Even that's not quite right."

Mark paused again, then went on to describe an experience during Centering Prayer when he was suddenly seized with terror at the prospect of actually coming close to God, the "fear of the Lord" in the King James translation of his youth. "It's like whenever I start to feel a presence I immediately go into evaluation mode and shut it down," he told me. "Like a neurotic couple too busy analyzing the relationship to let it happen. Close but not too close and always on my terms. Sitting with my grandfather slipped through the cracks before I saw it coming."

Mark identified with both characters in the dream, the fearful man who shoots on impulse and the wounded woman who does not seem to know she's hurt. He felt a surge of empathy for her desperation, an emotion he could definitely relate to. Her contradictions also felt familiar, a hippie professional who refers to herself as Dr. Rambo. "It's all right there," he told me, "The professional who sees still himself as a hippie, and the guy who thinks he's an action figure and goes around getting in street fights. She's in her early forties, the age when I quit drinking and started acting like a grownup. Well actually that's a bit of an overstatement since my job lets me keep living the sketchy life by proxy, like the joke in the rooms about the dry drunk bartender who gets other people to do his drinking for him."

"When you really look at it, the dream's kind of a mini autobiography, beginning when I was a teenager and I stormed out of church to be a revolutionary and discovered I wasn't not particularly into that either, just playing a part. I'm okay slouching in the hallway with my shoes off pretending to be important, but things fall apart when I straighten up and start taking my life seriously, same as they did when I quit drinking and turned into an asshole. But things really hit the fan when I had to face Dr. Rambo, and everything went to shit."

We both knew he was talking about the tumultuous changes over the last couple of years after he really began looking at his behavior in a serious way, in keeping with the "development project" he finds himself guarding. An aspect of the dream Mark found particularly excruciating was the obvious parallel between his meltdowns with Jennifer and the way the dream figure devolves from a composed professional to a melodramatic and self-mutilating child. Whereas an earlier dream had featured a heady child determined to impose her rules on an out-of-control world, this one loses her head and becomes a baby. As with the ghostly girl in the pursuit dream, there is no escaping her and he shrinks back in terror as she runs at him. That's when Jennifer enters the picture, in keeping with his recent realization about looking to her to manage his difficult feelings for him. "Still expecting women to save me," he said, "like a bad country song. It was always one or the other in the music I grew up with, either Angel's going to save me from myself, or she drove off in my pickup with my best friend and I'm playing the jukebox and drinking to forget her."

One way of approaching a dream is to assume that the characters represent different aspects of dreamer, and their interactions portray the relationship between various parts of the personality. This makes sense if you recall that a dream is that person's creation, a movie in which the psyche writes the screenplay based on characters it knows. On one level, Mark saw the dream ego's oscillation between terrified attack and desperate efforts at intimacy as a cartoon version of patterns he played out in his marriage. However, he also identified with the female figure and her contradictory identity as a hippie professional, not to mention her gradual regression into the child having a tantrum who expects Jennifer to hold her awareness for her. The macabre image of tossing Jennifer the severed head captured his raw emotional state in those moments when everything seemed to be disintegrating.

Although Mark identified with the tormented woman, she was also an enemy in the dream or at least an accurate representation of how others looked when he felt threatened. Among the most painful developments of the last few months had been coming to understand on a cellular level that Jennifer was not necessarily the way he saw her, any more than his childhood picture of a vengeful God defined the divine essence. This gap between his internal perceptions and actual people in his life was highlighted in a dream he brought to our next session. Before turning to it, however, there are a couple issues that I need to address.

I noted that the Rambo dream moves between Mark's marriage and his spiritual life. Later chapters will explore in more detail how human relationships shape our relationship with the divine, an insight at the heart of Jung's approach to spirituality.[167] For now, I'll focus primarily on the human side of the equation and the ways in which pervasive patterns formed in early relationships manifest in dream material.

A related issue, which I will also address later, involves the meaning of gender in relation to internal figures, a controversial topic within Jungian thought. Here the dream's grotesque exaggerations leave little doubt that it is not portraying the nature of women, let alone the "feminine"; rather it is an aspect of Mark's internal view of women. More specifically, it represents a strand in the fabric of internalized experiences of women he brought to his relationships.

The next dream came a few nights later, and Mark vacillated on its name, going back and forth between "In the Witch's Kitchen" and "The Night Kitchen," the title of a children's book about a dreaming boy who narrowly escapes being baked into a pastry.[168]

I'm sleeping with a group of people in my boyhood room, which has been converted into some sort of dormitory. We're all in our twenties, a group of students like a tour or study abroad. Most are women, although there may be another man present. A cruel woman owns the house. She pushes one young woman back in the room after she leaves it and enters some kind of administrative center elsewhere in the house. The girl falls down, crying, and I see she has scraped her knees. I calm her, saying I'll get bandages and medicine when the woman falls asleep. Jennifer, who looks perhaps ten years younger, is sharing a bed with our daughter, who is a child. She asks with a sort of smirk if I left the collard greens cooking on the stove, as if baiting me. I don't think so but once she says it I start second-guessing myself and figure I better check. I sneak out into the darkened house and go to the deserted kitchen

---

[167] C. G. Jung, 1945. "Psychotherapy Today," *The Practice of Psychotherapy,* CW 16, ¶¶212, 218–220.
[168] Maurice Sendak, *In the Night Kitchen.*

of my childhood. I see a crock pot and touch it to verify it's warm. I grope for the lid in the dark and lift it to check inside. A large cut bone is stewing in the broth. The witch bursts in screaming, "What did you do?" I'd expected to be able to face her, but she is huge, and I shrink back, terrified.

As in the preceding dream, the imagery of this one operates on multiple levels. The setting is Mark's boyhood room, and the narrative focuses on patterns from early life that were resurfacing in his marriage and other relationships. Here, his room has been converted into a dormitory for college students, a time of exploration and trying out new things. The detail suggests that Mark's maturing attitude was beginning to outgrow the confines of childhood. The students are on a study tour, a good image for the provisional quality of his adult life. The fact that their dormitory is located in his boyhood room indicates they haven't yet managed to leave home, as though they are asleep and only dreaming of growing up.

Apart from an unknown man, he finds himself in a female world, consistent with his tendency to distance from men and look to women for validation. Jennifer is present yet unavailable to him, preoccupied with their fictitious daughter. Similar to the lawyerly girl in the earlier dream, this one is around eight and content to stay close to her mother while a braver companion ventures outside the room. The adventurous young woman starts out as one of the college students, then regresses under pressure to an eleven-year-old, a transitional period between childhood and adolescence marked by initial forays into the larger world. Her effort to break out ends badly when the owner of the house throws her back roughly into the bedroom where she falls and skins her knee, crying like a disconsolate child.

Unlike his actual childhood home, this one is ruled by a cruel matriarch. Her malice seems to infect Jennifer, who smirkingly asks whether he left something cooking on the stove. "That's actually a bugaboo of mine," Mark admitted, "and it drives me crazy when I start obsessing over whether I turned on the burglar alarm or left the coffee pot on. But Jennifer wouldn't act that way, that's the weird part. Just not her style. Even on her worst days I've never seen her smirk. Plus it's not even clear if she's actually doing anything to me and or if I'm just blaming my anxiety on her, like getting mad when somebody whistles a melody you can't get out of your head."

Mark explained that collard greens were a comfort food, reminding him of his Southern grandmother, and he often cooked up a batch when he was feeling down, something he had been doing a lot lately. In the context of the dream, he associated them with the Rapunzel story about a dutiful husband who trespasses into a witch's garden after his pregnant wife declares she'll die without the greens growing there. When the terrified man is confronted by the witch, he surrenders his daughter to a sort of eternal childhood in which she's locked away in a doorless tower, at once coddled and imprisoned by maternal solicitude.

In psychological language, new developments are prevented from coming into the world, confined to a childhood room like the young people in the dream. As in the fairy tale, this impasse is disrupted by a knight in shining armor when Mark volunteers to help the injured girl. This version of him appears far less passive than in the previous dreams; however, like the cautious prince in the fairy story, he's still afraid to confront the witch directly. Instead, he sneaks out under the cover of darkness, hoping to get medicine for the girl and check the stove before slipping back into the safety of the room. Just as Pandora cannot stop herself from opening the box, he just cannot resist peeking inside the pot. This pulls the lid off whatever's going on in the house. It appears to be something cannibalistic, given his horror on finding the bone and his association to a children's book about a boy nearly cooked into a pastry. As in the Hansel and Gretel story, what's happening seems to involve him, as though he's somehow already in the soup. The discovery brings the witch storming into the kitchen and his heroism crumbles into cowering terror. Nonetheless, as her furious question makes clear, something fundamental has already changed, or, as Mark put it, "Rapunzel has left the building and the cat's out of the bag."

But there is still a witch to deal with. "That's what happens when you wake up," Mark decided. "Every alarm clock should come with a warning label." He went on to characterize the recent upheavals in his life as Rapunzel leaving her comfortable tower. "It's all there in three-part harmony, the tweener part of me who wants to wake up and stop making women take care of me but can't quite manage. Then the me character gives it a try, acting all heroic, after getting nudged along by Jennifer who is preoccupied with her own child."

"All these kid dreams remind me of the inner child stuff you used to hear in the eighties, protecting your tender young parts and all that.

Except here it's not about protection but the opposite—Rapunzel getting out of her tower. The first girl who tries to escape gets her ass kicked, maybe by the part of me that doesn't want to grow up, if that's not being too psychological. At the very least it's safe to say I seem to have a certain resistance to the idea. An old girlfriend once told me I suffered from a Peter Pan syndrome, something she read in a self-help book. I dumped her, of course, but even then I had a sneaking suspicion she was on to something. It's sort of embarrassing to talk about, even with you. I ran across the phrase 'King Baby' somewhere and that's what I call myself when I'm feeling particularly disgusted. Like I have a private exemption and get all butt hurt when things don't work out exactly how I want."

Mark was prone to extreme judgments, whether of himself or others, and I encouraged him to back up and view the pattern in the wider context of his life. Their couples' therapist had pointed out a dynamic that happens in many relationships, in which he pursued Jennifer and became angry or critical when she felt overwhelmed and retreated. There had always been a tension in the marriage between his need for emotional validation and her more reserved style. Lately, however, the convergence of his midlife crisis with its attendant anxiety and her growing need to define herself apart from the relationship had given rise to a perfect storm that threatened to swamp the marriage.

Her withdrawal not only threw Mark into a panic, reminding him of his depressed mother, but also pushed him back on his own resources. The effort to manage his feelings in a more mature way had forced him to reexamine adaptations he had made in early life, which allowed him to survive then but no longer worked. The feeling of specialness that his mother helped foster had sustained him through difficult circumstances. At this point, however, his driven quality and disappointed entitlement were interfering with adult relationships. This was the childhood enchantment from which he was struggling to awaken, in the imagery of the dream, as his sustaining sense of grand mission foundered on the realities of middle age. When Jennifer stopped carrying his head for him, the terror beneath his anger resurged.

"It's like I'm going to disappear if she doesn't see me," he said. "Stuff I knew abstractly from therapy but now it's coming to life. Like those psalms where God turns his face away and the psalmist cries out pitifully, why are you so far from me? Except now I know the problem isn't really

God or Jennifer or the church or my parents. It's all about me and not in a fun way."

Before moving to the next set of dreams, it is worth pausing to consider a fundamental shift in orientation that had broad implications for Mark's ability to weather the storms of change he was experiencing. The change was part of a developmental process extending across all areas of his life. I have noted before that his struggle to mature psychologically, and the self-understanding this facilitated, was inextricably interwoven with a similar developmental push in his spiritual life and the support he received there. Similar to the Mark figure in the last dream, the personal growth engendered by this struggle enabled him to face things he had previously avoided and to take more responsibility for his actions. That meant learning to tolerate the uncertainty and messiness of opening himself to situations and relationships on their own terms, not according to some childish fantasy of how they should be.

I have tracked this growing capacity in his primary relationship. It was also evident in his changed stance toward dream material. Early in our work together, he was determined to "make sense" of dreams by turning symbols into concepts or getting me to tell him what they really meant. He still fought the tendency to send his analytic mind on raiding parties to seize images that could be brought back and assembled into interpretations. By now he knew from experience this only turned living symbols into dead ideas, like stuffed animals arranged in a museum diorama.

Soon after we discussed his more open approach to dream material, *Mark dreamed he was walking along the tideline between the ocean and the land, clamoring over rocks to watch the amazing creatures moving in the tide pools around him.* I have heard countless variations on this motif over the decades, which offers a vivid image of what it is like to thread between the conscious and unconscious realms, observing its inhabitants in their natural habitat without trying to preserve them in jars. This requires surrendering to the dream and letting its images work in the imagination, listening to the bird sing instead of comparing its plumage to pictures in the bird book.

Unlike psychological systems with a fixed canon of dream symbols, Jung viewed dream images as unique expressions of shifting movements in the lives of his patients.[169] From this perspective, the woman who confronts Mark in the kitchen is not his depressed mother, let alone the "negative feminine," any more than the smirking Jennifer offers an accurate picture of the flesh-and-blood person. Dreams employ images in precise ways and are quite good at saying what they mean, albeit in an imagistic language foreign to day-world thought.

Earlier I suggested that the figures in Mark's dream can be seen as strands of his experience that became activated in certain situations, something on the order of "how Jennifer looks to me in those moments" or "the way a female authority figure can seem when I'm feeling attacked." One of the benefits of Jung's transpersonal perspective is how it allows us to incorporate the details of personal history while moving beyond them.

Humans do not create symbols in a vacuum, and the psyche searches out images from the surrounding culture that reflect recurring patterns across human experience, like the crock pot/witch's cauldron at the end of the dream. What's often startling is the subtle way in which these collective images are then blended and shaded with private symbols drawn from the individual's unique experience. The combination creates a nuanced vocabulary of "a man who looks like my father before I knew him" or "lying on the couch we had in the dorm except with the slipcover from my grandmother's living room." A particularly eerie aspect of working with dreams is how they watch you, sometimes offering ongoing commentary on a directee's response to previous dreams or even quoting our discussions directly.

Dreams also refer back to earlier dreams as images get reworked in a new context. New meanings emerge as the sequence unfolds, incorporating previous motifs much the way bits of melody weave through a symphony. This dynamic is apparent in a subsequent dream that tracked Mark's slow progress in reclaiming parts of himself he had projected onto Jennifer.

I have a small baby with a woman, and it is learning to walk, somewhat precociously given its apparent age. It keeps falling and banging his/her head and butt. I'm aware of its resilience and determination. Then we are climbing stairs. The baby is somewhat like a human infant and somewhat like a puppy or other mammal,

---

[169] Jung, 1961. "Symbols and the Interpretation of Dreams," *The Symbolic Life*, CW 18, ¶¶477, 483.

perhaps a baby seal. It's white, with long fur, like my childhood dog. I have a long leash that is also a phone cord, which seems to mean I'm connected to it by phone. We run out of cord on the flight of stairs up to the third floor, and I try to plug into another jack, aware this is the difficulty of being attached by a landline. A man and woman, perhaps Jennifer, go ahead. They seem to be a couple. They report that the third floor looks out onto Antarctica and the icebergs seem intact, suggesting global warming isn't as bad as we thought. A transparent phone jack breaks, and we will have to ascend without the phone, or perhaps I can find a new jack so we can go the rest of the way. I'm excited about this.

This was the first in a series of dreams about infants and toddlers, an apt image of new developments in Mark's life and his growing sense of himself apart from how he was viewed by others. It is always worth noting the dreamer's reactions within a dream, and here they reflect his increased self-acceptance. In contrast to his usual bitter self-criticism whenever his performance did not measure up to internal standards, he delights in the toddler's resilience and painstaking progress. The child associated with this emerging sense of self transcends gender and even species, combining dawning human awareness and animal instinct, with a sidelong reference to the hyper puppy of Jennifer's pet name for him. Both ends of human embodiment take their lumps as the toddler alternately bumps its head and falls on its ass, in Mark's usual pungent phrasing.

In contrast to the heady or headless children of previous dreams, this one keeps its head but does not live there. As a thinking type, Mark was most comfortable in the realm of ideas. There he was in control, for better and for worse, and whatever did not fit the thinking modality had to enter awareness by a different route. Usually this involved feeling, Mark's least developed function and so the most open to the unconscious.[170] As a result, the emergence of anything new and alive in his life was typically marked by overpowering emotion, including his spiritual awakening. Feelings compensated the dryness of his thinking; although they were not his strong suit and tended to come up in primitive forms that needed to be integrated with thinking to avoid disaster.[171] That was what he was

---

[170] Jung, 1921/1971. *Psychological Types,* CW 6, ¶¶905–907.
[171] Jung, CW 6, ¶85.

learning to do in his relationships, after the dual wakeup calls of his marital separation and the confrontation at the box store.

The puppy/baby reined in by a leash/phone cord is a complicated image that operates on multiple levels, spanning animal and human, instinct, and consciousness. Puppies are put on leashes for their protection, yet this creature is also human, the young part of himself he called "King Baby." Using a phone cord as a leash provides a link to human communication, although it is not clear who's on the other end of the line. The cord's range needs to be extended as he climbs, just as Mark himself was being stretched. The ascent is led by Jennifer and another man. Although encouraging the baby's progress, the pair give it space to find its own way. The fact they form a couple does not seem to bother Mark in the dream, which suggests the man is associated with his higher or future self.

In Jungian terms, both the ideal man and the miraculous child offer images of the Self, the ampler personality that guides growth toward greater wholeness, which sometimes gets projected on to the therapist in the early stages of treatment.[172] The dreamer's awareness within the dream also operates on two levels, simultaneously an observer and a toddler as he follows the couple up the third and final flight of stairs. This ambiguous location has been called the *third half of life,* a dimension that opens up when we leave the collective road and proceed without a path on the way to becoming ourselves. At the close of the dream, the dreamer has left the known world and the phone cord no longer reaches, as though he needs to plug into a higher connection.

The view from the top is encouraging, according to the couple guiding him. They call back down the stairs to say that things are not as apocalyptic as feared and the good news propels him forward. Something similar seemed to be happening in Mark's outer life as hopeful signs began appearing in his marriage, spurred in part by his increased ability to see Jennifer as a person in her own right and accept her strengths and limitations. In working with dreams, emotions often provide the most direct link to daily life and this one ends on a note of hope.

I do not have space to go into the other dreams from this miniseries, yet the shift from fear to optimistic engagement emerging over the course of their unfolding narrative mirrored another perfect storm in Mark's life,

---

[172] Jung, 1917/1926/1943. "On the Psychology of the Unconscious," *Two Essays on Analytical Psychology,* CW 7, ¶110; "Psychotherapy Today," CW 16, ¶218.

this one positive. His spiritual and psychological growth were coming together in an increased sense of personal wholeness, as his deepening spiritual life allowed him to loosen his emotional demands on Jennifer. The forces guiding this inner growth were personified in the first dream of yet another series, in which his interactions with unknown women provided an image of new internal relationships as he got to know previously hidden parts of himself.

> *I'm traveling alone on a train, sitting on the righthand side looking out the window with an empty seat beside me. The train stops at a station where we have a brief break, and I get off. I feel ambivalent about continuing, although I leave my stuff on the train. I meet my Evangelical sister in the corridor as I leave and explain this to her before continuing on alone. I walk into the station, looking for coffee. I ask an Indian salesgirl at a service counter and have difficulty understanding her answer. I think she says that they don't have coffee, but I can buy a gourd at another stand, apparently containing some other liquid. The dark-haired woman at this food stall is middle-aged with a spacey hippie demeanor. She says that all they have is tea and I say I'll take it. All this is taking a long time, and I worry the train will leave. I ask how to get back to the station and another woman behind the counter points the way, telling me to turn left at Sycamore Street. I go into a bathroom while I'm waiting. It's filthy with a single drain in the center of the floor like a shower stall. My tea still isn't ready when I come back out and the dark-haired woman tells me I can get it out of her gourd. This is inside a massive wooden cupboard with round holes for drinks and I go behind the counter to get it. Some drinks are in gourds, but mine is in a small glass jug. As I turn to go back to the train, she takes my hand and says she will meet me later. Her eyes are huge, dark, and luminous, reminding me of the Beatle's line about the girl with kaleidoscope eyes. I know the tea is mescaline, and I will drink it on the train.*

Mark found this dream especially meaningful and worked extensively with its images. As usual, I will only touch on a few high points and pass over more personal material. Like the start of a good novel, the setting of a dream establishes its psychological ambiance and hints at the themes to be addressed. This dream's initial scene would make a striking opening shot in a movie, evoking the classic motif of the journey as a lone traveler stares out the window at the world passing beyond the glass. An empty seat always points to its missing occupant, whether someone left behind or the mysterious person yet to arrive. Mark associated the vacant seat beside him with the unseen guest in a plaque above the kitchen table when he was growing up. "I forget the exact wording," he told me when we went over the dream together, "something about God being the unseen guest, the silent listener to every conversation. My dad used to point to it whenever we got boisterous. The idea of an invisible listener always creeped me out, like setting a chair for Elijah and cracking the door so he can sneak in."

Reflecting further on the dream, he realized it offered a concise synopsis of his spiritual journey to this point. The individual leg of this quest begins when he gets off public transport, which has come to a stop anyway, and ventures alone into the world outside. He says goodbye to his Evangelical sister, in keeping with the adolescent split from institutional religion that left him to find his own path. As then, the separation is less final than he thinks, and the dreamer leaves his things behind on the train, the baggage that awaited Mark when he reconnected with Christianity. He needs something to help him wake up and first tries a service counter staffed by an Indian woman. The elixir she stocks is not what he's used to and his difficulty understanding her reminded him of his brief forays into Eastern thought. The next woman does not have his usual beverage either; at least the one she offers is familiar. He finds her familiar as well, in fact too familiar, and writes her off inwardly, a middle-aged version of the spacey hippie friends he had been happy to leave behind.

Suddenly he worries about missing his train, a mini awakening like the sudden awareness of ticking time that led him to call me in the first place. He asks directions from a third woman. This figure is less defined, an indistinct presence who sends him to Sycamore Street. The name held several connotations for Mark, including the turnoff to my office and the Old Testament figure of Amos, the reluctant prophet and dresser of sycamore trees. Another association involved a song he remembered from Sunday School that I encouraged him to sing aloud during our session, in which the tiny tax collector Zacchaeus climbs a sycamore tree to catch a glimpse of the Savior *who looks up in the tree and says Zacchaeus you come down cause I'm coming to your house for tea.*

Before resuming his spiritual journey Mark has to deal with his crap, the unwelcome task currently demanding his attention. As with the earlier encounters with representatives of his Evangelical past and the hippie world of early adulthood, it is something that must be faced. Worse yet, the unlikely construction of the bathroom means his crap will not disappear quietly and he's going to have to learn to live with it. Perfect hygiene is out of the question, since he cannot flush it away and has no paper to clean himself. Jung maintained that the gold of spiritual growth is found in the messy stuff of life that we would like to ignore, something Mark had plenty of at the moment, the *prima materia* that alchemists dug from abandoned outhouses.[173] His own association to the dream image was more visceral—public restrooms he had seen in Third World hostels where the promised toilet turned out to be a hole in the floor surrounded by near misses and backed-up sewage.

His drink still is not ready when he emerges from the bathroom, but the dark-haired woman promises to give him one out of her gourd, an appropriately hippie phrase for getting out of your head, something he was learning to do. Mark's other association to the gourd was autumn, in keeping with his current life stage. His association to the cupboard with multiple compartments was more idiosyncratic, the verse in which Jesus reassures his followers that his father's house has many mansions, guaranteeing an individual place for everybody.[174] Consistent with this promise, his drink looks different from the others, housed in a glass jar as transparent as the train window he looked through at the beginning of the dream.

Up to this point, he's managed to maintain his autonomy, the classic hero steering his isolated journey. Now the spacey woman he has not taken seriously demands to be recognized. Apparently, she's not there just to serve his needs. She takes his hand in parting and assures him they'll meet again, suggesting an intimate connection between them. There is something magical about her after all—the mysterious woman with kaleidoscope eyes from the psychedelic anthem from his youth. And just in case he missed the drug reference, it dawns on the Mark in the dream

---

[173] Jung, 1937. "Religious Ideas in Alchemy," *Psychology and Alchemy,* CW 12, ¶421; Jung, 1942. "Paracelsus as a Spiritual Phenomenon," *Alchemical Studies,* CW 13, 209.
[174] John 14:2

that the tea contains mescaline, and he'll drink it on the train, bringing its altered perspective to public transport and the world outside.

A useful approach when working with a dream is to ask what it tells you that you do not already know, the crucial piece missing from the dreamer's conscious orientation. Was this one urging a recovering drug addict to take peyote? The idea cannot be entirely ruled out, given the substantial body of psychological research on psychedelic-based treatments; however, careful discernment was certainly called for. Every religious tradition contains shaggy dog stories about aspirants who take spiritual metaphors literally, like the heady Neoplatonist who bought a flute when advised to harmonize with the music of the spheres. In Mark's case, the reference to mescaline appears to function as a shorthand symbol for the broadened perspective he associated with his adolescent experimentation with psychedelics. It is always important to place dream images in the context of an individual's idiosyncratic experience to understand how they function in that person's symbolic world. In contrast to the largely negative impact of other drugs, Mark felt that psychedelics had played a mixed role in his early life, helping him reconnect with spiritual meaning while muddying the water with random distortions. "It's like the old stoner standup routine," he told me. "Oh no, not the waltzing giraffes again."

Stepping back a moment to view the dream in a wider context, speculation regarding how literally to take the woman's gift reflects two assumptions at the heart of Jung's approach. The first is a commitment to engage dreams seriously as potential carriers of deep meaning.[175] The second relates to the way human beings experience the world. Treating the woman in the dream as an autonomous person with motivations of her own reflects a core Jungian belief that has been borne out by subsequent developmental research. This is the premise that, from their earliest moments, people experience the world in relational terms, instinctively personifying the forces and situations they encounter.[176] This predilection drives the interpersonal response set I previously described as a relational template, which is forged in early relationships and applied to new interactions that reinforce it in turn.

---

[175] Jung, 1934. "The Practical Use of Dream Analysis," CW 16, ¶304.
[176] Jung, 1935. "Principles of Practical Psychotherapy," CW 16, ¶13; Jung, 1941. "The Psychological Aspects of the Kore," *Archetypes and the Collective Unconscious,* CW 9i, ¶¶314, 315.

The personifying reflex also extends to nature, cars, the weather, and events attributed to fate, not to mention our internal experience of ourselves and whatever we picture as God. Since human beings operate as a unified system, no area of life gets partitioned off. As individuals we bring to every situation the relational perspectives arising from early interactions with the environment. A downside of this perceptual quirk is the tendency to get trapped in traumatic narratives, bringing old wounds to new relationships, and superimposing unresolved conflicts on the situations we encounter as we remake the world and our experience of God in the image of ourselves and the people we carry inside us. As Mark was discovering, people also can alter their relational template when they open themselves to trustworthy others in a vulnerable way, sparking changes that can also shift the nature of future encounters.

In Mark's case, the changes emerging in his relationships with those around him were reinforced by extended dialogues with dream figures who personified the internal perspectives he brought to his interactions.[177] This quintessentially Jungian exercise is based on a third core assumption. Like Ignatius, Jungians believe there is a healing impulse acting within the psyche.[178] Prayerful and discerning attention to its movements can help heal distorted relationships, whether with people in our current life or those we have internalized.

Earlier, I described two perfect storms that rocked Mark's world, one positive and one negative. Both can perhaps better be seen as self-reinforcing feedback loops. Taken together, they comprised an ongoing process of disassembly and reconstruction in his life, as limiting patterns broke down to make room for new growth.

In developmental terms, the unified world of childhood must be gradually dismantled, a primal universe ruled by the preverbal maxim "I am the measure of all things, and everything revolves around me."[179] In order to relate to others as beings, with separate needs and desires, I need to be able distinguish them from me. This happens over time in the outer world, to varying degrees, but if I open fully to my experience, it also occurs in relation to the preconceptions and internal models I bring to relationships. Central to this shift is the dawning realization that other

---

[177] Jung, 1955-56/1970. *Mysterium Coniunctionis*, CW 14, ¶706.
[178] Jung, *Memories, Dreams, Reflections*, 324, 325.
[179] Jung, 1935. "The Tavistock Lectures," CW 18, ¶¶204, 205.

people are not my fantasy, and I cannot control what they do, for better or for worse.

Separating from early templates is a long and arduous process, whether it happens in a relationship with a spouse or with God, and is often portrayed in dreams through a series of interactions with inner figures.[180] A final dream, which bookends the love triangle in the dream at the beginning of the chapter, points toward the evolving nature of the ambiguous intimate other who Mark encountered in dreams as well as its partial differentiation from the outer relationship on which it had been projected.

> *I'm telling someone or they're telling me that I'm married to a transvestite, which is then corrected to a transsexual. I realize I'm also married to Jennifer. The three of us are together and I see we're doing fine. We stand together in a circle with arms linked, perhaps dancing.*

---

[180] Jung, "Psychotherapy Today," CW 16, ¶212.

Chapter 11
Intimate Strangers and the Inner Other

You've entered the realm of anima and animus, the most contested part of Jung's model and one of the slipperiest to grasp. In Jung's view, these inner figures, who show up in dreams and revery, personify unknown or undeveloped aspects of the personality.[181] They were traditionally seen as opposite in gender from the dreamer, although this view has broadened with time to accommodate the complexity of gender and the existence of multiple gender narratives in each person, an issue that will be discussed in the pages that follow. They have been described as the face of the unconscious and their expression changes depending on what face the conscious perspective turns toward them.[182] And those expressions vary wildly, as you saw in the last chapter, from fearful to loving, pitiful to overpowering. In Jung's map of the personality, they inhabit a middle kingdom between shadow and Self while incorporating elements of both. Like the shadow, they embody destructive patterns that play out in relationships with others or with oneself. At the other end of the spectrum, they serve as psychopomps or soul guides who draw us toward deep levels of the psyche that open out into the transpersonal expanses of the Self.[183] Besides appearing in dreams and waking fantasies, they are projected onto intimate partners and others in our lives.[184] They assume a myriad of shapes and personalities in art and mythology, from femme fatale to inspired prophet.[185] As with most aspects of Jungian theory, anima and

---

[181] C. G. Jung, 1951/1968. *Aion*, CW 9ii, ¶¶25, 26.
[182] Jung, CW 9ii, ¶26; Jung, *Memories, Dreams, Reflections*, 207.
[183] Jung, CW9ii, ¶¶33, 56.
[184] Jung, CW9ii, ¶¶24, 42.
[185] Jung, CW9ii, ¶¶24, 41.

animus were derived from observing the inner lives of actual people, including Jung himself, and are best conveyed through concrete examples.

Wracking my brain for a suitable illustration, I recalled a young woman who called for therapy. The voicemail said she had to see me right away because she could not make decisions. Lots of people have the same problem, but for her it had reached epic proportions, culminating in what she called the "shirt incident." She had just received her second formal warning for lateness and was on the verge of losing a mid-level administrative position after missing an important meeting because she could not decide which top to wear.

"I wasn't even trying to look good," she told me, "Just avoid being a bad person. Every shirt I own was piled on the bed and I'd tried them all at least twice. I knew I should just pick one already but the voice in my head wouldn't shut up. That one's too casual, this one too revealing, what would people think if I wore orange?"

She did not hear actual voices, of course; she did, however, have a vivid visual image of her inner accuser. Even though the nuns were long gone by the time she attended Catholic school, that's who she pictured—a pursed Mother Superior critiquing her every move. Time was of the essence if she was going to keep her job, so we met frequently.

As she pushed back against this critical voice, a boy named Jimmy began appearing in her dreams. She recognized him immediately, the designated bad boy in her fifth-grade class who smoked cigarettes, got in fights, and was expelled in middle school for flipping off the principal. "In case you hadn't guessed I had a crush on him that wouldn't quit," she told me, smiling at the memory, "but was way too shy to even look at him." Fortunately, this was not an impediment in her relationship with the daydream Jimmy who began cropping up at random times. I encouraged her to record their conversations, paying particular attention to what he said when Mother Superior tried to shush them. Passing a Bible bookstore one day soon after we began meeting, she saw a silver bracelet in the window engraved with the letters *WWJD?* She bought it on the spot and, although she opted against wearing it to work, consulted it mentally whenever difficult decisions or conversations loomed, asking herself, *What Would Jimmy Do?*

Her bracelet reminds me of a necklace made by another bad boy, a friend from my twenties who presented his girlfriend with a gold chain holding a gilded slug dug out of his hip. "Only two things have been inside of me," he explained as she held it up with a quizzical expression, "you and this bullet." Although the ex-con and the overly conscientious executive could not have been more different, both encountered what felt like an actual person inside them.

Jung had similar experiences, and the concept of the anima grew from his encounter with an inner female figure during his self-analysis.[186] Actually, there were a series of them who appeared in a variety of guises and roles, just as they did in Mark's dreams, enticing and befriending, tormenting, bullying, and guiding. Jung interpreted this shape-shifting proto-personality as a hidden aspect of himself that could only be seen in reflection as it surfaced in dreams and active imagination or was projected onto women in his life. He observed a parallel phenomenon in the dreams of his female patients, which he termed the *animus*, a male figure who carried unexpressed elements of the personality that needed to be dealt with.[187] In Jung's view, these inner figures constituted a soul-image, the not-me that is nevertheless a part of me. Like the shadow, they cannot be avoided; also, like the shadow, they rule our lives from below unless we can form a conscious relationship with them.

Jung found that although most people resonated with the idea of the shadow, they had a much harder time with the anima or animus in the absence of direct experience.[188] For today's readers, this difficulty is compounded by significant differences between his culture and our own, especially regarding gender. In keeping with the thought of the time, he structured his theory in terms of opposites: female and male, matter and spirit, dark and light.[189] Today's intellectual milieu is deeply suspicious of binary categories and overarching structures. Gender is placed on a continuum, and there is less talk of universal human characteristics. Later in the chapter, I will explore some of the challenges raised by these differences in perspective.

Despite such complications, the basic concept behind this part of Jung's system is quite simple and has to do with the human tendency to anthropomorphize, as I discussed in the previous chapter. Individuals who engage deeply with the unconscious often experience its core

---

[186] Jung, *Memories, Dreams, Reflections*, 186, 187.
[187] Jung, CW 9ii, ¶29.
[188] Jung, CW 9ii, ¶35.
[189] Jung, CW 9ii, ¶¶386, 390.

contents as personalities, some of whom appear as the opposite gender.[190] These figures incorporate an individual's accumulated experiences of men and women, supplemented by images from art, myth, and literature that encapsulate recurrent patterns in human relationships.[191] They take many forms in dreams and daydreams, including imaginary people and ones we've known. As with the shadow, they impose a template on experience that shapes our perception of those we encounter. When this process rises to awareness, I may say I like or dislike someone because they remind me of a sibling or grade-school teacher, or perhaps a fictional character like my client's Mother Superior.

In popular books and seminars, the anima is sometimes described as the woman inside every man and the animus as the man inside every woman, an idea that can be traced back to Jung.[192] If taken literally, this metaphoric way of putting things leads to all kinds of difficulties. I spoke earlier about the male group leader who dismissed objections from women in the audience by citing superior insight into female experience based on his access to the inner feminine.

It would perhaps be more accurate to describe anima and animus as images of relationship between the conscious and unconscious perspectives.[193] In this encounter, the unconscious often assumes the form of the opposite gender because an intimate relationship between a woman and man is among the most universal symbols of union with difference. It is also a place where core personality patterns are likely to emerge, including the kinds of unconscious complexes depicted in the dream Mark called "In the Night Kitchen."

Since these complexes differ widely, soul-images are as varied as the complications that bring couples to a therapist's office. I remember a man in his fifties who consulted me about his failure to put together a long-term relationship despite numerous false starts. I asked him what a long-term relationship would look like, and he painted a vivid picture of the space they would share, which he visited often in his fantasies. A giant bed dominated the room with hooks on the opposite wall for matching over-and-under shotguns, hers on the bottom and his on top. A nearby rack

---

[190] Jung, CW 9ii, ¶26.
[191] Jung, CW 9ii, ¶¶20–24.
[192] Jung, 1935. "Principles of Practical Psychotherapy," *The Practice of Psychotherapy*, CW 16, ¶17.
[193] Jung, *Aion*, CW 9ii, ¶40.

held matching bowling balls with his above and her smaller one below. "I don't ask for much," he explained earnestly, "just someone who shares my interests and will be a good fit." When I explored his fantasies in more depth, it became apparent that he was locked in a sort of internal incest reminiscent of the Rapunzel story, a demon lover no mortal woman could match. In the fairy tale, the doting captor only becomes abusive when the girl tries to leave. Mark's night kitchen dream concentrated on the negative side of this enmeshed relationship, in part because he was beginning to separate from it, but this man's fantasies were entirely positive, and he spent hours lost in a sort of emotional pornography that kept him bound in silken cords.

Anima and Animus in the Mirror

This discussion of the soul-image has moved back and forth between inner and outer relationships. The movement mirrors the way anima and animus slide effortlessly between the two, as inner figures blur with outer people until it is hard to tell where one ends and the other begins.[194] In the case of my ex-con buddy, his girlfriend brought a tenderness otherwise missing from a life marked by violence and betrayal. His own buried capacity for emotional closeness was awakened to the extent he took her inside, in the imagery of his bullet parable. Only she could unlock this part of him, and he needed her like a drug.

By contrast, what the anxious woman in the first vignette absorbed from those around her was not tenderness but perceived judgment that activated old tapes about her intrinsic inadequacy. Chronic self-doubt gave rise to carping criticism that she attributed to an omnipresent jury in the world around her and the equally inescapable one she kept inside. Personifying her inner critic allowed her to establish some distance from it. The imaginary figure of Mother Superior drew on her religious background, the relationship with her own mother, and archetypal images from the collective cultural storehouse. Unlike my friend's girlfriend, her lover was an internal personality who supplied what was missing from her conscious stance and day-world relationships. Whereas the ex-con's girlfriend introduced a note of vulnerability into his siege mentality, her dream lover brought much needed aggression. Forging a relationship with

---

[194] Jung, CW 9ii, ¶24.

this imaginary figure allowed her to fend off her inner accuser and push back against her reflexive deference toward those around her, a pattern graphically depicted in a dream in which she literally gave away pieces of herself. In Jungian language, this positive animus figure compensated deficits in the conscious perspective and brought forward a viewpoint that needed to be integrated in her growth toward wholeness.

Her relationship with this inner figure and the internal capacities he represented also made her less dependent on the men in her life. My friend never managed this kind of inner activation, in line with a long tradition of men who rely on women to carry their emotional life for them. In the extreme form of this arrangement modeled by my male patient, the hunger for mirroring was so exacting there was no room for his partner to have needs or interests that did not coincide with his. In this charged situation, a whiff of rejection can turn love to hate. Once projections start shifting, spouses complain their partner has been taken over by aliens, that they are suddenly an entirely different person. Others report feeling as though they are finally seeing them for who they really were all along, like the fairy-tale motif of being freed from enchantment.

I once worked with a pro-wrestling fan who compared the abrupt shifts in his perception of his boyfriend to the way wrestlers change masks to become a different character, instantly morphing from clean-cut American hero to fanatic terrorist. Borrowing a term from psychoanalytic theory, a therapist couple I saw for marriage counseling used to joke about becoming each other's *bad object*.[195] The phrase refers to the negative side of an infants' experience of the caregiver, so the spouse who accidentally pokes an ancient wound suddenly becomes the flaky father or the distant stepmother. Mark's dream about the night kitchen offers a prime example of this dynamic when he finds himself back in his childhood home and sees the resident witch's malevolence mirrored in an uncharacteristic smirk on his wife's face.

This happens in all relationships, to varying degrees, and frequently involves the very attributes that attracted the pair in the first place. Early in my career, I did premarital counseling in a working-class setting where the typical couple was a male carpenter and a female nurse's aide. Prior to the wedding, she might wax effusive about how her fiancée's ability to live

---

[195] The concept of the bad object is taken from the object relations theory developed by Austrian British psychoanalytic theorist Melanie Klein (1882–1960).

in the moment had introduced an element of magical spontaneity into her humdrum existence. For his part, he appreciated the way she brought much needed order to his life, motivating him to pay off old tickets and finally start studying for his contractor's license. As often as not, I received a call from the same couple a few months later. "He's bouncing checks everywhere," she would wail while he muttered from the other side of couch about her always ragging on him. The honeymoon was over and, like the pro-wrestling fan whose boyfriend suddenly seemed to change masks and personalities, the savior had become a devil.

The Negative Anima and Animus in Dreams

The complexes behind such shifts assume many guises, sinister images of the intimate other that Jung called *negative* anima or animus figures.[196] Some convey pure evil, like the witch in Mark's childhood home or the terrorists and Nazi torturers who regularly surface in dreams. Although the anxious woman at the beginning of the chapter felt liberated by her inner Jimmy, many of the masculine figures who appear in women's dreams represent oppressive male power intent on domination. Other dream figures are harder to classify, such as the ambiguous Dr. Rambo who was at once scary and vulnerable. Her regression into a headless-child points to her connection with tangled patterns dating back to Mark's childhood. And as he discovered, coming to terms with the traumatic early experiences that disrupt adult relationships requires opening to the original hurt. This sometimes grueling process often reminds me of Jesus's admonition to accept the kingdom of God like a little child, even when that kid is cranky, whiny, and needy.[197] In fact, an obnoxious child is precisely the image used in the series of dreams that chronicled Mark's burgeoning relationship with the buried parts of himself he had expected Jennifer to carry, one of many dream images I will reexamine in this chapter.

The young girl who pursues him clambering for recognition is typical of a genre of soul-image that tends to appear early in the process: threatened or malnourished children who personify lost aspects of the self that need to be reclaimed and nurtured. Neglected babies are a common motif in dreams reported by women, although men encounter them as

---

[196] Jung, 1955-56/1970. *Mysterium Coniunctionis*, CW 14, ¶539; Jung, 1936. "Individual Dream Symbolism in Relation to Alchemy," *Psychology and Alchemy*, CW 12, ¶192.
[197] Mark 10:5.

well. The infant may be unable to nurse or choke on the mother's milk. One woman described the sickening realization that she had set her fictitious baby's car seat on the roof of the car and forgot to move him inside when she drove away. Another was quite certain she had the baby with her when she began running errands but could not recall where she had left her, perhaps in a fast-food bathroom. Other infants slip through the cracks or are lost in toilets. A man I worked with dreamed of a huge fish tank containing hundreds of floating babies who might or might not be able to breath underwater.

If unaddressed, these starved and underdeveloped parts of the personality create havoc in intimate relationships. For Mark, they manifested in a hunger for recognition and soothing that quickly gave way to sullen resentment if his wife's efforts did not meet his standards. Unmeetable ideals are a third partner in many marriages, and I have learned to listen for their presence when working with couples, often heralded by the accusing refrain "I want to be with someone who ..." Whether their venom is directed at the partner or turned inward in self-criticism, as with the woman in the story at the beginning of the chapter, such hidden expectations inject poison into a relationship.

Where a traditional culture might talk about people being possessed by demons, Jungians describe being seized by a complex that throws a veil of illusion over perceptions of those around us.[198] This may shut off a person from others, like the man whose dream lover preempted relationships with real women or lead to a desperate search for connection that can turn violent if frustrated, the stance personified by Dr. Rambo. Folk tales are full of such enchantments, from the wizard who ensnares young women with a love potion to the warrior under an evil spell who sees his family as attacking wolves. Their psychological equivalent is found in Mark's encounter in the parking lot when he experienced the shopper who cut in line as a mortal threat and armed himself in response. It is not surprising that similar patterns came up in his marriage. Like a wrestler donning a sinister mask, Jennifer's smirking face in the night kitchen dream illustrates what happened when she became his bad object. If she was not the understanding wife who soothed his hurts, then she must be the rejecting stepmother who locked him in the emotional basement, the

---

[198] Jung, 1921/1971. *Psychological Types*, CW 6, ¶175.

childish attribution lurking beneath his elegantly phrased concerns about her lack of psychological attunement.

But things were changing for Mark, spurred in part by Jennifer's own changes. His increased ability to see her as a separate person with needs of her own first surfaced in the rather melancholy dream about her relationship with a female friend who claims her love. Although it left him feeling hurt and sad, the dream pointed to his growing capacity to accept her as she was. Coming to terms with a flesh-and-blood partner means surrendering the hope of an ideal soulmate, a disillusioning process in both senses of the word. In psychological terms, this requires reclaiming projections as we gradually separate our stuff from the actual person in front of us. Doing so opens the door to real relationship, with all its surprises and disappointments, and frees us from the doomed effort to find inner healing in outer relationships, a change Mark referred to as "learning to carry his own water."

His was a typical male pattern. A quick look at the movie guide shows women have their own variations on the theme of being saved by love. For both genders, this unrealistic expectation is fostered by many forces in the culture, including therapists. There is a standard routine I go through with long-term clients when they complain that their new relationship is not making them happy, and I gently remind them they were not especially blissful before it came along. It is often said that our culture puts tremendous pressure on partnered relationships, and this truism struck me with force when I returned from living in rural Latin America. There most people were embedded in a complex and sometimes claustrophobic web of family and peer relationships. Back in the States, the isolated couples I saw for marital therapy expected their partner to be their everything. The job qualifications would stump the best headhunter: hot lover, business associate, co-parent, therapist, talking head, event coordinator—the list goes on and on.

The Intrapersonal Anima and Animus

Thus far the discussion has concentrated on interpersonal components of the soul-image that are projected onto others, especially intimate partners. These internal figures can also be seen intrapersonally. By way of illustration, it may be helpful to revisit the dreams from the previous chapter. There I looked at them primarily from an interpersonal perspective, exploring their meaning in the context of the crisis in

Mark's marriage. However, the same dream images can be applied to the personality itself.

Jungians sometimes distinguish between a *subjective*[199] approach to dream interpretation that focuses on developments in the dreamer's outer life and an *objective*[200] approach concerned with internal relationships and deep levels of the psyche. Many dreams operate on both levels simultaneously, and those containing anima or animus figures are particularly likely to span the two domains because the same blocks show up in both places. Internal relationships have a way of replicating themselves in the outer world. Often there is a sort of dialogue between the two levels as the dream moves between uneasy relationships within the larger personality and complications in navigating outer relationships. Just as my female client's relationship with her inner Jimmy gave her to access previously denied aspects of her personality, the dream series in the last chapter portrays Mark's deepening relationship with split-off parts of himself, including aspects of the psyche that extended beyond the personal sphere. In order to get there he first had to deal with complexes that interfered in all his relationships, whether with people in his life, himself, or God.

Similar to Dante's epic journey in *The Divine Comedy*, the quest begins with losing his way.[201] The first female figure he encounters takes him to look at rings, none of which fit, and used billfolds, none of which are his. Mark's immediate associations were to IDs and wedding bands, an interpretation that rang true at a time when his identity seemed be lost along with his marriage. However, the dream woman is not Jennifer, as you might expect, but a disturbed female client on his caseload. Her unknown quality suggests she's actually an aspect of himself and points toward his relationship with the unfamiliar parts of himself that surfaced over the next several months, just as a long-forgotten classmate began haunting the dreams of the indecisive woman at the start of the chapter. She experienced her Jimmy as a positive force in her life, although Mother Superior would disagree. By contrast, in the shopping dream Mark saw his female companion as psychologically disturbed.

---

[199] Jung, CW 6, ¶812.
[200] Jung, CW 6, ¶779.
[201] Dante Alighieri, *The Divine Comedy*.

This raises an important issue regarding how much to trust the protagonist in a dream, what Jungians call the *dream ego*. The woman certainly does not appear to be acting crazy; in fact, she actually functions as Mark's guide. Like the literary device of the unreliable narrator whose account of events cannot be taken at face value, the dream ego's perception of the situation always needs to be questioned. In dreams similar to this one, in which the protagonist is the dreamer, the first-person perspective represents the conscious viewpoint with all its limitations. Sometimes the dream goes out of its way to highlight these distortions by using the narrator as foil, much the way many spiritual teaching stories feature a dimwitted disciple who gets everything wrong. I mentioned earlier that the unconscious turns the same face toward us that we turn to it, and most of the female figures in this dream sequence look pitiful or scary. That's hardly surprising at a time in Mark's life when he found himself doing things that made him acutely uncomfortable and violated his old way of seeing the world, whether joining a men's group or being emotionally vulnerable with Jennifer.

Jennifer makes an appearance in the next dream, along with an unknown female figure who informs him that the two women will become lovers. Earlier, I looked at the dream from an interpersonal perspective and explored Mark's struggle to come to terms with changes in his marriage as his wife reconnected with her lost sense of self and refused to continue carrying his emotional life. From an intrapersonal perspective, her growing independence forced him to reclaim parts of himself that he had projected onto her, and now this "inner Jennifer" is forging a relationship with a previously unavailable aspect of himself. Withdrawal of projections always frees up psychological energy, and Mark suddenly found himself able to do things that surprised them both, including the open-hearted way he encouraged Jennifer's growth even when it took her away from him. In the dream, he feels sad and hurt over changes in their relationship yet accepts them as inevitable, an accurate depiction of the new attitude he brought to both the marriage and his own shortcomings.

At this point, the dreams shift their focus to another pattern that interfered with his inner and outer relationships, the bossy eight-year-old who has to have things her way. When she and the dreamer meet and merge, the dream ego fears he's being taken over; actually she has been reabsorbed back into the larger personality. Mark's ability to see the lawyerly girl, and the corresponding parts of himself, with compassionate clarity diminishes their power to hijack his interactions with others. She's no longer running the show, in contrast to the actual girl forced to care for a psychotic mother. The inner growth catalyzed by confronting this complex is demonstrated in the subsequent dishwasher dream when the dreamer discovers he can manage the floods of emotion he had expected Jennifer to contain for him. A backhanded acknowledgment of his growing insight into old patterns comes at the end of the dream when the dream ego catches himself wishing the new behavior hadn't worked so he could go on blaming Jennifer.

Earlier, I described how the inner other spans the realms of shadow and the Self. These initial dreams and the issues they address operate mainly on the level of the dark or negative anima, as does the Dr. Rambo dream that followed them. However, that dream is already beginning to point toward deep levels of the psyche that opened into Mark's relationship with God, a focus that becomes more pronounced in the subsequent toddler and train dreams.

There is an implicit link between the dreamer's ambivalent behavior toward Dr. Rambo, the regressed woman who represents the primitive and disturbed parts of the personality that emerged in his relationships, and his equally ambivalent attitude toward the Christianity of his childhood. He disrupts an Evangelical church service by loudly mocking the preacher but then secretly consults a fundamentalist minister in his family. This uncle pops up in other dreams, representing the shadow side of the "inner Evangelical" who rejected the Christianity of his youth but resisted forming a more mature relationship with the God he encountered at this point in his life. It is true Mark was intellectualizing when he associated this attitude with "Ash Wednesday" and the "children … who will not go away and cannot pray."[202] However, the poetic image beautifully captures the passive demand to be cared for like a child that shadowed his marriage and his relationship with God.

The night kitchen dream chronicles his effort to break free of this childish attitude and provides a frightening image of the complex that kept him stuck in both relationships. It also documents his continuing growth. If the immature girl who tries to escape imprisonment represents an aspect of himself, so does the dream ego willing to risk defying the witch. This new stance was coming closer to consciousness, and although

---

[202] T. S. Eliot, *Collected Poems.*

that bid for freedom also seems to end in failure when he regresses to a cowering child, it turns out that yanking the lid off the complex has already loosened its stranglehold. Future chapters will explore how this new attitude reshaped Mark's relationships with God and the people in his life, changes already presaged in the last two dreams of this series.

Leaving for now the shadowy realm of negative anima, the dreams' tone becomes more positive. The Mark in these dreams is growing up fast, first a toddler climbing to a level where he can plug into a higher source and then a grownup capable of traveling on his own. In the toddler dream, the way upstairs is led by Jennifer and another man. Listening to Mark, I linked this internal Jennifer with the newly tapped levels of himself that had been freed by the changes in his intimate relationship. Now she's guiding him upward, accompanied by a male companion associated with his Higher Self and the new possibilities that were arising in the context of his relationship with me.

The train dream that followed is a "big dream" that traces the larger trajectory of Mark's spiritual life, as he immediately recognized. The major milestones of his spiritual journey are referenced, including his break with the religion of his childhood, the spiritual tourism that followed, and the current unpleasant task of dealing with his crap. This onerous chore accomplished, at least for now, he reboards the glory train with an expanded perspective helpfully provided by a new female figure, a decidedly unintellectual woman who embodies intuitive qualities he had previously scoffed at. The morally ambiguous elixir she provides to a recovering addict echoes a common dream motif of growth as theft, a criminal act that violates the old injunctions.

Criticism of Jung's Anima and Animus

Having sketched the broad outlines of Jung's concept of anima/animus and its application to dream material, it is time to consider some of the criticisms that have been leveled against it. The topic could easily be a book in itself and the discussion that follows will provide the most cursory of introductions to a complex and varied literature. For a more comprehensive overview of the subject and the issues involved, readers are encouraged to consult Susan Rowland's *Jung: A Feminist Revision* and

Andrew Samuel's *Jung and the Post-Jungians*.[203] Many of the criticisms directed against this aspect of Jung's work involve his concept of the animus. The fact that most of his core ideas originated in self-analysis gives Jung's work a distinctly male orientation.[204] Nowhere is this more apparent than in his theory of the animus, which arose as a sort of postscript to his own encounter with the anima.[205] He did not have nearly the same degree of relationship with the animus, and this shows in his writing. Although he fleshed out his original hypothesis of an analogous structure in women with case material from female patients, these descriptions lack the robustness of passages addressing the anima. Worse yet, they tend to emphasize the negative qualities of the animus, in contrast to the range and subtlety of his discussion of the anima.[206] In addition, feminist critics have noted that Jung's concept of the animus fails to account for the impact of patriarchal social structures on how women see themselves and are seen by others.[207] These deficits have been addressed by a number of subsequent Jungian theorists who provide a fuller account of the animus from a female viewpoint.[208]

Similar issues arise in regard to sexual orientation. For Jung, development of the personality is greatly facilitated by an emotionally intimate relationship that allows individuals to encounter unacknowledged aspects of themselves and reclaim what has been projected onto their partners.[209] His description of this process assumes a cross-gender relationship and the sparse mentions of same-sex relationships in his writings tend to have a negative cast,[210] although this bias is less pronounced than in most psychological literature of his time.[211] In the end, both problems stem from the same root, as does the way in which he largely ignores same-sex relationships between women. Although Jung was at the cutting

---

[203] Susan Rowland, *Jung: A Feminist Revision*; Andrew Samuels, *Jung and the Post-Jungians*.

[204] Jung, *Memories, Dreams, Reflections* 181–185.

[205] Jung, 186.

[206] Jung, *Aion*, CW 9ii, ¶29; Jung, 1928. "The Relationship between the Ego and the Unconscious," *Two Essays on Analytical Psychology*, CW 7, ¶¶335, 336.

[207] Demaris Wehr, *Jung and Feminism*.

[208] Rowland, *Jung: A Feminist Revision*; Ann Ulanov and Barry Ulanov, *Transforming Sexuality*; Polly Young-Eisendrath and Florence Wiedemann, *Female Authority, Empowering Women Through Psychotherapy*; Wehr, *Jung and Feminism*.

[209] Jung, CW 7, ¶¶309–310, 316–317.

[210] Jung, CW 9ii, ¶¶20–23.

[211] Jung, 1936/1954. "Concerning the Archetypes, with Special Reference to the Anima Concept," *The Archetypes and the Collective Unconscious*, CW 9i, ¶146.

edge of his culture in many ways, his perspective on men and women—
and the inner feminine and masculine figures he observed in their inner
lives—was still shaped by the mores and values of his society.

Beginning with his colleagues, there has been an ongoing effort to
expand the scope of his original formulations by looking at expressions
of gender across a range of groups and cultures. A rich Jungian literature
approaches the psyche from a feminine perspective, seeking to connect
contemporary women's experience with mythic analogues.[212] Jungian
theorists have explored images of the intimate other in the inner lives
of gay and lesbian individuals.[213] Among other conclusions, these works
support the common wisdom among therapists working with gay and
lesbian clients that, in comparison to heterosexuals, they bring to the
encounter a heightened awareness of the subtleties of gender and its social
ramifications. This is hardly surprising, as is the equally unsurprising
fact that the love interest in dreams is generally the same gender as the
dreamer, with opposite-gendered figures appearing in a variety of roles.

In my own work with gay and lesbian clients, I have noticed that dream
material also contains sexually charged interactions with the opposite
gender, just as dreams by heterosexuals contain intimate encounters with
the same sex. This points not only to the spectrum of sexual attraction but
also to the varied ways in which dreams use sexual union as an image of
deep joining, the same metaphor employed by many Christian mystics.
The transgender image in the previous chapter reflects a relatively new
gender narrative in the culture, at least in terms of broad awareness. It has
been showing up more frequently in the dreams of people I work with,
sometimes in reference to day-world relationships and sometimes as an
image of new internal relationships.

Over the decades, Jung's intellectual heirs have addressed many of the
gaps in his original articulation of anima and animus.[214] A more fundamental

---

[212] Jean Shenoda Bolen, *Goddesses in Everywoman*; Esther M. Harding, *The Way of All Women*; Clarissa Pinkola Estés, *Women Who Run with Wolves*; Sylvia Brinton Perera, *Descent to the Goddess*.

[213] Christine Downing, *Myths and Mysteries of Same-Sex Love*; Susan McKenzie, "Queering Gender: Anima/Animus and the Paradigm of Emergence"; Susan McKenzie, "Gender and Sexualities in Individuation"; Brennan J. Jung, "Revisioning Anima and Animus: A Paradigm of Queer Otherness in the Psyche."

[214] Samuels, *Jung and the Post-Jungians*; Rowland, *Jung: A Feminist Revision*; Ulanov and Ulanov, *Transforming Sexuality: The Archetypal World of Anima and Animus*; Irene Claremont de Castillejo, *Knowing Women: A Feminist Psychology*; James Hillman, "Anima" and "Anima II."

issue involves his failure to clearly differentiate between *gender* and *sex*. (In this context, the former refers to cultural norms and gender narratives whereas sex refers to biological expression, although gender theorists are quick to point out that to some degree sex is also a cultural construct. A third category, sexualities, addresses sexual behavior and orientation.[215]) Jung's discussions of gender often slide between describing femininity and masculinity as forces in the psyche and their application to individual men and women.[216] This blurring of boundaries is both a strength and a weakness in his theory of anima and animus. On the positive side, it allows the soul-image to bridge the inner and outer worlds, as internal patterns are expressed in outward relationships. More negatively, these models of femininity and masculinity fail to take into the account the variability of gender expressions in individual lives and can be weaponized against those who do not conform to traditional gender patterns.

A related criticism involves charges of *gender essentialism*, a phrase used to describe theoretical models that define gender in terms of core characteristics that extend across time and place. A prime example is the way Jung associates Eros or relatedness with the feminine anima and Logos or rationality/insight with the masculine animus.[217] This categorical approach was standard in his time but has been attacked by contemporary gender theorists, who also take issue with his selective use of cross-cultural material to support his theories,[218] a criticism also raised in regard to his treatment of race and ethnicity.[219]

Other issues arise when core characteristics attributed to gender are applied to individual men and women, an approach that finds its fullest expression in popular Jungian books and workshops that offer exercises to help people get in touch with the deep feminine or masculine.[220] Gender theorists who emphasize sociological factors have little patience with

---

[215] Brennan Jung, "Revisioning Anima and Animus," 16.
[216] Jung, 1934/1954. "Archetypes of the Collective Unconscious," *The Archetypes and the Collective Unconscious*, CW 9i, ¶62; *Aion*, CW 9ii, ¶¶22-23; *Memories, Dreams, Reflections*, 185–187.
[217] Jung, CW9ii, ¶29.
[218] Maryann Barone-Chapman, "Gender Legacies of Jung and Freud as Epistemology in Emergent Feminist Research on Late Motherhood"; McKenzie, "Queering Gender."
[219] Franny Brewster, "Wheel of Fire: The African-American Dreamer and Cultural Consciousness."
[220] Linda Hartley, *Servants of the Sacred Dream*; David Deida, *The Way of the Superior Man: A Spiritual Guide to Mastering the Challenges of Women, Work and Sexual Desire*.

anyone making sweeping pronouncements about the nature of women, let alone a man doing so in the case of Jung.[221] It is a short step from describing the feminine and the masculine as overarching principles in the personality to implying how men and women should act in daily life. Not surprisingly, these judgments tend to fall particularly hard on women. If the feminine is intuitive or emotional, this must be women's true nature and they need to get in touch with it. Because Jung's model associates the animus with rationality, women who rely on their thinking function are subject to accusations of animus possession.[222] This train of thought has been used to defend traditional gender roles by some of his adherents, not all of them male, leading to predictable pushback by Jungian feminists and writers from other disciplines.

Gender Identity and Jung

I noted earlier that Jung falls in an awkward period for a thinker, sufficiently distant from us in time to have lived in a different world but near enough to be judged by current standards. This is nowhere more evident than in his views on gender and non-Western cultures, two areas where he has been sharply criticized. Despite the rumblings of cultural change that partly prompted his reflections on gender, Jung lived in a time and place when gender roles were clearly differentiated and largely traditional, at least by current standards.

Needless to say, the range of gender expression in our society is far more varied. Instead of a bifurcated model of female and male behavior, theorists stress the existence of multiple gender patterns operating within a given culture.[223] In this context, it is not clear what it means to talk about "the feminine" in global terms, let alone the feminine in a man. Critics find Jung's rationale for the concept unconvincing, including a rather ingenious allusion to unexpressed chromosomes.[224] Of course, intellectual

---

[221] Jung, CW9ii, ¶29

[222] William McGuire and R. F. C. Hull, eds., *C.G. Jung Speaking*, 26, 27. Jung, 1940/1950. "Concerning Rebirth," CW9i, ¶223; Jung, 1911–12/1952/1967. *Symbols of Transformation*, CW 5, ¶272.

[223] McKenzie, "Queering Gender"; Downing, *Myths and Mysteries of Same-Sex Love*; Andrew Samuels, *The Plural Psyche*; Ulanov and Ulanov, *Transforming Sexuality*.

[224] Jung, "Archetypes of the Collective Unconscious," CW 9i, ¶58; Jung, 1938/1940. "Psychology and Religion" (The Terry Lectures), *Psychology and Religion: West and East*, CW 11, ¶48.

trends are not the only thing that's changed in the last century. Just in my lifetime, the press for gender and racial equality, along with LGBT rights, has led to profound changes in law, employment, education, childcare, and many other facets of society.

Jung wrote at the cusp of this paradigm shift, and many modern readers give him a mixed scorecard when it comes to gender and cultural plurality. The high value he accorded indigenous cultures was groundbreaking for its time but in hindsight can be criticized for romanticism and Eurocentric bias. His diagnosis of the problems associated with suppression of the feminine in Western societies and his hope for its reemergence, which he saw prefigured in the Roman Catholic doctrine of the Assumption of Mary,[225] helped lay the groundwork for an entire genre of Jungian goddess feminism that seeks to empower contemporary women by connecting them with ancient goddess myths.[226] However, critics point out that Jung's valuation of the feminine principle, which he believed was also available to men through their anima, did not translate into practical concerns about the status of women in modern society.[227]

Unlike Freud, Jung welcomed women into his inner circle. He gets kudos for taking women's experience seriously and treating feminine perspectives as a distinct and equal force in the psyche and society rather than a deviation from the masculine norm. Here too, he has been criticized for universalizing the values of his society and failing to recognize his own cultural embedment. At worst, this gives rise to a circular process in which the prevailing cultural views that shaped his description of feminine and masculine characteristics became normative and thus "normal" for men and women everywhere.

In Jung's defense, gender is notoriously difficult terrain for any personality theorist, a potential minefield where every assertion borders on stereotype and all statements are at some level autobiographical. Whether the pronoun of choice is she, he, or they, people view the world through a lens of gender. It is one of the first differentiations children make in organizing their world. Constructing one's own gender identity, however, is a long and complicated process.

---

[225] Jung, 1939/1954. "Psychological Commentaries on the *Tibetan Book of the Great Liberation*," CW 11, ¶625.
[226] Anne Baring and Jules Cashford, *The Myth of the Goddess*; Perera, *Descent to the Goddess*; E. B. Whitmont, *Return of the Goddess*.
[227] Rowland, *Jung: A Feminist Revision*, 44.

For both men and women, gender identity arises from comparing oneself with others who are different or similar along a range of dimensions, real or fictional characters who become internalized in various ways. The topic of male identity came up a lot in Mark's men's group, a mishmash of the men's experiences of themselves and other men, what women in their lives said about men, and a barrage of conflicting messages about what it meant to be a man in the culture, subculture, family, and profession where they found themselves. Such input comes mainly through unconscious channels, and individuals must sort through the myriad ideas and images floating around in the culture, a particularly difficult task during a transitional time when gender roles are changing.

An added wrinkle in Jung's approach is the way he links the opposite gender with unexpressed aspects of the self. In this view, internal male figures not only reflect a woman's experience of men but also the parts of herself she projects onto them. The woman in the story at the beginning of the chapter offers a typical example, in which the bad boy of her dreams personified elements of her personality she needed to claim for herself.

Although this can be a useful way to understand common patterns in dream material and unconscious life, it carries obvious risks. To the extent we encounter undeveloped parts of ourselves in the other gender, there is a real danger of confusing our unconscious with men or women as a whole, just as other cultures become a Rorschach card on which we project what's missing or undervalued in our own. Here, as elsewhere, the fact that Jung's theories arose from self-exploration opens him to criticism. Is he talking about "the feminine" or repressed parts of himself? Often there is a kind of slippage in Jung's writings between describing the male unconscious in female terms and characterizing women as closer to the unconscious, emotional and intuitive in a male-dominated society that values rationality over relationality.[228] Although many women might agree with this assessment, others would object to the way it defines feminine identity from a male perspective and projects this view onto women as a class.

Gender attributions come alive in intimate relationships. Like the carpenter and nurse's aide I saw for premarital counseling, people often choose partners who seem to complete them by embodying traits missing in themselves. This already tangled transaction is further complicated by the fact that it does not happen in a cultural vacuum. There is a complicated

---

[228] Jung, "The Relations between the Ego and the Unconscious," CW 7, ¶¶296–301.

interplay between individuals' internal dynamics and those in the larger society. The woman in the vignette at the beginning of the chapter affirmed traditional gender attitudes even as she struggled against them, and her inner male figure was credited with the decisive assertiveness she could not access in herself. For his part, Mark was well aware that holding his partner responsible for his emotional life reinforced gender roles that he rejected on principle; that knowledge only added to his shame.

Jung was comfortable making broad pronouncements about the nature of men and women. Contemporary Jungians struggle with gender in ways he did not. His theory of anima and animus has proved particularly problematic, prompting some Jungians to suggest deemphasizing these categories or scrapping them altogether.[229] Do they reflect intrinsic qualities or potentialities whose contents are imported from outside? And how exactly do they relate to biological sex? Multiple efforts have been made to tease out the various dimensions of the concept—sociological, developmental, relational, and symbolic—and the relationship between these inner figures and gender patterns in the culture.[230] Some Jungian writers keep the concept of anima and animus largely intact while stressing the distinction between gender and sex.[231] Others treat them as universal forces operating in both sexes, like yin and yang.[232] Often these are framed in terms of Jung's categories of Eros or relatedness, which he associated with the female anima, and Logos or meaning, which is linked to the male animus in his system.

In contrast to Jung, however, these theorists unhook those dimensions from biological sex so that individuals express them in a gender-neutral way, just as avatars in a role-playing game may not correlate with the sex of players. This approach resolves some of the difficulties in Jung's formulation of the soul-image but loses some of its strengths, including the ease with which it maps onto cultural images and interpersonal relationships. Other contemporary Jungians maintain that anima and animus are best seen as representations of the experience of difference,[233]

[229] McKenzie, "Queering Gender"; Singer, *Androgyny: Toward a New Theory of Sexuality.*
[230] Samuels, *The Plural Psyche* and *Jung and the Post-Jungians*; Rowland, *Jung: A Feminist Revision*; Ulanov and Ulanov, *Transforming Sexuality.*
[231] Ulanov and Ulanov, *Transforming Sexuality.*
[232] Gareth Hill, *Masculine and Feminine*; Samuels, *The Plural Psyche*; Singer, *Androgyny*; James Hillman, *The Myth of Analysis.*
[233] Samuels, *The Plural Psyche*, 96; Brennan Jung, *Revisioning Anima and Animus.*

an idea that has its roots in Jung's writings.[234] In their encounter with the other, men and women are having the same experience from different directions, just as couples in treatment can sometimes unite around their common experience of feeling misunderstood. Here, the main focus is on the otherness of an inner figure, which is not so much an embodiment of femininity or masculinity as a stranger sharing our table who chooses one entree from the vast smorgasbord of gender expressions.

Although Jung thought of gender in terms of binary divisions and core characteristics, the decentralized quality of this last model is actually more consistent with the composite nature of personal identity in his system. For him, the personality is not only a village but also a museum and a movie house. Every action and reaction, whether internal or expressed, involves multiple players representing an array of motivations, experiences, and cultural forces. The many layers and crosscurrents operating in every moment create their own kind of identity politics as each one lobbies for recognition.

My personal image for this kind of defuse identity goes back to a childhood fascination with adjusting the mirrors on the medicine cabinet and the bathroom door to create an endless line of selves stretching into infinity, none more real than the next. This splintered self-image fits Jung's dynamic view of human psychology, an ongoing negotiation between semiautonomous subpersonalities and external forces. It also fits the panoply of figures encountered in dreams, which give these personalities a (largely) human face.

The variations are endless. Some lend themselves to standard Jungian categories such as shadow or soul-image, but others do not sort neatly into any group. There is always a certain arbitrariness in categorizing dream figures, similar to the final stage of factor analysis when researchers examine the clusters emerging from the data, give them a name, and interpret them. Often those names say as much about the researcher as the data, especially in social sciences like psychology. In any statistical analysis, there are always random data points that do not fit in any cluster, outliers in the language of statistics. That's true of dream figures as well. The old wisdom in Jungian circles is that same-gender dream figures represent shadow whereas opposite-gendered dream figures are soul-

---

[234] Jung, 1928. "On Psychic Energy," *The Structure and Dynamics of the Psyche*, CW 8, ¶¶85–89.

images, with bonus categories such as the wise old man or woman. It is a useful template but does not account for everybody, including bit actors who advance the plot like non-player characters in a video game, those one-schtick figures who pop up out of nowhere with gnomic instructions about the gemstone under the zombie's hat. Contemporary theorists place gender on a continuum, and dream images do that with everything, blurring not just sexual categories but every conceivable division: hybrid figures that combine fish and birds, animals,trees, demons, humans, gods, and inanimate objects from rocks to refrigerators. Some dreams seem to go out of their way to push the boundaries at societal flash points, as though trying to work out the problem, gender in the case of Mark's final dream in the last chapter and ethnicity in one I will examine in a moment.

Just as early humans looked at the stars and saw constellations, dream figures tend to organize themselves into relational categories. Lover, enemy, friend, guide, neighbor, and a host of other roles, an endless parade organized nightly by the image maker who never quits. Often, not always, they reflect the main gender narratives in the culture, and the image maker seems to have a range of opinions about them. These are the roles children act out in play—you be the mommy and I'll be the daddy—without worrying too much about the sex of the players. The same ones adolescents try on for size and young adults begin to inhabit, awkwardly at first, then with increasing and sometimes deadening seriousness, while comedies and drag shows delight in turning them on their head. From this perspective, gender can be seen as a shared dream that straddles the inner and outer worlds, a game of dress-up we play with others. But that does not exhaust its possibilities.

Gender's many dimensions—biological, sociological, and inter-personal—provide the alphabet for a nuanced symbolic vocabulary that can be applied in many directions. Jung believed that dreams use gender to portray relationships that extend beyond the social roles individuals hold internally or play out with others, including their relationships with the deepest levels of the self and the realities that transcend it. As elsewhere in his model, it is not one or the other, internal and external, human and divine, but everything at once. This expansive view reflects the dual nature of the symbol, something that exists in actuality while pointing beyond itself. Unlike an arbitrary signifier like a stop sign, a symbol operates on two levels simultaneously—the thing itself and our experience of it as an image of something larger. You see this in movies and novels when unsettled weather or a broken water pipe mirrors a character's emotional state. In the same way, the details of our daily interactions—who we are and who we encounter, what we long for and what we dread—are appropriated and reworked as symbols for all kinds of internal and external relationships, from prayer life to how we see the government.

Ethnicity and Cultural Narratives in Dreams

Many of the concerns that have been raised in regard to Jung's treatment of gender also apply to his reflections on non-European cultures and ethnic minorities, an issue that has received increased attention in the Jungian community in recent years.[235] Over the last few decades, our society has been sensitized to ways in which majority cultures project their denied or undeveloped personality traits onto ethnic and cultural minorities. These projections can be negative or positive, from unbridled sexuality or a propensity for violence to creativity and sensuality. A standard example is the statistically unlikely number of Anglos professing Native American heritage, a roundabout way of claiming a bit of wildness and an intimate connection to nature.

Like gender, ethnicity plays a complicated role in dream material, both mirroring and challenging prevailing viewpoints in the surrounding culture while also serving as a symbol of internal processes. So far I have looked at the experience of otherness in terms of gender. Ethnicity offers an equally compelling example of how cultural narratives appear in dreams and assume new meanings in the internal world, including that of otherness. Like gender, ethnicity is a social reality, a shared dream and sometimes nightmare that offers a wealth of relational images, at once concrete and metaphorical, an inner symbol and a sociological construct. Also like gender, the perspective varies with the viewer and the images draw us into the equation in a personal way.

In an increasingly global and multicultural society, there is no home base to serve as a reference point. My office is located in a university town, and I hear the dreams of people from all over the world and various subcultures within the United States. The scientific research teams in which they participate tend to be international with no single group in the

---

[235] Fanny Brewster, *The Racial Complex.*

majority. Individual researchers bring different cultural perspectives to the encounter, and their dreams reflect the complicated interplay of these narratives, with all the tensions and surprises they engender in both the internal and external worlds. Here, as everywhere, the people encountered in the environment are assimilated into each team member's internal script, a long-running play about interpersonal relationships that started long before their lab mates showed up. Ethnicity gets fed into this drama in complicated ways, just as it does in many of the movies and television shows that come out each year. As there, the portrayal can hover on the brink of stereotype or contradict it by going against type. Either way, it elicits multiple reactions in the internal audience, creating a dialogue marked by complexity, even irony, as the following dream illustrates.

> *I'm bantering with two men in their twenties, one half and the other pure Chinese. I'm back in school taking advanced sciences classes. The mixed one teases me about my ability to understand the material, as though I'm actually doing quite well, and the teasing is affectionate. I say something and both go quiet. I wonder if I've offended them. I ask the mixed one, and he looks in my eyes for a long time while I study his face, which appears older, round, pale, and sad. He tells me no, as though after deliberation, saying we've talked for a while after the remark, and I haven't referred to race. The implication seems to be that I'm not obsessed, and some talk of race is normal in context. Despite this assurance, the feeling in the air is still uneasy.*

With its focus on science and the tensions among cross-cultural colleagues, the dream is typical of many I hear in the university community. I will not reveal the source yet, so you can play with how your perspective changes depending on who had the dream. What did it mean to the dreamer for someone to be Chinese or half-Chinese, let alone seen as racially preoccupied?

Obviously, a lot depends on context, which is why it seldom makes sense to look at dream material in a vacuum. The meaning of dreams is always sliding and relative, depending on where you are standing, and which part of the personality is talking. I spoke earlier about the existence of multiple cultural narratives within society. There are always plenty floating around on any research team. Scientists hail from every continent, bringing with them cultural values and styles that do not always mesh. Women from all backgrounds describe struggling to make their voices heard in a scientific community dominated by men, a challenge compounded by conflicting cultural views on gender.

In an increasingly multinational society, the issue of mixed identity raised in the dream comes up frequently, whether in reference to literal parentage, acculturation, or multiple affiliations. Bi- or triracial identities are common among the young people I see, including many that do not fit the boxes on survey forms, such as Pakistani-Laotian or Lebanese-Filipino-Latvian. Biracial individuals sometimes claim this as their core identity. Sexual orientation serves a similar role in organizing experience, sometimes in concert with other identities like Lesbians of Color in the Sciences.

American scientists, a multiracial group that includes many recent immigrants, frequently discover that ethnicity both unites and divides them in relation to international researchers. European Americans describe their complicated experience as a dominant group in the process of losing its majority, and they hold a range of views on the subject. Consistent with waking life, dreams reported by minority individuals tend to reflect a more complex sense of identity than those of people from the majority culture. Seeing yourself as the norm does not lend itself to reflecting on identity, an attitude epitomized for me by a North American retiree living in a remote Central American village who complained about being surrounded by foreigners.

Moving from the larger sociological context to specific dream images, the dream provides a good illustration of the complicated ways cultural patterns show up in inner life and assume new meaning as internal metaphors. Ethnic Chinese form one of the largest contingents on campus, and this group is divided, sometimes sharply, between Chinese Americans and Chinese nationals, with further regional and class divisions in each category. In the dream, it is unclear whether the man described as "half-Chinese" has a mixed Asian background or a non-Asian parent. Of course, Asian identity itself is a function of living in the West, a sociological designation that lumps together diverse populations with complex historical relationships. In the dreams of Westerners, Asia often functions as an image of the exotic and unknown despite the offensive nature of the association, decidedly un-PC in the language of the university community.

We are all symbols to each other, and racial stereotypes pop up in dreams from every ethnic group and across the political spectrum, causing no end of embarrassment to the dreamers. It often seems as though different strata of the personality have differing views on the matter, as what was learned in childhood bumps up against adult beliefs and relationships. "I can't believe I'm dreaming about the mysterious Asian woman," a female sociologist told me with chagrin, "the worst kind of Orientalist trope." Both Asian and non-Asian researchers reference the common cultural stereotype of Asians' scientific and technological superiority; the attribution is viewed differently depending on the individual's cultural and personal history, from racist jibe to oppressive expectation to point of pride—the same ambiguity it carries in the dream.

The dream gives a flavor of the complications and lingering unease that often emerge in cross-cultural relationships. For the actual dreamer, this complicated outer reality mirrored her internal divisions and the uneasy process of identity integration. The dream's portrayal of struggles around ethnicity depicts a very real interpersonal and cultural phenomenon while also providing an image of an equally tangled interior process. The dreamer was a young postdoctoral researcher who felt the outsider very much, both as a woman in the sciences and one of the few non-Asians on a research team primarily comprised of male Chinese nationals. The dream came soon after she spoke to a group of female undergraduates from STEM (Science, Technology, Engineering, and Math) programs. One asked about her experience as a woman in the hard sciences, and she had difficulty formulating a response. That night she lay in her hotel room mulling the question, which touched on a number of issues she had been struggling to articulate. As usual, her personal associations are critical in understanding the dream that came later that night. The most awkward of these involved a make-believe game about an upside-down world that she and a girlfriend played as children. Based on a comment by her immigrant grandmother, they dug holes in the backyard and pretended these went all the way through the earth to China, where everyone walked upside-down, and everything happened backward. This long-forgotten landscape had resurfaced in recent dreams, usually in contrast to the structured scientific world of her daytime hours.

Her second association came in response to the part of the dream where she looks into the eyes of her mixed colleague and sees his face morph and age, becoming round, pale, and sad. The man was not an actual person, and she did not recognize his altered face either until she suddenly remembered a pen-and-ink drawing of Lao Tzu on the cover of a copy of *Tao Te Ching* she kept on her bedside table in high school. She still recalled the opening line—*the way that can be spoken is not the way*—and bits and pieces of the text that followed. This paradoxical way of seeing the world made perfect sense to her back then and seemed to epitomize the intuitive and spiritual parts of herself she had left behind when she immersed herself in the sciences.

"It's like the old joke about converts being more Jewish than Moses," she told me. "A woman in the sciences has to be more scientific than Kepler. The guys in my lab are all business, at least the side they show me, and I need to be the same way for them to take me seriously."

The Chinese colleague in the dream was an actual doctoral student who personified this attitude, whereas the fictitious biracial researcher combined it with the side of her who lived in an upside-down world and had been out of touch for years, here represented by the *Tao Te Ching*. What did reconnecting with lost parts of herself have to do with the dreamer's worries about racism and whether her forgotten question had offended him?

She had done enough work with dreams to have a sense of how everything hangs together, like the details in a novel, and it bothered her that the two main threads of the dream did not seem to connect. She decided to dialogue with the biracial man, and his answer broke open the conundrum. *All I want is a human relationship,* he told her, *one that recognizes differences but sees the other as a person and not an abstraction.* On reflection, she realized this applied to her inner relationships as well, which brought together three parts of herself that had been living separate lives: the woman in the lab, the one who had a life outside the lab, and the mysterious stranger from the upside-down world. This process of integration was far from complete, as the uneasy feeling at the end of the dream indicates, but at least she now knew who they were.

Viewed through the lens of internal integration, the men in the dream function as animus figures. In traditional Jungian thought, animus and anima are images of relationship that give form to the encounter with an inner other who is also experienced in the outer world. Although Jung's model emphasizes gender, relationships occur along multiple dimensions. Here gender and ethnicity coincide, as they do in waking life, and together convey the sense of a multidimensional relationship. Lingering tensions surrounding ethnicity give interactions in the dream the same complexity and ambiguity as the woman's outer-world relationships and those between the different parts of herself, to the extent these can be separated.

In fact, anima and animus figures encountered in dreams are frequently a different ethnicity than the dreamer, and this characteristic tends to be emphasized, as it is in many accounts of sexual fantasies. Although Mark's dreams in the previous chapter lack this dimension of diversity, they give a good sense of the wildly varied forms these figures assume in inner life: mentor and tormentor, lover and betrayer, vulnerable child and tyrannical parent, witch and good fairy, sibling, friend, even an image of union with God. The male counterparts in the dreams of women are equally diverse, from golden-haired surfers to kidnappers, cops, gurus, and the ubiquitous man with a gun who shoots down hopes before they can unfold.

The possibilities do not end there, as the female researcher's dream illustrates. From a Jungian viewpoint, Lao Tzu functions in this dream as an image of the Self, the aspect of the larger personality that enters awareness as a God-image and opens into depths that extend beyond the individual consciousness.

It is All about Relationship

This brings me to final topic of the chapter. This discussion has focused on relationships, whether internal or with people around us, and you may be wondering what this has to do with the overall theme of the book—spirituality and its relationship to psychology. As often happens, the answer lies in more questions. What exactly would spirituality look like apart from relationships, and how can you separate spiritual life from the way we behave toward others, or for that matter, ourselves?

From the first, Christianity has maintained that you cannot love God in isolation from how you treat other people. Human relationships are viewed as places of spiritual challenge and growth. Relationships come up all the time in spiritual direction, as any director knows, the ones directees have and the ones they wish they did. When asked to define the spiritual path, Jesus described it as a love relationship with God and the people we are commanded to love as ourselves, an injunction that took on an ethnic dimension in his encounters with the centurion and the Canaanite woman. As with many spiritual teachers, his own life oscillated between two relational poles, withdrawal from the world and active engagement with others.

The traditional Christian image for the split between finding God in solitude and encountering Christ in other people is a pair of bickering sisters: Mary who sat raptly at Jesus's feet and Martha who bustled around making sure everyone got fed. Like characters in a dream, they have come to symbolize the two halves of Christian life: contemplation and service. But the Gospel vignette has multiple interpretations, as any good teaching story does, and commentators have debated the relative value of these stances for centuries. Most emphasized Mary's role. Others favored the active life, or combined the two, like Ignatius's call for contemplation in action and finding God in all things.

Whether you go with Mary, Martha, or both, it is all about relationship. From a psychological perspective, relationships are always present, whether in prayer or solitary confinement. Early ascetics such as St. Anthony fled human company to concentrate on God but wound up taking it with them. This happened literally when throngs of aspiring anchorites followed his lead and Anthony was called to help organize the fledgling community. Long before they arrived, however, his solitude was already crowded with voices as the silence unleashed a torrent of memories and inner figures.

Most of the preoccupations that haunted the Desert Fathers and Mothers, which later thinkers codified into the seven deadly sins, were relational in focus. Lust, envy, and pride pursued the solitaries into the silence, like the 1960s catchphrase "wherever you go, there you are." And not just you but the people in your mind, whether they are living, dead, or never were, like the fictitious Mother Superior at the beginning of the chapter. We carry our previous relationships inside us and have to keep working on them if we do not want the new ones to fall into the old familiar patterns.

This includes our relationship with God. We experience the divine through the lens of human relationships. Initial images of God are almost always parental, whether maternal or paternal. That does not mean God is just an introjected parent, as some psychological theories claim, but we still need to reexamine what we took from those early human encounters. Is God an overbearing patriarch, a depressed mother we need to cheer up, or a guilty weekend father who can be manipulated into giving us whatever we want? And, of course, parental images are not the only way to experience God, just as mom and dad do not encompass the entire range of a child's emotional development. There is a long tradition of seeing God as the beloved or intimate other—a soul-image in Jungian terms—whether in the person of the spiritual guide or a lover who awakens longing for spiritual union.

Meditations on this theme can be frankly erotic. From the canonical Song of Songs to Beguine[236] writings condemned by the Catholic Church, sexual relations offer a natural symbol of union with God. Deep human relationships open into the divine and always have, as our modern preoccupation with perfect mirroring and being saved by love makes clear. There is a long history in Western thought of seeing human love as a gateway to ultimate reality, beginning with Plato's idea of moving from beautiful bodies to abstract beauty and cosmic harmony.[237]

This optimistic view of the soul's union with God needs to be tempered with the reality of psychological projection. If relationships elevate our gaze, they can also cloud it. Every spiritual director knows the intense reactions triggered by images of God the Father or Mother Church. True love never runs smooth, and this includes the relationship with God, although believers can be fairly certain that the distortions are on the human end. Even though God's nature is not defined by human categories of relationship, our experience of it is. It is hardly surprising the same patterns show up both places. Fortunately, they also surface in dreams and inner figures, if you pay attention, shedding light on the underlying dynamics and giving them a crystalized form you can work with.

I have described these figures as images of relationship that reflect past experiences and expectations that shape our perception of those we encounter. Engaging them in a conscious way, not just insights but personalities, diminishes their distorting power and can help guide the path forward. Taking back projections in our relationships with other people forces us to acknowledge our darkness and own our wounds. We are constantly being challenged to assume responsibility for ourselves, what Mark called "carrying his own water." Others cannot save us, and our

---

[236] The Beguines were lay religious orders of women that flourished between the thirteenth and sixteenth centuries in Western Europe. Their status outside the formal authority structure of the church brought them under suspicion and sometimes led to persecution by clerical authorities.

[237] Plato, "The Symposium," *Plato's Complete Works,* 492–493, sections 210–212.

enemies are not just out there in the world; they are in our own house, and we must separate from them, according to one of Jesus's more unsettling pronouncements.[238]

Another verse in a similar vein informs us that no one can follow him who does not hate parents, siblings, spouses, children, even their own lives.[239] In psychological terms, this is not so much an early diagnosis of family dysfunction as an accurate description of the process of withdrawing projections. Doing so forces us to take up the cross of ourselves, in one of Jung's most compelling images—a Eucharist in which we eat our own flesh and drink our own blood.[240] Once we stop defining the world on our own terms, we discover it no longer revolves around us. "King Baby" is dethroned, in Mark's phrase. Then, not unlike Jesus's parable about the entitled wedding guest who sits at the head table and is asked to move down, the ego must find its way to a humbler seat.[241]

And it turns out we do not get to define God's nature either. The spiritual path is littered with outworn God-images that no longer capture our experience, as projections fall apart, and human models break down in wonder. The remainder of the book will track this process of deepening relationship with the divine as it manifests in internal images of union, the traditional and spontaneous religious symbols that Jung referred to as God-images.

---

[238] Matthew 10:36.
[239] Luke 14:26.
[240] Jung, *Mysterium Coniunctionis,* CW 14, ¶512.
[241] Luke 14:7–11.

Chapter 12
Not Bad for a Baptist Boy

Months passed. Mark was learning to be patient. He and Jennifer went through a period of wrenching conflict in couple's therapy and then settled into a long slog through accumulated problems. "It's like we're opening up the rooms we sealed off to avoid arguments," he told me, "All the unresolved stuff we gave up on. That works okay in the short run but pretty soon there's nowhere left to go, like those hoarder houses on reality shows where there's just a narrow path between the kitchen and the bathroom with boxes in the shower. Now that we've dragged out the worst of the rat-infested garbage it's a matter of sorting through what's left to see what's salvageable, if we still have a marriage."

As usual, his dreams did not answer the question directly. Instead, they played out different scenarios and examined the situation from all angles. *In one, he and Jennifer were young again and splitting up after just nine months together. He was telling her how much he appreciated the relationship, even if they weren't soulmates but broke off bewildered before a vision of a complicated connection stretching across many lifetimes. There was no baby in that dream, despite the reference to nine months; however, the next night he dreamed they had a tiny infant who kept spitting up. That worried the dreamer, although the baby seemed alright otherwise, and the three of them went on a trip together, Mark holding the baby while Jennifer carried her own load. He joked that the baby needed to carry a load too and it laughed, as though it understood.*

"I guess you could say I'm the one carrying the relationship at the moment," he decided, "which is only fair considering all the years Jen did it for me." Mark saw my confused expression and shot me an exasperated look. "I'm just going off what you said—that babies are something you make together in a relationship, new possibilities, and all that. This one's a little sickly but getting stronger, or at least that's what I hope the dream means."

At their therapist's suggestion, the couple began going on dates. The first one felt awkward and self-conscious. "Like being back in high school," he told me, "Stupid and nervous and excited at the same time. Except now I can't get high first." Next, they planned a weekend away together, but wound up returning early when they got in a fight. Mark told his men's group about it and was touched when they listened intently for the better part of an hour without giving advice. "That seems to be the lesson right now," he told me, "Listening instead of dictating. No more Mr. Dictator for me."

His changed attitude extended to work, where he often found himself in the role of mediator. "Talk about a thankless job," he told me with a smile, "and a whole lot less fun than being the rebel without a clue." He had shared about it at an AA meeting and caught himself slipping into a familiar routine—"Whatcha rebelling against? I dunno, whatta ya got?"— then pulled short to talk about it in a more vulnerable way.

His involvement in AA had increased along with his growing participation at church. He began working the steps again, took on a couple of sponsees, and started chairing a meeting at a local shelter. "It's not like I'm turning into Mr. AA," Mark assured me, "just doing my share." He paused a moment to reconsider. "Actually, it's more complicated than that. I realized in doing step work that I've always held the program at arm's length, same as I did with Christianity. Never actually quite in the room, rolling my eyes at the *Big Book* thumpers or being tolerant and above it all. 'Terminally unique,' we call it, or 'terminally special,' I've heard that too. Always wanting to skip ahead, like the guys in the first week of detox who decide they're going to be alcohol counselors and have to be reminded they have eleven more steps to work first. AA may not completely contain my spirituality—any more than it did for Bill W.—but I really do hear something useful every time if I actually listen, just like they say. Last week I was complaining about my new supervisor at a meeting and this old-timer said, 'Pray for the SOB.' Well I tried it, just so I could tell my sponsor I made the effort and damned if it didn't work. That's the pisser. When all's said and done, AA is where I need to be right now, and it even turns out I have something to offer. After all that drama about discerning a call, it was right under my nose the whole time, just not as exotic as I hoped. So much for the ashram."

The next weekend away with Jennifer went better. He told his men's group about it and shared again in AA. "Talking about the good stuff was harder than I expected," he said at our next session. "I'm great at bad news but laying out my hopes and maybe looking stupid next week, that's tough. Not everyone who came up afterward was especially insightful but that's OK; it doesn't have to be perfect. You can't always have it your way, there or anywhere else, certainly not my marriage." Mark paused.

"I've been so quick to judge, that's another thing coming up in step work. The program's big on letting go of resentments, not for the other schmuck's sake but for our own, and I've been carrying a ton of them. Speaking of which, I've been thinking a lot about my dad lately. His rigidity drove me crazy, but it's what held him together, like the exoskeleton on a crab, and I realize I'm the same way only with different contents. I may roll my eyes at the hairsplitting permutations of dispensationalism that kept him awake nights, but I have my own obscure fundamentalisms, not all of them religious. He did his best—both my parents did—and their lives weren't just about me. My dad was way more complicated than the story I tell myself, a better father than his dad and maybe that's as good as it gets. Plus I know for a fact he helped a lot of people and not just in his church, preaching at the jail and arranging jobs and housing for guys when they got out. I've been having more positive memories of him lately too, or maybe I'm just more open to them. The two of us cooking scrambled eggs before anybody else got up, the only thing he knew how to make, or me pretending to be asleep when I was little, and we got home late so he'd carry me up to bed."

Mark continued doing Centering Prayer and extended the time whenever he woke up early and could not get back to sleep. At the suggestion of another member in his men's group, he added the Welcoming Prayer, praying to be open to whatever happened in his life instead of automatically clenching himself against change. He attended another retreat, this one a little longer. "It had its ups and downs," he recounted with a shrug at our next session, "but I'm learning not to take them so seriously. Like Eliot's line about 'teach us to care and not to care / Teach us to sit still.'[242] That's the big epiphany in my notebook, just sitting with whatever comes up without making a big deal of it. The last night of the retreat *I dreamed I was living in the woods next to a tiny spring that had*

---

[242] Eliot, "Ash Wednesday," 95.

just enough water for my needs. I worried it would run dry during the night but when I looked the next morning, I saw a couple inches of water at the bottom of the pool."

Mark referenced this dream frequently over the next few months, a perfect image for this period of his life. "Like Elijah in the desert," he said, "I think he's the one who got fed by ravens. Just enough for today and he had to trust they'd be back in the morning. Basically, one day at a time, I guess."

Other dreams were more disturbing. *In one, he and Jennifer were cleaning house and found dead bodies in the trunk of the car and a skull at the base of a potted plant.* "Which is how it sometimes feels in couple's therapy," he confided, pulling a face. One featured the cataclysmic weather common in dreams during times of transition. *A huge storm was blowing in. He was stranded in a hotel with a group of strangers and led them to an upper story after grabbing bread from the half-submerged kitchen.* Another dream snippet left him puzzled: *I have to locate something that is and isn't there and can't find it. This seems like a phrase in something written and I'm afraid God will be upset at me over the failure.*

"Does everybody dream in Zen koans?" he asked rhetorically.

The dream baffled me as well, and I told him so when he pressed for an interpretation. My lack of answers clearly irritated him. His edginess mounted as we circled the dream without getting anywhere. I remarked that the wording reminded me of the language in mystical accounts, looking for something that could not be located with precision.

"Yeah, I got that part already," he snapped and caught himself. "Sorry, I guess I was hoping you'd be more insightful … um, that didn't come out quite right."

I said I understood his frustration, and we ended a few minutes later. After he left, I sat awhile before writing my notes, aware I had disappointed him and feeling like a failure as a spiritual director. Halfway home it occurred to me that was exactly the attitude in the dream, failing at an impossible task and worrying God would be upset.

I brought this up at our next meeting and wondered aloud about his experience, whether feeling like a failure rang any bells for him. "Only belfries full," he replied. "Actually, that's been coming up a lot in couple's therapy. Having to get everything just right and not trusting Jennifer to manage her part, correcting her on stupid stuff that doesn't even matter. She says she's always in the wrong, which is how I feel inside most of the time. Our therapist calls that playing it forward, treating other people the way we were treated and treat ourselves." Mark went on to connect his pervasive sense of failure with messages he had received in his family. I agreed but then noted that the dream talked about God being upset, not his parents. He grew quiet, saying he would have to think about. That night he had a particularly vivid dream that he brought to our next meeting.

> *I'm with a woman, probably Jennifer. I am clearing out a muddy place in the garden, shifting large rocks out of the way. The space is located inside the Accord, as though the floorboards somehow open downward. Moving the boulders, I discover there's a spring underneath. It's warm, as though thermal, and mildly sulfurous. I show Jennifer and start to plug it back up with rocks but decide to open it further and let it flow. Water begins welling up, filling the cab of the car. I realize this is a problem but don't feel panicked, more curious how to solve it. Water wells out the top of the window without quite filling the cab completely. I puzzle how to move the car, wondering if it will start, but am excited about the spring.*

He called the dream "Holy Springs," his childhood name for a tiny granite basin he used to pass on his way to elementary school. "It couldn't have been more than a yard in diameter," he told me, spreading his hands to demonstrate. "The place was magical for me. Shaded and dark with pollywogs and little water creatures swimming around. I used to imagine it led down into the earth and sometimes I'd stand there picturing the journey until the school bell rang and I had to run for it."

The woman in the dream also had something magical about her, although he could not quite put his finger on it. She was Jennifer, but not quite, the two identities overlaid like a double exposure. It is a pattern I have seen frequently in my years as a therapist. The doubling can be subtle, as here, although sometimes a character will completely change identity over the course of the narrative: so that now she is an aunt, now a female coworker. A common variation involves two people who are somehow linked, one factual and the other unknown, like Mark's earlier dreams about Jennifer and the female friend who was edging him out of the relationship. Other dream figures combine identities: the policeman who looks like an old school friend or a coworker who is simultaneously a public figure.

In the last chapter, I examined these multilayered images in terms of the many people present in any relationship, whether inner images or ghosts from the past. Owning those projections not only brings the actual person into focus, as Mark was discovering with Jennifer, but also opens a path to the inner world, in the imagery of his "Holy Springs" dream. It is only when people begin to disentangle their fears and longings from the person in front of them that they discover the deeper level within what they sought in the relationship, a mysterious quality that predates it.

I kept these thoughts to myself, knowing a theoretical discussion would only get us off track. For his part, Mark was struck by the idea of pulling out boulders so he and Jennifer could start a garden, an image that reminded him of their hard labor in couples' sessions. He got a kick out of the reference to a Honda Accord, not a car he had ever owned, though it is the kind of pun dreams love. "Cars are how we get around in the world and present ourselves to others," he said, "at least according to Guru Google or maybe something you said. With me it's always been split screen, pickup or Prius, my weekend identity, and the workweek self. Neither one's going anywhere at the moment, in deep waters with nothing to do but wait. Trusting more will be revealed, as we say in the rooms. It's like when I first got sober and had to start doing life as me, except this time I'm not flailing around quite as much. Sort of like in the dream, oddly calm and mostly curious. Not sure the car will start, even if we get it unstuck, but excited about finding the spring."

We spent the rest of the session on water. When Mark closed his eyes and entered the dream image, his thoughts went two directions. *One was downward into the interior world where the spring led, just like the one from his childhood. The other was upward with the rising water that stopped just short of the roof of the cab.* "With barely enough room to breathe," he said when we talked about the visualization afterward, "which is pretty much how it feels at the moment."

I encouraged him to forgo the various interpretations of water he had found on the internet, most of which revolved around its status as a symbol of the unconscious and stick with his own associations. His first thought was the living water Jesus offered the Samaritan woman he encountered at the town well in John's Gospel, a favorite sermon text when he was growing up.[243] "Look, the dream's even got wells," he told me delightedly, "if you count verbs when *water wells out the top of the window.*"

---

[243] John 4:1-42.

Details always matter, and I asked what he made of the water being thermal, even sulfurous.

"I don't know," he replied with a hint of the same irritation I had seen the last time we met. "What do *you* make of it?"

I told him I was more interested in his thoughts and the room went quiet.

"Sorry," Mark said a minute later. "I seem to be a little cranky lately."

I asked him if something was going on and he shook his head.

"Well maybe," he said after a pause. "Look, I know where you're headed with the sulfur thing." He switched to scholarly intonations, as though reading from an encyclopedia "… sulfur, denoting the infernal or diabolical, fire and brimstone, whatever the hell that is. My grandfather still called matches a box of lucifers. I know damn well that's where you're going, but I don't see what it has to do with the dream."

"I'm not sure either," I told him, struggling not to get defensive. I tried to explore the feelings coming up for him without getting anywhere. We talked some more about the dream. I speculated that when something new comes up it can feel diabolical to the established order, like the religious authorities who accused Jesus of having a demon, adding this might explain why the dreamer initially debated whether to plug the spring up again. Mark said the interpretation made sense yet did not ring true, and I assured him that was what mattered—what fit for him and not my ideas about it. The session ended on an unresolved note, and he left me a conciliatory voicemail a few days later, saying he had had another dream that continued the series.

I'm in church with Jennifer in a sanctuary like the ones in churches I attended as a child. It's dim, with only a few people in attendance. The speaker announces that men and women will sing alternate verses of a hymn. Jennifer jokes with me about my reluctance to sing. The women go first. When we get to the men's verse, I largely mouth the words but to my relief a group of men somewhere to my right sings strongly and well. The versus are mildly sexual in a joking way, something jaunty about touching under the covers etc. The mood in the sanctuary is light. I'm surprised this is a religious song.

He had worked with the dream on his own by the time we met and shared entries from his notebook. The image of sanctuary stood out for him, and he listed places of refuge in his present life, including the men's group and Centering Prayer. "The woods were a sanctuary for me when I was growing up," he said, looking up from his journal, "in both senses of the word. Church too, especially on communion nights when everyone sat in silence while the organ noodled softly."

Mark was also struck by how the men and women in the dream sang alternate verses. "Both getting their separate say," he decided, "like me and Jen learning to take turns in therapy and say our piece without second guessing what the other one's thinking. And she's teasing me again, that's good news, not just in the dream but when we talk on the phone or text during the day."

"The part about mouthing the words pretty much sums up my teenage years," he continued, "whether we're talking about hymns at church or the Pledge of Allegiance at school. Going through the motions so everyone would leave me the hell alone. In the dream, I want to sing but can't find my voice and feel self-conscious, but the chorus of men does it for me. Which feels super supportive, like my posse's got my back. Actually, that's one silver lining of the last few months, connecting with men and learning to trust a little, which doesn't come easy. The line about touching under the covers makes me think of something going on beneath the surface, like the new playfulness with Jennifer. Both of us shy and flirting a little. Which is wonderful, of course, but not exactly what I think of when it comes to hymns. Back in the day we went for blood and guts, a mighty fortress is our God or Jesus bleeding on the tree for me. A make-out hymn is a bit of a disconnect, to say the least."

We spent the remainder of the time on that disconnect. Just talking about this part of the dream made Mark uncomfortable, as though he was somehow blaspheming. Religion had been a serious business in his childhood and still was, like most parts of his life. He knew intellectually that there was a long tradition of framing the relationship with God in erotic terms. The idea of singing about sex in church offended his inner Evangelical, however. "It's like a conversation I had with an old friend who grew up in the same church," Mark added. "I think I told you about it. He's got no use for religion now, but when I told him about my spiritual journey, he just shook his head and said, 'Well that's not the kind of Christian I'm not.' Maybe it's what you said last time about new things looking demonic.

Sleazy even, the way Jesus's disciples muttered among themselves when they saw him talking to the woman at the well, the prototypical pickup spot in the Hebrew scriptures. Everybody loves a taboo breaker except when it's our taboo, like the way we used to rail on the Pharisees when we weren't busy damning and smiting over playing cards or rock 'n' roll. Progressives too, for that matter. We all do it, just in different ways."

We came to the end of the session and arranged our next appointment. Mark paused on his way out the door, looking awkward. "Look," he said, "I thought about last time when you asked if there was something going on. A therapist I saw in my thirties used to talk about falling into my daddy trap when I maneuvered him into taking over and then criticized whatever he said. It's like I can't agree even when I agree. I actually think it's more of an authority trap than a daddy trap," he added, "although it does happen more with men. We talk about competition a lot in my men's group and I'm starting to realize how much it colors every part of my life. I never pictured myself as a jock, but the truth is I have to win at everything, even Centering Prayer. I tell myself it's about personal bests but that's a crock. I'm even competitive with God if that makes any sense."

"I imagine he just smiles," I told him. "Like a dad taking pride in his kid pushing back, his beloved son in whom he is well pleased."

Mark stood there a second more, his eyes welling. "That's totally humiliating," he said with a smile, "just so you know."

Although I did not realize it at the time, that moment in the doorway crystalized many of the themes that were to unfold in Mark's life over the next several months. With a therapy client, I might have spent several sessions exploring the pattern and ways it played out in *our* relationship. Here I was clearly just the finger, not the moon. Even so, Mark's comment put a name on the push/pull I experienced when he pressured me for answers and then bristled if I gave them. Although he talked about this happening mainly with men, the same dynamic came up in his marriage. The couple's therapist had pointed out how his need to control the relationship pushed away the very intimacy he demanded. Jennifer withdrew when she could not be herself and nothing she did was right, leaving him more desperate and lonely.

Mark had often described a similar loneliness in his spiritual life, and I found myself wondering if something parallel happened there. He had always been adamant that the relational aspect of Christianity was a stumbling block for him, although it crept in any way from time to time.

"That whole concept of a relationship with Jesus just doesn't compute," he declared in one of our first meetings. "How can I relate to a dead Palestinian guy?"

He described his experience of God as more of a place or a feeling. "Perhaps a place with a feeling," which he sometimes reached and sometimes could not find. That was fine as far as it went, yet he missed the sense of personal connection with God he had felt in childhood. This longing had grown more pronounced in the last few months as he leaned less heavily on Jennifer for support.

"You know I actually used to see him sometimes on communion nights when I was a kid," he confided a few weeks later. "Jesus, I mean. The ushers would pass out little cups of grape juice, and we'd all drink them at the same time, 'doing our shots,' we joked as teenagers. Then the organ would play, and we'd sit there praying as twilight fell outside. I just knew he was there, so close I could touch him, a dim presence like the hologram in the haunted house at Disneyland. I told my mother, and she said it was just my imagination, which was probably true in a way, but after that I kept it to myself. Well, lately he's back for weekend visits, and I realize how much I've missed him. Not necessarily a guy in robes this time but definitely a presence. And a place too, if that makes sense, like floating in an ocean that talks to you. Whatever metaphor you choose, it's an intimacy that goes where no one and nothing else can, like the line in the Koran about God being closer than your jugular vein. Some of the street people I advocate for describe voices telling them what to do and it's not like that, but there's definitely a way God rummages around inside and points stuff out, kind of shining the flashlight around."

This theme of intimacy with God had looped throughout our time together, a little different each time it surfaced, and it always elicited a certain shyness in Mark. At the same time, he described relief at being able to talk openly about experiences that would have seemed ludicrous to most people he knew and often felt that way to him. He played with different images for this new closeness, none of which seemed quite right, before settling on a warming trend as his need to control interactions with God loosened.

"Looking back, I can see I treated him like an event at a theme park," he confided. "Okay, I've paid for my ticket in prayer and it's time for the five o'clock showing. Now there's more of the continuity you get in a relationship, like going through my day knowing Jennifer's out there even if we're not texting. That's how it was with Jesus growing up, but it had this magical element too, black magic really, where you said the right prayer and he had to save you. Except you had to really mean it—that's the catch—and you were never really really sure you did completely. Not so much true intimacy as topping from below, if you know what that is, when the bottom runs the show through passivity.

"I've got a million ways of managing people to make them safe, and I use them all on God—the same subtle competition that keeps everybody at arm's length. One up or one down, whatever works best at the moment. Either running things myself and feeling lonely as hell or being placating and secretly contemptuous. Telling people what they want to hear, precocious and charming or sad and pitiful so they have to take care of me, the patterns go back a long way.

"I've got plenty of ready explanations for why I do what I do, all the old tapes from childhood about how nobody likes me the way I am, so I have to game the system, but none of that matters anymore. I keep thinking of those bible verses about sons versus slaves, basically taking the power element out of the relationship. But relinquishing control goes against the grain, especially if I don't get the reaction I want. I do my stuff and when it doesn't work I'm outraged, like Jennifer not paying me the right kind of attention or what happened that day in the box-store parking lot. But God just smiles when I try that crap on him, like you said about a father chuckling fondly when he sees his little son getting full of himself. It's humiliating, like I said, but a good humiliating—at least most of the time."

The dreams slowed for a while and then one day Mark walked into the room waving his notebook, saying he had had another installment in the series.

I'm at a festival like a company picnic, where a large crowd is celebrating. A middle-aged male colleague, quite extroverted with lots of energy, announces his engagement. He's a gay man with close-cropped hair. He gives me the nod, and, on cue, I ask who the lucky girl is. This is a joke we worked out together beforehand. He tells the crowd I was raised Baptist but have come a long way before announcing his partner's name. Then he nods at a huge Black man with dreads, the fiancé he's marrying, who picks up Jennifer from the edge of the crowd and carries her to the table or stage where we are. He announces that I'm getting married too and says, "Not bad for a Baptist boy." Someone asks who the Black man is, and he says, "Mr. T. grown old."

The first thing I noticed when Mark read the dream aloud was its emotional tone, always a good indication of the dreamer's relationship to the themes in a dream. Here the atmosphere is lighter than before, as if the new playfulness in his relationship with Jennifer has spread to his dream companions. Apparently, this warming trend even extends to the torturous relationship with his Evangelical past, softening the hard edges of the conflict with gentle ribbing. The festival is a company picnic, and the mood is celebratory and communal. Since his actual work environment was anything but festive these days, Mark decided the dream probably had more to do with the new warmth in his personal relationships across a range of settings, including AA and his men's group. He was intrigued by the gay male colleague, who did not correspond to anyone in his day-world life.

The man's effusive personality was opposite his own intense and introverted style. It resonated, however, with the new spirit of openness emerging from his increased "engagement" with those around him, in the imagery of the dream. Sitting with the dream, Mark noticed how much attention it paid to hair, not usually something he thought about much. The man's hairstyle reminded him of a young guy in his men's group, a look he characterized as "gay professional," claiming his sexual identity without making a big deal of it. It suddenly occurred to Mark that he had a similar haircut himself since he cut off his ponytail, what he called the "'balding boomer buzz,' too proud for a comb-over but not shaved like a tough guy."

Mark's hair linked him to the man in the dream, but their connection appears to go far beyond coiffure, enabling them to accept and even joke about their differences. In keeping with the festive atmosphere, they've arranged a comedy routine in which Mark plays the straight man in both sense of the word, content to give his colleague the limelight without competing for attention. The humor comes at his expense and hinges on his cluelessness as a naive Baptist boy.

Banter turns to slapstick when the man's fiancé picks up Jennifer and carries her forward to join them in front of the crowd. In a typical dream equivocation, they are either at a table or on stage, breaking bread together or playing a public role, with the added punning implication of a life stage. Mark puzzled over the figure of Mr. T., who'd been on television when he was young, the epitome of an in-your-face tough guy during what now struck him as a very innocent time. He was being uncharacteristically careful in his associations, and I commented on this unusual reticence.

"Well, you've got to admit it's a little awkward," he said, "the gay yuppie and his dark alter ego. Why couldn't he have been a cowboy?"

I related a suitably disguised version of my exchange with the sociologist who'd been aghast to find herself dreaming of a mysterious Asian woman and Mark laughed.

"I guess they do make a cute couple," he decided, "like something out of a bad rom com. Opposites attract and all that."

I wondered aloud how these two figures mapped onto his life.

"I *knew* you were going to ask that," he smiled, shaking his head, and it occurred to me that the playfulness in the dream was spreading to our relationship as well. "I think it's what I said before," he continued, "about the split between the button-down professional and the tough guy. Not that I was ever actually tough, more playacting like Mr. T. and definitely a hero in my own mind. You always say if I don't recognize somebody in a dream, they're probably a part of me, and these guys are my Prius and pickup, two halves of me coming together."

Mark's interpretation rang true on a psychological level. I encouraged him to sit with the image to see what else emerged. He closed his eyes a few minutes before replying. "Well, this is kind of a long train but what came up first was hair again. Mr. T. had a mohawk, which looks kinda silly now but packed a lot of shock value back in the day, rebellious and over the top. Now he's mature and wearing dreadlocks, which seem a lot less adolescent, like when I finally cut off my poor threadbare ponytail. His new hairstyle is spiritual, assuming he's Rasta, part of a religious tradition and not just making a personal statement. The opposite of when I grew my hair long as a teenager and people at church called me Sampson or John the Baptist, who probably looked a lot like the guy in the dream, dreads and all. That's actually what came up for me, Mr. T. changing to John the Baptist, which sounds weird I know."

Mark hesitated and I nodded, knowing how dream images can morph into each other. "I told you about my soul connection to John the Baptist," he added, "even after I left Christianity. This great lonely hippie on the edge of something new he could see but couldn't quite reach, like

Moses peering into the Promised Land. I used to joke he'd be my patron saint if I was Catholic, not just the Baptist part but being stuck between worlds. Like I said, it's a long train of thought, but it fits my general feeling these days of reconciliation and different parts of me coming together. Including not having to be the center of the universe anymore, riffing on the passage where John says Jesus must increase as he decreases, one of my favorite verses. Letting someone else take the wheel without feeling stupid or humiliated."

As in many dreams, this one moves seamlessly between the psychological and the spiritual, not so much distinct domains as two facets of an integrated growth process. In developmental terms, the adolescent part of Mark who got in street fights and poisoned his marriage by acting like a spoiled teenager was coming into dialogue with his grownup self. Bringing the two parts together allowed him to be where he really was, instead of forever standing apart and telling himself his real identity lay somewhere else. Ever the intellectual, Mark described the shift as moving from Dostoyevsky to Tolstoy, taking his place in the larger society instead of hiding in his garret obsessing about how different he was. From a psychological perspective, having a reference point outside himself made it possible to have real relationships and see others as separate people with needs of their own. All these themes wove through the dream, or at least his reflections on it, along with the strong implication that the wild part of him was bringing its energy to his mature workday self instead of popping out in parking lots, another new hybrid of Prius and pickup.

The growth unfolding in Mark's life did not end with psychological integration, any more than it began there. For him the outside reference point that enabled him to see himself from a wider perspective was not just a developmental milestone, or what psychologists call "the observing ego," the part of you that sees yourself. It was also a presence, an otherness that showed up interiorly but was not him and took him beyond himself. His image for the resulting demotion of the small self was the recognition by John the Baptist that he must decrease as Christ increased.[244] This same theme is found in every spiritual tradition—the encounter with a larger reality that puts the ego in its place.

From a Jungian standpoint, this relativizing relationship is reflected in the very structure of the dream, which fits the archetypal pattern of

---

[244] John 3:30.

the double marriage that shows up in myths and folktales, even Disney movies. This multidimensional symbol, which I will discuss more fully in the next chapter, depicts intimate connection with an otherness that is integrated into one's life on multiple levels. The players vary yet there is always a double wedding between two interconnected couples from different groups or ranks—sometimes royalty and their chief aides, sometimes two set of siblings from different social strata, or even an entirely different species altogether, such as a human pair marrying into the elven kingdom or the prince's stallion mating with the princess's mare. Jung believed that the folktale motif of the double wedding offered a mythic representation of the union between inner and outer realities, in which a human relationship in the outside world facilitated a parallel process of internal integration.[245] The dream references a prime example. Mark's growing intimacy with his partner both mirrored and supported his deepening connection with an inner presence that put the small self in proper position.

In practice, this sharp distinction between inner and outer is not entirely accurate since intimate relationships always operate in multiple dimensions, a sort of hinge between internal and external life. Every important interpersonal connection contains a village of other relationships, as the last chapter described, the ones you had, the ones you missed, and the ones you dream about. But the union of inner and outer symbolized by the double marriage is not merely a matter of human relationships. What comes together are not just different parts of the personality—Mark's adolescent and professional selves—or even different levels of it, such as conscious awareness and deeper levels of consciousness. In common with mystics across spiritual traditions, Jung believed that real healing occurs when the individual self comes into relationship with the larger whole of which it is a tiny part, as in Mark's image of floating in a living ocean. For Jung, the goal of human existence was the kind of transforming relationship with the divine that mystics like Teresa of Avila described as spiritual betrothal leading to spiritual marriage.

I half expected Mark to plunge into these deep waters during our session. For once Guru Google missed a trick, however, and I kept my thoughts to myself, not wanting to spark an intellectual discussion. For

---

[245] C. G. Jung, 1946. "The Psychology of the Transference," *The Practice of Psychotherapy*, CW 16, ¶¶425–434.

the same reason, I chose not to comment on the gender of the couples, two men and a mixed pair. Unlike many such dreams, the internal otherness Mark encounters here is not sexual but racial. I wondered whether the predominance of men in the dream was a way to spotlight the new integration of his male identity that was being nurtured in the men's group. Here I could only speculate, as often happens with dreams, pondering these things in my heart.

Meanwhile, dreams about mysterious women proliferated, even as the couple reconciled, and Jennifer moved back into the house. *In one, he distanced himself from a disheveled young woman who was staggering home from a night of partying and instead went home with a middle-aged woman. When she commented on this choice, he explained that he wanted to be with someone his own age, adding that sex isn't everything and besides, what would we talk about afterward? The older woman told him she wasn't interested in a serious relationship, and he felt disappointed but thanked her for letting him know so he could adjust his heart accordingly. Then the narrative skipped ahead to the next morning, when he was delighted to discover that she also did Centering Prayer. He accompanied her to Catholic mass, which wasn't his church, though it felt close enough. Afterward, she invited him to move in with her, and he realized that her previous talk about not wanting a relationship had been a test.*

In another dream, *Mark found himself deeply drawn to a slight woman with an engaging manner who was not his type and appeared to have a cold. He kept his distance for fear of catching it, but they wound up embracing over an empty chair, and he knew instantly that she was his soulmate, and he would never let go. She assured him that her sniffles were due to allergies. He said he wouldn't mind sharing her cold,* a strong statement indeed since avoiding germs was somewhat of an obsession for the day-world Mark. This image of contagion suggests lingering ambivalence on the part of the dream ego, which surfaced again at the end of the dream when *the dreamer experienced a momentary surge of panic the woman didn't share his feelings after all, despite knowing intellectually that she did.*

The dream could be interpreted in terms of moving toward a more realistic relationship with Jennifer; however, Mark woke with the certainty that it was about joining God and God being sufficient for all his needs. Reflecting on it further, he found himself drawn to the image of embracing over an empty chair, which took him back to his earlier train dream and the seat left empty for Elijah as well as the mercy seat atop the Ark of the Covenant where Yahweh was said to appear between two golden cherubim. My own thoughts went to the third chair in spiritual direction, a common image for God's unseen presence in the room. This triadic structure resonated with the dream he brought to our next session.

I'm at some kind of retreat where we are camping in a city park. Martin Luther King is there and has spoken earlier. It's late afternoon and I'm getting settled in the campsite. Returning from the communal faucet with water, I see MLK hurrying along in a suit with a well-dressed Black woman. They are carrying plants from a nursery, probably rosemary. The plants look a little bedraggled, and he is carrying his plant carelessly so it scrapes on the pavement. One of them carries a shovel. I assume they're planting the shrubs and ask if they need help. After hesitation, they accept. I am barefoot and grab my tennis shoes so I can dig. Then MLK drops away and I follow the woman. We begin climbing a long ladder. I wish I had put on my shoes first, which I carry in my hand. I accidentally bump her hip with the plant, and she jokes about the view from below as she climbs ahead of me. I say it's nothing new as I'm a married man. All this is in good fun. The ladder is very tall, and I'm nervous of heights, although at least there are posts to lean against. I realize she would be with MLK if I hadn't volunteered and apologize, since I know it's hard to find a chance to be alone with him. She acknowledges this good-naturedly, and I say she doesn't have to make nice on my account. We are getting along well, chatting as we climb. I'm glad since this cuts my nervousness about the height. We will plant shrubs at the top of a mountain where there are three elevated receptacles, like Olympic torches. Our two plants go in lower pots on either side. There is a higher one in the middle, and I ask if we forgot a plant. She says MLK will be lowered in a helicopter with that plant. When we get to the final stretch, there is no support behind us, and I tell her to go on ahead as this will make me less nervous. I wonder what coming down will be like, then wonder if we can get a ride. She asks if I want to be above her when we come down, and I say no, as I don't want to take her down if I fall. I feel that will somehow be alright if it happens, part of a greater event.

This turned out to be a watershed dream for Mark, one of those rare overviews of the developments that had been building in his life and the path that lay ahead. As in the previous dream, archetypal motifs abound. Private spirituality and community life come together in the image of being on retreat in a city park. It is late afternoon, in keeping with Mark's developmental stage. By any math he was well into the second half of life, when focus shifts from individual accomplishment to finding one's place in the larger whole.

Like many of his generation, he saw Martin Luther King Jr. as a leader of almost mythic proportions. From a Jungian standpoint, the minister serves as an image of the Self, a revered figure who represents a higher perspective that calls us beyond narrow ego preoccupations. In folktales and mythology, this part is often played by the king, which is one component of his name. Although Martin Luther King was a political leader, his main role in society was prophetic, even messianic. In a novel, he might be viewed as a Christ figure who sacrifices himself for the good of others, absorbing humiliation without retaliating and dying a martyr's death. That was actually Mark's first association, which suggests that Martin Luther King functioned as a God-image in his inner world, a figure who embodies the highest spiritual values for an individual or a culture.[246]

Named for another religious prophet and reformer, MLK's message was deeply rooted in the Protestant tradition of Mark's childhood. Like his namesake, Martin Luther King was a very human man with feet of clay and his share of weaknesses. Here he looks exhausted, similar to the drooping plant he carries, his strength flagging as the shadows lengthen. In Jungian terms, this suggests the motif of the aging king, an image that appears in dreams and myths when the ruling paradigm no longer adequately captures the lived reality of an individual or a people. When the aging king is associated with a God-image, it is usually an indication that the religious perspective needs to widen and deepen. Losing a comforting religious structure can be experienced as a kind of death, as the shovel implies, but rebirth requires sacrifice and the seed must fall to ground for new life to emerge, in the imagery of the premonitory egg dream Mark brought to our first meeting.

Mark asks the couple if he can aid in the planting, and they agree. The great man fades from the scene as he steps forward, the sort of tag team

---

[246] Jung, *Aion*, CW 9ii, ¶170.

substitution often seen in dreams. Mark has taken the place of the failing king and now the quest is personal—no longer worship from afar but a matter of life and death. A common image across spiritual writings is the image of an ascending stairway, like Jacob's dream of a ladder reaching to heaven depicted in the book of Genesis.[247] What this dreamer faces is a hard scrabble up a shaky ladder.

The details in a dream are always noteworthy, and there is much attention to the shoes Mark carries in his hand but does not put on. In many spiritual traditions, going barefoot is associated with the humble role of mendicant and connotes remaining close to the earth, as Moses must remove his shoes to approach the burning bush.[248] Mark's association was more idiosyncratic, the cover of a Beatle's album from his youth. According to the interpretation circulating widely in pop culture of the time, the barefoot Paul McCartney represented a corpse and the other band members were officiants at his funeral, including an undertaker, a priest, and a gravedigger. This obscure reference fits the imagery of the dream and the cycle of death and rebirth associated with the aging king when the reigning paradigm loses its grip. On a more prosaic note, Mark could be careless in his approach to life and not stopping to put on his shoes before climbing might also indicate excessive haste or approaching the task too lightly.

Barefoot or not, he begins the perilous ascent accompanied by the woman previously associated with the king. He apologizes for not being the messiah, a realization that was gradually seeping into Mark's awareness with the help of external events. From a Jungian perspective, the woman functions as a soul-image, the inner other who complements and challenges the conscious viewpoint while serving as a bridge to the transcendent Self. As an anima figure or soul-image, she gives a human face to Mark's deepening relationship with his hidden depths. This element of relationship is central to most forms of Western mysticism as God stirs within the inmost part of the soul, the place where the seeker encounters the sacred presence.

Jung believed that reflections of this divine movement in the depths enter consciousness as God-images. These are not necessarily the God of theology but a personally meaningful image like the dream figure of

---

[247] Genesis 28:10–17.
[248] Exodus 3:5.

Martin Luther King, God "as we understood him" in the language of Alcoholics Anonymous. The God-image is a representation of something inexpressible, not the moon but the finger, pointing beyond itself to the vastness of God beyond human understanding. The soul-image also leads beyond itself. Like the woman in the dream, it has an intimate connection with the God-image and serves a bridging function in relation to the ego. This dual role is depicted in the narrative. On the one hand, the nameless woman accompanies the God-image as companion, like Sophia who was God's playmate in creation.[249] On the other, she leads the dreamer upward to where the God-image descends from on high, the origin and conclusion of the journey.

But for the soul-image, this upward end of the bridge is only half the story. The soul is no angel and not every part of the spiritual path is elevated, a point emphasized throughout spiritual writings. As the lotus's roots reach into the muck, connecting with the deep self is an exercise in self-knowledge that sometimes requires a strong stomach. The depths within run the gamut and, as with any marriage, an intimate relationship with them brings out the best and worst in everyone. As humans we are embodied creatures rooted in biology, a point driven home by the sticky imagery of the Nicodemus dialogue about entering again into the mother's womb.[250] We are made in the image of God with mammal brains and troop monkey psychology. Consequently, the soul-image must operate on many levels. Like Mark's previous dream about bawdy hymns in church, the message here seems to be that he needs to join the different parts of his experience together and bring them into the daylight. The mysterious woman grows steadily more familiar as they climb. Things get a little coarse when she jokes about the view from below. For his part, Mark tells her not to be nice on his account, suggesting it was time to get real in his spiritual life, even down and dirty.

Along with the motif of the journey, ascending to meet God on the heights is a universal image of the spiritual quest. Like Beatrice in Dante's quintessential Christian epic, the woman can only take him so far. He must make the final ascent on his own, climbing one-handed with the shrub across his shoulder, an image he associated with taking up his cross. Their task is to plant shrubs on either side of the raised pot in the

---

[249] Proverbs 8:22–31.
[250] John 3:4.

middle. Mark googled rosemary and found it was associated with Mary and Christ, marriage, and death. It grows near the sea, suggesting the vast unknown, and should be planted by women. It draws elves into church, a thought that tickled him, and drives away witches.

In keeping with Mark's religious background, the dream is full of Christian iconography. The summit reminded him of the barren hill of Golgotha, the place of the skull where three crosses are planted. Christ was hung on a tree, and Mark's shrub stands in the position of the dying thief crucified at his side, a central figure in altar calls of his childhood.[251] It is a place of shame and ignoble death, a stumbling block for disciples who expected a triumphant campaign of conquest.

As we worked with the dream, Mark realized part of what needed to die was an outworn heroic attitude that he associated with the militant faith of his childhood, where Christian soldiers marched onward to evangelize the heathen. That martial imagery was safely distant, somebody else's fault; a more uncomfortable realization involved the many ways in which his own spirituality was shot through with power motives.

As he climbs, Mark ruminates on the hard path back down, bleakly wondering if he can hitch a ride. With no help arriving from on high, it looks like he's on his own. You cannot live on the heights, as Peter learned when he wanted to prolong the Transfiguration by subdividing Mount Tabor.[252] The trip down the mountain is always harder, as any experienced climber can attest, and this includes coming down to earth after a mountaintop experience. Reentering the world is a perilous time in every spiritual tradition. After his enlightenment, the Buddha despaired of communicating his realization to others, and it was on the way down from Mount Tabor that Jesus told his disciples of his upcoming humiliation and death.[253] In the final line of the dream, Mark reaches his own point of surrender, and a strange sense of peace ensues. He's no hero and there is no woman to break his fall. It is crunch time and he cannot charm his way out of this one. Taking his life into his hands, he places himself in a one-down position, assuming responsibility for his stumbles and determined not to endanger anyone else. He who hangs onto his life will lose it, seems

[251] Luke 23:39–43.
[252] Matthew 17:1–8.
[253] Matthew 17:9–12.

to be the message, and in giving his all he discovers he is part of a larger whole.

The next dream continued this process of union with the divine using imagery that shocked his inner Evangelical to the core.

My nephew is getting married to God. I'm in a large group of people at long tables working on invitations and preparations. I begin addressing my nephew's invitations, working on his side of the preparations.

Chapter 13
The Self: Wholeness as Relationship

So exactly what is the *Self*? Although the term has come up frequently, its meaning is probably still far from clear. Unfortunately, lack of clarity is inherent in the concept. The Self has been characterized in diverse and seemingly contradictory ways: the source and goal of psychological life,[254] the unifying force within the larger personality and the unity itself,[255] the archetype of meaning,[256] and the totality of human potentialities encompassing both conscious and unconscious life.[257] On one hand, its expanse is immense—an entire universe of images, thoughts, sensations, and emotions spanning the full range of human experience, both positive and negative.[258] On the other, it is experienced interiorly as an intimate sense of purpose and meaning.[259] The pages that follow will draw on all these models, coming at the topic from multiple directions, so readers can line them up with their own experience.

Big Self and Small Self

Despite Jung's insistence on the scientific basis of the Self,[260] its closest analogues are religious concepts that point to an ineffable reality that

---

[254] C. G. Jung, 1942/1954. "Transformation Symbolism in the Mass," *Psychology and Religion: East and West*, CW 11, ¶¶391, 397–400; Jung, 1928. "The Relations between the Ego and the Unconscious," *Two Essays on Analytical Psychology*, CW 7, ¶404.

[255] Jung, 1927/1931. "The Structure of the Psyche," *The Structure and Dynamics of the Psyche*, CW 8, ¶396.

[256] Jung, 1934/1954. "Archetypes of the Collective Unconscious," *The Archetypes and the Collective Unconscious*, CW 9i, ¶66.

[257] Jung, 1935/43. "Introduction to the Religious Problems of Alchemy," *Psychology and Alchemy*, CW 12, ¶¶20, 247.

[258] Jung, CW 12, ¶¶20, 21; Jung, CW 7, ¶274

[259] Jung, CW 12, ¶22.

[260] Jung, 1951/1968. *Aion*, CW 9ii, ¶123.

defies precise definition and so winds up being expressed in paradoxical terms, at once the center and the circumference.[261] The word itself adds to the confusion since the Self does not refer to our ordinary sense of who we are but to a deep knowing that goes beyond the personal perspective, what has been called the *big Self* as opposed to the *small self*. This distinction was lost on many of Jung's Christian critics who accused him of divinizing the ego, the very opposite of his meaning.[262]

Jung devoted much attention to the complicated relationship between the big and small selves, both of which play a crucial role in the growth of the personality. The ego may not get the final word in his model, yet it still needs to have a strong voice.[263] A common sentiment across religious traditions is that individuals need to develop a sufficiently solid sense of self so that they can surrender its supremacy without falling apart. There is an ongoing dialogue between the two selves, and the quest to form a conscious relationship with the depths that sustain us continues throughout the lifespan, engaging every aspect of the personality.[264]

On the level of personal psychology, healing requires coming to terms with our wounds and blind spots while taking responsibility for the ways we wound others, a process facilitated for Mark by his involvement in therapy and twelve-step groups. This effort sets up a feedback loop, as intimate relationships help connect us with the deepest parts of ourselves and withdrawal of projections onto those around us makes us more present for others. But the healing does not stop there.

Becoming truly whole requires connecting to depths that open out into the mystery beyond representation. Every effort to describe it ends in paradox, at once the landscape and the light that illuminates it, the goal of the journey and the guide who accompanies us along the way.[265] Its numinous power exerts an attractive force that expands our narrow perspective and draws us toward greater wholeness.[266] This guidance may be experienced as a personality, a palpable sense of purpose, or a pattern that emerges over the course of a lifetime and only becomes evident in hindsight.

---

[261] Jung, CW 12, ¶44.
[262] Jung, 1916/1948. "General Aspects of Dream Psychology," CW 8, ¶432.
[263] Jung, CW 9ii, ¶¶11, 45.
[264] Jung, CW 9ii, ¶42.
[265] Jung, 1936. "Individual Dream Symbolism in Relation to Alchemy," CW 12, ¶247.
[266] Jung, CW 12, ¶¶328–330.

Such vastness cannot be swallowed whole, however. Jung believed that the small self plays a crucial role in filtering the transpersonal power of the Self and integrating what can actually be assimilated into a given human life.[267] I mentioned before that his insistence on the ambivalent nature of the Self led to conflicts with Christian theologians who objected to his claim that the larger unity contains both good and evil, at least from a human vantage point.[268] His concept of the God-image was less controversial, a sacred symbol capable of drawing together disparate elements within the Self in a unifying image of totality.[269] With no illusions of resolving the questions they raise, I will explore both these concepts and their implications for Christian thought further in subsequent chapters.

Given the immensity and ambiguity of the Self, there is no easy way to approach the topic. If the difficulty in delineating shadow is the fact that I cannot see my own blind spots and the shape-shifting nature of the soul-image prevents me from ever pinning it down, the problem in describing the Self is one of scope. It is simply too big, like trying to see the Earth without a spaceship.

Jung's solution was to come at the subject from the perspective of the individual relationship with the Self, what happens in a human life rather than a God's eye overview of the terrain. For him, growth toward wholeness is all about relationship.[270] These relationships extend in all directions, connecting us with ourselves, our inner community, the people, and objects that surround us, and the mystery that transcends personality but approaches us in relational terms. Jung believed that humans are fundamentally relational beings. The child psychiatrist D. W. Winnicott famously claimed that there is no such thing as a baby, only a mother/child dyad, because the infant does not yet exist outside the mother's gaze.[271] Regardless of our age, it is only in relation to another that we can experience ourselves, whether a person out there or someone we carry inside us.

You see this illustrated in the individual spiritual journey I have followed through these pages. Mark's journey unfolded through a series of encounters with outer and inner figures. It began when God entered

---

[267] Jung, CW 9ii, ¶¶45, 46.
[268] Jung, CW 11, ¶232.
[269] Jung, CW 11, ¶238; Jung, 1952. "Answer to Job," ¶558; Jung, CW 9ii, ¶170.
[270] Jung, 1946. "The Psychology of the Transference," CW 16, ¶503; Jung, CW 9ii, ¶42.
[271] Donald Winnicott, The Child, The Family and the Outside World, 88.

Mark's life in an unexpected and intensely personal way. At the same time, conflicts with those around him spotlighted distorted relational patterns he carried from childhood. Tensions in his marriage forced him to see his partner as a separate person and reclaim aspects of himself he had projected onto her. Intimate relationships can be especially helpful in this regard because they bridge the inner and outer realms, a point stressed in the last chapter, at once the flesh-and-blood person out there and our image of them, which is itself shaped by previous relationships. Put another way, they provide access to disclaimed and unseen parts of ourselves that are reflected to us as though in a mirror.

The Double Marriage

We are surrounded by a great cloud of witnesses, as the writer of Hebrews reminds us, a vast interpersonal web connecting us with others and our many selves, the outer world, our inner depths, and the vastness at its core.[272] The motif of the double marriage discussed in the last chapter draws together the multiple dimensions of these relationships with the image of a wedding celebration. It is a particularly apt symbol. In John's Gospel, Jesus's public ministry begins with the wedding feast at Cana,[273] and it is hard to imagine a better image of our relational nature than two lovers enacting their union in the context of a gathering that brings together family, friends, and the larger community.

This image of the double marriage plays a central role in the deeper levels of Jung's psychological model, and I will explore various configurations in the pages that follow. It is based on a quaternity, four individuals or two individuals with dual levels of being who are connected by a complex set of bonds.[274] A typical example of a double marriage involving four individuals is the common folk-tale device in which the marriage of the prince and princess is mirrored by a simultaneous marriage between two of their servants or closest companions. The more psychological application of this archetypal motif described by Jung involves an intimate relationship between two individuals, which always happens on two levels. In terms of the folk-tale example, the prince and princess represent the part of the relationship that takes place on

---

[272] Hebrews 12:1.

[273] John 2:1-12.

[274] Jung, CW 16, ¶¶420–425; CW 9ii, ¶42.

a conscious level whereas the marriage between their servants or close companions represents the part of the relationship that occurs on an unconscious level.

Most of the time, this level of relationship remains unconscious while exerting tremendous influence on the conscious relationship. It is not until couples begin to separate their actual partners from aspects of themselves they have projected onto them that they become aware of the multiple levels of the relationship, the process described in Chapter 11. In Jungian terms, the unknown parts of the self that are projected on the partner include the anima or animus. Withdrawing the projection allows each to see their partner more accurately while gaining access to undeveloped aspects of themselves. As often happens, Mark found that the two processes built on each other as his deepening relationship with himself allowed him to see his partner more clearly while his growing relationship with her threw into the sharp relief the previously unseen aspects of himself he had expected her to carry.

There is another dimension of the human person that extends far beyond personal psychology. This dimension represents another level of the relationships portrayed by the quaternity image, the divine dimension. In theological language, as humans we are created in God's image and carry its imprint within us. In terms of the model of the double marriage, this is another unseen aspect of the larger personality that can be projected onto people and situations around us. Most religious traditions employ images of exile and separation, just as many spiritual journeys begin with the feeling of something missing. As the path unfolds, this elusive something is sometimes experienced as a place, a lost homeland, and sometimes as a personality, the lover of our soul. Christianity is deeply relational, and, as with many directees, Mark entered spiritual direction with a vague longing for deeper connection in his relationship with God. The journey toward what we yearn for takes us out of ourselves, or at least out of our everyday way of seeing ourselves, while guiding us toward our center, which is somehow more than us—the transpersonal Self that opens into the mystery of Being.

This chapter and those that follow will address this dimension of the double marriage and the union that draws us into intimate relationship with the depths in which we live and move and have our being. I will approach the subject from two perspectives. The first involves images of the relationship itself, like the interaction between Mark and his fellow climber in the ladder dream recounted in the previous chapter. The second reflects the goal of that guiding relationship, what Jung calls the *God-image*. That part was played by Martin Luther King in the ladder dream, but other God-images transcend human form or form itself. Both perspectives are implicit in Mark's image of floating in an ocean that spoke to him. On one hand, he experienced an enveloping sense of connection and, on the other, a personal relationship with the larger whole that surrounded him. The previous chapter focused primarily on the former, images of connectedness that assume many faces and forms in leading toward the center. Subsequent chapters will focus on the center itself and the dream images, not all of them human, through which the inexpressible enters human awareness to guide us toward itself.

Traditionally, this journey to the center has been described in religious terms. Most traditional accounts of the spiritual path also contain a human component that would today be called *psychological* because movement toward God requires us to address the internal obstacles that get in the way. These obstacles, specific to the individual and the culture, are the wounds and weaknesses that typically have distorted relationships at their root. The modern discipline of psychology systematized and reinterpreted problematic personality patterns that previously had been viewed as sins or character flaws and placed them within a developmental framework that traced their origins and tracked their unfolding across time.

Contemporary Westerners tend to think in terms of early influences on the growing child, including cross-generational trauma, but that perspective is absent from most religious literature prior to the twentieth century. Jung's contribution to the standard psychological model was a spiritual dimension largely missing from earlier psychological theories. He conceptualized human development in terms of the deepening relationship between the small self and the large Self, typically the domain of spirituality. Using very different language, he and Ignatius of Loyola both offer practical suggestions for movement toward this larger wholeness, at once the source and the endpoint.

If Jung's contribution to psychology was his emphasis on spirituality, what he added to the traditional spiritual model was a developmental dimension that resonates with a more psychological view of human growth. His writings detail the lifelong journey through which we construct an individual self by partially separating from our inner and outer environments and then reconnecting with the larger whole, a process he calls *individuation*.[275] At times, Jung described the evolving relationship with the Self in traditional spiritual imagery, a journey to the center that reveals itself in new religious symbols as outworn forms are discarded. But he also framed this deepening connection in developmental terms, in keeping with his psychological orientation, and placed it within the larger context of personality development over the course of a lifetime. His approach to personality development stresses the interplay between the conscious and unconscious viewpoints as ego emerges from the unconscious and consolidates a solid sense of the small self, which then comes into conscious relationship with the larger Self in its journey toward wholeness.[276]

The Self over the Lifespan

I mentioned at the outset that this chapter will approach the Self from various angles. This section looks at it from the perspective of lifespan development, highlighting some of the relevant challenges associated with each phase of life. Here a caveat is needed. The topic could easily be a book, in fact many books. A vast scholarly literature addresses human development from multiple perspectives: neurological, physiological, cognitive, psychological, social, moral, and spiritual. Even a cursory summary of their complicated interactions is beyond the scope of this chapter so I must content myself with an impressionistic overview of the topic while noting some of the major trends and principles that guide the process.

In keeping with Jung's model, my discussion will concentrate on the relationship between ego, or *conscious awareness*, and the unconscious from which it arises, which includes both personal and transpersonal dimensions. This dialogue between the conscious and unconscious perspectives is the context in which the voice of the Self emerges, although it also can be said to guide the entire process.[277] After summarizing personality development over the course of the lifespan from a Jungian perspective, I will concentrate on the later stages of the journey when the

---

[275] Jung, 1928. "On Psychic Energy," CW 8, ¶111.
[276] Jung, "The Structure of the Psyche," CW 11, ¶¶292, 293; Jung, 1916/1948. "General Aspects of Dream Psychology," CW 11, ¶¶414, 448.
[277] Jung, CW 11, ¶400.

relationship with the Self predominates. This is the part of the path Mark was trudging along, and I will use examples from his journey.

I have mentioned that a key component of Jung's model is his emphasis on the changing relationship between the small and big selves over the course of a lifetime and the developments appropriate to each life stage. In the pages that follow, I will cover this same ground from the perspective of basic human development, albeit from a Jungian orientation. Since Jung was mainly concerned with the second half of life, the discussion will draw on the thought of other Jungian theorists, especially the work of Michael Fordham.[278] To begin at the beginning in my brief exploration of development across the lifespan, a major goal in the first stage of life is the formation of a sense of self distinct from the vast sea of unconsciousness from which it develops. The infant's initial relationship with the world is thought to be one of fusion with no separation between self and others, sensations and the environment, internal states and the external world. Two main tasks in the first months of life are connecting with caregivers and differentiating self from not-self. Both operations have multiple components—relational, cognitive, and sensorimotor—and both are shaped by a growing subject/object differentiation that enables the infant to distinguish its body from the environment and gain a working knowledge of its capabilities and how it interacts with other bodies.

Figuring out where I stop and the world begins is largely a matter of trial-and-error and anyone who spends time around small children knows the raw questing physicality with which they bounce off their environment. The instinctual nature of this developmental stage may explain the nearly universal fascination with animals during this intensely physical phase; even urban kids who have never seen a farm can tell you with great authority that their hypothetical pigs say *oink*. In the interpersonal arena, a central, if somewhat paradoxical task, involves connecting with others while carving out a boundaried sense of self that allows children to distinguish themselves from inner promptings, other people, and the world around them.

Exterior demands grow ever more complicated over time. Soon the child is expected to understand that his baby brother did not really make

---

[278] Michael Scott Montague Fordham (1905–1995) was an English child psychiatrist and Jungian analyst who did much to integrate Jung's thought with child development research and the objects relations school of psychoanalytic theory. His major works include *Children as Individuals*.

him break his spaceship, and he must resist the urge to hit him, something many adults have trouble remembering. Magical thinking prevails and the child's perspective on the world is profoundly egocentric, a point brought home to me by a seven-year-old boy I saw for therapy. As usual, I opened our first session by asking what brought him to my office, and he tearfully confided that he made his parents get divorced. I asked how and he told me by spilling his juice. At first, I worried about his reality testing. As we spoke, however, things became clearer. Apparently, he had tipped over his glass for the second time that night, no doubt made clumsy by the tension at the dinner table, and his father yelled at him. His mother yelled back to stop yelling at the children and his father stormed out saying he was leaving. That was not an unusual event in the family, but this time his father really did not come back. The little boy was drowning in grief and the guilt of knowing it was all his fault.

Ideally, small children develop not only an identity capable of meeting the world but also a core sense of specialness that will need to be renegotiated in midlife, if not before. In fact, most of the initial lessons in life will be challenged in later developmental stages, including the rigid subject/object division that allows children to make sense of the world in the first place. As the child gradually differentiates from her caregiver, she gains a sense of independent agency that also may need to be reworked in old age when caregivers reappear.

Let's zoom out for a moment to the larger trajectory across the lifespan. Whereas early development stages enable a child to create a separate sense of self, the challenge in late adulthood is bringing this individual identity back into relationship with the larger whole. These two forces—differentiation and connection—drive every relationship, whether we are pleasantly surprised to discover similarities with somebody who had previously seemed totally alien or are shocked to encounter what feel like unbridgeable differences with someone we thought was our soulmate. Over time, the comforting childhood division of the world into good people and bad, friends and enemies, must be surrendered along with the hope of being perfectly understood.

Like most people, Mark found that a major challenge in midlife was separating from old childhood messages and the unconscious early patterns he played out in his current relationships. Reclaiming the parts of himself he had projected on to people around him led to a more integrated sense of self and allowed him to connect with others while respecting their individuality. In a similar way, distinguishing his actual experience of God from his tangled religious legacy opened the door for a relationship beyond his projections. Or perhaps it would be more accurate to say it illuminated the doorway, since he came to recognize that the relationship was initiated and sustained by God, the driving force behind a journey leading to Itself.

Returning to my whirlwind tour of the lifecycle, developmental psychologists often describe the process of self-definition during early life in terms of *ego consolidation*. The word *ego* carries negative connotations; here it simply means the *center of conscious awareness*, the everyday sense of self that enables you to balance your checkbook, navigate relationships, and maintain a relatively stable sense of identity across time. You might picture the ego as a diplomat who mediates between the inner world and external reality, or perhaps an internal cabby who steers you through the world by the route most likely to get you where you want to go. Anyone who has ever watched a baby at the instant she finally manages to get the cheerio all the way to her mouth knows the jubilation that comes from bending the environment to her needs, literally putting herself on top of the world.

This life stage is marked by three developmental acquisitions that organize experience: an ability for the child to see himself as a separate being, a workable mental map of the outside environment, and a sense of continuity across time that enables him to connect isolated moments of experience into a continuous sense of self. A common metaphor for ego consolidation during childhood is a chain of islands rising from the sea of unconsciousness to form an archipelago, which then grows into a peninsula, the same image I have used to describe Mark's spiritual development.

The developing self is still quite tenuous in the early stages of life. The body sometimes has a mind of its own, like the little girl who told me she had been sent to therapy because her hands sometimes hurt people. From a Jungian standpoint, a child still has one foot in the realm of the unconscious where everything is symbolic and has a life of its own, so chairs reach out to trip you and candy in the checkout line literally calls your name. I will always remember the tone of outraged betrayal on the part of a small boy when he related an incident that had happened earlier that morning. He had been instructed not to open the packages under the tree until Christmas came and was overjoyed when Christmas finally walked in the door, only to vanish when his mother called his name reproachfully. This magical perspective overlaps with everyday awareness so that children half believe they really are pirates, and a stuffed elephant is their best friend. There is a fascination with mythic stories that help give form to the inner world and claims of royalty surface in the most democratic families. William Wordsworth maintained that babies come into the world "trailing clouds of glory," and many people describe particularly vivid spiritual experiences during childhood.[279] Most of these reflect the child's cultural tradition, such as seeing God as father with all the overlays of the relationship with the personal father. Spiritual sensibilities can also surface in stirrings of something outside the collective religious framework, for instance, the solitary moments in nature Mark remembered the rest of his life.

As children gain a more solid sense of themselves in relation to the physical world, attention turns to the realm of social relationships. Focus fluctuates between differentiating a separate self and identifying with others. In fact, these are two sides of the same coin since belonging to one group means not being in another, a third grader not a first grader, a girl not a boy. Children observe each other closely and have a sophisticated grasp of power hierarchies. They can tell you off the top of their head who is the shyest boy in the class, the tallest, and who has the most freckles. There is a lover's fascination with learning everything there is to know about their new best friend. Belonging is everything, whether this means being part of a family, a friend group, or a school class.

Most children are moving between multiple environments by this time, and they are generally quite concerned to learn the rules of each. Typically, they want to do the socially acceptable thing and can tell you what it is, although conflicting allegiances and unconscious urges sometimes interfere. These "good citizen" adaptations are renegotiated in adolescence when the maturing child no longer has the luxury of coasting on family values. Often there is a dip in judgment, at least from an adult point of view. Working in the schools I saw kids who only a year earlier had spoken with real insight about the dangers of drugs and gang life dive into them with both feet.

---

[279] William Wordsworth, "Ode: Intimations of Immortality from Recollections of Early Childhood," published in *Poems, in Two Volumes* in 1807, https://www.poetryfoundation. org/poems/45536/ode-intimations-of-immortality-from-recollections-of-early-childhood.

In psychological language, the teenager experiences a resurgence of the unconscious marked by magical thinking and personal omnipotence— nothing can hurt me and deciding something makes it true, from utopian politics to musical genius. The line between pretending and real life gets blurry again, but this time they actually can kiss the prince and carry a real knife instead of a plastic light saber. In terms of my island metaphor, the tide is rising along the coastline. This inrush of unconscious material is partly driven by a new ability to conceptualize alternate realities. Teenagers experience the same intoxication in learning to navigate the hypothetical world that babies do in relation to the physical world. There is often a fascination with altered consciousness, with or without drugs, and fantasy of all sort flourishes—science fiction, horror movies, and video games. Many adolescents express strong spiritual interest, either within their own tradition or one guaranteed to alarm their parents.

If all goes well, this burst of creative imagination is gradually grounded in real life accomplishment as teenagers move into early adulthood. Now the main developmental arena is interpersonal and societal, finding one's place within committed relationships and the larger society. Just as infants must differentiate themselves from the surrounding environment, young adults often struggle to separate their beliefs and aspirations from those of their family and childhood community. Focus typically shifts to the outer world and fantasies of perfect love and unlimited success.

Young adulthood is often described as a heroic phase of life defined by effort and struggle. An endless parade of coming-of-age movies depict protagonists moving alone to a strange city, encountering obstacles, forming alliances, and experiencing setbacks and betrayal before accomplishing their goal, which may or may not be the one they arrived with. Rewards are often quite tangible, even bankable, and the core skills that someone uses to achieve them are reinforced whereas others fade into the background. There is a growing danger of becoming one-sided, like a body builder who only exercises one muscle group.

As young people enter the adult world, they assume an outward personality that matches their role in society. Jung called this social face the *persona*, a word that literally means *mask*.[280] Such roleplaying is essential for social relationships, a neurosurgeon shouldn't talk like a drug dealer or vice versa. Hopefully, the mask they choose bears some resemblance to

---

[280] Jung, 1940/1950. "Concerning Rebirth," CW 9i, ¶221.

the face underneath and is worn loosely, since ministers who sermonize to their spouses are not likely to stay married and administrators who issue executive orders to adult children soon find their texts unanswered.

In terms of my image of an emerging land mass, by middle adulthood the island has become a continent, often lined with seawalls to keep out unpredictable waves from the unconscious. Although this kind of rigid separation made sense when the adult ego was still shaky, it becomes increasingly problematic as midlife approaches. To extend the geographic metaphor, the personality starts resembling the Netherlands as more and more resources go into shoring up the ego and keeping the unconscious at bay. The image is apt because dreams during this period often contain images of flooding and crumbling dikes.

The later stages of life call for an arrangement more on the order of Venice, as ego and unconscious learn to interpenetrate. Of course, this adaptation is temporary as well since, not unlike Venice, the land of ego is gradually sinking back into the sea as adults move toward old age and death. At this juncture mortality becomes increasingly personal: I am literally going to die and sometime in the foreseeable future, a realization that throws accomplishment into a different light. I cannot take it with me, and who's going to give a damn about it when I am gone? Sooner or later, progressive losses trigger yet another round of disconnection from the previous way of being. In a typical coming-into-old-age movie, the protagonist finds him- or herself alone in the world after losing both partner and professional identity. Like young adult movies, these films depict the struggle to establish a new identity, but this time identity is often less tied to outer achievement and coupled relationships, as focus shifts to the inner world and the larger whole.

The Second Half of Life

Jung's primary interest was the second half of life when the heroic stance wears thin and something new is called for.[281] As with any psychological theory, his account of this phase needs to be taken with a grain of salt since different individuals experience the dynamics that he associated with it at different points in the lifespan. Mark's story offers

---

[281] Jung, "The Stages of Life," CW 8, ¶¶768–795; Jung, 1931. "The Aims of Psychotherapy," CW 16, ¶110.

a good example of a typical pattern that happens when individuals crest the ridge of life in late middle age and begin reassessing their values in light of mortality. At this point, I will lay aside my overview of lifespan development to concentrate on the problem of its impending end. The first rumblings of this crisis often come in midlife. Sometimes these are subtle, as the identity that was woven in the first flush of adult life begins to fray around the edges. Other times, a crisis such as the one Mark experienced threatens the very foundations of a person's life. These threats take many forms. A chronic illness hits, a marriage crumbles, a child dies, or a couple discovers they cannot conceive. Perhaps the promised recording contract never materializes, or a job ends and there is nothing else available in the field. Suddenly, the person encounters an obstacle they cannot power through and no one else can resolve it for them. Coping mechanisms that have worked so far will not solve this problem and may make things worse. Mark's story offers a good example of how ego strategies that are initially positive can turn tyrannical over time. The self-discipline that enabled him to quit drugs and establish himself as a productive member of society gradually morphed into a slavedriver who made life miserable for himself and those around him.

In Western culture, midlife crises often propel people into therapy. Every school of psychology frames the core problem differently, but all agree on the need for fundamental change, whether this is described as coming to terms with the shadow, softening rigid ego defenses, or altering distorted thinking patterns. However, like Mark, many people who initially find therapy quite helpful gradually discover that the difficulties at the heart of what they are experiencing cannot really be resolved in the framework of traditional psychology. His crisis was certainly psychological—it involved relationships with himself and others—but it also had a spiritual dimension. At the same time that internal conflicts and problems with others were challenging his basic approach to the world, he experienced a growing sense of something outside himself calling him to a new way of being. Impasses in the outer world required him to engage with an inner realm that also was not within his control. As the center of balance shifted toward the interior, he discovered things there had a life of their own, just as they did in the day world, and equal care was needed in negotiating his relationships with them.

To move forward, he had to get reacquainted with parts of himself he had denied or left behind. Coming to terms with his "inner Evangelical" allowed him to reconnect with his early religious experience and begin integrating it into his current spirituality. The relationship with "King Baby" was rockier, what Jungians call the *encounter with the shadow*, and forced Mark to claim his darker motives instead of projecting them onto others.[282] The sea change that began in a box-store parking lot spread to his relationships with coworkers and family. His sense of control was further challenged when a crisis in his marriage forced him to confront the power motives that were poisoning the intimacy he craved. Although he had understood this on an intellectual level ever since his first therapy decades before, the insight did not keep him from repeating the pattern.

This time around, however, his growing connection with God allowed him to surrender longings that could not be satisfied in any human relationship, including the desire for perfect mirroring that would make up for past disappointments and misattunements. From the perspective of depth psychology, this fundamental human yearning for wholeness had been transferred to his partner, along with baggage from early relationships. Accepting her as she was, a separate person with her own needs and flaws, introduced uncomfortable unpredictability. It also made a real relationship possible and allowed him to reclaim parts of himself he had projected onto her, including the squirming vulnerability he had wanted her to manage so he did not have to see it. Loosening his expectations enabled him to hold the timeless moments in the marriage more lightly, which were not his wife's job to re-create, since these were stirrings of an ancient longing that extended far beyond the relationship.

Beginning to separate his projections from the person in front of him not only saved Mark's marriage but also brought him face to face with hidden parts of himself he had expected her to embody, whether they fit or not. This growing connection with "his" mysterious depths found expression in dream images of unknown women who seemed somehow familiar. In Jungian terms, their appearance represented the second level of the double marriage, in which intimate connection with another person enables us to encounter aspects of ourselves that are otherwise hidden. Often this is a partnered relationship, but any close connection that reflects our unseen self back to us can open the door to depths beyond the world of the ego, whether with a friend, a relative, a therapist, or a mentor.

---

[282] Jung, CW 9ii, ¶14.

In the previous section, I used the metaphor of a rising landmass to illustrate how the personal self differentiates itself from unconscious immersion in the inner world and then comes back into conscious relationship with its origins. In traditional religious terms, this mysterious inner domain comprises the spiritual realm, a place as complicated and morally ambiguous as the outer world and just as difficult to negotiate. Every spiritual tradition offers detailed guidelines for relating to it. It can neither be controlled nor made to go away, nor can it be embraced blindly. We need to exercise judgment in responding to the powerful forces the spiritual realm contains.

The discussion thus far has described the developmental process whereby the conscious self defines its borders by separating from the unconscious, only to have its autonomy challenged with the discovery of other rooms and inhabitants in its house, a common dream image as midlife approaches. These interlopers include denied or discarded parts of the personality associated with the shadow as well as an aspect of the deeper personality that approaches as an intimate stranger who feels at once foreign and familiar. But that's not the end of story. I will now turn to yet another of the multiple relationships represented by the double marriage, which emerges in later life stages when the ego runs up against its limits in a yet more profound way as the Self makes its presence felt.

The Self in Relationship with Itself

Before moving to the relationship between the ego and Self, I need to make another pass at the question that opened the chapter: what do I mean by the Self? Unfortunately, it cannot be answered with any precision because the Self is what has been called a *horizon concept*, which points beyond itself and tries to put in words an experience that transcends human conceptualization. From what's been said so far, it may sound as though I am equating the Self and the unconscious. That's what many of Jung's early critics claimed. However, the relationship between them is more complicated than that.

The Self encompasses both conscious and unconscious aspects of the person as well as the personality that arises in the interaction between them.[283] Once the conscious self has consolidated, growth beyond it

---

[283] Jung, "Individual Dream Symbolism in Relations to Alchemy," CW 12, ¶247.

can only come from what is unknown, the part of experience that lies outside conscious awareness. This is the unconscious, by definition, and the dialectical relationship between the conscious and the unconscious— along with the vast scope of the Self and the limitations of the conscious perspective—helps explain the seeming non sequitur in which the Self is at once the unifying principle and the unity itself, the whole and its core, a paradox familiar to mystics.[284] Since the Self represents the sum total of possible human experiences, it includes conscious and unconscious contents in both their personal and transpersonal dimensions. It is also the heart of this totality, the dot within the circle, a felt sense of meaning that assumes a position of authority in psychological life.

This paradoxical breadth accounts for the contradictory nature of the Self in Jung's model, which contains both sides of any argument and all points in between, a fullness that swallows opposites. Jung's image for this underlying or overarching unity was the *pleroma*,[285] an archaic term that Gnostics applied to the spiritual universe and early Christians to the fullness of godhead present in Christ as logos, based on Paul's use of the word in his epistles.[286] Both uses of the word point to the aspect of the Self that Jung called the *archetype of meaning*, the structuring impulse that meets us as a guiding force or a personality, the God-image that gives form to divine reality beyond all form.[287]

Mystics through the ages have lamented how hard it is to talk about the things that matter most, the gap between the concept of unity and the actual experience of interconnectedness. Jung struggled with the same issue, and his account of the Self bounces between psychological and religious language while managing to offend both fields. He acknowledged this awkwardness but maintained that both vocabularies are needed to adequately describe the experience of the Self, since the separation between them is more a function of different intellectual disciplines than any real divisions in how the deepest level of reality is actually experienced.[288] In Christian terms, we carry divine treasure in earthen vessels and see

---

[284] Jung, "Introduction to the Religious and Psychological Problems of Alchemy," CW 12, ¶20.

[285] Jung, *Dream Analysis: Notes the Seminar Given in 1928–1930*, 131; Andrew Samuels, Bani Shorter, and Fred Plaut, *A Critical Dictionary of Jungian Analysis*, 109.

[286] Colossians 1:19, 2:9.

[287] Jung, "Archetypes of the Collective Unconscious," CW 9i, ¶66.

[288] Jung, 1950. "Foreword to Allenby," *The Symbolic Life*, CW 18, ¶1495.

God through human eyes, with all the astigmatism of personal history.[289] This disjunction creates obvious friction points so it is not surprising that contemporary spiritual teachers across the religious spectrum report that the majority of difficulties brought to them in consultation straddle spirituality and personal psychology.

The pull to integrate these two dimensions of experience becomes increasingly strong in the second half of life. In early adulthood, the center of gravity in the personality is usually concentrated in the conscious realm. This balance tends to shift with age, as the ego discovers its limits and recognizes its dependence on the depths in which it is rooted. Growing connection with this unconscious center often finds expression in dream images of intimate union like those in the previous chapter.

These highly charged symbols operate on multiple levels. On the personal level, they portray psychological integration, as the conscious part of the personality comes into relationship with the larger portion that lies beneath the surface. Beyond the level of the individual personality, images of intimate union resonate with mystical writings across spiritual traditions, from Sufi love poetry to the biblical Song of Songs. You can find similar imagery in the dreams of contemporary individuals and ancient sacred texts that portray the connection between the small self and the larger reality in terms of human relationships, whether with mothers, fathers, sisters, brothers, friends, or lovers.

The dreams in the previous chapter centered mainly on the latter, images of romantic intimacy ranging from flirtation to sexual union. The tone of those dreams is erotic, in the fullest sense of the word, yet their emotional complexity and spiritual overtones indicate they are not just about sex. Neither is sex, for that matter; instead, it is a deeply symbolic connection that resonates on many levels of the personality. Jung's expansive view of eros was a key driver in his split with the early psychoanalytic movement. For him, libido is a creative force that expresses itself in every aspect of life, including spirituality,[290] which is not merely a redirection of frustrated sexual energy but a drive in its own right.[291] Drawing in part on the long tradition of sexual imagery in Christian mysticism, Jung interpreted the ubiquitous images of physical union he encountered in

---

[289] II Corinthians 4:7.
[290] Jung, 1911–12/1952/1967. *Symbols of Transformation*, CW 5, ¶324.
[291] Jung, CW 5, ¶¶197, 332–334.

his patients' dreams as a very human symbol of the yearning for inner integration and connection with the larger wholeness. As such, they offer a visceral reminder that spiritual growth must be grounded in creaturely life, our biological and instinctual core.

Sexual union is an obvious image of intimate interpenetration. Thus it is hardly surprising that it has been applied to spiritual life. From Carmelite bridal mysticism to tantric tankas, mystics have often used images of romantic yearning and physical merger in ways that make the orthodox squirm. Jung's self-exploration and his work with patients convinced him that a deepening connection with the Self can be described as an intimate relationship in which the larger whole whispers through the unconscious in a highly personal way to draw us toward itself. A long tradition in Christianity depicts the believer's relationship with God as courtship leading to marriage. It is an apt metaphor. Like the detailed accounts of inner life found in the spiritual autobiographies of mystics, marriage spans the extremes of human experience—the lofty and the petty, eye-rolling irritation and oceanic love. There is a real person out there, sometimes totally familiar, and other times utterly strange to us, a separate reality beyond our control.

As the unknown woman in the Martin Luther King dream led Mark to the shaky ladder, intimate relationships can lead to scary places and nudge us along our solitary path. This is the individual journey that couples walk in the middle of intimacy as they come into relationship with the mystery of themselves. Its unfolding brings spirituality together with human psychology and physiology, as transcendent reality enters an embodied personality with all its kinks and ticklish places. Although sexual union offers a handy symbol of this merger, the spiritual path is in some ways even more intimate since it happens from within. It often seems as though the mystery beyond all representation is taking advantage of its inside view to rummage the memory for images meaningful to that individual, clothing itself in idiosyncratic symbols drawn from personal history like children trying on old clothes in the attic.

In Jungian terms, these images of union lend form to the conscious personality's experience of deepening relationship with the Self. Movement toward this center is typically described as a progression in which the ego enters ever more deeply into the unconscious, encountering first the shadow, then the soul-image, and finally the core of meaning associated with the Self. I have followed this sequence for simplicity's sake, but it is important to remember this is only a visual aide. Progress is never that linear.

Because consciousness is ultimately a unified whole, any discussion of its parts is purely theoretical. In the end, there is no such thing as an ego or a shadow, a point that I have stressed repeatedly in an effort to undercut the natural tendency toward reification. The conscious and unconscious are not really two different entities, let alone places; instead, they are a spectrum of shifting states of awareness.

The contradictory nature of Jung's concept of the Self illustrates the pitfalls in trying to categorize these states. From one perspective the Self represents the entirety of consciousness and from another the guiding core of meaning within it.[292] This conundrum is familiar to theologians, for whom God is both the source of all and a spiritual force encountered in the physical world, with or without a burning bush. Unfortunately, analogies are all that humans have to describe what is beyond words.

This book has followed a well-worn path in characterizing the ego's growing relationship with the Self in terms of a spiritual and psychological journey marked by common landmarks. Like dream images, spatial and temporal metaphors enable us to visualize an amorphous reality that cannot be reduced to concepts. I have also talked about the Self in temporal and spatial terms when I could describe it more precisely as a hypothetical extrapolation from a recurring set of experiences, a bloodless characterization that does violence to the vividness of those experiences.

Like the motif of the journey, the image of the double marriage offers a metaphor for this central mystery, a symbol that captures the relational nature of the experience of the Self. By way of quick review, earlier chapters focused mainly on the personal level of the quaternity, which links human relationships and the initial stages of internal integration. This is the domain of the individual personality, which includes not only the conscious awareness that navigates the world but also the unconscious aspects of the personality associated with the personal shadow, that unpleasant side of us that pops out at inopportune moments and always feels like somebody else's fault. The realm of individual psychology also includes unconscious attitudes absorbed from family and culture, along with some aspects of what I have called an *inner otherness*, the parts of

---

[292] Jung, CW 12, ¶20.

ourselves that can only be seen in reflection as they show up dreams and fantasy or are projected on those around us.

As with every phase of personal growth, coming into conscious relationship with these hidden parts of us involves a process of differentiation followed by integration, as the boundaries of the personality are enlarged and renegotiated. The first step in forming a wary relationship with the shadow is gaining sufficient separation from compulsive unconscious patterns to begin realizing when we are acting them out in the world. By the same token, recognizing when unexpressed parts of ourselves are being projected on to partners and those around us allows us to see them as separate people while simultaneously facilitating connection with our unseen depths.

Standard psychological approaches that enable people to gain insight into their interpersonal patterns are quite useful in improving outer relationships. However, they offer little help in relating to these autonomous inner forces. This limitation in no way diminishes the importance of psychological counseling, whether from a secular or religious standpoint. Relationships with others comprise a crucial component of daily practice in every religious tradition and the self-awareness and behavioral change that comes from understanding our interpersonal patterns is a vital part of spiritual growth. Mark profited immensely from his time in therapy, but the kind of fundamental change in orientation needed at this point in his life required coming to terms with internal realities inaccessible to psychological insight. Working within the conceptual framework of his time, Ignatius of Loyola developed a nuanced system for negotiating this inner realm based on discernment between good and evil spirits.[293]

The Western model of the world has changed significantly over the intervening centuries, and Ignatian spirituality has become increasingly psychological as it adapts to the current zeitgeist. Although directees still express concern about the impact of good and evil forces in their lives, our culture's view of the inner realm is more complicated and less binary than in Ignatius's time. Jung appreciated Ignatius's recognition of the autonomy of spiritual forces operating within the personality and articulated a parallel process of discernment regarding the archetypal

---

[293] Joseph Munitiz and Philip Endean, The Spiritual of Exercises of Saint Ignatius in *Saint Ignatius of Loyola: Personal Writings*, 348–353, ¶¶313–336.

forces experienced as internal presences.[294] Previous chapters explored the need for discernment in relation to the primal forces associated with the shadow, impulses that are neutral in themselves yet can manifest in destructive ways. Similar discernment is needed on the level of the Self, the larger wholeness that presents itself to us in a God-image. Human beings always see the divine through the filters of culture and personal history, with all the power politics of their primate heritage, and a glance at the headlines offers ample evidence of horrors done in the name of God.

Ego and Self in Relationship

Jung devoted much attention to the relationship between the individual ego and the Self, a topic that has been further developed by subsequent thinkers.[295] For purposes of discussion, you can picture the connection between the ego and the Self in terms of a series of Venn diagrams, those familiar overlapping circles that illustrate how different entities relate to each other. Four possibilities present themselves. In the first, the two circles are separate. In the second, the smaller one disappears into the larger. The third is harder to visualize, as the little circle tries to contain the bigger one. This relationship is reversed in the fourth option when the smaller circle is contained within the larger without entirely disappearing, although its edges may be blurry and sometimes fade from view. Although the Self remains constant in all these configurations, each arrangement has different implications for the ego.

I find it useful to categorize these in terms of Goldilocks' decision tree regarding the bears' porridge: too cold, too hot, and just right. "Too cold" corresponds to the first Venn diagram in which the circles do not overlap at all. Ego rules, or at least thinks so, and wants no part of inner depths and spiritual reality.[296] The universe is mechanical and the worldview literal with little room for symbolic expressions that point beyond the physical world. In Dickens's Christmas classic, *A Christmas Carol,* this gray existence describes Scrooge's life before his encounter with the spirits when a ghostly visitor is just a bit of undigested beef.[297]

---

[294] Jung, 1944. "The Holy Men of India," CW 11, ¶¶937–941.
[295] Edward Edinger has been especially influential, see, for instance, Edward R. Edinger, *Ego and Archetype.*
[296] Jung, CW 9ii, ¶44.
[297] Charles Dickens, *A Christmas Carol,* Stave 1, "Marley's Ghost."

At the opposite end of the spectrum, the ego completely identifies with unconscious depths and gets burned in process, to use my porridge metaphor. This can happen in both the second and third possibilities. In the second Venn diagram, the tiny circle of the small self disappears into the larger Self.[298] Here a poorly consolidated ego loses itself in the inner realm and can no longer navigate the outer world. Psychosis sometimes ensues, as thoughts become realities, and I begin to think the CIA is monitoring me through my dental fillings.

A more forceful ego may attempt to master the inner world and bend it to its will, a scenario I described as the little circle trying to contain the larger.[299] Sooner or later, the effort backfires and things get too hot for the ego overwhelmed by archetypal forces, the meltdown depicted in the story of the *Sorcerer's Apprentice*.[300] Although trying to embody the Self can be a little like trying to drink the ocean, some people pull it off for a while and even attract a following. History is littered with examples of messianic figures who saw themselves as the hand of destiny and convinced others to follow them off a cliff. All spiritual paths warn against becoming a guru, in the negative sense of the word, a temptation illustrated in the Gospel story of Jesus's ordeal in the desert. Whereas the saint surrenders the ego to be filled by God, the dark magician seeks to rule the spirits by an act of will and usually pays the price. Fame compounds the problem when public figures start identifying with the projections showered on them, a drama played out by doomed rock stars who attempt to channel Dionysus and the steady trickle of televangelists arrested in public bathrooms. On a lighter note, I will always remember a woman in my childhood church who informed her startled fellow committee members that she had been blessed with the Spirit of Truth, which basically meant everything she said was beyond question.

To summarize my little Venn PowerPoint, the relationship between ego and Self goes wrong at the extremes. On one end of the spectrum, the ego tries to cut off from the unconscious, which leaks through anyway, like water through an earthen dam. On the other, it winds up being swallowed, whether through weakness or hubris. Either way, the ego is locked into

---

[298] Jung, CW 9ii, ¶45.
[299] Jung, CW 9ii, ¶47.
[300] Johann Wolfgang Goethe, *The Sorcerer's Apprentice*.

a single position when personal growth requires moving back and forth between separation and connection, independence and merger.

The "just right" Goldilocks option balances extremes, a working relationship between ego and the unconscious as in my earlier image of Venice and the surrounding ocean. The smaller circle is contained within the larger while continuing to function, as the ego recognizes its subordinate position in relation to the Self. Aligning itself with the deepest core of being, the ego exercises discernment regarding the forces stirring within the larger personality.

The degree to which the small self remains distinct from the larger whole is hotly debated in mystical writings, which struggle to express the ineffable and often speak in paradoxes. Jung followed the primary strand of Christian thought in emphasizing distinction in union.[301] The saint may lose herself in God, but she knows there is still her humanity to deal with. The union of human and divine depicted in the double marriage is never fully realized on Earth. The Christian image for their final convergence in the afterlife is the beatific vision, in which death removes the mortal veil and the believer gazes directly on God's face. In the meantime, Paul exhorts us to keep our eyes fixed on the divine image dimly reflected in our awareness, as it slowly transforms us toward its likeness.[302] Meister Eckhart, the great Christian mystic and theologian whom Jung cites throughout his writings, called this spark of the eternal at our center *the ground of being*. Although encountered at the deepest level of the internal world where we are most permeable to God's movement, it is not actually part of the individual personality, rather the core from which it arises.

As usual, Jung describes our movement toward it in developmental terms. In his model, our life journey brings us face to face with the shadow, the "not-me" who really is, and the soul-image, that internal stranger who leads us beyond ourselves and ultimately toward the Self, the wholeness in which we live and have our being. Jung maintained that the encounter with this core reality could not be distinguished from the experience of God, although as a psychologist he could not comment on the existence or nature of the deity.[303] His mix of religious and psychological language did not sit well with either camp and still makes some readers uncomfortable.

---

[301] Jung, CW 9ii, 43–47.
[302] 2 Corinthians 3:18.
[303] Jung, 1943/1948. "The Spirit Mercurius," *Alchemical Studies*, CW 13, ¶289; Jung, 1942/1948. "A Psychological Approach to the Dogma of the Trinity," CW 11, ¶231.

I will explore the issue further in a later chapter. For now, a few quick caveats are in order. Since spiritual growth occurs within the personality, it can be described in psychological terms, although this lens only brings into focus a tiny corner of the larger mystery. Every effort to bridge disparate perspectives, in this case psychology and spirituality, runs the risk of reducing one to the other or doing violence to both by calling very different things by the same name. The intent here is not to equate psychological and spiritual growth but to track how the two interlocking processes unfold together in a human life.

Journey to the Self with Others

The obvious question when considering how these processes unfold in a human life is what this deeper connection with the Self looks like in practice. As with most questions in psychology—and spirituality for that matter—the answer is "it depends." The Self manifests within the personality in highly individual ways; it is like light shining through a crystal whose impurities give it a distinctive hue. The same internal light may prompt some people to express their spirituality in forms that challenge religious orthodoxy whereas others move deeper into received tradition as their personal relationship with God deepens. Still others may find their spiritual life vitalized by something outside formal religious practice, such as artistic expression or immersion in nature.

Jung referred to this journey to the Self as the *path of individuation*, in which people gradually become more themselves as they separate from inner compulsions and societal expectations.[304] Contemporary critics have pointed out this element of individualism tends to be exaggerated for Jung, who often failed to recognize just how embedded in his own cultural context he remained. None of us ever really gain a complete overview on ourselves or our culture, and Jung was no exception. However, when we begin to recognize unconscious patterns of relating to the world and our projections on those around us, we gain a kind of relative freedom that makes us somewhat less likely to get swept up in mass movements and inner compulsions, the individuation Jung described. In everyday speech, we often talk about people who seem comfortable in their own skin, able to accept themselves with all their flaws, and claim their specific vantage point on the world without having anything to prove. If all goes well,

---

[304] Jung, CW 11, ¶233.

this becomes part of the normal aging process as we stop sweating the small stuff and feel less bound by appearances, like the poet Jenny Joseph's humorous threat to respond to aging by wearing a purple dress with a mismatched hat, gobbling free samples in stores, and generally throwing propriety to the winds.[305]

Knowing ourselves, warts and all, makes us more accepting of others, forgiving as we have been forgiven. There is a charming story about Moses the Moor, an early Desert Father and former brigand, who arrived late to the disciplinary hearing for an errant monk.[306] Everyone else was already seated in the communal hall, and his tardy entrance was rendered still more dramatic by the fact he carried a wicker basket dribbling sand across the floor behind him. When asked what he was doing, Moses replied that he could not judge another's sins when his own kept leaking out like the dirt in his wake.

Perceiving others more accurately, as separate people and not simply extensions of ourselves, increases empathy and the capacity to nurture. This is a feedback loop since relationships with other people are usually what force us to look at ourselves in the first place. Paradoxically, becoming less identified with cultural norms and expectations often strengthens an individual's sense of responsibility to society. For some, this can mean assuming the mantle of uncompromising prophet whereas others function as bridging agents in times of change, as their orientation to a deeper center allows polarizing societal projections to fade and new solutions to emerge. This happens on an individual level when we gradually realize that our political party is not the savior after all and everyone who disagrees is not necessarily out to get us, a perspective that is especially hard to maintain in a polarized environment. That humbling realization, which usually comes with age and a certain amount of disillusionment, does not diminish the need for social engagement but makes the goal less a matter of winning than mutual problem solving whenever possible. The same patterns play out in the religious sphere, where power motives also have an insidious way of intertwining with selfless service to others.

The Self Is in the Details

---

[305] Jenny Joseph, "Warning," *Selected Poems*, 42.
[306] Ishak Yacoub and John Paul Albdelsayed, *The Strong Saint Abba Moses: Hermit, Abbot, Martyr*, 44.

I have been speaking in general terms about some of the ways that deepening connection with the core Self affects relationships with ourselves, those close to us, and the larger society. This kind of conceptual overview is helpful in providing a comprehensive picture of a process that's always partial and fragmentary in an individual life. Despite those limitations, it is only in the details of an individual life that the full nuanced richness of the transformation can be seen, the reason I have included examples from Mark's life.

By this time, you are familiar with his challenges and vulnerabilities, the sort of human failings that ground theoretical discussions in everyday life. When visualizing the spiritual journey, we tend to intimidate ourselves by fast forwarding to its endpoint: Paul's assertion that "it is no longer I who live, but it is Christ who lives in me"[307] or Meister Eckhart's account of "living without a why" when the ego is utterly transparent to God's will.[308] Although inspiring, such lofty exemplars can make us doubt our own banal experience as we stumble down the spiritual towpath. Mark's progress is typical in its absence of great revelations or epiphanies. It came in fits and starts, as isolated and momentary experiences of God's presence slowly seeped out into the corners of his life. Over time, this fleeting awareness went from otherworldly to ordinary, what he called the "duh" realization that spiritual life was not actually an alternate reality he somehow had to find. In Ignatian terms, this allowed him to begin finding God in all things.[309] Instead of trying to somehow transcend his flawed self, he could engage with himself and the people around him as they were. Not that he could change them if he tried, as the confrontation in the parking lot and his marital struggles made clear.

Mark's quandary around finding his religious charism offers a good example of this unremarkable blend of inner and outer, psychological blocks and spiritual illumination. He felt called to spiritual service, yet nothing seemed spiritual enough. Actually, not important enough, he slowly came to realize. Over time, the healing relationship with God that was growing unobserved enabled him to gradually surrender what he ironically dubbed "his secret mission" and what psychology might

---

[307] Galatians 2:20
[308] Meister Eckhart, *Meister Eckhart: Teacher and Preacher*, 120, ¶247; Bernard McGinn, *The Mystical Thought of Meister Eckhart*, 153–161.
[309] Munitiz and Endean, The Spiritual Exercises of Saint Ignatius in *Saint Ignatius of Loyola: Personal Writings*, 292, 348–353, ¶¶39, 229–230.

term a messiah complex based on parental projections and a core sense of inadequacy. As often happen, once these expectations loosened, he suddenly discovered opportunities for ministry right under his nose. He assumed a more active role in the twelve-step groups and faith community he had always held at arm's length while also making himself more available to receive support from others in a vulnerable way.

In fact, the kind of earthshaking spiritual contribution he dreamed of making generally happens by accident anyway, at least from a human perspective, when people's private spiritual struggles happen to mirror conflicts in the larger culture and their responses fill a need for society as a whole.[310] In Jungian terms, the Self moves within individuals to bring forward what's needed for wholeness, both for them and the larger collective. Martin Luther and Francis of Assisi were not trying to start spiritual revolutions; they were troubled souls seeking God in the circumstances of their lives who came perilously close to the fate of other potential reformers who disappeared in smoke. We can never know the ultimate value of our contribution and must leave the fruits of our labor to God because praise does not ensure profound insight and being reviled does not necessarily mean we are right.

The Self and the Helper

Over the course of this chapter, I have explored how the Self manifests as relationship, both internally and with others. Before wrapping up, there is one more relationship I need to examine. Although Jung's model of the double marriage can be applied to a range of interactions, its original context was the relationship between therapist and client. Specifically, the double marriage provides an image how the Self is projected onto the analyst and slowly reclaimed over the course of treatment, as clients strengthen their own connection with the deeper Self.[311] In that setting, the image provides a pictorial representation of the concept of transference shared by many schools of psychology, in which patterns arising in important early relationships and the emotions connected with them are transferred onto the therapist where they can be worked through in a conscious way. Manifestations of transference in the therapeutic

---

[310] Jung, CW 5, ¶¶98–101.
[311] Jung, "The Psychology of the Transference," CW 16, ¶¶441, 445–449.

relationship range from *passive dependence*, when clients resist claiming their own authority, to *open hostility* as they seek to deflect intimacy or rage against past disappointments.

On the other side of the coin, therapists are people too and bring to the encounter a range of reactions rooted in their own life experience and cultural background, all of which shape the therapeutic relationship and the experience of being two embodied humans in the room together.[312] Traditionally, this was called *countertransference*, as opposed to *transference*. These categories have blurred with time as depth psychology came to view the interaction as a single transferential field to which both members contribute.

Jung did not try to cultivate transference in his clients and described feeling relieved when no intense reactions emerged, although recognizing this is the exception, not the rule.[313] His writings contain some of the earliest discussions of various transferential patterns and the complications they raise for treatment. He stood apart from most of his psychological compatriots, however, in insisting that the ultimate aim of therapy is not working through human relationships but connecting with the core reality that goes beyond them. This is the Self, in his terminology, and to varying degrees the analyst becomes its representative within the relationship, a role shared with spiritual teachers as they seek to facilitate students' own connection with the Holy.

To the extent the Self is projected onto the analyst, it is often mixed with parental projections. In Jungian terminology, the God-image is experienced in terms of human relationships—punishing father, loving mother, competitive sibling, or indifferent spouse. This means that carrying the Self is not all sunshine and roses, any more than parents relish the developmental shift when teenagers begin debunking childhood idealizations so they can claim their own authority.

Projections of the Self onto the analyst can be particularly powerful. You can picture therapists' reactions to them in terms of my Goldilocks rubric. On the one hand, they can deny them, whether by ignoring them entirely or pointing out how illogical they are. A given therapist may have a blind spot for either positive or negative projections, depending on personality, since both can feel burdensome. When these projections are

---

[312] Jung, 1929. "Problems of Modern Psychotherapy," CW 16, ¶163.
[313] Jung, "The Psychology of the Transference," CW 16, ¶359.

denied or minimized, the client winds up feeling crazy and rejected. They know perfectly well it does not make sense to see the therapist as godlike and yet that's how they feel. If this minimizing response on the part of the therapist is "too cold," identifying with the projection soon becomes "too hot." Being seen as cosmically wonderful can be gratifying for the therapist but leaves clients stuck in a position of childish dependence. The relationship can overheat as clients becomes more regressed or erotic energy floods the room. The "just right" option involves being willing to carry the projection until it can be returned to the client, like the mother of a panicked three-year-old who needs to believe that she really can protect him from all harm.

It is often claimed that therapy emphasizes the relationship with the therapist, whereas spiritual direction focuses on the relationship with God. In part, this reflects a misunderstanding of the nature of transference, which is not an end in itself but a door into clients' relationships outside the office, whether with themselves, their inner figures, or the people in their lives. It is true that the ultimate focus of direction is the relationship with God, yet this cannot be separated from addressing those same relationships.

Despite vehement disclaimers in the literature, all the transference patterns I have discussed can show up in the spiritual direction relationship, although usually in less intense forms. Supervisors often assure new directors that meeting less frequently ensures that they will not have to worry about the kind of transference that arises in therapy. Unfortunately, the actual content of spiritual direction supervision sessions and peer consolation groups suggests otherwise. Since any new interaction is experienced in terms of past relationships, directors do not get off the hook that easily. To the extent the director is seen as nurturing or an authority figure, patterns formed in early relationships enter the room. Directees may praise them to the sky or be subtly undermining, demanding to be told what to do and then complaining the guidance is not sufficient or does not work. Infrequent contact can even contribute to intense projections when meeting with the director is seen as climbing the mountaintop to speak with the guru. In dealing with these situations many directors and supervisors quietly borrow from the psychological understanding of transference, often without realizing it.

The same parental projections that color a directees' view of God also shape their perceptions of God's representative, a role directors share with clergy whether they want to or not. This was not a major factor in my work with Mark. Flashes of it emerged in the session described in the previous chapter when my limitations as a director activated his own internal sense of divine judgment and failure. Part of the reason many directors resist the idea of transference in the relationship is the simple fact that no sane person wants to be identified with God. The spiritual direction model is quite correct in doing everything it can to guard against this possibility. The image of having three chairs in the room is a very helpful one, reminding director and directee that they are in the process together and God guides the outcome, but the reminder wouldn't be needed if there was not something to guard against. Like it not, the entire process of direction, including the unfolding relationship with God, is mediated through a human relationship and boundary lines are bound to blur.

So, what's a director to do? The first answer, as always, is prayer. But we pray best over what we can see and that requires being sensitive to the nuances of relationship stirring beneath the surface. Unlike therapy, the goal is not necessarily to explicitly name and explore these patterns, although that may be necessary if they are disrupting the relationship or blocking the person's movement toward God. More often, the director guides directees back to their own experience or gently deflects a projection without examining its roots in detail. However directors may feel led to respond, they first need to recognize the pattern, like the old saying that if you think a cobra is loose in the room the first thing to do is turn on the light. Fortunately, God is not a venomous snake, despite how it sometimes feels to directees, and directors can rest in the knowledge that the light that illumines the room will guide them both forward if they can get out of its way.

Chapter 14
Space Aliens and Dish Dryers

The last chapter provided an overview of the personality's growth in relation to the Self over the course of the lifespan. In keeping with the alternating format used throughout the book, this chapter will examine how a deepening relationship with this core reality manifested in an individual life. Like previous "Mark" chapters, it will present dream images that helped to illumine his spiritual path. This time, however, instead of looking at a specific leg of his journey I will track how one aspect of it surfaced in dreams over the course of our work together. Not just any aspect but a fundamental one—Mark's evolving relationship with God and his Christian heritage.

The discussion will move between three interrelated themes. The first two are his relationships with Christianity and the institutional church as he struggled to come to terms with his upbringing and forge an adult relationship with his religious tradition. The third involves the highly individual ways in which his unique relationship with God found expression in dream images that gave shape to his inner experience.

These expressions took two primary forms. One was an ongoing conversation in which dream figures voiced various religious perspectives within him, including his "inner Evangelical." The other involved what Jung called *God-images*, symbolic expressions through which the Holy presents itself in human awareness. I must stress that these are not snapshots of divinity itself; rather they are representations of ways that Mark experienced the Holy at a given time. Some employ traditional religious symbols. Others use earthier images, much like biblical passages that compare God to a rock or a mother hen. Unlike those universal metaphors, these symbols are specific to Mark's experience. Some are not images at all but sensations and emotions familiar to him from moments of deep connection in his prayer life, including what he called "the feeling of the real." These too are highly individual and complicated. Any relationship brings up mixed feelings and Mark's relationship with God was no exception, evoking not only the tangled emotions associated with his childhood faith but also ambivalent feelings about his deepening connection with God and the loss of ego control it entailed.

Because I am looking at a specific dimension of the dreams, I will focus on that with minimal attention to events going on in his outer life, which I have addressed in previous chapters. I will examine some dreams in detail; with other dreams I will just present enough images so that you get a sense of their flow across time. The chapter will move sequentially through Mark's journey during the time I knew him, noting dreams he found especially meaningful.

In the very initial stage of our work together, these included the two "Egg Dreams," *in which he was given something of great value but must pay the price*, and the "Guardians Dream" *in which he followed a path to the sea and encountered three women who demanded a sacrifice.* I explored these dreams in previous chapters as well as the meaning they held for Mark at that point in his journey, insights that deepened over time as new meanings emerged. As often happens, these early dreams were broad in scope and offered an overview of the journey ahead. Such initiatory dreams can feel especially magical and may evoke a kind of giddiness like the first flush of religious conversion.

The next dreams come from a slightly later stage of my relationship with Mark and represent what might be called the "sophomore slump of inner work" when directees buckle down and begin slogging through their "stuff," the everyday conflicts and frustrations that have been called the lumpiness of life. This demanding and sometimes tedious period often comes as a disappointment after the euphoria of the honeymoon phase. In hindsight, those lofty preliminary dreams can feel like a tease, a letdown Mark compared to walking the first few steps of the labyrinth when it looks as if you are headed straight for the center, only to have the path veer to the periphery. Doubts and second thoughts begin to bubble up, and the initial sense of grand adventure fades as the small self realizes what will be required of it.

One of Mark's dreams from this time painted a vivid picture of the ego's queasiness over being pulled into the depths. *In it, he was visiting an aquarium and casually leaned against the wall of a large tank only to have the glass give way, leaving him stuck inside.* I have heard many variations of this motif through the years; sometimes the dreamer is fishing and gets yanked underwater, whereas other dreams feature sea monsters such as the one who swallowed Jonah. A subsequent dream, which I discussed briefly in an earlier chapter, followed up on this image of being plunged into deep waters and offers an accurate picture of Mark's bleak internal experience during this period.

I'm meeting with someone who tells us of ecological disaster; the energy is all used up, and the world is falling into chaos. We are in a sort of hellish swamp world, immersed in water and trapped inside a series of underground rooms, pursued by bears that periodically devour members of my group. The woman in charge, a nurse who reminds me of the head nurse in the movie "Cuckoo's Nest,"[314] *is talking to a nurse in our group who pushes back verbally as they speak. The conversation ends when the woman in charge says, "I guess you don't want to look behind you." A sort of white ghost closes in on the second woman and devours her as the staff laughs. Night falls, pitch black, and I argue with someone who tells us to keep moving instead of waiting to be eaten. I say that moving blindly will only attract the attention of the bears. We come to a dry room with Hebrew writing that is scrawled like graffiti on the wall, a spell that will save the world if we can pronounce it correctly. I see sunlight outside and can hear traffic, pressing myself despairingly against the grate. People try to read the passage on the wall, which translates "Hear oh Israel, the Lord thy God is one," interspersing it with snippets of conversation like a beat poem. Someone says son of a bitch in a European accent. Nothing seems to be working. I know we won't get out before nightfall but am optimistic for tomorrow.*

The dream fits a classic pattern of underworld dreams that come during times when people feel trapped in darkness, with all the energy used up and the world falling into chaos. Placing himself back inside the dream, Mark felt the primal explosiveness of the bears in his chest, the same

---

[314] "Cuckoo's Nest" refers to the 1975 film *One Flew over the Cuckoo's Nest*, which was adapted from the novel of the same name by Ken Kesey. The screenplay was written by Lawrence Hauben and Bo Golden. Miloš Forman directed the film.

sensation he experienced during the bursts of berserker rage that snuck up from behind to threaten his established life. The ghosts reminded him of the moment in the video game Pac-Man when the field suddenly reverses, and pursuer becomes pursued as harmless dots transform into ravenous specters. He saw the ghosts in the dream as old dead patterns that wouldn't stay buried—like the one that seized him in the parking lot—forever waiting to rise from their graves and swallow him mind and body.

The only solution at such times, Mark had discovered, was to freeze and wait, resisting the urge for frantic action—like the old joke from the men's movement, "don't just do something, stand there." In the dream, his willingness to stop blundering forward blindly catalyzes a shift. The group comprising different parts of himself reaches an island of dryness and relative safety. This oasis of sanctuary is presided over by the *Shema*, the traditional prayer at the heart of Judaism. God is one, the source of all, and humans are invited to love and serve this unity with all their heart and soul and strength.[315] Only then can they prosper, a correct expression of their humanity that will renew the world, in the imagery of the dream.

But it is not a matter of simply saying the words. The biblical text stipulates that the prayer must be worn on their foreheads and written on their gates and doorposts.[316] In other words, awareness of this central unity must be integrated into life, interspersed with daily conversation in the imagery of the dream. That will take time and for now the way is blocked by an iron grill that reminded Mark of the barred cave exit that kept the murderer confined underground in *Tom Sawyer*.[317] The group will not be out before nightfall. A dark period lies ahead, yet he finds himself optimistic for the future.

This optimism was eventually rewarded, just as the dream promised. In the meantime, the predicted time of darkness found expression in grim dream images. Terrible storms were brewing, flooding the Earth. In one, *raindrops hatched as they landed, giving rise to swarms of carnivorous locusts.*

Christian imagery looped through his dreams, often in ambivalent or negative ways. In one, *a mixed group of religious people were discussing*

---

[315] Deuteronomy 6:4–5.
[316] Deuteronomy 6:5–9.
[317] Mark Twain, *The Adventures of Tom Sawyer.*

how to present their faith in ways that wouldn't be off-putting to others. A minister with pale waxy skin who moonlighted as a mortician talked about shading the truth about his second profession so it wouldn't get in the way of his Christian message while Mark recoiled, disgusted by the smell of formaldehyde. In another, *he arranged to have dinner with an Evangelical mentor from his childhood, one of the few church members he remembered fondly. He left abruptly, however, when the older man showed up with a choir director with a reputation for molesting teenage boys.*

Other dreams voiced his uncertain relationship with the Christian tradition through internal dialogue. In one, *he defended his Christian faith to a dubious meditation teacher.* In the next, *a Christian acquaintance demanded to know whether he had become a real Christian yet, and Mark replied that he had, meaning in his own way, while his friend eyed him challengingly.*

Many of the dreams from this period interwove difficult situations in his life with questions of faith and religious identity. In one, *he confronted his wife about difficulties in their relationship, only to have her remind him that he was late for an appointment with a fictitious female therapist. Grumpy at the implication that he might be the problem, Mark began driving to the woman's office in a distant city and was touched to find his wife had filled the tank. The trip stalled when he couldn't remember how to get onto the freeway, and he left the car in search of an on-ramp. He soon found himself in a group of young people touring Rome. As they climbed the Spanish Steps, Baptist ministers in black suits were preaching to the crowd. His preacher uncle was leading the group in prayer. Mark tried to sneak past while everyone's eyes were closed, but his uncle caught his arm and demanded he come along to hand out Gospel tracks in San Francisco. Mark resisted, saying he was in a class and needed to get back to his cohort. Some of the younger Evangelicals seemed to understand but the old man was adamant. Eventually, Mark broke off the conversation and walked away, worried he had lost his group.*

"I guess all roads really do lead to Rome," he quipped, "only my Rome happens to be Christianity. Which also just happens to be headquartered there, at least historically." In a typical piece of dream foreshadowing, the couple's looming relationship issues and his wife's role as an image of his inner self are already present in miniature. There is gas in the tank for the journey, thanks to her; however, he cannot go there yet and takes a detour into his past instead. There is no sneaking around his religious problem, as Jonah discovered before him, and it is no use protesting that he's just studying the issue academically. Mark associated San Francisco with worldly life and new age spirituality, although the saint for whom the city was named represented, for Mark, the true heart of Christianity. St. Francis was the little poor man of the people who preached to birds and sultans. So where did Mark stand in relation to these alternatives? This was the question that came up when he reflected on the dream. At the end of the dream, it remained unanswered, as he broke off the conversation with his Fundamentalist uncle and found himself alone and worried he would never find his flock.

The confrontation with his religious background intensified in another dream in which avoidance proved equally unsuccessful. *He found himself in a Christian convention or training center, standing by a swimming pool enclosed in glass. Leaving the safety of this enclosure, he picked up a dagger that was either a poignard or sharp triangle of mirror like the weaponized shard in the movie* Black Swan.[318] *The dagger belonged to a man who was supposed to be studying theology at the center and picking it up meant Mark had usurped his place. He threw it over the fence to his right, where the man wouldn't find it, and sprinted to the left to hide from him. A group was gathering for a marathon but let him pass, perhaps fearful. He needed to reach the trees to his right for cover yet feared the man would ambush him there at the stations of the cross. He pictured his assailant, a middle-aged Protestant minister in a white t-shirt who seemed very respectable, and the dream broke off on an unresolved note.*

Mark worked extensively with this dream. I will only hit a few of the high points. Several images stood out for him, and he illustrated them in his journal. One was the enclosed swimming pool, which he associated with baptism. "I had two of them actually," he recalled, "baptisms I mean, not counting getting sprinkled as a baby. One when I turned twelve and the second a couple years later, a typical summer camp experience when I found Jesus yet again after doing mushrooms and decided on a redo, the last hurrah of my childhood faith."

On a symbolic level, baptism marks a death/rebirth cycle of initiation in which the old self dies and a new one is born. Apparently, a new initiation is needed, and Mark can no longer stay in the safe enclosure

---

[318] *Black Swan*, 2010. Screenplay by Mark Heyman, Andres Heinz, and John McLaughlin. Directed by Darren Aronofsky.

of his old religious model. Because this leaves him vulnerable, he arms himself against attack. The word *poignard* seems to come out of nowhere, as often happens in dreams, and he had to look it up. A *poignard* is a slender parrying dagger carried by knights in the Middle Ages. He puzzled over this oddly specific detail but never arrived at a satisfactory explanation, apart from the idea of knights on a quest or else parrying, as you would in a debate. More generally, he associated it with Paul's admonition to arm yourself with the sword of the Spirit, "which is the word of God."[319] He had taken this advice to heart after forming an adult relationship with his Christian faith, a return to sources in which he devoted himself to study. He developed a better working knowledge of biblical scholarship than many ministers, the underpinnings of what he referred to as his "unsystematic theology."

This devotion to scripture study was not entirely surprising. Mark's original call had been to become a preacher, or at least that's what everyone in his childhood church assumed he would do with his life. Now it was time to come to terms with that discarded identity, according to the dream, the respectable middle-aged minister he should have been, at least from the perspective of his inner Evangelical. He had thrown it away in adolescence, like the knife he feels compelled to pick up and heave over the fence in the dream. This time around he cannot get rid of it that easily—it is a marathon, not a sprint, and there is no way to dodge the denied self who waits to ambush him, as he discovered in an active imagination that dreamed the dream forward.

Mark drew several versions of the dagger, which was used only in hand-to-hand combat. The shard of mirror was even more mysterious, so he watched *Black Swan* again, trying to get at the meaning of the image.[320] The film is filled with mirror images, shattered mirrors, and the shock of encountering a sinister reflection in the mirror. As in the dream, the film portrays a similar confrontation with a threatening double. A virtuous ballerina is haunted by a dark counterpart who usurps her place in the performance and attacks her with a piece of broken mirror. Or at least she thinks she does, an illusion shattered when she encounters her unharmed double and discovers she has stabbed herself. In Jungian terms, this is the

---

[319] Ephesians 6:17.
[320] *Black Swan,* 2010.

encounter with the shadow, the denied self who is part of us and demands a hearing.

In the dream, the anticipated showdown will take place in the Stations of the Cross, which was not part of Mark's own religious heritage, lending the symbol freshness. He first encountered the Stations of the Cross when his agency held an offsite planning day at a Catholic retreat house. The Stations were strung along a gravel trail in the woods. He had only intended to stretch his legs before returning to the meeting room after lunch but found himself unexpectedly moved as he walked along the trail. The experience stayed with him; the steep walkway with its chipped plaster statues became an image of the spiritual path for him, as it has for countless Christians through the ages, as every vestige of identity is progressively stripped away until all that is left is the lonely figure naked and exposed. This crucifixion motif recurred in another dream that followed soon after.

> *I'm discussing scripture with a group of others. I'm surprised to discover that Matthew 1:12 says I need to be crucified with Christ. I argue against this interpretation but see it is correct. Looking at myself in the mirror, I notice that I am old and heavy, bent almost double. I straighten painfully. This requires great effort and makes me dizzy. The dream came after lying in bed one night overwhelmed by what a failure I am, that I will never win renown etc.*

This highly compressed narrative was one of several dreams with explicitly theological content that came as Mark struggled to integrate his childhood faith into his current relationship with God. His initial take on the dream centered around the opening image of discussing scripture in a group, which he associated with his effort to establish an individual connection with Christianity in the context of the larger tradition. The meaning of the Crucifixion was a point of tension for him. The cross was literally the focal point in his childhood church, filling the bare wall behind the pulpit, and Jesus's saving sacrifice formed the core of every sermon, the whole point of Christian belief. As a teenager, he struggled with the concept of atoning death, Christ dying in his place so he could avoid hell. Back then, it rang true for him on a cellular level, whereas cognitively the doctrine made no sense whatsoever.

The unresolved argument resumed where it had left off when Mark reconnected with Christianity as an adult, and he immersed himself in *soteriology*, the branch of theology that deals with salvation. He soon grew conversant with the major interpretations of the Crucifixion, several of which criticized the idea of sacrificial death on various grounds, including the claim that it justified passive acceptance of oppression. From this perspective, his childhood attitude seemed masochistic, a matter of kowtowing to superior force. In the end, he felt most drawn to an interiorized interpretation of the Crucifixion in which being crucified with Christ was an image for dying to the egocentric dictates of the small self.

Mark assumed this was the point of the dream, and the narrative seemed to support this interpretation. I had the feeling something more might be going on and encouraged him to look at the actual verse. It falls midway through the genealogy of Jesus at the beginning of Matthew's Gospel and references a tragic mini saga spanning three generations. Jechoniah assumed the throne of Israel as a young man, the last king before the Babylonian Exile. He was cursed by Jeremiah, apparently for the sin of being his father's son, and the prophet proclaimed that his progeny would never rule. Taken to Babylonia as a captive, Jechoniah had a son, Salathiel, who likewise died in captivity. This ended the direct royal bloodline. The lineage then passed through a cousin, Zeubabbel, a shoot from the severed stump of David's bloodline, in the imagery of the Hebrew prophets, the ruler who led the people back to Israel and began construction of the Second Temple.

In Mark's childhood church, the Hebrew Scriptures were interpreted in light of the Christian message. This allegorical way of reading scripture still shaped his thinking. In this brief history of exile and return, he saw a parable of his own tangled relationship with Christianity, which felt right intuitively, but when he tried to work out the details the dots wouldn't quite connect. He was left with a string of images that interrelated in ways he could not flowchart. He needed to be crucified with Christ, that much was clear. The idea resonated with the interiorized view of the Crucifixion he espoused in waking life; his dream self, however, objected to this psychologized interpretation of Christ's sacrifice. The dream pushed back against the objection, citing scripture.

Here Mark's reflections came to an end, leaving him frustrated. Instead of trying to solve the puzzle logically, I encouraged him to reenter the dream and see where the images led him. Almost immediately, the words "Christianity is your cross to bear" rose in his mind, and he saw himself bent beneath its weight. His reflection in the mirror showed that he was aging, no longer the angry teenager who had stormed out of church in an earlier dream. Addressing his image in the mirror, he encouraged himself to straighten up. This was a loaded phrase, what his father used to yell at him as a teenager when he was devoting himself to doing exactly the opposite. Looking back, Mark saw that much of his life had been lived in reaction to his minister father and his Fundamentalist upbringing, a reverse identity like a photographic negative. In Jungian terms, he had lived out his Christian shadow. Now he was a grownup and arrested adolescence was no longer working.

The long exile was over, father and son both dead in Babylon, along with the power struggle between them. In his mind's eye, he saw himself straighten painfully to face the situation. The change in perspective when he stood upright felt dizzying as the whole childhood drama imploded before his eyes. It turned out he was not special after all, neither a prince of darkness nor a prince in disguise who was going to be famous someday, the deflating realization that preceded the dream.

This fantasy of unlimited greatness had taken many forms in Mark's imagination through the years, its latest incarnation being the grand spiritual mission God was supposed to arrange for him. On his terms, of course, an irony that was not lost on Mark. His magical secret identity had sustained him in childhood. Now he needed to let it go, a sacrifice that felt like death. Being crucified with Christ was not a safe spiritual abstraction after all, the defeat for the ego that Jung called taking up the cross of ourselves.[321] The next dream continued the dialogue.

An older man is teaching a group of young men, including me, about the nature of Abraham's covenant with God. He says Abraham was supposed to sacrifice a man to mark it and unfortunately killed the man's young son by accident when he intervened on behalf of his father. Only I know this isn't the real story, and he focuses his teaching on me. He asks what really happened, and I give a couple versions, including a burnt offering

---

[321] C. G. Jung, 1935/43. "Introduction to the Religious and Psychological Problems of Alchemy," *Psychology and Alchemy*, CW 12, ¶24.

or animal sacrifice, which he negates. I say that God gave him the dream about progeny numerous as the sand, realizing as I speak that I don't actually know what Abraham did. The man tells me to stop babbling, Abraham didn't just wake up from an intriguing dream saying, I think I'll tell my spiritual director. I wake up still wondering.

This dream also became a parable for Mark. Its story line mapped onto his family history with uncanny accuracy, the long intergenerational chain through which his father's childhood abuse was transmitted to him. Over the years I have spent working with families, I am often reminded of the biblical warning that the sins of the father will be visited on the sons unto the third generation, less a punishment than an empirical observation.[322] By linking this traumatic legacy to the Abraham story, the dream pinpoints how abuse colored Mark's view of God.

As a child, he had identified with Jesus, the son of an abusive father willing to sacrifice his son, the grim dynamic foreshadowed in the Isaac story. As often happens, personal history interwove with what initially seemed to be strictly theological questions regarding Jesus's death and the different meanings attached to it. In the dream, Mark offers up various models like a dutiful student until his internal teacher brings him up short. He has come to the end of explanation and wakes up wondering, itself a kind of awakening.

Like a Zen koan that pushes the disciple beyond reason, its logic forced him to sacrifice the rational explanations he so loved and the security they promised. It turned out the desire for "mastery over mystery," which he associated with fundamentalism, was not confined to his childhood church. He carried it within himself and accepting the limits of his understanding was a painful sacrifice. Apparently, he could not wrap his mind around God after all, his interpretive models only "signposts and not a topo map," as he put it in one of his usual vivid phrases.

Despite, or perhaps because of this lack of resolution and the consequent necessity of living in uncertainty, his preoccupation with theological explanations faded. As usual, the shift found expression in dreams. Its melancholy tone was captured in a dream *in which a man identified as "God's Slob" sat hunched in a library gazing longingly out the*

---

[322] Deuteronomy 5:9.

window at a celebration going on in the courtyard below. In another, *Mark found himself in a cluster of students urgently debating the afterlife and gradually drifted away from the group in boredom.*

As theological debate faded from his dreams, new images of divinity began appearing. In one, *a female pope, a diminutive woman with dark hair, walked down the aisle of a large Protestant church shaking hands with congregants. The men in the row ahead of him refused her proffered hand but he pressed forward as she joked with a small boy about kissing her ring. When Mark reached out for her hand, she pulled it back playfully and smiled at him invitingly.*

Another dream found him *meditating on a point of silver light with rays of white light emanating from it. Suddenly it occurred to him this wasn't the meditation exercise he was supposed to be doing. It was followed by the realization that he wasn't was on his meditation bench but reclining as though asleep. As he straightened, a gold circle came into view. It began to glow as he focused on it, emanating a sense of holy presence.* He woke with the thought that straightening up seemed to be working. Ever the scholar, his mind went immediately to patristic descriptions of God as a circle whose center is everywhere and circumference nowhere.[323]

In a subsequent dream he was staying at the retreat center where he had walked the stations of the cross. *He couldn't find his room and wandered farther and farther afield in search of it. As he passed a recreation area, a group of young men pushed past, intent on beating him to the only open tennis court. Resisting the urge to compete with them, despite the fact he didn't even have a racket* [itself an evocative phrase], *Mark came to a giant underground lake. Passing a cluster of pines, he saw it wasn't yet dawn. The moon was high, giving off magical light. The trees were covered in snow and the branches looked like starched lace. He sensed that he was seeing things as they actually were, the "feeling of the real" familiar from prayer. The scene was exquisite, and he felt moved to call out "take me God," then worried someone would overhear and misunderstand, interpreting the comments in a sexual way when he meant death. That thought brought him up short and he reflected that his death wish also seemed overly dramatic and out of keeping with the peace and wonder of the scene.*

---

[323] From the *Liber XXIV Philosophorum* or *Book of the Twenty-Four Philosophers*, an anonymous book dating from the eleventh century CE.

We spent some time going over this dream, which was marked by an increase in self-awareness on the part of the dream ego that mirrored Mark's day-world growth. Consistent with his shift away from intellectual speculation, it emphasized felt experience, the bodily sensation of holy presence. Feelings often offer the best way into a dream, and this particular chain of emotional responses was familiar from waking life. Entering back into the dream, he connected immediately with the urge to beat out his competitors, whether or not he cared about the prize, and the rueful feeling of letting it go, something he was learning to do in daily life.

The experience of God's presence in nature had always been especially palpable for him, just as it was on the shores of this underground lake, a string of vivid moments stretching back to childhood. As he rested in this magical image, Mark felt a jolt of fear, not the emotion he was expecting but a familiar one from waking life. His fearful reaction to the numinous scene in the dream echoed the way he yanked himself out of the intimate moments with God he so craved by switching into what he called his "voiceover," a running commentary on what was happening like the opening scene of a movie when a character walks down the street narrating his experience aloud.

There was something contrived about his response to divine presence in the dream that also felt familiar, an exaggerated show of surrender bordering on melodrama, as though God had to be carefully stage managed. Apparently, the issues of power and placation that preoccupied him on a theological level were not strictly theoretical, let alone confined to Evangelicalism. The God of his dreams demanded death or at least knuckling under. "Which is how I got through childhood," he realized on reflection. Here the demand for subservience certainly was not coming from God, who silently filled the world with beauty. Their wordless connection brought up a jolt of panic, and he squirmed out of the embrace, leaving a self-conscious actor in his place.

As the active imagination continued, this sense of intimacy with God triggered a chain of ruminative worries familiar from daily life. Could it be trusted, will someone misunderstand? The lines leading back to childhood were all too clear, feigning closeness while he detached internally, a relational template he had transferred to God. But the response was becoming less automatic, both in human relationships and with God, leading to moments such as the one in the dream when he pulled up short and viewed his distancing behavior with a kind of puzzlement.

Early in our work together, Mark quoted a Buddhist maxim about reaching a point on the path where awareness of our true nature is a red hot ball we cannot swallow and cannot cough up.[324] He had reached a similar juncture in his relationship with God, in which he could not stay away and could not stand to be close. "Right now, I feel like I'm egg bound," he told me, backtracking when he saw my confusion. "It's a condition that affects laying hens, like being constipated only with eggs, and can be quite serious. I guess you could say something's trying to be born but can't get out."

The impasse in his relationship with God extended to the church and the Christian tradition. He sampled various faith communities with Jennifer, feeling like a picky eater who cannot decide what he has a taste for. This conundrum was reflected in a series of dreams.

In one, *Mark tried to squeeze into a pew, but the seat was only three or four inches wide, and he had to search for somewhere else to sit as people around him laughed.* In another, *he found himself in the administrative offices of the Evangelical college associated with his childhood denomination, the school he'd planned to attend as a kid. The offices were deserted, and he passed into an empty inner courtyard with a stained-glass window at the far end that made him think of a church. The building seemed familiar, somewhere he'd been before, perhaps even lived, and he entered an open door before discovering he was in a private residence. Sensing people to his right, he hurried toward the front door to escape. His path took him through a living room that reminded him of the home of a friend from church when he was growing up, a stable Evangelical family he'd envied as a child yet found stultifying as a teenager. When he reached the front door, it turned out to be fake and the door behind him closed, leaving him stuck in a windowless vestibule. He realized he was trapped, literally facing a brick wall, and woke up terrified.* The dream captured his sense of being nowhere and did not require much interpretation. There was no going backward. He did not belong in an Evangelical college, and besides, theological studies did not grab him anymore. Although he had left the old model behind, he did not have a new one and no way to connect his private spirituality with the larger tradition.

His fear of being imprisoned in constricting religious structures, which he associated with finding himself trapped in the windowless

---

[324] Koum Yamada, *Gateless Gate,* 17.

vestibule of his boyhood friend's house, surfaced in other dreams. Often, it ran together with fears about losing his coolness, the rebel persona he had adopted in adolescence. Mark had a visceral repulsion to the religious world of his childhood yet found himself returning to the faith of his fathers. Could he keep his edge, something he valued more than he liked to admit?

One dream *found him in a group discussion about the difficulty of seeing God in everyone. Somebody brought up the example of a dangerous person, like a young gangster, and he replied that the real problem for him would be seeing God in a middle-aged woman who wasn't particularly interesting or articulate, picturing the church pianist when he was growing up.* In another dream, *he entered a church where a secular event was being held prior to the service. A wild friend from his youth walked in ahead of him and waved away the usher's proffered bulletin contemptuously, as he was obviously there for the other event. When nobody offered Mark a bulletin, he took one from a container by the door, averting his head to slink past his friend who gave him a sardonic look, shaking his head with a smirk.*

Mark's internal selves were arguing it out. A key dream a few months later placed his struggle with the Christian tradition in the context of his extended family. *As it opened, he found himself back at his grandparents' farm where a large group of relatives were gathered for a midday dinner. He realized with a shock that all of them were dead except an elderly female relative, and he wondered what she was doing there without questioning his own presence. She scolded him for passing her by on the road to the house. He justified his hurrying by, saying that he needed to get somewhere, perhaps to turn in a rental car. Taking his place at the table, he ate what seemed to be an innocent piece of toast and realized it was drenched in butter, something he had given up along with other animal products after his heart attack. He remarked that it looked like his grandmother's fry bread and wondered aloud whether it had pork in it, another food on his list of prime offenders. Instead, the morphing entre turned out to be a rolled tortilla containing a whole fish. This didn't look particularly appealing but he ate it anyway, not wanting to be rude. To his surprise, he found it delicious. He asked why they were all there together in the house, which had been sold long ago, and his grandfather smiled mysteriously, saying nothing. Mark realized that he couldn't speak, perhaps due to death, yet he felt his warmth, a glow of acceptance that stayed with him when he woke.*

The dream heralded a change in his relationship with Christianity that would unfold gradually over the next several months. As he reflected on it, the images took on a life of their own. The setting transported him back to the world of childhood. His grandparents' farm had been the heart of family life when he was young, a sort of lost ancestral home. It was also the place where he had felt most comfortable as a child. This was mainly due to his grandfather, who emanated an uncomplicated acceptance missing from other family relationships. His grandmother was another story, a mean church lady who represented for Mark the negative pole of his early religious experience, a role taken over after her death by the same female relative who upbraided him for passing her by on his way to the house. It seemed he had returned home for a visit but could not stay long. It was not yet time to join the ancestors, who were feasting in the afterlife along with the aging female relative who died soon after the dream. Apparently, he needed to turn in his rental car first, a temporary means of getting around the world that he took as an image of earthly life. This was not the only obstacle. He did not completely fit anymore, as the tension around food made clear. Butter was poison to him, according to his doctor, and his grandmother's innocent-looking bread was a good image of the malice under her saccharine demeanor, the hidden aggression that formed the shadow side of his early religious experience.

At this point a shift occurred, the hinge on which the dream turned. His remark about his grandmother's fry bread requires some unpacking. It refers to another grandmother, this one highly positive, the matriarch of a large Navajo family he had advocated for in the course of his work. She had taken a liking to him and began including him in family gatherings where he developed a fondness for her lard-soaked fry bread in those innocent days before cholesterol became an issue. The cook had changed for the better, although that did not resolve his food issues, as his concern about pork made clear. Pork was on his forbidden list. Mark's associations also went to similar prohibitions in Islam and the Jewish idea of keeping kosher.

Sitting with the image, he recalled a Buddhist ceremonial feast, or *puja*, he had attended in his twenties, where even strict vegetarians were required to eat a token sliver of meat. The idea of ritual taboo violation is shared by many spiritual traditions and lies at the heart of tantra, where it mirrors the larger task of transmuting carnal poisons into spiritual food. Something similar was happening in his relationship to Christianity, transforming toxicity into the Eucharist. In the dream, this change in perspective happened when he lay aside his negative preconceptions and actually looked at what he was eating. Fish is a central image in Christianity, the symbol for Christ and the school of believers, the food Jesus served his disciples[325] and ate himself after the Resurrection to prove he was alive.[326] It is also the main course at the messianic feast at the end of time when Leviathan is served up to the elect.[327] Mark, however, was not relying as much on Guru Google these days and was less interested in obscure mythological references than what dream images meant for him personally. Something had opened inside him that enabled him to rejoin the tribe while still remaining himself. His grandfather's smile blessed the prodigal's return. The ancestral homeland was not lost after all, and he was invited to the feast. "So, it turns out you really can go home again," he told me, "Although not necessarily your literal place of origin."

Over the course of the next few months, a series of dreams amplified this change. In one, *he was walking down a country road carrying a medium-sized black dog in a backpack. The landscape looked oddly familiar. He seemed to be returning the dog to its home, although he didn't know where this was, as if the dog had been lost or in treatment. He encountered an empty church and released the dog, which ran across the lawn as though it knew where it was going. A huge golden dog bounded forward, and he feared the black dog would be attacked but the second dog seemed friendly. Then a brown mastiff appeared, and the two new dogs began fighting in earnest, doubling back up the road behind him while the black dog continued unmolested. The two dogs were ferocious and evenly matched, and he woke fearing one would kill the other.*

"It's a case of the empire strikes back in my spiritual life," he decided, "for every action an equal and opposite reaction." Fortunately, Mark's day-world reality was less apocalyptic than his dreams. His internal religious perspectives continued to battle it out but that did not stop him from settling on a reasonably compatible church with Jennifer, a development that showed up in another dream.

---

[325] John 21:9–13.
[326] Luke 24:41–43.
[327] Babylonian Talmud, Tractate Baba Bathra 75a.

I'm with a group. We are fixing the wood floor of a church to level it, a massive project in a huge, dilapidated building. Jennifer points out this is unnecessary since we've decided to dig out the median strip in front. I agree and yet we continue work on the floor. I see it is raised. The pastor of our old church comes in and opens a window. A man points out a pivot on the floor, off to one side. We try to figure out what it is and if it's necessary.

As often happens, this dream extended and developed many of the themes and images from the previous one. There, a nondescript black dog returns to an empty church by slipping past warring opposites, one golden and the other the color of earth. The action now moves inside where Mark is working with others to repair the abandoned building. The timing of this dream coincided with his efforts to repair his relationship with institutional Christianity and establish himself in a faith community. Seen in this light, the flow of the narrative seemed relatively straightforward, but some of the images assumed new meanings for him over time, including Jennifer's encouragement to focus his energy on the median strip in front.

The dream came after Mark joined a key committee and took an active role in church governance. The usual interpersonal conflicts arose. This time, instead of storming off in a huff, he finished his term before declining another. Although he remained an active church member, his main involvement shifted to the AA meeting in the basement, a sort of median strip where the church interfaced with the outside world. As in the dream, a window had been opened to let new air into his relationship with the church and institutions in general, the same metaphor used by the Catholic Church to describe the changes associated with Vatican II.[328]

Mark was becoming more flexible, learning to pivot, and come at things from his own perspective, in the imagery of the dream. This allowed him to retain his individuality and bring his unique talents to the relationship, in contrast to his usual pattern of over-joining followed by violent disentanglement. In Christian terms, he was learning to be open to the guidance of the Spirit instead of deciding ahead of time what should happen. This change in his relationship to religious institutions was one

---

[328] Pope John XXIII introduced the idea of Vatican II in a speech that called for a major council that would "throw open the windows of the church and let the fresh air of the spirit blow through." This quote is widely cited, although some have questioned its authenticity.

more piece in a larger process of relinquishing control. His prayers had been answered after all; he was in relationship with something larger than himself. God was real in his life, yet the longed-for breakthrough brought up mixed emotions. One dream captured this ambivalent experience.

I see a chain of rolling hills and buttes being leveled, as though by dynamite, leaving bare earth. I hear the phrase from Handel's "Messiah" about every valley being exalted and every hill brought low but am confused, as this seems like a negative process in the dream.[329]

The change in his religious orientation felt cosmic, as the dream imagery made clear, but it also had a relational component. Throughout our work together, Mark's experience of the divine had vacillated between two perspectives, both of which had a long history in Christian spirituality. He was most comfortable with the idea of God as ambiance, an enveloping presence like his image of floating in an ocean that talked to him. Although this appealed to him on an intellectual level, it left him emotionally unsatisfied. His personal relationship with God had been central in childhood, when Jesus was a constant companion and conversation partner, and he still found himself praying in the old way. Actually, he had never stopped. These automatic bursts of inner conversation had been a source of secret shame once he left Evangelicalism, like the childhood superstition that still kept him from stepping on cracks in the sidewalk. God's nature was not merely a theological issue. Over time he realized it had a psychological dimension as well. He longed for a personal connection with God and resisted it fearfully, the same push-pull that emerged in his human relationships. Another dream involving a fictitious daughter portrayed the scary side of this intimacy with an image of colonization.

I'm sleeping in a strange and communal place with Jennifer and our daughter. Aliens come into the atmosphere and drain all the power from an electrical line, which also disappears. I know the aliens have passed close before but didn't stop and now will

---

[329] Handel, "Every Valley Shall Be Exalted," *Messiah*, 1907. The lyrics, taken from Isaiah 40:4, are "Ev'ry valley shall be exalted, and ev'ry mountain and hill made low; the crooked straight and the rough places plain."

drain the planet of resources. Some kind of negotiation is going on, and I describe what's going to happen to my daughter, as if I have inside knowledge. I know the aliens will agree to restore the infrastructure but will keep the power and return for further exploitation at their convenience.

All spiritual traditions describe the small self's ambivalence over moving closer to the divine, a complicated dance of longing and avoidance in which spirit is willing but flesh resistant. Here Mark was no exception. As every spiritual guide knows, this dance plays out differently for everyone, depending on temperament, life circumstances, and formative experiences.

Union with God is a relationship, and our experience of human relationships does much to shape the interaction. Here the Jungian perspective is helpful in integrating personal psychology and the universal spiritual path, which looks a little different for everyone. For Mark, the prospect of loosening the ego's control, having the power drained off in the imagery of the dream, elicited an intense reaction. His relationship to authority was a complicated one, especially when it had a parental feel. At a fundamental level, he felt as though his very survival depended on keeping a core part of himself separate and hidden, even in close relationships. The pattern dated back to childhood, when he molded himself to others' expectations outwardly while distancing internally, escaping in plain sight. This dynamic was evident across his relationships. He merged on the outside while a part of him pulled back coldly, scanning for vulnerabilities.

But God was not buying it and the pattern did not work any better in his spiritual life than it did in his marriage, where having a relationship with a partner of his own creation was not enough anymore. Both relationships called for more, and the prospect of unpredictable closeness with a real person beyond his projections felt good and scary at the same time. A dream discussed in an earlier chapter captures both sides of the equation. *Distancing from a disturbed young woman, he went home with an age-appropriate woman who turned out to be his soulmate, alike but still different. She had the sniffles, and he worried about catching her cold, then decided she was worth it before she informed him it was only an allergy, a good image for his response to intimacy.*

Coming to terms with the new reality entering his life required changing his view of God, or what Jung termed the *God-image*. This shift was reflected in a series of dreams that came several years into our work together. *One began in a grubby church basement where a young male relative tasked him with carrying a payment to the man's father in the empty belfry. This top story could only be accessed by squeezing through a narrow tube, a sort of vertical birth canal so tight it required him to raise his arms in a gesture of surrender. Even then he couldn't fit through until he noticed there were two tubes, one for children and the other for grownups, and moved over to the adult entrance.*

This image of being born into an adult relationship with God through an act of surrender became a sort of leitmotif for Mark. Several dreams highlighted the need to surrender childish expectations in his relationship with God, just as loosening his unrealistic projections onto Jennifer gave that relationship room to breathe. Among other things, this meant not demanding from his marriage the kind of honeymoon glow he had experienced in the initial stages of the relationship, the same welling of deep feeling he encountered on his return to Christianity. Mark's experience of God was less emotional now, perhaps because the relationship had lost some of its newness. This change sometimes left him disappointed but also relieved that he no longer embarrassed himself by breaking into tears in the middle of communion.

Reflecting further on the dream, Mark became aware of a secret inner demand for the sort of personal relationship with God he had known in childhood. Their current interaction was not personal in the companionable way he had felt back then, although there was definitely someone or something there in the dark with him. The conflict over surrender, which came up whenever the relationship began to feel more personal, also emerged in relation to the twelve-step practice of "turning things over to God" when they are too hard to deal with in the moment. Mark's sponsor had suggested he construct a "God box" to stick his worries in, which felt to him like a craft project from Christian summer camp. He never actually built the box. However, he did experiment with doing the practice mentally and was surprised at the result.

"I always figured turning it over was just a form of compart-mentalization," he told me at our next session, "like telling my insomniac 2:00 AM self that 9 o'clock Mark will handle the court appearance. Which is true as far as it goes but it isn't the whole story and that's where things get murky." He paused a moment to reflect. "How can I put this? Placing yourself in a larger context gives you a toehold outside the whirlpool, like you always say, the same thing that happens in Centering Prayer. But there's something else going on too, a sense of assurance from someone or something like 'relax, I got your back.' That's not very articulate but it's the best I can do."

Something new and startling was entering his life, a bewildering development that found expression in an important dream that came near the end of our work together. Because the first part of it contains a great deal of personal information that I will omit in the interest of privacy, I have summarized this part before sharing Mark's own description of the dream. Unfortunately, this makes it harder to understand some of the conclusions Mark reached in working with the dream, like a math student who answers the problem without showing her work.

The story line centers around a fictional encounter between Mark and a girlfriend from his early twenties. *In the dream, they have broken up but remain friends, in contrast to the permanent breach that occurred. As with many dream figures, she has a dual identity, sometimes morphing into a female friend from the same era who was also a casual sexual partner. He and his ex-girlfriend are getting together to work out a problem in their relationship after she called to express concerns about the way he treated her during their last exchange. The meeting takes place in a Mexican restaurant where they are helping out in the kitchen. The construction of the building is subcode, with a dirt floor covered by gravel, and its location is unclear, either Latin America or a place run by immigrants to the United States. As they work, Mark tells his ex-girlfriend a story that had been told to him by the female friend she sometimes changes into, a humorous anecdote about a bonding moment when she was washing dishes with her father. In the story, her father was in charge of drying, and when she apologized for leaving a spot on a plate, he told her it's a poor dish dryer who can't get the dishes clean. At this point, the dream shifts location and theme.*

> *...We move to the front of the restaurant to watch a performance by a group we're with, perhaps from a church. This has to do with the nature of God. A giant figure reclines, filling the entire back section of the building. At first, it seems like a prop but then I realize it is living and may actually be God. It appears to be a young white man in his early twenties who looks a little dazed.*

He turns his face back toward the curtain covering the entrance to the kitchen and then turns back with another face. This one looks less human, like a statue of a Hindu deity. Then the scene shifts, and God's giant face is reaching into the room from above to create God, a smaller version of himself. He does this by licking it into existence, like the Nordic creation myth about the primordial cow.[330] I'm blown away by this. It seems brilliant on the part of the people putting on the play, completely true, although I wonder how others will see it, especially more traditional Christians."

In the dream, Mark worried how traditional Christians would react to the play. In waking life, he was the one scandalized by its imagery. To reassure him, I quoted Augustine's remark about being grateful God does not hold us accountable for our dreams, which has always made me curious about his.[331] Despite qualms, Mark moved back into the dream and began letting the images work in his imagination. The narrative revolved around three different pairs, he soon realized, or rather three figures with two faces: the composite woman, the dual deity, and God who licked a smaller double into existence. The first pair deftly captured his bifurcated view of women as a young man. His girlfriend had been idealized, placed on a pedestal so high he could not see the actual person, whereas he did not take the other woman seriously enough. A fog of maternal projections obscured both, the same mist that shadowed his marriage. "It's like their sole purpose in life was to meet my needs," he remembered with embarrassment, "perhaps even save me—I think I actually may have said that."

The couple has broken up, suggesting that projections are loosening but there is still a relationship problem to be worked through. They meet in a restaurant, a nurturing place run by immigrants which is not up to code, as though something from a foreign culture is coming into Mark's life but has not fully acclimated. The good news is that the couple can work together now, and their collaboration sparks the anecdote on which the dream turns, which Mark came to call "the parable of the forgiving dish drier."

---

[330] Auoumbia, the primeval cow who licks the imprisoning ice to free Buri, the ancestor of the gods, can be traced back to the Prose Edda written by Snorri Sturluson in the early thirteenth century.
[331] Augustine, *Confessions*, 314–316.

In psychological terms, his increased capacity for internal and external relatedness had catalyzed a new relationship with the father, including the internalized father who treated him and others with harsh judgmentalism. This new dispensation was marked by tolerance and affection, the sort of winking acceptance he received from his grandfather in the previous dream. Mark may not have cleaned the plates perfectly, but the dish dryer is on his side and does not hold his imperfections against him, a beloved child in whom he is well pleased. This attitude of acceptance heals divisions, both within himself and in his relationships, and the reconciled couple moves to the front of the restaurant where a ritual drama is taking place.

It concerns the nature of God, an abrupt change in theme that seems to come out of nowhere. Or does it? The spirit of reconciliation emerging in the first half of the dream had direct implications for Mark's view of the Heavenly Father, which itself had been heavily influenced by the relationship with his human father. Mark played out both sides of their conflict in his own relationships, the rebellious teenager and the exacting patriarch, an eternal rebel who was merciless in punishing mistakes.

The split between idealization and undervaluation illustrated by the dual female figure occurred throughout his relationships, including how he treated himself. In his spiritual life, it showed up in the divide between isolated moments of transcendence and everyday existence, the waste sad time stretching before and after he complained about in our first meeting.[332] Mark's marriage improved dramatically when he began focusing less on his own emotional experience and more on his partner, accepting their inevitable highs and lows as part of being human. Just as he had grown more tolerant with himself and others, Mark was becoming more accepting in his relationship with God, trusting their ongoing connection instead of forever evaluating whether he was getting his needs met.

These changes were happening simultaneously, a feedback loop across his relationships. High and low were coming together—valleys exalted, and mountains brought low, in the imagery of his premonitory dream. In Christian terms, this is the process of incarnation when the heavenly quickens the earthly. The second half of the dream chronicles its sloppy birth. Here Jung's concept of the God-image proved helpful in allowing

---

[332] T. S. Eliot, "Burnt Norton" from "The Four Quartets," 181.

us to explore together Mark's changing view of God without speculating about God's intrinsic nature, a distinction his Inner Evangelical tended to forget.

Given its lofty theme, one of the things Mark found startling about the second half of the dream was its setting. The restaurant was public and ordinary, even gritty, a long way from his private meditation room. At first in the dream, he does not really take the show seriously, assuming the giant reclining figure is only a prop. He then realizes with a shock that it is a living being, perhaps even God. What a bizarre epiphany this turns out to be, weirder even than being born in a barn. The deity is a dazed young man about Mark's age when he knew the two women, a time he had spent wandering around in a daze himself. The pitiful figure reminded him of his boyhood image of Jesus, the suffering son of an abusive father who knew firsthand what he was going through and always had time to listen. That view seemed tacky and maudlin to him now, an obvious projection, but made perfect sense back then.

Suddenly, the old painful emotions came welling up. The averted face reminded him of Jesus's abandonment on the cross and the disciples' own sense of abandonment, despite their master's assurance that his departure was necessary so they could come to maturity. The curtain across the doorway unleashed a flood of associations, from the veil of the temple torn at the Crucifixion[333] to the line in *The Wizard of Oz*[334] about paying no attention to the man behind the curtain.

When the figure turns back to the room it wears a new face, the other half of the polarity. This one is less human, reminding Mark of a strange figurine he had seen in the Asian section of a metropolitan museum, a syncretic depiction of the supreme deity Vishnu with the face of the human Buddha emerging from the back of his head. A creepier association to the image was a scene from a Harry Potter movie in which a stammering junior professor unwraps the scarf covering the back of his head to reveal the face of the arch-villain who has taken over his body.[335] Like the alien

---

[333] Matthew 27:51.
[334] *The Wizard of Oz*, 1939. Screenplay by Noel Langley, Florence Ryerson, and Edgar Allan Woolf, based upon L. Frank Baum, *The Wonderful Wizard of Oz*, 1900. Chicago, IL: George M. Hill Company. Directed by Victor Fleming.
[335] *Harry Potter and the Sorcerer's Stone*, 2001. Screenplay by Steve Kloves, based upon J. K. Rowling, *Harry Potter and the Philosopher's Stone*, 1997. London, UK: Bloomsbury. Directed by Chris Columbus.

dream or his earlier association to the fraudulent wizard's admonition not to look behind the curtain in *The Wizard of Oz*,[336] this grotesque association conveyed the negative side of his ambivalent feelings about God's entrance into his life.

In working with the dream, Mark came to view this complicated dream symbol as an incomplete incarnation in which the opposites remained far apart, the human and transcendent facing opposite directions. The final dream figure unites these halves in a decidedly earthy image, a cow licking its newborn calf. The dream references a Nordic creation myth in which the cosmic cow licks the primordial human from imprisoning ice.

Mark's associations were less elevated, freezing nights in the barn where birthing cows gently licked slime from their newborn calves. The image is not especially heterodox as God-images go and could easily have come from the Hebrew scriptures if the Israelites had been cattle herders instead of shepherds. What offended his inner Evangelical was not so much the figure itself, but the interpretation supplied by the dream, in which God licks human beings into existence in his own image, that of a calf bound for slaughter, the very image rejected at Mount Sinai when Moses ground up the apostate Israelites' golden calf in water and forced them to drink it.[337] It is one thing to talk about a spark of divine presence at our core, but the idea of God creating human beings as a smaller version of Himself scandalized the traditional Christian in him.

Dreams often use shocking images to force the issue, such as Peter's vision of unclean animals lowered from the heavens.[338] Reflecting further on the dream, Mark realized that what bothered him most was not even the interpretation supplied in the dream, the same one Paul used when he talked about being transformed into Christ as he gazed on the divine face, but the reality of what this meant in his life.[339] God was not going to beam him out of the world; instead God would nuzzle him tenderly in the muck, inviting him to rest in Christ who rests in God, like a series of nesting Russian dolls, an image from another dream that came a few nights later and echoed the farewell speech in John's Gospel.[340] Christ was his companion again, but the relationship brought an embarrassing intimacy

---

[336] *The Wizard of Oz*.
[337] Exodus 32:20.
[338] Acts 10:9–16.
[339] 2 Corinthians 3:18.
[340] John 17:21–23.

he had not expected. Another dream around the same time portrayed this growing intimacy in human terms.

Here the inner Christ was depicted as his best friend from childhood, in keeping with his boyhood picture of Jesus as an intimate companion. Best friends have a particularly tight bond in the latter half of grade school, treated almost like a married couple by their classmates, and he still remembered the relationship tenderly. In the dream, *Mark was all grown up and working on a broken car in his father's grimy garage, an image that resonated with his general sense that the wheels had come off his old way of getting around the world. Looking out through the open garage door, he saw a submarine suspended in air and realized that he was dreaming, quickly deciding to take advantage of the opportunity to understand reality from this perspective. Gazing at the moon obscured by clouds with self-conscious devotion, he prayerfully wondered where God was before deciding that perhaps this rarified state wasn't the doorway to absolute truth after all.*

The realization sparked a compressed dream journey that began with studying at a college. This was hardly surprising, given Mark's intellectual bent, *but the school turned out to be a community college where he wandered the common room looking for a bathroom, carrying blankets from his bed like a sleepwalking street person. He started up the stairs before discovering he couldn't get there from here, a common experience for him over the past few years. He headed back down to the ground floor and exited the building before realizing that he had forgotten to find a bathroom, apparently not as grounded in his body as he thought. As he walked away from the college, Mark felt an arm around his shoulder and turned to find a young Latino man walking beside him, a grownup version of his lost childhood friend. The man told him he would be his companion and Mark flashed on his childhood picture of Jesus, the longhaired portrait that hung in his Sunday School room.*

The scene changed and they were driving in the country with others in the back seat, so apparently the broken car was running again. Mark was having difficulty staying on the road and realized the car was slightly elevated, as though it was skimming the asphalt, more down-to-earth than the flying submarine but still a good image of his tendency to get ungrounded. His friend talked about the difficulties of driving as though his presence would help, a discussion that also seemed to be a commentary on navigating life. He used a word Mark couldn't understand to describe the natural tendency to stray from the path and Mark asked him to repeat it, still not understanding and telling him so, a disconnect he took as an indication of final unknowability. He woke with the image of his friend's dark eyes gazing into his and a deep sense of connection, the familiar feeling of the real that had been a touchstone of God's presence throughout his life.

That would be a good note to end on; however, I need to address a couple of points before closing. There is a tendency in Jungian circles to speak about the relationship with the Self in reverential tones suggestive of spiritual enlightenment. Mark was not enlightened by any means, just as intimacy with Christ hardly implies perfection. His dreams pointed the way forward, but a long path still lay ahead of him.

As you saw in the last chapter, everyone has a relationship with the Self, whether they are aware of it or not, just as everything ultimately rests in God from a Christian perspective. The sequence of topics I have covered over the course of the book may suggest a progression culminating in relationship with the Self. Like most people, Mark's actual experience was a mélange of shadow material, intimate otherness, and God-images, although different themes tended to predominate during different periods of our work together. What made his journey so interesting was not the presence of extraordinary events in his inner or outer life, let alone reaching his goal, but the way his dreams charted its major milestones with particularly arresting imagery.

This book tracks a portion of this path, but real life is not a novel that moves to an inevitable conclusion. I do not know where Mark's journey took him, in this life or the next. This dream marked the end of the stretch of road he and I walked together. Leaving his still unfolding story behind, the next chapter will offer a brief and speculative discussion of the relationship between Jung's spiritual vision and the Christian tradition, followed by a summary chapter and a brief epilogue.

Chapter 15

Jung and the Christian Tradition:
Implications for Spiritual Direction

How does the mind grasp the inconceivable? How does the imagination depict what is beyond representation? Mystics throughout the ages have struggled with this conundrum, the same one faced nightly by the inner prophet who guides our dreams. Jung devoted much attention to the question, and this chapter will examine his views against the backdrop of the Christian tradition.

God beyond Image

Every major spiritual system agrees that no metaphor can contain divine mystery because it is forever spilling beyond images. Christianity, Judaism, and Islam all wrestle with this dilemma, which takes a different form in Hindu and Buddhist thought. Each religion has framed the issue in its own way and generated its own set of interconnected symbols that point toward the unrepresentable reality. These religiously sanctioned symbols are shared across a given culture.

Jung believed that the psyche also mediates divine mystery personally for everyone, constantly generating new symbols to represent its presence in human awareness.[341] These God-images assume a multitude of forms in dreams and revery, shocking or comforting, depending on what's needed at the time to draw or prod individuals toward their source. Earlier chapters looked at God-images that express divinity in terms of human relationships, as the divine presence they point toward transforms our relationships with those around us. Examples from Mark's dreams include

---

[341] C. G. Jung, 1961. "Symbols and the Interpretation of Dreams," *The Symbolic Life*, CW 18, ¶¶480 591–595.

fictitious female partners and the young Latino man who reminded him of a childhood friend.

The God-images in this chapter portray the experience of the Holy in less human terms, like Mark's dreams about space aliens or mountains being leveled. As with any attempt to categorize God-images, the distinction between human and nonhuman images needs to be taken with a grain of salt. Humans see everything through human eyes, no matter how alien, and always form some type of relationship with it. After all, if you cannot relate something to your experience how do you even know it is there? So, what happens if that something is God beyond all images? This enigma harkens back to my opening question: how do human beings connect with what is beyond human conception or categories?

Although this quandary is traditionally framed as a theological issue, Jung started with the human side of the interaction and approached the problem from a psychological viewpoint to examine the subjective experience of transcendence and the ways it presents itself in awareness. This endeavor features prominently in his later works, which draw on various religious traditions to flesh out his ideas. Since this book comes at the issue from the vantage point of Christian spiritual direction, the question becomes how divine reality beyond representation enters human awareness from a Christian perspective.

By grace, theologians agree, and after that, things get messy. There is revelation, of course, not to mention Incarnation, and an underlying affinity between God and humans that makes communication possible in the first place. But there is a disconnect as well; therefore, symbols are crucial in translating divinity into limited human consciousness. Jesus taught in parables, practical stories people can still relate to, like losing money somewhere in the house[342] or nagging an indifferent bureaucrat until he takes our call just to get rid of us.[343] Every human image of God runs the risk of remaking God in our image and the Gospel writers show Jesus going out of his way to reiterate that the Kingdom of God is like this or that but not really, multiplying examples to come at mystery from all angles.

Turning to scripture, the range of God-images is unimaginably broad. The first that spring to mind are often derived from family or

---

[342] Luke 15:8, 9.
[343] Luke 18:1–5.

social relationships: God as Father[344] or Lord.[345] God is also compared to a shield,[346] the wind,[347] a high rock,[348] running water,[349] a jealous lover,[350] a mother hen,[351] turning wheels,[352] the boundless ocean,[353] and vast sky.[354] Of these examples, jealous lover and mother hen are overtly relational, whereas relationship is implied in the images of a shield or high rock where enemies cannot reach. Here God is protector and savior. But what about Ezekiel's turning wheels, or yet more amorphous images of water, wind, and sky?

Although human beings anthropomorphize everything, some things are easier to form a relationship with than others. And yet, across spiritual traditions, empty space and darkness are standard images for divine reality beyond all categories or definition. "Neither are your ways my ways, saith the Lord,"[355] and a dark cloud covered the mountaintop where God met Moses face to face.[356] Try as we will, we cannot imagine nothing. Empty space quickly takes on a location and a color or sensation, perhaps a sound, and we even have feelings about it. Ultimate reality may be beyond concepts, images, or analogies, but we need all three to guide us toward it.

Relational images predominate in the Christian tradition, although a strong undercurrent emphasizes the God beyond form or definition. Theologians talk about *cataphatic* and *apophatic* approaches to God, a distinction that occurs across the religious spectrum. The *cataphatic path*, which tends to be devotional in tone and active in approach, encounters God through sacred images people can relate to. The *apophatic path* is more contemplative, a stance of passive receptiveness to the God beyond all images, the ineffable reality unlike anything imaginable. This is some-times called the *via negativa* or *negative path* because it approaches

---

[344] 1 Corinthians 8:6.
[345] Psalm 100:3.
[346] Psalm 28:7.
[347] John 3:8.
[348] Psalm 27:5, Psalm 62:7.
[349] John 7:38, 4:14.
[350] Deuteronomy 32:21.
[351] Luke 13:34.
[352] Ezekiel 10:9,10.
[353] Psalm 36:6.
[354] Psalm 36:5.
[355] Isaiah 55:8.
[356] Exodus 24:15, 16.

God through a process of negation, not this and not that, as all human conceptions of God fall away one by one.

In practice, most Christian mystics describe a combination of both in their own spiritual lives as images of God derived from human experience lead them to the very margins of human awareness. There sacred images dissolve in formless wonder and brilliant theological concepts become so much straw, the image Thomas Aquinas used to describe the mystical insight that led him to hang up his quill.[357] Conversation ceases because there is nobody left to talk as prayer collapses in undifferentiated unity. This silence gives way in turn to renewed awareness of the other, a gradual coming-into-focus sometimes compared to the moment after lovemaking. The mystical literature tends to focus on such moments of merger, yet alternating experiences of union and separation are part of a continuous process, an ongoing revelation by approximation in which limited God-images guide us toward the real thing through a sort of holy game of Marco Polo. From this perspective, formless God-images are simply those that arise when we are being held too close to see who is embracing us, a lover's game played in the dark where there is no way of knowing what we are holding, or rather who is holding us. And the game goes on forever because God's nature is beyond comprehension. Fortunately, we have all the time in the world and out of it as well.

What do these lofty musings have to do with Jung and dreamwork? This brings me to the topic of the current chapter in which I take a closer look at Jung's concepts of God-images and the Self, filling out the picture with practical examples. A second and more speculative discussion will place his model in the context of traditional Christian thought and examine the fit between the two approaches. It is an issue I have glossed over in my account of Mark's unfolding path, which can be understood from a Christian standpoint as a deepening relationship with God and from a Jungian perspective as a deepening connection with the Self that he experienced in Christological terms.

Form and Formlessness, Image, and Imagination

The previous chapter used Mark's dream material to illustrate God-images that represent this connection in imagery taken from human

---

[357] Brian Davies, *The Thought of Thomas Aquinas*, 9.

relationships. The current chapter also draws on dream imagery to explore the interplay of form and formlessness that shepherds the seeker toward a glimpse of presence beyond representation. This distinction between form and formless can be applied to individual God-images, the difference between Mark's dreams about characters with elaborate backstories and dream images involving silver light or the feeling of the real. Jung also differentiated between God-images of every kind and the indefinable reality toward which they point, the unrepresentable wholeness he called the *Self*.[358] Some of the God-images in Mark's dreams are abstract and some earthy, others bizarre or explicitly theological as he worked out his relationship with God and the Christian tradition. Whatever form or lack of form they assume, the real question is how the images got there in the first place, the guiding process that operated beyond Mark's awareness and the mystery behind Jung's concept of the Self.

Jung's insistence that ultimate reality transcends all images is hardly unique, although he was one of the few psychologists to speak in these terms. His contribution to the larger dialogue between religion and psychology stems from the awkward fact that individuals' relationship with God cannot be separated from their psychological makeup and the patterns that play out in the rest of their relationships. Dreamwork has always been part of spiritual direction. Jung's addition to this age-old practice was a systematic application of the very modern realization that the God we encounter is always seen through the eyes of personal psychology and cultural heritage. In his view, healing the wounds that distort a person's view of God is part of an overall growth process whose psychological dimensions cannot be separated from spiritual healing.[359]

In the letter to Pastor Bernet discussed in an earlier chapter, Jung describes the process through which successive dream images lead to the hollow square at one's core, the spark of divinity that he calls the Self.[360] Sometimes this happens all by itself when an irresistible force bursts into a person's life with blinding force, like Paul's encounter on the road to Damascus.[361] For most people, however, epiphany is incremental and interactive, facilitated or impeded by how they respond to intimations

---

[358] Jung, 1951. *Aion*, CW 9ii, ¶¶59, 60.

[359] Jung, 1943. "Psychotherapy and a Philosophy of Life," *The Practice of Psychotherapy*, CW 16, ¶¶182–185.

[360] Jung, *C. G. Jung Letters, 1951–1961*, 258.

[361] Acts 9:1–8.

and images of the divine presence. Innumerable spiritual practices seek to deepen awareness of this invitation, the same goal described in Jung's writings.

The fact that his model parallels many of the roadmaps found in formal religious systems is hardly surprising since he saw depth psychology as a spiritual path for contemporary individuals, including those no longer contained within any religious tradition.[362] Although many people find Jung's approach helpful, I feel it is important to temper the claims advanced by some of his more enthusiastic adherents. No system or technique can lead us to God or connect us with the divine image within. That comes on its own terms, an act of grace in Christian parlance, and the most we can do is cultivate an attitude of receptivity. Such openness is a central aim of spiritual direction and the techniques it employs, which are carefully tailored to individual temperament and cultural context.

All spiritual traditions rely on images and imagination to symbolize what cannot be conceptualized, the familiar something we haven't yet seen. Ignatius of Loyola based much of his model on this symbol-making capacity, the graced ability of divinely guided imagination to bridge the gap between God and human. Jung was a close, if not always accurate, reader of Ignatius and employed similar techniques.[363] Both believed that divine guidance emerges through the free play of images, a process Jung called *active imagination*. Such claims were far riskier in Ignatius's day, yet he was fearless in trusting God's leading in emotional stirrings and internal images. At the same time, he insisted that multiple spiritual forces were at work in the personality and recommended active discernment of spirits, an ongoing process of prayerful and clear-eyed scrutiny.[364] Here, too, there are parallels with Jung and his emphasis on the crucial role of ego in establishing a dialogue with the unconscious, not dominating the conversation but not entirely passive either.[365] In keeping with modern sensibilities, his perspective on the symbolic world is less dichotomous than Ignatius's view, for whom discernment was a matter of deciding whether a good or an evil spirit was behind a given image or feeling.

---

[362] Jung, 1935. "Principles of Practical Psychotherapy," CW 16, ¶22.

[363] Jung, *Jung on Ignatius of Loyola's Spiritual Exercises: Lectures Delivered at ETH Zurich, Vol. 7, 1939–40.*

[364] Joseph Munitiz and Philip Endean, "The Spiritual Exercises" in *Saint Ignatius of Loyola: Personal Writings*, 348–353, ¶¶313–336.

[365] Jung, *Aion*, CW9ii, ¶11.

Given the vast differences in their respective worldviews, what's surprising is how much their core premises align. Both believed that the inner world contains a spiritual dimension that manifests in ambivalent ways, and both stressed the need to engage the images and emotions arising from its depths in an open though careful manner. This kind of nuanced approach to inner images does not come easy in any epoch. Earlier eras tended to take religious visions at face value and judged them accordingly, angelic, or demonic. The modern tendency is to dismiss them out of hand, at worst pathological and at best meaningless, or else swallow them whole with new age credulity. By contrast, Jung encouraged dealing with them much the way we might approach the new neighbors in deciding how to relate to them.

Working with Symbolic Material

The dream images recounted over the course of the book chronicle Mark's deepening relationship with God and neighbor. Engaging deeply with images of divinity challenges the ego's supremacy, a threat depicted in his dream of being pulled into an aquarium. The small self defends against the encounter in various ways. These play out differently for everyone. His journey highlights some common complications in working with symbolic material.

Whereas many people have difficulty taking dream symbols seriously, Mark lavished them with intellectual attention, but he had trouble forming a personal relationship with them. He had a natural affinity for symbolic thought and loved playing with images, turning them this way and that in light of cross-cultural material. In many ways, his stance toward them repeated the very childhood patterns he complained about. Back then, religious truth was expressed conceptually and was not something you monkeyed with. A preacher might speculate about the meaning of a given scripture passage. However, putting yourself into the story, as Ignatius suggested, would have been unthinkable. The choice was clear in his childhood church, either everything in the pages of the Bible is a historical fact or the whole thing is a lie. That did not leave much room for symbolic truth and its absence left him disillusioned when he spotted inconsistencies between different scripture passages as a teenager or encountered textual criticism as an adult. For all his intellectual grasp of hermeneutic theories of interpretation, Mark treated symbolic images in the old familiar way. Although he might wax eloquent about cross-cultural analogues; actually, opening a dialogue with them left him feeling uncomfortable and self-conscious.

Meanwhile, untouched by all this rarefied spiritual reflection, the same old unconscious patterns continued to disrupt his life. Mark had been sober for decades, but impulses from the darker parts of his inner world functioned like a drug to touch off the familiar cycle of emotional intoxication, defensive blame, and impotent remorse. Fistfights and ruptured relationships were not something he was anxious to talk about, particularly in spiritual direction. Gradually, however, the destructive patterns beneath them began creeping into his dreams.

Like the drunk uncle at Thanksgiving dinner, dreams have a habit of dredging up whatever you do not want mentioned. Mark's dreams became ever more insistent when he ignored them, and they had something to say about everything: his marriage, the way he treated coworkers and strangers in parking lots, his secret fears, and grandiose dreams of greatness. The same tired patterns showed up everywhere, like the old cliché about meeting yourself wherever you go.

Having his nose rubbed in shadow material was bad enough; worse yet were the dreams that spotlighted his distorted relationship with God. According to them, he treated God the way he treated his supervisor at work, any authority for that matter, including me—the same outward acquiescence and passive resistance. To make matters worse, these dreams incorporated sacred images in disturbing ways, mixing and matching promiscuously, plaids and stripes, the Second Coming and parking tickets. He liked to joke that they offended his inner Evangelical, but in truth his grownup self was equally appalled.

Mark liked to complain that his early religious training had been like walking through a museum, everything neatly labeled and under glass, and at first the new and imaginative way of engaging sacred images he found in spiritual direction felt like a breath of fresh air. As time went on, what began as an elevated spiritual exercise was getting uncomfortably close to home, like the old joke about the church elder who shouted hallelujah when the preacher railed against murder and adultery and then waddled out of church when the sermon turned to gluttony. The more Mark reflected on these dreams the more complicated they seemed, everything weaving together like a good novel—personal history and geopolitics, religion, and lunchmeat. It was not just a matter of the images themselves but his relationship to them, which turned out to be extremely complicated. Was the dream pointing in the direction he needed to go or where he had strayed from the path? Neither, for the most part, he discovered to his disappointment. Most simply laid out the situation from a particular perspective and left him to draw his own conclusions, although a kind of gentle directionality did gradually emerge over time.

Where Is God in All This?

At this point the reader might well ask, so where is God in all this? That's always the underlying question in spiritual direction and a good way to orient when things get confusing. Given this ambiguity and blending of images, what constitutes a God-image and what does it have to do with the God of traditional faith? I will address the first question now and take up the second at the end of the chapter.

So, what is a God-image and how does it function? On the level of individual personality, it symbolizes the person's experience of the divine and represents the highest value for a given individual, like theologian Paul Tillich's definition of religious faith as that which is of ultimate concern.[366] It does not necessarily correspond to what a person tells herself about religion but what matters at the core of her being. As a unifying symbol of wholeness, a God-image creates order and meaning while drawing together diverse parts of the personality.[367] It balances opposing perspectives within the individual, like the struggle between Mark's everyday self and what he termed his "inner Evangelical."

This ability to mediate contradictions reflects its function as a symbol of totality that leads us beyond our limited human awareness, as successive God-images guide us toward the divine reality beyond all images.[368] Observant readers may have noticed that the description of God-images sounds a lot like Jung's definition of the Self. In fact, there is considerable overlap between the two concepts.[369] A God-image expresses the deepest levels of the Self for an individual or culture, thereby giving form to the transcendent core at the center of the human personality.[370] According to Jung, the figure of Christ has been the primary expression of

---

[366] Paul Tillich, *The Dynamics of Faith*, 1.
[367] Jung, 1950. "Foreword to Allenby," CW 18, ¶1495; CW 11, ¶233.
[368] Jung, *C. G. Jung Letters*, 258–260.
[369] Jung, 1952. "Answer to Job," *Psychology and Religion*, CW 11, ¶757.
[370] Jung, 1942/1948. "A Psychological Approach to the Dogma of the Trinity," CW 11, ¶231.

the Self throughout much of Western history, a God-image that still exerts a profound effect on believers and unbelievers alike.[371] Consequently, he saw the secularization of Western culture as a spiritual and psychological crisis, as the absence of a meaningful God-image makes it increasingly difficult for people to connect with higher values and puts the very human personality at risk.[372]

At such times, Jung almost sounds like a Christian reformer, a sort of modern-day Ignatius who employed psychology to develop a spiritual practice for contemporary individuals. This is the side of his thought that his Christian proponents like to quote. For his theological critics, however, the devil lies in the details of his concepts of the Self and the God-image. A major sticking point is his insistence that as a symbol of totality, the Self needs to include both good and evil, a caveat that extends to the God-images that represent it within human awareness.[373] Not surprisingly, the idea was roundly denounced by Christian thinkers, including several of his early supporters. Jung dismissed such criticism, saying he was merely talking about the God-image, not God,[374] but his critics remained unconvinced he could do one without the other, especially when he went on to describe the Christ-image as incomplete because it does not include shadow.[375]

Christian critics found this problematic, to say the least, and the dispute illustrates a key difference between the two perspectives. Like much else in his approach, Jung's argument regarding the ability of the Christ-image to capture the human experience of transcendence rests on the crucial distinction between God and the God-image.[376] We see God in a glass darkly, according to Paul's letter to the Corinthians,[377] and what we know empirically of divinity is limited to its partial reflection in the dingy mirror of limited and divided human consciousness, where it is subject to the same distortions that cloud our perceptions of those around us. From this perspective, a God-image that reflects the full range of human experience needs to contain these same ambiguities, divisions that may

---

[371] Jung, *Aion*, CW 9ii, ¶79.
[372] Jung, CW 16, ¶216.
[373] Jung, CW 9ii, ¶¶77, 185; "Answer to Job," CW 11, ¶567.
[374] Jung, *C. G. Jung Letters*, 260.
[375] Jung, CW 9ii, ¶74.
[376] Jung, 1938/1940. "Psychology and Religion" (The Terry Lectures), CW 11, ¶144.
[377] 1 Corinthians 13:12

say more about the human subject than divinity itself. Then as now, this sort of argumentation did little to assuage his Christian interlocutors and the issue remains a source of conflict between the two approaches, although it does not preclude adapting Jungian methods to Christian spiritual direction. I explored similar questions in the chapter on the shadow without reaching any conclusion. They will not get resolved here either. Before plunging into that thorny theological thicket, I will survey the overall territory and examine how the concepts of the Self and the God-image function in Jung's system.

Symbols and the God-Image

Like every aspect of his thought, Jung's concept of the God-image rests on his understanding of symbols and their role in organizing the world. At this point, a quick review of his distinction between signs and symbols may be helpful.[378] A stop sign offers a good example of the former, an arbitrary mashup of red color and octagonal shape that becomes associated with the act of stopping through repetition and the threat of traffic court. By contrast, symbols point beyond themselves in an organic relationship between what they are and what they represent,[379] like the image of sowing seeds in the New Testament.[380] Seen in this light, ordinary objects and situations take on new meanings that allow us to glimpse the depths beneath our everyday reality. This neat division between signs and symbols is complicated by the fact that what starts out as an arbitrary sign may become so entrenched in awareness it takes on symbolic meaning, like a directee's dream about a heavenly stop light that flashed with rainbow colors.

Symbols come in many forms, from natural features like mountain ranges to elaborate literary metaphors that paint a vivid picture in the mind. To be meaningful, they must convey a level of experience that cannot be represented in conceptual terms. In a movie, this can be as simple as the way a character puts milk on her cereal or parks her motorcycle, gestures that perfectly capture how she moves through the world.

Religious rituals contain a particularly rich set of symbolic actions and images that resonates on multiple levels. Because rituals draw upon

---

[378] Jung, 1921/1971. *Psychological Types*, CW 6, ¶¶814, 815.
[379] Jung, CW 6, ¶814.
[380] Matthew 13:31.

the symbolic structures of the society in which they occur, a given religious ritual can only be understood within its cultural context. The Christian ritual of infant baptism offers a good example. A visiting Martian attending a christening might see a bunch of chatty people gathered around to wash a protesting baby's hair. From a Christian perspective, every element of the ritual—the white garment, the consecrated oil, the water, and the lit candle—is rich with meaning that stretches back across centuries of scripture and tradition.

Most religious rituals have a communal aspect, and a christening is no exception. Ritual dimensions of the ceremony blend seamlessly with everyday conviviality as friends and family gather at the church and celebrate together afterward. Godparents participate in two realms at once, channeling the Heavenly Father and Mother and, in many cultures, functioning as literal parents if the infant is orphaned. The symbolism gets even thicker when the service includes Communion. The token amounts of food and intoxicant distributed to the congregation are everyday sources of sustenance and enjoyment. As such, they offer a natural symbol of spiritual nurturance, just as godparents support both physical and spiritual welfare. And beyond the level of human relationships, bread and wine are central symbols of the core Christian mystery, the self-sacrificing deity who assumes bodily form to feed us with its flesh and blood.

The familiar ritual illustrates the complex matrix of interrelated images at the heart of religious practice. Each image helps interpret the others and together they create a vocabulary of symbolic meaning that organizes inner experience and gives us a way to talk about something that cannot be put into words. When I was growing up, it was not unusual for speakers at secular events to weave in biblical references, not just about being a good Samaritan[381] but also about finding a pearl of great price[382] or casting your bread upon the water, an image that still eludes me.[383] Society is less religious now, and when working with young people I sometimes find this role has been filled by movies, memes, or online games. These serve their purpose although they lack the richness and nuance of sacred texts and rituals. Scripture has something to say about everything, and

---

[381] Luke 10:29–37.
[382] Matthew 13:45, 46.
[383] Ecclesiastes 11:1.

Bible narratives have all the complexity and ambivalence of daily life, although not necessarily the ones we used to read in Sunday School.

Mark and I spoke the same religious language and fished from the same teeming pool of biblical images: the Witch of Endor[384] from the Old Testament and the whiny man at the pool of Bethesda[385] in the New Testament, Jesus's morally ambiguous family tree that includes characters such as Rahab, Ruth, and David. These vignettes and personalities are vivid, yet they are always in danger of being just about themselves and not us. Symbols operate in two worlds, the one we see and another that we barely glimpse, but it is hard to keep both in sight. Much as a spring stretches with age, the tension between them goes slack, and we land on one side or the other—cold fact or bloodless abstraction. Mark's spiritual journey had taken him from one extreme to the other, from literal beliefs he could not make sense of, to lofty principles that left him cold. Although he had a good intellectual grasp of theology and scripture, he struggled to rebuild the heartfelt connections he experienced in childhood.

Losing touch with the physical side of a symbol turns images into ideas. Without a real-world context, they become free-floating concepts that can be rearranged like building blocks to construct theoretical superstructures. This is the reason spiritual symbols need to be rebottled in new wineskins from time to time. Religious systems are always in danger of becoming self-referential, every image supporting the next yet none of them grounded in daily life. What exactly does it mean to be washed in the blood of the lamb in a culture where priests do not routinely splash the blood of sacrificial animals onto worshipers? Jesus' invitation to munch his flesh so disgusted his listeners that many abandoned him on the spot.[386] The image does not even register with present-day congregants who are more likely to be concerned about whether the Communion wafers are gluten free.

Salt loses its saltiness, according to the Gospels, and symbols cannot point beyond themselves if all the sharp edges have worn off.[387] Then ritual objects turn into collectables, mind-spraining parables are reduced to truisms, and miraculous events become empirical facts operating under a different set of physical laws. In his autobiography, Jung describes his

---

[384] 1 Samuel 28:7–25.
[385] John 5:1–18.
[386] John 6:52–57.
[387] Matthew 5:13.

childhood disillusionment when he was finally allowed to participate in the mystery of Communion, only to encounter mumbled words and poor-quality wine.[388] Of course, loss of symbolic meaning is not unique to religious systems. Every societal institution from the family to the military is held together by symbolic structures that are always in danger of losing their glue. And although sacred texts can be put to murderous uses, Jung believed that post-religious cultures lacking a mythic framework that connects them to their depths run the even greater risk of losing their humanity.[389]

Humans think in images, and these can be imprisoning if they turn into abstractions that substitute for experience. But if symbols decay, they also regenerate, the process Jung devoted his life to studying.[390] Mark's dream about an older man teaching a class on Abraham's sacrifice offers a case in point. In his childhood church, the shocking story of the binding of Isaac[391] had been reduced to allegory, its images demoted from symbols to signs. It stood for Christ's redeeming sacrifice and the details of the narrative were irrelevant now that its real meaning had been revealed. The dream came at a time when Mark was struggling with the prospect of having to sacrifice the sense of specialness that had sustained him through childhood. Riffing on the familiar Bible story, it raised questions regarding divinely sanctioned child sacrifice that resonated with his own family history and the view of God he took from it. In the process, it revived and personalized the timeworn myth with an ambiguous narrative as disturbing and enigmatic as the original.

This creative reworking of religious symbols can be seen all the time in art. For example, in the classic movie *Cool Hand Luke*, a decidedly un-Christlike convict is explicitly depicted as a Christ figure.[392] This unsettling portrait is probably closer to the view of Jesus held by many of his contemporaries than the Sunday School version. Like a close reading of the Gospels, it raises uncomfortable questions about what it means to imitate Christ.

---

[388] Jung, *Memories, Dreams, Reflections,* 53–54.
[389] Jung, 1945. "Psychotherapy Today," CW 16, ¶216.
[390] Jung, CW 6, ¶¶824, 825.
[391] Genesis 22:1–18.
[392] *Cool Hand Luke.* 1967. Screenplay by Donn Pearce and Frank R. Pierson, based upon Donn Pierce, *Cool Hand Luke,* New York: Scribners, 1965. Directed by Stuart Rosenberg.

To some extent, God always wears the face we place on "him," and dreams work overtime to make sure we do not get too comfortable with the projection. The last few chapters presented a series of dream images drawn directly from Mark's everyday life that provided him a sort of personalized training video on seeing God with new eyes.

After forty years of dreamwork, I am still amazed by the resourcefulness of this internal cinematographer. Humans cannot stop the process of generating new symbols or direct its output, any more than they can control peristalsis. Anyone who's ever tried to write a group ritual knows how clunky and labored these can sound, yet spontaneous rituals happen all the time when no one is looking, from the way chairs get arranged and who's in charge of making coffee to the hearty "Hi Barbara" that follows the first faltering admission of addiction in a twelve-step meeting.

Humans are symbol-making animals, or perhaps symbol-sensing animals. Symbols organize every aspect of experience. They join and divide people, give life meaning or make it seem pointless. In the case of religious symbols, believers are lifted out of their earthbound perspective and returned to the world with heavenly eyes able to glimpse the kingdom of God spread out among them. Jung referred to the powerful religious images that take humans beyond themselves as *symbols of transformation*.[393] Some offer variations on traditional images that help revitalize religious practice within the larger culture, such as the visions of Mary or the Sacred Heart of Jesus that gave rise to new spiritual movements. In a herding culture, Mark's image of God giving life like a cow licking amniotic fluids from its newborn calf might become an icon. Other images, such as mystics' descriptions of Christ himself placing the wafer on their tongues or handing them a cup of his blood to drink, are too personal to resonate in the larger culture. Claims of still more intimate contact with God often lead to conflict with the religious establishment, just as they did in Jesus's time.

A wide variety of Christian practices work directly with these spontaneous images. Ignatian spirituality offers a prime example and illustrates what I have called a top-down approach, which takes as its starting point a sacred text or traditional image of God like that of the crucified Christ. Ignatius encouraged directees to form a new relationship with familiar biblical narratives and characters by inserting themselves in a

---

[393] Jung, 1911–12/1952/1967. *Symbols of Transformation*, CW 5, ¶¶343–346.

Bible story or engaging the "risen Christ" in conversation.[394] In addition, the spiritual exercises he gave his directees included imaginative visualizations that employed God-images taken from their shared cultural context, such as the "Meditation on Two Standards" that drew on his extensive military experience to depict the world as a spiritual battlefield.[395] The images and emotions arising in response to these imaginative exercises were carefully recorded by the individual and became a source of prayerful reflection. All were taken seriously, however unusual their content might seem, and carefully examined in the context of the person's life and relationship with God. Whether Jesus stepped out of the biblical narrative with a personal message for the retreatant or nothing happened at all, everything was grist for the mill.

By contrast, I have described Jung's methodology as a bottom-up approach that focuses on spontaneous images that appear in dreams and imagination. In practice, this up/down distinction is blurrier than it sounds. Highly individual images arise during Ignatian work and the dream images examined in Jungian practice often include traditional religious symbols. These may be from the dreamer's own religious background or completely outside it, as if the psyche is trying to find an image which has not been dulled by use. Such unfamiliar religious symbols can be remarkably specific, like a directee with no background in Egyptian mythology who dreams the underworld deities Anubis and Ammit are waiting at the bottom of her basement stairs.

In contrast to Jung's era, this sort of esoteric image is readily available within the culture, usually with the click of a mouse. What remains astounding, however, is how often obscure details of a given religious image resonate with the dreamer's experience, the way Mark derived personal meaning from the genealogy contained in a seemingly random Bible verse referenced in a dream. During our work together, he was more drawn to Jung's bottom-up methodology than Ignatian meditation on sacred texts or holy figures; however, many directees benefit from both. The two approaches can be used separately or in combination, whether by applying Jungian techniques to Ignatian reflection or employing Ignatian methods to treat a dream like a sacred text.

---

[394] Munitz and Endean, "The Spiritual Exercises" in *Saint Ignatius of Loyola: Personal Writings*, 299, ¶71.
[395] Munitz and Endean, 310–312, ¶¶136–148.

The God-Image vs. the God of Traditional Faith

It would be nice to end on this conciliatory note but that wouldn't be entirely honest.

Creating a Jungian/Ignatian synthesis implies that the two approaches are doing more or less the same thing. This begs the question I deferred earlier regarding the relationship between Jung's concept of the God-image and the God of traditional faith, especially given his insistence on the morally ambivalent nature of both it and the larger whole to which it corresponds. That's the topic I will turn to now with the understanding it could easily be a book in itself. Given the complexity of the subject, my exploration of it will be not only cursory but also highly speculative, and the chapter will conclude on an unresolved note. In the end, I am not asking whether Jung's religious writings are orthodox from a Christian perspective, something he never claimed; I am asking what his approach can bring to Christian spiritual direction.

I have mentioned before that many of the more serious concerns raised by Christian critics have to do with Jung's model of a divine core at the center of the human personality and its relationship to divinity. It is worth noting these are debated areas within Christianity as well, and a number of theological models overlap substantially with his view. This is particularly true in the mystical tradition, as you'll shortly see in regard to Meister Eckhart. Jung's entire system is predicated on the existence of a dimension of the personality that participates in divine mystery.[396] The idea also has an extensive history in Christian doctrine, based on the scriptural claim that human beings are created in the image and likeness of God.[397]

An influential early interpretation differentiated between the terms *image* and *likeness* to posit that humans share in God's nature, but the imprint has been smudged or partially erased by the fall from grace recounted in Genesis. This gives rise to *split consciousness*, the contradictory state described by Paul in which we both do and do not want to do what we know we should.[398] Jung's model of the personality is similarly split, a dynamic interplay of competing instincts and forces that helps account for the diversity of God-images. Here, as elsewhere, the underlying structure

---

[396] Jung, "A Psychological Approach to the Dogma of the Trinity," CW 11, ¶¶231, 237.
[397] Genesis 1:26–27.
[398] Romans 7:15.

of his thought reflects the Christian culture that shaped it, even when specific elements fall outside the pale of traditional dogma. In this case, however, his belief in a divine core at the center of the person is entirely orthodox, as is his insistence that it offers intimations of the divine source from which it derives.

Over the course of its history, Christian spirituality has generated a vast literature that seeks to articulate how this inner guidance toward our source manifests within human awareness. Details vary across accounts, partly depending on the model of the personality prevalent at the time. By placing this journey back to the center in a contemporary psychological and developmental framework, Jung offered a new twist on an old tradition of applied spirituality that includes the work of Ignatius and others. His assertion that the divine core not only participates in the divine nature but also is indistinguishable from it—a smaller version of the original—is more controversial, although not entirely foreign to Christian thought.[399] In Jungian language, the Self that gives rise to transforming images of wholeness is transpersonal in nature, a limited manifestation of the larger whole. You might call this view of divine reality holographic since each part replicates the whole, whereas another metaphor for the relationship would be a tiny puddle reflecting the vast moon.

Such images suggest the classic Vedantic formulation—Atman is Brahman—in which the individual, or inmost soul, is the same as the universal soul, or ultimate reality.[400] Numerous analogues also exist within the Christian tradition. The idea that God became human so humans could become God goes back to the early Christian fathers.[401] Christians are committed on principle to the idea of divinization but disagree passionately on the details, including the role of human initiative and self-knowledge in the process, the theological question of acquired and infused grace. Are human beings sundered from God by an unbridgeable gulf, at least from their side? And conversely, what part do they play in connecting with the internal reflection of the deity whose image they bear?

These issues loomed large in Mark's spiritual odyssey as he struggled to translate his childhood Christianity into his adult understanding of the world. The journey was mirrored and presaged in dreams whose content

---

[399] Jung, *Aion*, CW9ii, ¶¶60, 73.
[400] Jung, 1935/43. "Individual Dream Symbolism in Relation to Alchemy," *Psychology and Alchemy,* CW 12, ¶137.
[401] Athanasius of Alexandria, *On the Incarnation,* 107, section 54.

ranged from dense theological arguments to a lengthy conversation with a nephew of Meister Eckhart he found living in a shabby bungalow in Berkeley, an image that anticipates my next topic. The reference to Meister Eckhart is especially interesting since Mark hadn't read the highly cerebral German theologian until the dream piqued his curiosity. His own intellectual bent notwithstanding, Mark found himself drawn instead to more heartfelt mystics like Julian of Norwich or Teresa of Ávila and her spiritual soulmate, John of the Cross. This unlikely preference suggests the Jungian principle of compensation, in which the unconscious seeks to balance the limitations of the conscious viewpoint, just as dream images supply what's missing from the everyday perspective.[402] People tend to concentrate on what they are good at, and the conscious perspective grows more one-sided with time. Despite Mark's intellectualism, or perhaps because of it, the growing edge of his spirituality had to do with movement away from a faith based in intellectual understanding toward the kind of deeply felt personal relationship with God he remembered from childhood.

This budding relationship found expression in dream images of union similar to those I explored in an earlier chapter. Many involved physical intimacy, in keeping with the long Christian tradition of bridal mysticism whose imagery derives from the Song of Songs. Despite scattered exceptions, the dimension of divine mystery that transcends form played a less prominent part in Mark's spiritual journey, perhaps in compensation for his tendency to become ungrounded. A similar preference is seen in Christianity as a whole. Given the religion's strongly relational focus, spiritual approaches that emphasize the unknowable nature of God hold a minority position in the spiritual literature, especially in the Western Church.

Nevertheless, apophatic spirituality has a long history in the Christian tradition, from the highly influential writings attributed to Dionysius the Aeropagite, who maintained that unlikely images of God are safer because at least we know they are images,[403] to the twentieth-century mystic Thomas Merton. Among its most articulate theological proponents in Western Christianity was the fourteenth-century German mystic Meister Eckhart. Despite posthumous condemnation of some of his ideas by church authorities, a move partially driven by political considerations, he remains a major figure in Christian spirituality.

---

[402] Jung, *Psychological Types*, CW 6, ¶¶693–695.
[403] Pseudo-Dionysius, *The Complete Works*, 150.

He was a favorite source for Jung, who references Eckhart throughout his work. This affinity highlights the many parallels between the two and gives an indication of where Jung's ideas might fit on the spectrum of Christian thought. His use of Eckhart, although accurate, made no effort to be comprehensive. Jung took from his writings ideas pertinent to his own approach. Of course he was not alone in this since a number of other modern religious and secular writers did the same thing, including the influential German philosopher Friedrich Hegel. Given the striking similarity in their views regarding the spiritual aspect of the personality, Eckhart offers a natural bridge between Jung and the larger Christian tradition, the topic of this chapter. In the section that follows, I will briefly summarize Eckhart's complex model, a daunting task under the best of circumstances, highlighting areas of overlap with Jung as well as divergences that reflect their very different cultural contexts.

Meister Eckhart's Model of Personality

At times, Eckhart sounds surprisingly psychological for his era. He describes three descending levels of the human personality: an outer aspect that relies on basic functions such as instinct and sensation to navigate the world, inner qualities such as will and higher reason, and an innermost level that he refers to as the ground of being or the spark of God in the soul.[404] This innermost core transcends the individual personality and shares in God's nature. Like God, it is beyond all images, nameless and empty in the sense of transcending definition, an apophatic desert where Christ dwells at the center of personality, bridging human and divine.[405]

Although Christ lives in this inner nowhere, the presence encountered there is beyond characteristics, in keeping with Eckhart's famous love of paradox. Its formlessness resembles the undefined unity at the heart of reality that he calls the *Godhead*, a boiling creativity that gives rise to the triune God in a joyful dance of relationship whose creative energy spills out in Creation.[406] From a psychological perspective that would be quite foreign to Eckhart's time, a modern reader might speculate that the

---

[404] Meister Eckhart, "Sermon 83," *Meister Eckhart, The Essential Sermons, Commentaries, Treatises and Defense,* 206–208; Bernard McGinn, *The Harvest of Mysticism in Medieval Germany,* 88–90.
[405] McGinn, *The Mystical Thought of Meister Eckhart,* 47–52.
[406] McGinn, 72–79.

triune God represents Godhead seen through human eyes, its relational nature rendering divinity accessible in ways that can be grasped if not comprehended.

In contrast to the nothingness of humans who derive their very being from God, God's nothingness is a matrix of pure being and potentiality.[407] As the spiritual journey nears its goal, our emptiness receives God's fullness and the Son is born in the manger of the soul as the pilgrim comes to rest in this undifferentiated nothingness beyond time and place.[408] The soul's return to essential unity continues as the believer breaks back into God and distinctions fade as God becomes all in all.[409] The inner and outer worlds come together, Earth and Heaven joined so that God is as present in the stable as the cathedral. Eckhart describes this non-dual way of moving through the world as "living without a why," a radical form of contemplation in action that offers a new twist on the traditional view of the unitive life.[410] Reversing the standard clerical justification for the superiority of cloistered life, Eckhart favors the active Martha who bustles around making dinner for Jesus and his disciples over the passive Mary sitting raptly at his feet.[411]

This brief synopsis does violence to the power and subtlety of Eckhart's thought, just as my earlier characterization of him as "cerebral" fails to recognize the emotional power of his German sermons. Nonetheless, it illustrates key parallels with Jung that help locate the latter's thought within the Christian tradition, especially his concept of the Self and its relationship to the larger wholeness. Whether Jung drew on Eckhart in formulating his model or found in him a post hoc analogue for his own conclusions, the parallels are often striking.

Like Eckhart, Jung believed that the divine core at the center of the person transcends the individual personality and shares in the essential unity from which it derives. It is empty, in the sense of remaining undefined while embracing all possibilities, a hollow square that gives rise to the plethora of images that represent it within human awareness.[412]

---

[407] Meister Eckhart, "Sermon 4," 250; McGinn, 81.
[408] Meister Eckhart, "Sermon 4," 251–252.
[409] McGinn, *The Mystical Thought of Meister Eckhart,* 147–151.
[410] Meister Eckhart, "Commentary on Exodus," *Teacher and Preacher,* 120, ¶247; McGinn, 153–161.
[411] Meister Eckhart, "Sermon 86," *Teacher and Preacher,* 338–345.
[412] Jung, *C. G. Jung Letters,* 258.

Like the Christ encountered in Eckhart's innermost center, it is at once personal and beyond personality. Jung believed that its prime expression in Western culture is the Christ figure who unites human and divine.[413] In Jungian terms, Christ operates as a symbol of the Self, embodying the intimate reciprocity between this inner core and the wholeness from which it springs and toward which it leads. The small self rests in the greater Self on which it depends, reminding me of Eckhart's memorable phrase, "The eye with which I see God is the same with which God sees me."[414]

Here I need to pause and ask, can Jung's concept of the Self really be equated with Eckhart's idea of the Godhead beyond God? Both point to ultimate wholeness, the creative center beyond definition or personality, but we must be wary of easy equivalencies.

My comparison of Jung and Eckhart demonstrates where Jung might fall within the larger Christian tradition. Religious ideas, however, do not operate in a vacuum. Although there are many parallels between the two models, it is not clear whether these carried the same meaning in the very different conceptual and religious environments in which they arose, the eternal problem in cross-cultural comparisons. Making Christ a symbol of anything, rather than the ultimate reference point, offends traditional Christian sensibilities. In the end, the deepest correspondence between the two men may not so much lie their theoretical models as in their similar stance toward the spiritual reality that underlies them.

Both spent much of their time as spiritual directors and this gives their work a practical orientation, a fact sometimes obscured by the complexity of their writings. Both were concerned with the transformation of the personality through a living connection with the inner core where divinity manifests in emotional stirrings, images, and intuitions. Over time, ongoing communion with this center gives rise to a life no longer directed by purely personal concerns, lived at the behest of the Self in Jung's language, or living without a why for Eckhart. The latter's valuation of the active life echoes Jung's insistence that individuals have a responsibility to bring what they have learned back to the larger community. Both prioritized direct experience—even when it seemed to contradict traditional religious thought—and incorporated events in their own spiritual lives into their models. For Eckhart, doing otherwise

---

[413] Jung, *Aion*, CW 9ii, ¶79.
[414] Meister Eckhart, "Sermon 12," 270.

was like covering Christ with a cloak and stuffing him under a bench, an image that could well have come from Jung.[415] The vividness of this earthy metaphor illustrates another area of overlap. Despite Eckhart's apophatic orientation, he relied on images to guide him toward divine reality and communicate his vision to others. These included dreams and imaginative reflection, what Jung would call active imagination. In one illustrative passage, he recounts how a man, probably himself, became pregnant with nothing in a waking dream and gave birth to nothing in which God was born, another image suggestive of Jung.[416]

Similarities abound yet there are also key differences in their stance toward ultimate reality, divergences that highlight Jung's ambivalent relationship to the Christian tradition. These reflect not only the very different times in which they lived but also a fundamental divide between the theological and the psychological perspectives that continues to the present. Reading their works, one is immediately struck with the different focus each brings to the journey. Eckhart offers a grand and soaring overview that embraces the entire universe whereas Jung's model is grounded in specific images and clinical material. It is as though Eckhart fixes his eyes on the distant mountain whereas Jung is far more interested in charting the twists and turns of the trail.

Is There Any There There?

I have talked frequently about Jung's emphasis on the progressive images that lead individuals toward the hollow square of Self. Although he had much to say about this journey, he spoke far less about what they find when they get there—the imageless emptiness beyond psychology. This reticence points to a fundamental distinction between the psychological and theological viewpoints, a difference I have characterized as bottom-up versus top-down. As a psychologist, Jung maintained he could not speak about the divine nature apart from what could be inferred from its impact on human beings.[417] The caveat seemed disingenuous to his critics, especially when his intense interest in religious issues led him to write in explicitly theological terms. Professional theologians complained that

---

[415] Meister Eckhart, "Sermon 13b," *The Complete Mystical Works of Meister Eckhart,* 110.
[416] Meister Eckhart, "Sermon 19," 140.
[417] Jung, 1946. "The Psychology of the Transference," CW 16, ¶537; Jung, "Psychology and Religion" (The Terry Lectures), CW 11, ¶11.

he was out of his depth, and there is truth to the charge, at least from the perspective of systematic theology.

However, Jung was approaching traditionally theological topics from a different angle than revealed religion. For his purposes, theological statements are best viewed through the lens of personal and cultural psychology rather than taken as free-floating ontological truths. They become a living reality to the extent they correspond with the psychology of an individual or culture and resonate with its unconscious dimensions while balancing deficits in the conscious standpoint. A given religious symbol can have many different meanings depending on the shifting needs of the times, just as the central tenets of Christianity have been interpreted in radically different ways across the centuries. In Jungian terms, transformative symbols are protean and inexhaustible, disclosing new facets in response to the shifting developmental needs of individuals and cultures.

In chronicling the encounter between human and divine, Jung concentrates on the human side of the equation. Whether he is writing about his own spiritual journey or the evolution of a given God-image within the larger culture, he's less concerned with eternal truths than religious experience grounded in a specific psychological context. It is hardly surprising that his theology is psychologically driven. He wrote passionately from his own history and responded to the religious atmosphere of his time.

This vantage point helps explain one of the more problematic aspects of his thought from the perspective of traditional Christianity, his insistence on the moral ambivalence of the Self and the God-images that represent it in human awareness. On a cultural level, this dark view balanced the overly sunny optimism of his childhood theological climate, darkness that gained substance as the twentieth century progressed. Jung's insistence on the mixed nature of the God-image also reflects his understanding of religious perception itself, a bottom-up perspective in which the greater wholeness is always seen through human eyes. We cannot know its real nature apart from our experience, at least from the viewpoint of psychology. Revelation is always partial and fragmentary, the God-image ambivalent because that's how it appears within limited human awareness.

There is an inevitable tension between this psychologically informed approach and the top-down orientation of revealed religion from which theology draws its authority, although the gap narrows somewhat in experientially based writers like Teresa of Ávila and John of the Cross.

Is Christ a symbol through which the larger wholeness expresses itself in human awareness, or the human manifestation of the Trinity, the image of the invisible God in the words of Colossians?[418] In a similar vein, do parallels between sacred myths from different cultures tell us about God's nature or our own? Put another way, does God choose to appear to us in forms that match our human categories, or is our experience of the divine determined by our own innate structures? Or is the question itself meaningless, a nursing infant trying to analyze the fit with her mother's breast? Formless experience of God can lift us beyond the limitations of human perception, at least momentarily, but how can we possibly conceptualize that experience?

Paul is seldom at a loss for words yet all he could say about his heavenly vision was that it could not be spoken of.[419] If the Jungian concept of the Self represents divinity as seen from a human perspective, I might speculate that from the standpoint of Christian dogma God is to the Self as the Self is to the ego. Jung himself had little patience with such views, judging by his exasperated tone in the letter to Pastor Bernet, who had objected to his concept of the Self on theological grounds. At one point, Jung demands testily how his own "ultimate" is somehow not as good as the minister's "absolute ultimate."[420] The exchange puts the clash of perspectives in a nutshell, as Jung speaks from the experiential vantage point of psychology whereas the pastor invokes the God of faith from the position of revealed religion.

Living in the Zigzag

So where does this leave us? I have noted before that my job is not to determine the state of Jung's soul, a task best left for God, but to explore whether his psychological approach can be fruitfully used in Christian spiritual direction. Part of the answer is practical. Whether you like it or not, our cultural perspective is deeply psychological. If psychology is not invited to the table, it will sneak in through the basement window, and Jung offers the most comprehensive available model for integrating psychology and religion.

---

[418] Colossians 1:15
[419] 2 Corinthians 12:2–4.
[420] Jung, *C. G. Jung Letters*, 259.

Was Mark's agonized struggle with the Father God and the doctrine of vicarious atonement a religious struggle or a psychological one? Both perhaps, depending on the lens through which the theological quandaries that preoccupied him are examined. Mark's spiritual journey demonstrates that while the psychological and theological viewpoints stand in tension, they also complement each other. Healing is always a mysterious process beyond human control, and it happens on multiple levels, as seen in the Gospel accounts where Jesus cures the suffering mind and body while proclaiming the sufferer's sins are forgiven.[421]

Mark's healing was equally multifaceted. His deepening relationship with God assumed both cataphatic and apophatic dimensions, the former expressed in reflection, worship, and prayer, the latter in his increasingly rich practice of Centering Prayer. However, his spiritual practice also took on a psychological dimension as he discovered that working with guiding images and the complexes they revealed helped clear the ground for a new receptivity in all aspects of his life.

What I am calling the psychological dimension of spiritual direction has been expressed in many vocabularies and assumed many forms over the centuries. Jungian methods represent a contemporary variation on an old theme, imaginal work grounded in a spiritual anthropology that is deeply attuned to the underlying religious reality. Spiritual direction operates on this same boundary between divine reality and individual psychology. As a director, I am constantly called to reconcile psychology and religion, not by reducing one to the other but by viewing directees' unfolding process from different angles—wave and particle in the tired analogy. As luck would have it, spiritual directors are accustomed to working from multiple perspectives. In a given session, the conversation zigzags freely between personal struggles and religious truths as we follow the path of God's transforming presence in a given personality, with all its quirks and wounds. Fortunately, as the empty third chair helps remind me, this dizzying process of integration and incarnation is guided by the Holy Spirit who uses me despite myself in ways beyond my understanding.

---

[421] Mark 2:1–12.

Chapter 16
The Spiritual Path: Jungian and
Christian Perspectives

The previous chapter addressed the relationship between Jung's model of the spiritual dimension of the personality and parallel formulations in the Christian mystical tradition, most notably in the work of Meister Eckhart. By way of illustration, I examined these two perspectives in the context of Mark's deepening relationship with God. Despite areas of overlap, Christian mystics such as Eckhart have a fundamentally different orientation toward the holy than Jung and appeal to very different sources of validation, a distinction I characterized as top-down versus bottom-up. At best, this makes the two approaches complementary; at worst, mutually unintelligible. The current chapter will explore the relationship between them in more detail as I compare Jung's concept of individuation with the traditional model of spiritual growth in the Christian mystical tradition.

Individuation is Jung's term for the process through which individuals come into right relationship with the holy and become more themselves as they are less ruled by unconscious internal and societal forces, which also leads to right relationships with the natural world and those around them.[422] From a Jungian standpoint, this journey can be loosely described in terms of successive encounters with the shadow, the inner other or anima/animus, and the Self, the progression I have been tracking throughout this book.

The classic Christian model of spiritual development, a sequence that has been applied to other religious traditions as well, also divides the

---

[422] C. G. Jung, 1935. "Principles of Practical Psychotherapy," *The Practice of Psychotherapy*, CW 16, ¶¶11–13.

path into three stages: *Purgation, Illumination,* and *Divine Union.*[423] Here spiritual growth can be described as a process in which separating from sinful patterns allows individuals to open to Divine Illumination as they move toward fuller union with God, a relationship that also expresses itself in loving relationships in the world around them.

As before, I will consider these Jungian and Christian models of spiritual development in relation to Mark's journey. Although examining his experience in depth brings the topic to life, it does limit my ability to look at the larger gestalt since each person's spiritual path is only one trail through a vast landscape. In an effort to gain a fuller perspective, I also will apply the two approaches to the prototypical account of the spiritual journey in Western culture, Dante's *Divine Comedy.*[424] As before, the goal is not to decide between competing models or create a schematic that correlates their stages; rather I want to draw on both to better understand how the divine unfolds within a human life.

Viewing spiritual development from these two perspectives, the traditional religious model and Jung's more psychological approach, brings me full circle to the questions about the relationship between psychology and spirituality that prompted the book in the first place. Consequently, this chapter will also serve as its conclusion, retracing the ground that has been covered and reviewing key concepts. Given the unresolved nature of the issues I have been examining, the point is not to pull together a book's worth of material in a tidy summary but to revisit the highlights and make tentative conjectures about a process that remains far from complete, both in Mark's life and in my effort to understand it.

Coming Full Circle

As we near the end of our journey together, it may be useful to look back at how it began—with a blurry morning in a busy airport and the issues it raised. If it was a dream I would linger over the setting, a transitional space for travelers headed in all directions. In fact, the entire scene did have a dreamlike quality, beyond the fact I was operating on four hours sleep. As if in a nightmare, I was searching for a quiet corner to do my morning devotions but blaring television screens chased me

---

[423] Evelyn Underhill, *Mysticism: A Study in Nature and Development of Spiritual Consciousness.*
[424] Dante Alighieri, *The Divine Comedy: The Inferno, The Purgatorio and the Paradiso.*

everywhere. A talk show was in progress and religion was on the docket, mirroring my thwarted devotions in classic dream fashion.

Two groups were featured, true believers and contemptuous skeptics, who were not so much debating as talking past each other to the camera. In a dream the two sides might represent parts of me, aspects of the larger social dialogue, or both at once. That's how I viewed them at the time, in keeping with the Jungian admonition to read outer events like a dream. Beneath the jargon and slogans lurked questions that haunt any attempt at contemporary religious dialogue, the same ones that have shaped this discussion. The combatants did not seem to know they were arguing about the relationship between psychology and religion, yet that's where the argument kept winding up.

Is God just the unconscious, as one woman claimed, thereby replacing one unknown with another, or the source of consciousness itself? In other words, is God out there, in here, or nowhere at all? Put another way, is God our psychological projection or are we God's and how would we ever know? Does "He" look like a big daddy in the sky because we are afraid to be alone in the universe, as the young man with the nose ring insinuated? Or is God perceived as a parent because childhood relationships are a natural way to visualize an intimate connection with something beyond our comprehension? If ultimate reality is truly beyond understanding, then the whole idea of describing it is absurd, like toe cells debating the shape of the face above them. More to the point, were the skeptics in the audience right in asserting that modern scientific and psychological models have accounted for what used to be called God, a hypothesis that's no longer needed? (Like a screen door on a submarine, one of my philosophy teachers used to joke.) And how do believers account for those same well-evidenced realties, especially when they contradict received religion? And, most importantly for my purposes, how can believers avoid living in two worlds at once, the workaday world ruled by science and a biblical one shaped by a premodern worldview?

That was the problem of my childhood, or at least one of them, although I could not have articulated it at the time. It went on to shape the trajectory of my adult life, something else I did not realize until much later, as I struggled to integrate the worldview that I inherited from traditional religion with the one I used to navigate daily life. Jung had encountered the same dilemma nearly a century earlier and reading him felt like coming home.

His particular problem was how to reconcile his intense inner experiences with the two competing systems that dominated his culture: traditional religion, on the one hand, and scientific empiricism on the other.[425] Neither helped much in understanding them, he soon discovered, and this disappointment set him on his quest. At a time when many theologians were trying to demythologize religion, he dedicated himself to re-sacralizing everyday existence in a world that he believed had lost connection with its mythic roots.[426] If Freud's big discovery was the unconscious, as many have claimed, Jung's epiphany had to do with its religious nature. For Jung, divine mystery is a living force in every human being, forever disclosing itself through new images.[427] His effort to personalize religion is a goal shared by spiritual directors everywhere as, like them, he sought to decrease his patients' emotional suffering and facilitate healing through direct experience of the holy. And although theologians have raised various objections to Jung's understanding of God, Jung's account of the human side of the divine/human relationship follows much of the same well-worn path described by spiritual guides across religious traditions.

Jung's word for this unfolding spiritual development, *individuation*, is unfortunate as it suggests an inflated notion of individualism, as though people can somehow transcend their time and place, the matrix of culture and relationships that defines them. Even if this were somehow possible, the result would be an inhuman monster. That sort of ego-driven specialness is exactly the opposite of what Jung meant by individuation— the gradual reorientation to a deeper reality that loosens the grip of complexed reactions and allows people to open to those around them in a less egocentric way.[428] Individuation is not a matter of developing one's full potential through an act of will but a process of surrender, *kenosis* in Christian terms, that preserves the personal viewpoint while relativizing its power. As people become less ruled by personal history and societal narratives, awareness shifts to the larger picture and the actual people and situations in front of them. They do not transcend their humanity;

---

[425] Jung, *Memories, Dreams, Reflections*, 72, 73.
[426] Jung, "Psychotherapy Today," CW 16, ¶216.
[427] Jung, 1961. "Symbols and the Interpretation of Dreams," *The Symbolic Life*, CW 18, ¶¶589–592.
[428] Jung, 1942/1948. "A Psychological Approach to the Dogma of the Trinity," *Psychology and Religion: West and East*, CW 11, ¶292.

they become fully human, with a deep responsibility to the surrounding community.

In Christian terms, the shift Jung is describing could be compared to putting on the mind of Christ, the way God lives through a particular person in her or his unique life circumstances, just as divinity was fully expressed in an itinerant peasant prophet in Roman-occupied Palestine. For Jung, imitating Christ does not mean doing what Jesus did back then but what Christ would do now, given who we are and what's happening around us.[429] In this view, people become themselves to the extent they embody the particular qualities that the larger Self would bring to their specific situation, given their unique gifts and personality, much the way light shining through a crystal highlights the idiosyncratic character of a given stone, flaws and all.

So what does this look like in practice? I have tracked an example of its partial unfolding over the course of the book. My account of this journey is drawing to a close, not because Mark's story was over but because that's as far as he traveled with me. His spiritual development, although incomplete and often stumbling, serves to illustrate a number of universal themes that offer a natural point of comparison between the Jungian and traditional religious models.

Before examining these in detail, it is worth noting a couple of overarching trends in his spiritual and psychological development. Over time, Mark became less reactive to those around him, an outward manifestation of his increased freedom from inner compulsions. In Jungian language, such compulsions are *complexes*, distorted reactions based in earlier relationships that become virtually reflexive. Their expression runs the gamut from caretaking to mass murder, and another era might describe their most extreme forms in terms of *demonic forces*, an idea not entirely dissimilar from Jung's concept of *autonomous complexes*.[430] Mark's complexes came up with a vengeance once he began engaging the images arising from his unconscious, just as St. Anthony was tormented by demons in the silence of the desert.[431] As these gradually eased their

---

[429] Jung, 1929. "Commentary on the Secret of the Golden Flower, Alchemical Studies," CW 13, ¶¶80, 81.
[430] Jung, 1934. "A Review of the Complex Theory, The Structure and Dynamics of the Psyche," CW 8, ¶204; Jung, 1926. "Spirit and Life," CW 8, ¶¶582–584.
[431] Athanasius of Alexandria, *The Life of Saint Anthony of Egypt.*

hold, the internal narratives through which Mark defined himself and others became more nuanced and open to change.

This shift happened in relation to those around him as well as in his relationship to God and his Christian upbringing. Mark's harsh view of his early life softened as he felt less need to steel himself against it. Painful memories remained; however, he also saw the good in difficult family relationships. As his worldview grew less polarized, the people in his life seemed to become more complicated. And as his relationship with God deepened, his perspective became less dogmatic, whether the dogmas he had grown up with or those he acquired in adulthood. He had less need for others' testimony now because he had experienced God directly, as the Samaritan woman's neighbors told her once they met Jesus for themselves.[432]

I haven't focused much attention on Mark's relationship with the larger social world around him but that also grew less rigid and polemic, "less Manichean" in his words, a sardonic reference to a highly dualistic religion that was an early competitor with Christianity. This new openness allowed him to discover opportunities for service in familiar settings he had previously written off, such as church or AA, now he had less need to safeguard his uniqueness by focusing on their shortcomings.

Having identified a few broad themes, I will take a look at some of the frequently cited milestones he passed along the way. The roadmaps I am using are Jungian and Christian, not because these are the only ones available but because they best fit my journey with Mark. The Jungian map is not necessarily Christian, of course, any more than the Christian map is intrinsically Jungian. The two can work well together, however, as I have attempted to demonstrate.

Purgation: Encountering the Shadow

The first step on the spiritual path is often to lose one's way and Mark's path was no exception. At some point, the accustomed ways of doing things do not work anymore and the old world starts falling apart. This change can be sudden, as with the death of a child or loss of livelihood, or incremental, like growing estrangement in a marriage or the gradual

---

[432] John 4:42.

erosion of religious faith. People then make various efforts to reestablish equilibrium but eventually these become untenable.

At this juncture there are two choices: they can deny the problem and blame those around them or admit they are lost and take responsibility for their predicament. In twelve-step language, the road to healing begins when addicts admit their life has become unmanageable, spinning out of control in ways they are helpless to fix.[433] Mark had come to this realization many years earlier in regard to his drinking; now he was forced to admit that major parts of his life were not working for reasons other than alcohol, although he had no clear idea what those might be. As with his addiction, he knew deep down that he was the problem, but his attempts to change only left him more frustrated and irritable. Achieving sobriety had required depending on a higher power. That's what he thought he was doing during the early stages of our work together. As time went on, however, Mark uncovered layer on layer of ways he still tried to impose his will on the world, attempts at control that even extended to God.

Religious writers often describe the spiritual journey in terms of three stages: Purgation, Illumination, and Divine Union.[434] The first, Purgation, begins with a transforming awareness of one's capacity for evil, the dark side of the personality that Jung called the *shadow*. Coming to terms with shadow requires learning to accept, even love, one's weaknesses and limitations without excusing the havoc they wreak. The process is never-ending and resurfaces in new forms throughout the spiritual journey.

Seekers enter this stretch of the path from many directions. St. Anthony's spiritual warfare in an abandoned desert fort, an iconic image that set the tone for the emerging Christian contemplative tradition, involved literal withdrawal into a solitary world. By contrast, Mark remained engaged with society and encountered the shadow in relation to those around him. Hell is not really other people, as Sartre famously claimed, but that's where shadow is most likely to rear its head.[435]

Mark's confrontation in the box store parking lot took on mythic proportions in his symbolic landscape and became a touchstone in our work together. Although it was not any worse than previous incidents—in fact it was better than most since no blows were actually exchanged—he

---

[433] Anonymous, *Twelve Steps and Twelve Traditions*, 21.
[434] Underhill, *Mysticism*.
[435] Sartre, *No Exit and Three Other Plays*, 45.

now saw it through new eyes. Despite feelings of shame, there'd always been an undertone of self-admiration as, with a sort of giddy amazement, he watched himself explode. This time he saw himself as others did, a middle-aged man being a jerk. As with other such incidents, it had a dreamlike quality. One moment he was arguing in the checkout line, and the next he found himself stalking the parking lot with a club in his hand. It was not as though he had blacked out, however, or did not know what he was doing, the excuse he had given himself in the past. He was dimly aware of making choices along the way, all of which seemed justified at the time. They still did, for that matter, when he reconnected with his rage at being treated as though he did not matter, a hackneyed action movie always running in some internal multiplex about the ordinary guy who's finally had enough and goes rogue.

Meanwhile, his grownup self could only hang its head in embarrassment, glumly wondering whatever possessed him. This tug-of-war between rage and shame was nothing new and always ended in stalemate. Mark bounced between suicidal self-recrimination and grim determination to do better in the future until the whole thing faded from awareness, at least until the next time he felt slighted. But this time it was not going away.

Another voice had entered the argument, a calm firm presence who was not buying it. Like the parents of a teenager who refuse to get sidetracked by drama, it gently refocused him on the need to take responsibility for his actions. It was not enough simply to wonder helplessly what had gotten into him or invoke psychological explanations he had learned in therapy. These were true as far as they went—his violent overreaction really was a trauma response, and he really did flip into abused child mode whenever he felt threatened, whether by strangers, supervisors, or people close to him. Although this knowledge was important, it did not change things in the moment, any more than knowing about alcoholism keeps people sober. Therapists talk about using insight as a defense when clients invoke their psychological issues to justify their actions, such as the compulsive philanderer who's quick to cite feeling unloved as a child. Mark's shame over his anger outbursts functioned in a similar way, eclipsing the actual event in a suicidal spiral that quickly took on a life of its own. But that was changing.

In Christian terms, this new voice entering his awareness presaged the illuminative phase of the spiritual journey. To invoke a different model, he had entered the *Dark Night of the Senses* that descends when we stop projecting godlike qualities on our human selves, a shift that happens naturally with age if we are honest with ourselves and so become less self-centered in our relationships with God and others.[436] The more profound *Dark Night of the Soul,* or *Spirit* comes later, if at all, when the human characteristics we project onto God fall away, leaving us floating in nothingness.[437]

At this point in his journey, Mark still felt the old patterns tugging at him, yet something had shifted. He had a hard time articulating the change and finally decided it was the difference between Judas and Peter, an insight that took on increased importance over the course of our work together. The idea first surfaced during an imaginative engagement with scripture after I encouraged him to try the Ignatian technique of placing himself in the characters' shoes and taking their stories as his own. Gospel accounts of the Crucifixion set up a contrast between the two errant disciples, something I had never noticed until he brought it to my attention.

Both men betray their friend and mentor, not to mention the presence of God within themselves, but their responses to the ensuing guilt go in very different directions. Judas could not live with this new awareness of his darkness and hung himself to keep from facing it.[438] When Mark looked at the incident through Judas's eyes, suicide preserved his idealized picture of himself, still the tragic hero of the story. It also kept control firmly in his own hands: judge, jury and executioner, as assistant DAs like to say at murder trials. Things looked very different when he saw the world through Peter's eyes. The account of his triple denial of Jesus in the high priest's courtyard is repeated in all four Gospels, a central narrative in the emerging Christian story. Each writer highlights different details. All of them linger over the moment when Peter first took in the full extent of his perfidy and cowardice. In Luke's cinematic version, Jesus's eyes search out his own at the very instant when the prophesied cockcrow fills the air.[439] We are left to guess the content of that glance; however, it changed everything for Peter, who went out immediately and wept bitterly.

---

[436] John of the Cross, "Book I: Night of Sense," *Dark Night of the Soul.*
[437] John of the Cross, "Book II: Night of the Spirit," *Dark Night of the Soul.*
[438] Matthew 27:5.
[439] Luke 22:60–62.

Just as Mark's parking lot meltdown was for him, the event appears to have been a turning point in Peter's life. The fact his private moment of shame is recounted in all four Gospels suggests he not only took personal responsibility for his actions but also claimed them publicly. In Jungian terms, he embraced his shadow. As we know from the rest of the New Testament, this does not mean he excused his darkness or justified his actions; rather he squarely faced the humbling knowledge of what he was capable of. Opening himself to Jesus's compassionate gaze, which saw him completely with eyes of love and acceptance, allowed Peter to acknowledge his flaws and repent.

That's what Judas could not bring himself to do. In Mark's version of the story he simply could not humble himself to receive the proffered forgiveness. Mark had added a final dialogue between Jesus and his betrayer to the standard Gospel account, a technique encouraged by Ignatius, one last effort on the Savior's part to reestablish relationship. As the scene really came to life for Mark, he joked about getting in touch with his inner Judas. He found the archetypal traitor disturbingly easy to relate to, proud and self-possessed to the end.

Peter's story also spoke to his experience, and the apostle's wordless exchange with Jesus struck a chord. Mark associated Jesus's piercing gaze with the new voice that had entered his own internal dialogue, disrupting the old pattern of suicidal rumination and ruining his self-pity. This process had actually begun in the parking lot when he first saw himself through these new eyes, not a tough guy after all but a grown man acting like a brat. In the past, this vision would only have fed his self-loathing. When Mark viewed himself through Jesus's compassionate eyes, he saw the frightened child underneath, a part of himself he could hardly stand to look at.

Mark told me about an apocryphal anecdote from Peter's later life that he had run across somewhere in his random reading. In this account, Peter was the acknowledged leader of the fledgling church when a new wave of persecution hit Rome. He managed to escape by the skin of his teeth and was headed out of town when a familiar voice gently inquired if he was going do it all over again. At this he *turned around,* a phrase that connotes repentance and conversion in the original Greek, returning to face his own inverted crucifixion.

A less dramatic kind of death awaited Mark, not martyrdom or suicide but the long hard road of Purgation. Many Jungians see suicide as a misguided literalization of the necessary process of diminishment that feels like death to the reigning ego.[440] Although the small self may grudgingly accept its limitations and allow the larger Self to take precedence, it never cedes ground without a fight. "He must increase, and I must decrease,"[441] John the Baptist said of Jesus, who in turn called him the greatest of men but least in the Kingdom of Heaven.[442] Something similar happens over the course of this renegotiation, a coming into right relationship that puts us in our place. Jung described this slow relativization of ego as a painful communion in which we eat our own flesh and drink our own blood.[443] It is a long slog, in most cases, and he stressed the need for Christian virtues such as patience and perseverance in sticking with it, the same self-discipline traditionally associated with the purgative stage.[444]

In twelve-step terms, Mark was being challenged to admit his powerlessness[445] and make a searching and fearless moral inventory,[446] turning over unresolvable conflicts to his higher power and surrendering resentments, forgiving as he was forgiven. Over the course of this slow and demanding soul work, more and more levels of ego disclosed themselves, pockets of willfulness that played havoc in his relations with others, including his marriage and his relationship with God.

The laser beam of scrutinizing light was not confined to current events. During prayer and at odd moments during the day, cringeworthy memories he had not thought about in years bobbed to the surface like bubbles in a stagnant pond. Petty and hurtful incidents ran like movie clips, a phenomenon Thomas Keating refers to as unloading the unconscious and Buddhists call emptying the karmic storehouse.[447] From the perspective of Christian spirituality, God's light was highlighting his darkness as long forgotten meannesses rose to the surface just as a log will sweat, smoke, and sputter when fire penetrates its depths, the earthy image John of the Cross used to describe this process.[448]

---

[440] James Hillman, *Suicide and the Soul,* 201.
[441] John 3:30.
[442] Luke 7:28.
[443] Jung, 1955-56/1968. *Mysterium Coniunctionis,* CW14, ¶512.
[444] Jung, 1946. "The Psychology of the Transference," CW 16, ¶¶385, 522.
[445] Anonymous, *Twelve Steps and Twelve Traditions,* 21.
[446] Anonymous, 42.
[447] Thomas Keating, *Open Mind, Open Heart: The Contemplative Dimension of the Gospel,* Chapter Seven, 95–114.
[448] John of the Cross, "The Living Flame of Love: Stanza 1," *The Collected Works of St. John of the Cross,* 649.

The humbling slideshow was rendered just bearable by the compassionate gaze that saw and loved him as he was. It felt as though every defense was being dismantled, a stripping process he associated with the Stations of the Cross where every protection is taken from Jesus, from legal status to his loincloth, leaving him naked, alone, and exposed. One of the trickiest parts of our work together involved helping Mark discern when this process of repentance tipped over into *scrupulosity*, the same excessive self-castigation that led Ignatius to keep confessing past misdeeds until his confessor finally ordered him to stop.[449]

At this point it might be useful to pause a moment and take stock of where we are. I have been examining Mark's story through two lenses. The first is Jungian, especially Jung's concept of the encounter with shadow. The second lens is the purification process associated with Purgation, the first stage of the spiritual path in the traditional religious model, although I have also noted elements of the later illuminative stage. Such conceptual models are useful, though they can feel a little bloodless and do not convey the ambiguity and messiness of what happens in an actual life. Here mythology and literature are vital in creating a vivid vocabulary of images and stories that capture the universal human experience in all its complexity.

The preeminent portrayal of the spiritual journey in Western literature is Dante's *Divine Comedy,* which not only provides a sweeping overview of the Christian vision of the spiritual path but also places it within the larger framework of Western culture and illustrates its every turn with arresting imagery. The epic's amplitude offers a rich counterpoint to my exploration of an individual spiritual journey, filling in the gaps of what happens in a single human life and explicating in lush detail what may be only suggestive hints in a given person's experience.

The next section will review Mark's spiritual odyssey against the backdrop of this quintessential account of the journey, which provides yet another lens through which to view the spiritual path, a less conceptual perspective grounded in religious imagination. Because Dante's opus offers a detailed map of the Christian model of the spiritual path, it will also serve as the framework for exploring the next two stages, the illuminative and unitive phases. I will examine these aspects of Mark's

---

[449] Joseph Munitiz and Philip Endean, "Reminisces or Autobiography of Ignatius Loyola," *Saint Ignatius of Loyola: Personal Writings,* 22, 23.

experience in the context of the poem and explore parallel stages in Jung's more psychological model.

Mark's *Purgatorio*

By way of a quick refresher for those who haven't thought about it since high school, the *Divine Comedy* famously begins when the narrator finds himself lost in the dark wood of middle life.[450] Wild animals associated with primal instincts such as pride, lust, greed, violence, and deception bar his ascent to the spiritual heights, just as manifestations of shadow block access to the Self in Jung's model. The only way forward requires descent. Accompanied by his poetic mentor, Virgil, Dante is plunged into the underworld where they literally go through Hell.

Descent into the underworld is a classic motif across mythological traditions, a pattern Jung saw as an archetypal symbol of being drawn into the unconscious.[451] Whether in mythology or the dreams of contemporary individuals, the first things encountered there are usually disturbing. Many of Mark's early dreams were set in the underworld, and he ran across Dante's imagery while researching dream images on the internet. A particularly grotesque set of engravings spoke to him, so he ordered the translation with those images. Although he had been exposed to the *Inferno* in a freshman literature class, he had a very different experience reading it now. The first thing that struck him about Dante's Hell was the self-absorption of its occupants. Characters whose speeches had once sounded grandly tragic now seemed merely myopic and full of themselves. Jungians call this *negative inflation*, the kind of maudlin posturing Mark associated with his suicidal "inner Judas."

The second thing that impressed him about the damned was their stasis. Nobody was going anywhere; they either wandered in agitated circles or stood rooted in place, calling out to Dante as he passed. Like robots in amusement park rides that spring to life when you approach them, Mark pictured Hell's inhabitants delivering the same impassioned speeches over and over. His description reminded me of what psychoanalytic writers call a *repetition compulsion*, in which destructive behaviors are repeated ad

---

[450] Dante, *The Divine Comedy*, 16–18.
[451] Jung, *Memories, Dreams, Reflections*, 181.

nauseam.[452] In Jungian terms, Dante's Hell represents the circular world of complexes where maladaptive narratives are reenacted without insight or change, much the way people may play out the same self-defeating patterns in relationship after relationship.

As do many readers, Mark relished the dark pathos of Dante's Hell and the gruesome poetic justice of its punishments. He soon bored of Purgatory and skipped ahead to the culminating vision of the epic. It is hard to beat the box office draw of articulate evil, but the processes depicted in the *Purgatorio* are the prime crucible for transformation in most accounts of the spiritual life. This place of rehabilitation for the soul is located on an island rising out of a sea of unconsciousness, a very Jungian image, and the climb represents the first leg of the long and arduous ascent that will take Dante to the heavens.[453] The two poets' upward movement balances their previous descent to the pit of hell, where Satan's hairy flank provided an inadvertent bridge along which they crawled out of his domain.[454]

If you look at this image from a Jungian perspective, the way to the Self lies through the shadow, and opening to this experience of darkness and alienation is the first step toward spiritual transformation, like the twelve-step idea of hitting bottom. The view of sin in the *Purgatorio* is surprisingly modern and accords well with Jungian thought. Contrary to the usual stereotype of medieval spirituality, the poem emphasizes the positive impulse behind various transgressions, which represent the product of unbalanced desires that are basically healthy yet misdirected.[455] Purgatory is where these diverted motivations are redirected and purified. The antidote for a given sin usually involves internalizing the opposite quality, "conviviality for wrath"[456] and "exertion for sloth,"[457] in keeping with Jung's core principle of psychological compensation[458] and Ignatius's

---

[452] The psychoanalytic concept of a repetition compulsion was introduced by Sigmund Freud in a 1914 article entitled "Remembering, Repeating and Working-Through," which described the unconscious need to repeat a traumatic experience or situation. See Sigmund Freud, "Remembering, Repeating, and Working Through: Further Recommendations on the Technique of Psychoanalysis II," SE 12, 145–157.
[453] Dante, *The Divine Comedy*, Canto III of *Purgatorio*, 302–307.
[454] Dante, Canto XXXIV of *The Inferno*, 264–269.
[455] Dante, Canto XII of *Purgatorio*, 430–432.
[456] Dante, *The Divine Comedy*, Canto XVII of *Purgatorio*, 429–432.
[457] Dante, Canto XIII of *Purgatorio*, 438–440.
[458] Jung, 1921/1971. *Psychological Types*, CW 6, ¶¶693–695.

idea of *agere contra*,[459] in which we do the opposite of whatever disordered desires urge us toward.

Insight enters the picture when the inhabitants of Purgatory surrender to a fuller perspective that takes them outside their solitary prisons of resentment and self-justification. This kind of insight into the bigger picture is a central feature of the inner Illumination associated with the second phase in the spiritual journey. In Purgatory the dead are not isolated anymore, as in Hell. Instead, they work together in groups and are integrated into the larger whole.[460] Unlike the damned, they are willing to accept direction from their angelic guides. Dante himself has enjoyed personal guidance from the beginning of his journey, not just Virgil's mentorship but intimations of the divine awareness that is choreographing his entire spiritual odyssey.

An unseen current moves beneath the surface of the poem, reminding Mark of his retrospective awareness of a guiding presence throughout his own life, even during times when he felt completely abandoned and alone. There had always been isolated moments when a sense of meaning broke through, often in his darkest hours. Looking back he now sensed that it had been there all along, too big, and too close to see. An incident when he was backpacking alone in the mountains became a metaphor for this mysterious guidance, and he referenced it frequently during our sessions. Not unlike Dante, he lost the trail as the temperature fell and had to scramble up a steep incline in the dark to find a flat place to camp. Peering down the crumbling rock face in the morning, he could not believe he had managed to thread his way up without a flashlight. He literally could not visualize his route and had the uncanny sense of an unseen providence directing his feet.

Reading the *Purgatorio* as an undergraduate, or rather Cliff Notes from the college bookstore, he had assumed that the ministering spirits who train the dead like high-school coaches were a literary device on the part of the poet. Now he was not so sure. As his inward journey deepened, Mark sometimes encountered what seemed to be actual personalities, such as the helpful dream figures who engaged him in intense dialogue during active imagination and popped up at key moments during the day. They came and went, hanging at the edge of his inner peripheral vision,

---

[459] Munitiz and Endean, "The Spiritual Exercises," 286, Annotation 16.
[460] Dante, Canto XIII of *Purgatorio*, 438-439.

but the ongoing sense of a deeper presence remained. He could see it had been there in various forms throughout his life, beginning with his childhood certainty of Jesus's companionship. Later, a similar feeling of benevolent presence surfaced in nature, in positive drug experiences, and even during moments of despair.

Its continuity across widely divergent circumstances, looping in and out of his awareness on a timetable of its own, illustrates the pitfalls of trying to conceptualize the spiritual journey in terms of neat categories. Dante's epic, like most models of the spiritual path, presents stages that are clearly delineated and occur in sequence. In real life the path is usually far less linear. My account of Mark's journey has shown how stages blur and overlap. Flashes of what spiritual writers call *Illumination* may show up early, often prompting the journey in the first place, and there can even be glimpses of the culminating experience of Divine Union. Mark's dream of a hellish underworld populated by devouring ghosts offers this kind of revelatory foretaste when the small band of survivors comes to a barred exit and finds the words of the Shema written on the wall, a guiding image of essential unity.

Spiritual writers readily acknowledge this variability. Most still find it useful to divide the spiritual journey into rough stages based on the themes that predominate during each phase and its emotional tone. Many employ the image of an ascending spiral to portray gradual progress in which the same issues are confronted at each turn of the path. Jungian writers also speak in terms of successive phases when describing the process of individuation, with similar caveats regarding the uniqueness of individual experience.

I have been using the basic sequence articulated by Jung to examine developments in Mark's life, moving from shadow material to growing relationship with the inner/outer other and then to the larger unity that Jung called the Self. Like the three stages of the traditional religious model, these divisions can be helpful in understanding what's going on in a person's life; however, they need to be taken with a shaker of salt, as the zigzagging course of Mark's spiritual and psychological development illustrates. The shadowy parts of the personality never stop cropping up; they just get sneakier. As in Mark's case, the initial painful phase of reckoning with shadow is often punctuated by guiding intuitions and flashes of a deeper awareness. To the extent the Jungian Self represents the image of the God in human consciousness, these are instances of what the traditional religious model calls *Divine Illumination*, the second stage of the spiritual journey.[461]

Jung's description of the difficulties encountered in dealing with shadow material maps well on the concept of Purgation, the first leg of the traditional spiritual roadmap. His work adds a developmental dimension to this model by considering a person's life stage and the challenges associated with it. Although these stages reflect the biological realities of maturation and aging, their expression is partly determined by culture.

And then there is the personal piece. In keeping with the image of a spiraling spiritual path referenced earlier, people tend to encounter the same complexes at every stage of the journey. The adolescent dynamics Mark played out in his parking lot encounter took a different form in his marriage, spanning the Jungian categories of shadow and soul-image. Life transitions are typically a point of increased tension and serious problems can occur when individuals refuse to relinquish patterns associated with an earlier phase.

In terms of personality growth across the lifespan, Mark entered Dante's dark wood of middle life at the developmental juncture when it becomes increasingly clear to most people that not every talent comes to fruition and they are never going to be all they dreamed, whether this involves financial success or spiritual enlightenment. By midlife, the burst of grandiose optimism that enables adolescents to break free of childhood starts wearing thin. Psychologists talk about a series of necessary losses that challenge the ego's view of itself, whereas spiritual writers employ concepts such as the Dark Night of the Senses to describe this humbling experience of human limitation.[462]

As people age, the tension between intimations of eternality and mounting evidence of mortality intensifies, an experience of feeling suspended between Heaven and Earth that Jung compared to crucifixion.[463] Failure to surrender the intoxicating sense of endless possibilities appropriate to adolescence leads to what Jungians call the *puer dilemma*, a conflict Mark diagnosed in himself.[464] The reckless charm of the teenage years looks increasingly silly by middle age. The transition to adulthood

---

[461] Jung, 1952. "Answer to Job," CW 11, ¶558.
[462] John of the Cross, "Book 1: Night of Sense," *The Dark Night of the Soul*.
[463] Jung, 1935/42. "Introduction to the Religious and Psychological Problems of Alchemy," *Psychology and Alchemy*, CW 12, ¶24.
[464] Marie-Louise von Franz, *The Problem of the Puer Aeternus*.

can be a slow and painful process, especially in an affluent culture that makes it easy to preserve the illusion of youth. Mark liked to quote a line from a vintage rock song about hoping he died before he got old, which made perfect sense when he was young but became increasingly ironic with each passing year.

Like all psychological models, Jung's theory of the personality operates at the interface between universal developmental processes and personal history. A distinguishing feature of his contribution was Jung's insistence that personal psychology extends far beyond the individual person, an idea that anticipated later developments in the field. Historically, psychology has focused primarily on distorted attitudes developed in the family of origin. The last few decades have seen increased attention to the impact of the larger culture on the personality. Contemporary theorists stress the many dimensions of psychological history, encompassing personal, familial, and cultural experiences of success and trauma as well as individual temperament and vulnerabilities. Early relationships with crucial figures play a prominent role in personality formation, so does an individual's role within the family and the fit with caregivers and the surrounding community. Social psychologists stress the importance of factors such as immigration history and whether an individual belongs to a scapegoated minority group or grows up with the unreflective sense of identity typically associated with majority status. Cultural and familial trauma extends across generations, as I have witnessed for myself over several decades of working with Shoah survivors and their descendants.

At this point in Western society, psychological and sociological perspectives are so much a part of the cultural wallpaper that we do not even see them. Across denominational lines, there is a growing tendency within religious settings to frame problematic parts of people's lives in terms of psychological and cultural history. In effect, this represents a new perspective on sin that does not eliminate the importance of personal choice but emphasizes the unique challenges and temptations faced by every person and group. By contrast, most models of the spiritual path were developed before the rise of the social sciences and exist in a psychological and sociological vacuum, which we reenter through a kind of unconscious code-switching. Here Jung can be helpful in bridging disparate worldviews, although much work remains to be done in updating his understanding of cultural forces and their impact on the individual personality.

Illumination and the Soul-Image

With these overarching themes in mind, it is time to return to the specifics of the Jungian and religious models of spiritual growth. I have lingered over shadow and Purgation, parallel concepts that fill a similar niche in the two models. This demanding portion of the journey takes up the bulk of the space in most accounts of the spiritual path, just as it has in this discussion. I now turn to the remaining stages: Illumination and Divine Union in the traditional religious model and, for Jung, deepening relationships with the soul-image and the Self. Although parallels between them are less obvious than in the case of shadow and the purgative stage, there is a similar progression across the two models.

As before, I will use Dante's vision of the spiritual journey to bring the two systems into dialogue, moving back and forth between them to view the path from multiple perspectives. The task is made easier by Dante's habit of marking major transitions in his spiritual journey with a change of guide, figures who give a human face to each new phase he enters. Virgil leads him through Hell and Purgatory, but the pagan poet cannot enter Heaven, a prohibition that demonstrates the limits of unaided human reason in Dante's religious worldview.[465] In Jungian terms, the ego perspective can only take us so far, no matter how insightful we may be.

Dante's path of purgation has led him back to the Garden of Eden, the site of human beings' initial alienation from their divine source, and now another kind of guidance is needed.[466] At the threshold of Heaven he is met by his beloved Beatrice, perhaps the best-known expression of the soul-image in Western literature.[467] In theological terms, she represents human understanding illuminated by divine revelation, and, as such, she's the perfect guide for the illuminative phase of the spiritual journey. According to Dante, he only met the earthly Beatrice on two occasions, yet her presence haunted and inspired him for the remainder of his own life.[468] This devotion at a distance followed the pattern of courtly love celebrated by poets of his time, a cultural movement that helped shape the modern notion of romantic love. But, for Dante, Beatrice was not just an image of the ideal woman. She was also his salvation, according

---

[465] Dante, Canto XXVII of *Purgatorio*, 523–524.
[466] Dante, Canto XXVIII of *Purgatorio*, 527–532.
[467] Dante, Canto XXX of *Purgatorio*, 548–551.
[468] Dante, *La Vita Nuova (Poems of Youth)*, 3–6.

to the poet, an embodiment of divine love.[469] At one point in his journey through Heaven, Dante describes seeing the divine image reflected in her eyes, in keeping with a long tradition of the beloved guiding the soul toward God.[470] In Jungian language, she exemplifies the soul-image as a psychopomp or guide of souls, an internal figure that gives human form to the larger personality that opens into the deepest levels of the transpersonal Self.

In Western thought, the concept of human love leading beyond itself reaches back to Plato's claim that love for the beauty of the beloved is the first step toward the ultimate love of beauty and goodness in themselves.[471] The classical Platonic progression resonated with the deeply relational nature of Christianity. The idea of relationship with God as a love affair has taken many forms in Christianity through the centuries, including the image of Jesus as the lover of the soul. On the human level, Christian mystics make frequent reference to a soul friend or spiritual companion, often involving a spiritual romance with a soulmate of the opposite sex. Early examples include recurring speculation regarding Jesus's relationship with Mary Magdalene and *The Acts of Paul and Thecla*, a second-century work modeled on secular Roman romances. This rather breathless narrative, which circulated widely in the early Christian Era, chronicles the many perilous adventures and deep affection between the Apostle Paul and his female traveling companion.

More prosaic examples of spiritual romances abound in the spiritual diaries of many key figures within Christian spirituality. Often these describe a lofty spiritual kinship between mature mystics. Another genre of religious texts emphasizes the need to purify a spiritual connection tainted by inappropriate desires. In most of these, a male aspirant encounters a heavenly female figure who confronts him regarding his mixed motives toward her before going on to instruct him on spiritual themes. Examples include *The Shepherd of Hermas*, a second-century work included in several early canons of scripture. In these narratives, putting love in order on the level of human relationships allows the seeker to progress toward love of God, just as Dante must confess his past misdeeds to Beatrice before entering Heaven.[472] By this point in the poem, his period of Purgation has

---

[469] Dante, *The Divine Comedy,* Canto XXXI of *Purgatorio,* 554–559.
[470] Dante, Canto XXVIII of *Paradiso,* 842–847.
[471] Plato, "The Symposium," *Plato: Complete Works,* 492–493, Sections 210–212.
[472] Dante, Canto XXXI of *Purgatorio,* 554–559.

prepared him to receive the loving Illumination she represents, and he continues to grow in understanding and wisdom as the divine guidance embodied by his heavenly lover leads his pilgrim soul toward union with itself.

Allowing for very different language, you can find a similar progression in Jung, who drew on early Christian sources in his effort to understand the imagery in his patients' dreams. Jung's observation that the same relational patterns occur in people's dreams and their waking lives led him to conceptualize the soul-image as an inner/outer phenomenon that finds embodiment in flesh-and-blood relationships with human partners.[473] Intimate relationships offer particularly rich ground for mutual projection, intensifying the interplay between external presentation and internal expectations, which happens in every interpersonal exchange.

You've seen this over and over in the Mark chapters. The internal templates he brought to interactions with others led to similar conflicts and disappointments across his relationships, not only in his dealings with authority but also in his marriage and his relationship with God. Like reflections on water, images of these distorted patterns surfaced in dreams and reverie as alluring or terrifying figures. Their connection to his day-world relationships only became visible when Mark opened to the counterintuitive idea that he might be helping to create the misunderstandings that seemed to dog him everywhere, similar to the old joke about people who bring their own banana peels to slip on. Coming to terms with his unrealistic expectation of being perfectly understood and nurtured amounted to a kind of purgation. Other complexed relational patterns manifested in his instinctive gravitation toward the role of misunderstood rebel, a stance that narrowed his options in any situation and blocked him from assuming adult authority. This pattern was particularly hard to see because it always seemed to come from outside, a scripted dance of group dynamics that pursued him wherever he went. It reminded me of a patient I saw for anger management who complained about bar fights in every club he went to, an association I kept to myself.

Although Mark found it difficult to separate outer events and internal templates in his interactions with supervisors, complications multiplied when it came to his marriage. Where does projection end and the real person begin? The question comes up constantly in my work with couples.

---

[473] Jung, 1951/1968. *Aion*, CW 9ii, ¶¶24, 42.

There is no answer, of course, because our experience of intimate partners is always a mixture of internal longings and moment-to-moment encounters with a separate being who has moods, needs, and vulnerabilities of her or his own. By definition, partners embody the ideal man or woman, even when this gets expressed in terms of how they are not measuring up. Partners also carry all the negative images and expectations we bring to relationships, some of which have little to do with the actual person. In Mark's case, these were personified in dream images of frightening female figures with superhuman strength and malice, such as the witch in the night kitchen or the woman who tosses her severed head.

These nightmare images decreased as the couple began sorting through their relationship with the help of a couples' therapist, trying as best they could to figure out what belonged to whom. Getting in touch with his own vulnerabilities allowed Mark to see that he had burdened the relationship with a weight it could not possibly carry. Jennifer was not Beatrice. She was not going to save him, as silly as that sounded when said out loud, and she was not responsible for meeting his deepest longings or taking away his basic aloneness. Seen in this light, her human limitations were not such a deal breaker after all.

He was finally learning to manage his own emotions and nurture himself, the standard psychological interpretation of this internal shift, which was definitely true but not the whole story. For Mark and many like him, this change was made possible by a different kind of union that did not have anything to do with improving himself or his partner or seeking other relationships. As he reclaimed his most blatant projections onto Jennifer, mysterious female figures began appearing in his dreams. Often, they displayed very human idiosyncrasies and flaws, like the aging Catholic soulmate with the sniffles, an endearing detail that reminded me of the way he was learning to tolerate the imperfections that made Jennifer who she was. Over time, these inner figures assumed explicitly religious overtones and he came to understand that his engagement with them mirrored his deepening connection with God, a relationship with all the unpredictability of a marriage and the only one that could actually address his core sense of painful separateness.

Divine Union and the Self

In the Jungian model of spiritual growth, the soul image leads our conscious awareness toward the larger Self and the God-images at its core.

The God-images encountered there also point beyond themselves to the living reality beyond naming, which expresses its presence in the unique symbolic language of each particular person. Gradually or suddenly, the individual ego comes to realize it is not the master of its fate after all and assumes its smaller place within the larger unity. You find a similar surrender of separateness in the religious concept of Divine Union with God that comprises the final stage of the traditional model of spiritual development. This has been described in terms of *unitive awareness*—a profound sense of oneness as boundaries drop away and there is no division between self and others, me and the created world, God and human beings.

Because sexual union offers a natural image for this experience of longing and intimate merger, images of uniting with God in the form of a lover have a long history in Christianity and other spiritual traditions. Writers have used various metaphors to portray the stages of this progressively deepening union. By way of example, Teresa of Ávila and John of the Cross drew on courtship mores in the Spanish society of their time to track the soul's movement from spiritual betrothal to marital consummation, supplementing this relational imagery with such traditional mystical metaphors as a log becoming fire or seeds sprouting in the darkness.[474] A particularly important strain of mystical thought interpreted the biblical Song of Songs in terms of a love affair between God and the soul. Bernard of Clairvaux helped lay the groundwork for this branch of mystical theology when he characterized the different kinds of kisses mentioned in the text in terms of deepening spiritual maturity, from maternal suckling to sexual union.[475]

Like the Song of Songs, Dante's epic is a love poem, and love imagery pervades every phase of the journey, from the disordered love at its onset to its culminating vision of the loving intermingling of persons within the Godhead. An act of love sets Dante's quest in motion in the first place when Beatrice sends Virgil to save him from the deadly impasse at the beginning of the narrative and lead him safely through the terrors of the underworld.[476] For Dante the poet, the young woman he adored from afar has been transformed into an internal figure able to guide him

---

[474] Teresa of Avila, *Interior Castle;* John of the Cross, *The Dark Night of the Soul.*
[475] Bernard of Clairvaux, *Commentary on the Song of Songs.*
[476] Dante, Canto II of *Inferno*, 25–27.

toward salvation. After taking over from Virgil at the border of Purgatory, Beatrice delivers him to his final guide after an ascending path of deepening illumination. This last heavenly mentor is Bernard of Clairvaux himself, the mystic who helped establish the Christian tradition of God as lover. In the symbolic framework of the epic, he represents *contemplation*, the culminating stage of the spiritual progression that takes Dante from human reason to reason illuminated by divine wisdom and, finally, to ineffable reality beyond conceptualization.[477]

In keeping with the relational focus of the poem, two final visions of loving union complete Dante's spiritual voyage. In the first, he glimpses the entire created universe as an interrelated whole, a vast living rose with the Virgin Mary at its apex and the throng of heaven arrayed around her.[478] Jung would call this a *mandala*, a Christian example of circular forms that appear across spiritual traditions and enclose a sacred space representing essential unity, in which apparent opposites—female and male, divine and human—are contained and reconciled.[479]

In Dante's religious world, it is only natural that the human mother of God provides the focal point of the mandala, the God-bearer who births divinity into the world. From a Jungian standpoint, the anima leads toward the Self, and as this journey nears its goal Mary offers a more archetypal image of the inner guide than Dante's personal soulmate, Beatrice. Archetypes always span opposites, and the paradoxical Virgin Mother bridges the divine and human realms, an ability confirmed by her bodily assumption into heaven, according to one of Jung's more controversial pronouncements that offended secular critics and Protestant theologians alike.[480]

This bridging role becomes explicit in the next section of the poem when Bernard offers a fervent prayer to the Holy Mother on Dante's behalf.[481] Invoking her aid opens the way for the second and highest vision, in which he witnesses the internal dance of the Creator as the persons of the Trinity move in an endless exchange of mutual love.[482] The stanzas

---

[477] Dante, Canto XXIX of *Paradiso*, 875.
[478] Dante, Canto XXXII of *Paradiso*, 880–885.
[479] Jung, 1955. "Appendix: Mandalas," *The Archetypes and the Collective Unconscious*, CW 9i, ¶¶717,718.
[480] Jung, "Answer to Job," CW 11, ¶¶748–757.
[481] Dante, Canto XXXIII of *Paradiso*, 889–891.
[482] Dante, Canto XXXIII of *Paradiso*, 891–894.

that describe this sight are uncharacteristically abstract, the imagery less sharply defined than usual. At the threshold of Heaven, Dante the poet has warned us about the impossibility of describing what cannot be put into words[483] and nowhere is this truer than in his vision of the inner workings of the Godhead,[484] which can only be conveyed through metaphor. In Jungian terms, the Self expresses itself to us in images, transforming symbols that point toward the numinous reality beyond representation, which cannot be communicated directly.

This final image of dynamic unity represents the culmination of Dante's journey and ends my brief examination of the *Divine Comedy*. Before moving on, I want to reiterate a point made earlier. The point is not to subject a literary masterpiece to Jungian analysis, like sophomore English papers offering Marxist or post-colonial critiques of *Beowulf*. Dante's epic cannot be reduced to Jungian categories, any more than the biblical God can be reduced to the Jungian Self. My more modest goal has been to use Dante's rich imagery to help flesh out the Jungian and traditional Christian models of the spiritual journey, just as dream images turn psychological forces into human figures.

From a Jungian perspective, the *Divine Comedy* can be seen as a Christian active imagination that tracks the soul's spiritual development using images drawn from Dante's life and the culture in which he lived. It is a mark of Dante's genius that these images are both highly specific and universal in ways that reach across time and culture. His ability to integrate his life journey and the events that shaped it into the larger framework of Christian cosmology allows the poem to function as a sort of Rosetta Stone that translates between theology and individual psychology. In this way, its imagery provides a symbolic language that has enabled me to bring two disparate perspectives on the spiritual path into dialogue—Jung's model of an individual's movement toward their transpersonal depths and the Christian model of the soul's journey to God.

Being Himself in the Life He Was Already Living

Having followed Dante to his destination, it is time to step back and look back on our own journey. Over the course of these pages, I have

---

[483] Dante, Canto I of *Paradiso*, 596–597.
[484] Dante, Canto XXXIII of *Paradiso*, 893–894.

explored the disconnect between psychology and religion and ways in which Jung's model can help bring them together. It is not a perfect fit, by any means, but the Jungian framework remains a useful bridge, at least for some people. There is not a unified field theory of human unfolding, so any perspective is binocular at best. When it comes to ultimate reality, the only way to approach the inexpressible is to look at it from multiple angles, a kaleidoscopic viewpoint that disorganizes limited models and provides new metaphors for what cannot be put into words.

Something similar happens spontaneously in the human psyche, as Mark's dream material illustrates. Using images from his personal and cultural storehouse, the imagination helped draw him into relationship with the deepest reality by creating a symbolic and interactive roadmap of the soul's journey. Similar to the "You Are Here" signs in malls and parks, it showed him where he was and guided him along the way, an individual version of what Dante gave to Western culture. Following its flickering track, Mark established a personal relationship with God that was both like and unlike what he had known in childhood.

The long interior journey that began in the dark wood of middle life took him through a personal underworld peopled with figures both factual and imaginary. In Christian terms, he experienced Purgation and Illumination in his interactions with external and internal figures, including a life partner who spanned both realms. Like Dante, he found that the messy details of relationships in his outer life could not be separated from his spiritual journey. And also like Dante, he discovered that working through distortions in his human relationships helped clear impediments in his relationship with God. In Jungian terms, this is the path of individuation, a progressive separation from inner and outer compulsion that makes us more open to the leadings of the Self. The changes in Mark's general attitude described at the beginning of the chapter give a taste of this developmental shift, including a new openness to others and growing ability to live from his depths. His journey was far from complete when our work ended yet his path had already offered intimations of union with mysterious depths beyond anything he could imagine or conceptualize.

Is this the same as movement toward God? The question has come up repeatedly during our sojourn together, and the answer probably depends on what is meant by God, the Self, and the God-image at its core. All three are notoriously hard to pin down; essentially, they are names that point beyond themselves to something that transcends definition. In the end, it is probably safest to say that the paths toward them appear to lead in the same general direction, at least in the early stages of the journey.

That being said, Christian spirituality is not inherently Jungian any more than Jung's thought is inherently Christian, despite being stamped by his Christian culture. I could have approached the spiritual quest from any number of directions. Jung's atlas is not the only available guidebook, and there is nothing sacred about the traditional division of the spiritual path into Purgation, Illumination, and Divine Union. In terms of overlap with Jung, I have mentioned several prominent Christian mystics who also emphasized the sacred imagination, including Ignatius of Loyola, and many more could be added to the list.

What Jung brings to this rich legacy of spiritual guidance is a developmental and psychological perspective that resonates with our current understanding of the world. For spiritual seekers coming out of the Christian tradition, his way of grounding the spiritual journey in everyday life can breathe new life into traditional religious formulations. I witnessed a striking example of this convergence when Mark was undergoing his period of darkness. He was reading Jung by then and took comfort in the Jungian maxim that the path to the Self lies through the shadow.

Relationships are often where shadow makes its presence felt. Seeing his distorted relational patterns for what they were did not mean he could change them. He was powerless, in AA terms, and his sponsor's only advice was to turn them over to God and wait, a less than edifying prospect. Reflecting on this helpless feeling during one of our sessions, he remembered sermons he had heard in childhood about Paul's mysterious thorn in the flesh.[485] Whatever this unnamed affliction may have been, Paul tells us that he prayed repeatedly to have it removed and God's answer was always the same: my grace is sufficient for you and my power is made perfect in weakness.[486] Accepting this, Paul came to glory in his infirmity in much the same way that Jung speaks about our wounded places being the entryway of the Self. Suddenly a concept Mark espoused in a creedal way was coming to life before his eyes, illuminated from multiple directions, and all he could do was bow his head in gratitude.

---

[485] 2 Corinthian's 12:7.
[486] 2 Corinthians 12:9.

Virgil was not around to guide Mark's journey, so he had to make do with what he had. Fortunately for him, the limitations of his human guides, a group that included me, were balanced by internal guidance that showed up in dreams and intuitions, not to mention providential developments in the outer world. I did my best to read the signs, comforted to know that new ones would make up for those we missed. The real guide sat in the empty third chair.

From a Jungian perspective, Mark was largely contained within the Christian myth, yet it was not fully alive for him. He did not experience quite the same split between Sunday reality and the rest of the week that marked my childhood, but he had his own difficulties reconciling the two. In Jungian terms, this seemingly intractable conflict of values could not be solved but only outgrown through movement to a more comprehensive viewpoint, with the help of unifying symbols generated by the transcendent function.[487] This process can take many forms, and for him the first rumblings of spiritual renewal came through emotion, surges of religious feeling that baffled and embarrassed his intellectual self. Feeling was Mark's inferior function, in Jungian terms, and thus most open to messages coming through the unconscious. However inconvenient they might be, these perplexing experiences were too real to ignore and sparked a long quest to integrate what he knew and what he felt. It was not just a matter of bringing together different sides of himself, however. Another level was operating in him or through him, as he discovered when he found himself struggling not to sob out loud during a perfectly ordinary worship service. This was not simply a religious part of him that he had stowed away in adolescence, Mark slowly came to realize, but a living connection with a force beyond his understanding.

In Jungian terms, Mark's journey during the years I knew him helped integrate these preliminary intimations of transpersonal reality into ordinary life, as his conscious awareness recognized its limits and came to rest in the larger reality. His deepening relationship with God helped reconcile him to himself, including depths that opened into Divine Mystery. Guidance comes in various forms and a remarkable series of dream images translated religious truths he had known in childhood into a living language that could speak to his everyday experience.

---

[487] Jung, *Psychological Types*, CW 6, ¶¶824–829.

God works with everyone differently, the whole point of a personal relationship, and the imaginal aspects of Mark's journey were particularly strong for him. They were also confusing since they did not match his picture of how God leads believers, any more than the deity he encountered resembled the God of his childhood. Actually, the two had many similarities, which he realized as the relationship grew closer; they just looked different on the surface.

This God was personal as well, although not in the way he expected. This God definitely knew him inside out and was able to turn the intimate details of his life into personalized religious symbols. Perhaps most surprising of all, the whole experience of spiritual renewal turned out to be oddly ordinary, something he struggled with given his desire for dramatic change. As often happens, Mark's spiritual growth did not so much introduce anything new into his world as enable him to see it with new eyes. In the end, God appeared to expect him to simply be himself in the life he was already living, albeit from a broader perspective, a shift he described as having a new center of gravity. For my part, I was grateful to witness a portion of this transformation, one of the sacred perks of being a spiritual director, with the usual human curiosity about what happened next. But that is another story, which is not mine to tell.

Chapter 17
Epilogue

Five years after we began working together, Mark took a job in another state. Jennifer was in the process of a career change and a particularly good opportunity opened up in the Midwest. He was ready for change himself and soon found a position with a community-based organization in the same city. It meant a pay cut, but the cost of living was lower there and Jennifer would be making more. He was excited about the job itself, which gave him free rein to develop programs for high-risk families and allowed him to follow them long-term. "This isn't like my impulsive moves in the past," he assured me, "what we call a geographic in the program. It's true I'm itching for something new, I always am, but the move makes sense in lots of ways. We can even afford a house there if we want."

He and I discussed various options for continuing spiritual direction, including meeting remotely or finding a new director once he got settled. After reflection, Mark decided to take a break from direction altogether and see where things stood in a few months. "Right now I feel like this boa constrictor I saw in a clip on the internet," he told me. "It had swallowed some large animal, probably a deer calf, and could barely move. You could see the outline under the skin, like some weird kind of whole-body pregnancy, and according to the caption it was going to take weeks to digest. That's how my spiritual life feels at the moment, like I've swallowed the ocean and need awhile to metabolize it." Mark and I spent our final sessions reviewing his experience over the last few years, an enlarged version of the Ignatian repetition in which directees go back over the ground they've covered to see how God has moved in their lives. I told him I would be praying for him and encouraged him to feel free to contact me in the future.

He emailed a few times soon after they arrived, describing the new job and their search for a faith community. I hadn't heard from him in several months when I received an email marked "Salutations From The Heartland!" with a lengthy letter attached. He started with news. Jennifer was enjoying her new career and the relationship was going well. They had found a church they both liked and were hosting a small study group in their home. Mark was taking an active role in the local twelve-step community. He had begun chairing a meeting at a recovery center and was scheduled to cofacilitate a recovery-based workshop at a nearby retreat center. He found his new job challenging yet satisfying and felt like he was really making a difference in his clients' lives. Mark went on to describe his spiritual life over the past few months. The waves of cringe-worthy memories that he referred to as "psychological night sweats" were coming less often now, although they still happened from time to time. He also felt less flooded during Centering Prayer and frequently had the sensation of resting in a peaceful place beneath the churn of thoughts and emotions.

"Like when I used to dive," he continued, and I smiled to myself, remembering his vivid metaphors and similes. "I'd swim down a ways and then roll over on my back to look back up at the surface where the light got all chopped up by the waves, like a fractured sky overhead. But no matter how rough things were up there everything was calm and cool down where I was, drifting gently back and forth in the little currents playing along the ocean floor. My life's calmer all the way around these days, and I'm slowly adjusting to the idea that's not necessarily a bad thing. I don't get the soaring highs I used to when God and I first started dating but that's OK. We have our ups and downs, but most of the time it's just steady, like an old married couple who know the other one's there even when they're in different rooms. Now the honeymoon's over I don't have to worry as much what God thinks of me or if I'm holding up my end of the conversation if that makes sense. Assuming you can marry the wind or the landscape you're walking in (sounds like a line from a bad sixties folk song)."

After sharing a few more details about recent developments in his inner life, Mark moved to a couple dreams he wanted to share. He already had a good working relationship with them and said he was not looking for input but wanted to pass them along because they seemed related to the work we had done. He thought they might be a reaction to our wrap-up sessions, the psyche weighting in with her response and not pulling any punches as usual. The rest of the chapter is in his words, although I have edited out some of the more personal parts.

Dream 1

I'm giving an impromptu lecture on Gandhi's ethics to a small group in an upstairs room, probably at a church. It's late evening and I'm tired. I talk about his religious orthodoxy, saying he read the Vedas and the Upanishads and supported a Muslim colleague's call for sharia. I emphasize ritual aspects of his practice as a traditional Hindu and tell the usual joke about him reading the New Testament and saying Christianity would be a great religion if only it had been tried. As I talk, I feel something on the floor in front of me and pick it up idly with my left hand before discovering it's dried dog shit and letting it drop. I can't wash my hand and hold it away from me uncomfortably. I say it's getting late for people and ask what they'd like to hear about before we close, aware I'm losing the audience. Someone asks what all this means in practice, and I begin speaking on ahimsa. I warm to the topic and rise to my feet, pacing excitedly as I talk. I describe Gandhi's ethics as incarnational, in Christian terms, and talk about joining with your opponent, holding him close, and absorbing his violence against you without opposing him. I picture this vividly, moved to tears as I speak.

That's the dream, thought you'd get a kick out it. I won't do a systematic exposition—especially given its opinion of my lectures—but had a couple thoughts I wanted to share. Starting with the location, which is obviously significant. An upstairs room recalls the last supper, of course, and Jesus's final teachings, but it seems my own teaching isn't going so well. (So maybe I'm not Jesus after all???) It's "probably" a church so there's an ambiguous relationship to institutional religion like the twelve-step groups in the church basement. Timewise it's late evening and I'm tired. I haven't reached the sunset of life yet (hopefully), but anyway you do the math, the shadows are definitely lengthening. A new day may be dawning, but I've come to the end of the phase I was in when I first met you. The old way of doing things is getting tired—what you used to call an outworn attitude—but I just keep plugging away at my lecture like a cranky kid who won't go to bed (which reminds me, Jen's niece and nephew are coming to spend the summer with us and—before you ask—yes, I'm looking forward to the visit).

An impromptu lecture in a lowkey setting is definitely the right tack now I've finally accepted I don't have the background or attention span to be a scholar (ergo the Eleventh-Step workshop scheduled later this year), but in the dream I'm droning on like a tenured professor anyway. Apparently, I'm not even listening to myself since I completely miss the contradiction (at best paradox) between Gandhi's supposed religious orthodoxy and doing things that went beyond it, what got him killed in the end. That's Jesus's story too, of course, and much of my journey with you was figuring out what orthodoxy means for me (let alone orthopraxy since truth is in the doing, at least for me). Practically speaking it mainly meant unlearning most of what I thought I knew. Correct interpretation of scripture was everything when I was growing up, including about topics the Bible never addressed and things we couldn't possibly know—which is probably why our churches kept splitting like beehives. The dream equates orthodoxy with pluralism, yet another shock to my poor inner Evangelical. Ecumenism isn't theoretical in a country like India that takes its religion very seriously and Gandhi's ethics were all about praxis (to the best of my very limited knowledge), but I launch into bloodless abstractions anyway. My quote growing edge over the last few years has been putting intellect in its place but apparently the "dream me" didn't get the memo. By the time I get to my canned joke about Christianity never having been tried I'm far too enamored of my own cleverness and the kindest interpretation would be that I've lost sight of my audience—which is where the whole concept of ahimsa comes in.

That's when the unconscious weighs in with a pointed critique. (Or should I say the Holy Spirit delivers a critique via the unconscious?) My father loved to quote Paul about all our righteousness being as filthy rags, but the message here is all my pontificating is so much dogshit, dry and stale as my one-liners. Talk about being brought down to earth, probably the reason we keep dogs in the first place. I drop the turd when I see what I'm holding but the feeling of contamination remains. You and I talked lots about how the notion of ritual impurity shaped my concept of sin and salvation but in this soteriology there's no way to clean myself. A coworker of mine with OCD said part of treatment was getting his hands muddy and not being able to wash them as the mud slowly caked and smeared all over everything he touched, which still gives me the shivers. The left is typically the unconscious side, like coming out of left field or the left pillar of the Sephirot, and the left hand is the "bad hand" in lots of cultures, the one you use to wipe yourself according to Guru Google. Of course there's always the verse about not letting your right hand know what your left hand is doing but I'm not as good at that as I used to be.

In the dream I try to preserve my platonic purity like a good Pharisee. It turns out I'm just another guy with dirty hands like that spooky Gnostic text I showed you about waking up to find your hands covered with blood. It's interesting to think about Gandhi having dirty hands. He couldn't't escape the ambiguities of his political situation any more than MLK (or Jesus for that matter!), the inevitable byproduct of incarnation. It's the difference between handwashing and foot washing in John—being pure versus being useful. Jesus was all about opening fully to our ambiguous situation and reaching out to others from our brokenness, as they say. I used to think living the social Gospel got me off the hook—before I even knew what it was—but the truth is I don't like taking a fearless and searching moral inventory any better than the next guy. Not the giant of our dreams or the dwarf of our nightmares, as we used to say in the program back in the bad old days before political correctness.

But I pontificate. Again. Acknowledging the shit on my own hands wakes me up and I actually see my audience for the first time. I finally get around to asking what they want and realize they're tired too. Turns out I need to stop being smart and give them something useful. I start crying, which is usually a good sign (at least in sobriety). So the obvious question is what does all this have to do with ahimsa and why am I dreaming about a Hindu concept I don't really even understand?

I've never actually read Gandhi beyond spiffy quotes, but I heard the phrase somewhere along the way and assumed it was just a fancy word for nonviolence. Turns out to be more complicated than I thought, like most things actually. Near as I can tell ahimsa is a whole other way of relating to people and the natural world, not setting yourself apart or against but accepting them fully even when they're trying to kill you. It extends the concept of nonviolence to a general attitude of noncoercion, the core dynamic behind all forms of violence. That's exactly what I'm doing when I fail to recognize my audience's existence, rattling on self-importantly and losing touch with the people in front of me. Self-absorption is a form a violence, like me repeating Gandhi's snarky joke about Christianity in a church.

From the perspective of ahimsa other people's viewpoints have equal weight to our own and you hold even your enemies close, absorbing their violence without anger or retaliation. That's what Gandhi did with his dying breath when he said, "Oh God" and literally reached out to his assassin after being shot. It's also the attitude in the beatitudes, of course, which gets embodied in the passion narrative. That's why the dream implies that orthodoxy is pluralistic, like the story about Gandhi telling a Hindu man who wanted to atone for killing Muslims during the riots to adopt a Muslim orphan and raise him Muslim (at least according to the movie). Which is all well and good when it comes to India, but it also means loving my Fundamentalist neighbor without trying to change him, including my inner Evangelical, which brings the whole thing home to roost.

That's even harder than it sounds, probably on a neurological level. Not just the standard guy thing of me-against-the-world but how we mammal folk perceive reality. So once again, why am I dreaming about a utopian concept I don't even understand? The longer you look at the dream the more levels it has (like most dreams) and all of them apply to me (which is less flattering than it sounds). They say life is the teacher and the first lesson I've had to learn is I'm not the king of the world. Not a prophet or one of the sons of the prophets, as old Amos said (sounds like a Christian boyband). Not just having to be smart and funny but the smartest and funniest in the room—not to mention the humblest. And then there's my internal audience to wow and they're the toughest crowd of all. But once you adjust to being nobody special it's a huge relief not having to win them all.

I know it's too early to tell for sure, but I actually seem to be getting along with my supervisor, for the first time in my life. That's the social level of the dream, not in the sociological sense but how I relate to the people around me. I've been so inward focused the last few years it always catches me by surprise. Something new is coming to life, I can feel the difference but it's hard to put in words. Activists are famous for loving people in the abstract and detesting them in person, but occasionally you meet one who seems unpolarized somehow, even in advocacy work. Not quite on one side or the other, even when they take a stand, but coming at things from a whole different angle like the angels in C. S. Lewis's space trilogy who walk at a slant because they're oriented to another world. I'm not there myself but sometimes get hints of it, hearing myself say something and wondering where the hell did that come from? (But without back-patting or the old familiar sinking feeling of, oh shit, did I really just say that?) It's probably relevant that I'm still doing the Welcoming Prayer when I center, and it's a game changer even when I don't entirely mean it, sorta fake it till you make it like in the program. Just accepting what comes up—or at least opening to it—without a million ruminations about what it should be (not that I have a choice anyway, of course).

On the psychological level, accepting human limitations fosters an attitude of nonviolence toward myself and others. Noncoercion means not trying to pressure or please others but accepting them fully even while you're encouraging attitudinal change, something Gandhi modeled to a T. And of course it means noncoercion toward yourself, which turns out to be at least as hard. I really can't be better than I am no matter how hard I try. That's what the program is all about, of course, seeing ourselves for who we are with no do-overs and letting go of the past so we can live in the present (which is all there is anyway, om shanti, etc.). Leaving judgment to God for others and ourselves and let posterity take care of itself. On a spiritual level not having to justify my existence to God opens the door for moments of closeness that aren't as self-conscious or self-evaluative, aren't even about me for that matter. All this is getting pretty abstract (my sin of choice). In the end I don't think the dream is intended as some grand revelation about religious pluralism—not that there's anything wrong with that—but respecting different viewpoints in me and others and trusting that God welcomes them all even if they aren't "Christian." I know that sounds glib and new-agey but accepting ourselves on all our levels is no picnic as you well know. I'll probably go to my grave still trying to be someone different and better than I am. Maybe that's where afterlife comes in, if there is one, not so much purification as acceptance in all its dimensions. Well I could perseverate but promised not to, so I'll get to the other dream.

Dream 2

I'm in a bedroom with Jennifer, sitting on the bed and studying the Bible together. We're in someone else's house. It's well decorated but comfortable with wood paneling. It's daytime. The bedroom door is open, and others are having a Bible study in the living room. It's a fairly conservative group. The passage we're studying is Romans 3:23, although in the dream the verse actually talks about going the way of sin or accepting Christ's guidance, like the straight is the gate logion. Jennifer sees the passage in terms of an Evangelical theory of atonement. I agree it is that and also a more dynamic process involving two choices in every moment, like process theology, going the way of narrow self-interest or following the example set by Christ's sacrifice. I feel a kind of excitement, as though opposing perspectives have been bridged.

I rattled on longer than intended with the first dream, so I'll try to be succinct (I know I know promises promises). You always encouraged me to name my dreams and I gave this one the brilliant title "Reading the Bible in Bed." The setting tells the story as usual. I'm reading the Bible in bed with Jennifer (hence the title). Actually we're not exactly "in bed" but sitting on a bed together in somebody else's house. And not just reading but studying scripture. Jen and I come at spirituality differently and don't actually sit around reading the Bible together so we're probably talking about my inner Jennifer. But the dream still says Jennifer and you need to pay attention to what it actually says (I hear your voice in my head) so probably both Jennifers are in the mix. That makes sense in dream logic since most of what I've learned about being in relationship has come from my marriage and it carries over into spiritual life, the permeable membrane you used to talk about.

The fact we're studying is important on a couple levels. Historically my spiritual life bounced from intellect to emotion with nothing in between, dry pontificating (as the last dream so kindly points out) punctuated by wild flights of Romantic poet agony and ecstasy. Study means serious engagement with something you care about beyond just getting good grades or publications leading to tenure. Even Rimbaud couldn't dispense with intellect, but it definitely needs to be put in its place, which turns out to be in relationship. A love relationship to be precise, although it's actually more complicated than that since marriage has everything all mixed together—like you and I talked about a million times—love and hate and splendor and tedium and the undramatic blending of lives once the fairytale ends and you learn to see another human being in a million micro-contexts. So apparently that's also the context for studying God's word whether we're talking about the outer marriage or the inner one or getting married to God, like the dream about my nephew.

It's daytime—always a good sign in the Gospels but especially John— and the room is comfortably furnished despite being well decorated, a good picture of the Christian tradition. My spiritual life has definitely gotten more commodious over the last few years, and I'm finally not afraid to pick out curtains. I'll admit my association here is pretty idiosyncratic, the bare walls of my childhood churches and my proclivity for living out of boxes without unpacking even when I've lived in a house for years. (You know me, footloose and fancy free and don't tie me down, living on the transcendental plane and forgetting to flush the toilet.) But I digress. Again. The obvious question is whose house we're in, and my immediate thought is the House of the Lord. Again lots of levels. One is the flesh-and-blood faith community now I'm not too cool for school anymore but also the mystical body of Christ where the whole inner and outer world is all the House of the Lord. Wood paneling reminds me of the Jerusalem temple, probably based on illustrations in Sunday School worksheets when I was kid. I remember it was lined with shittim wood (or was that the Ark of the Covenant?), which delighted us as fifth grade boys. Like the "probably" church in the last dream, we're in and out of the institutional church. It's a "fairly" conservative one (with a nice play on words) so we're in and out of traditional religion too but still on the general premises since my father's house has many condos.

The passage we're studying was a prime text in my childhood church, basically one of the pillars that held the theological roof up. Romans 3:23, for all have sinned and fallen short of the glory of God, the proof text for total depravity and our complete inability to do anything on our own to reach God. Except not quite Romans 3:23 because the passage actually sounds more like the "strait is the gate" verse (another childhood pillar) about choosing salvation or damnation (admittedly the paraphrase is pretty loose). You always said to notice when a dream waffles between options, trying to have it both ways because something transcends neat categories.

Actually having it both ways is the whole point of the dream— Paul and James, faith and works, inner and outer, immanence and transcendence, female and male, yours and mine, God and human, etc. But I'm getting ahead of myself. Jennifer and I are divided on the meaning; she's upholding the Evangelical view of atonement while I opt for process theology. She's less traditional in real life (or at least less theologically obsessed) so we're probably talking about the inner Jennifer, the one who got raised Evangelical instead of tepid Presbyterian. The dream puts its thumb on the theological sore spot (per usual), the whole soteriological quagmire of atonement and what it means to be "saved." Vicarious atonement has always been a bete noire for me (as you well know) and spelling it at-one-ment doesn't solve the problem. As a kid the process was completely literal, a magical transaction my sophisticated teenage brain found preposterous, presto chango I switch my death for yours and pay no attention to the left hand. I now realize my obsession with substitutional death was partly a straw man (as you kindly pointed out early in our relationship—I could have killed you), an elaborate evasion to keep God at bay. But there's a real kernel of truth beneath my drama, that old red-hot ball I can't swallow and can't cough up. (How's that for mixed metaphors?) Because when all's said and done Jesus's death is still the central Christian rite, sacrifice and resurrection its central mystery.

The dream me holds out for process theology, which (unlike ahimsa) I actually know a little bit about. I think I mentioned reading it before we left, especially the newer feminist authors. What grabbed me most is the part I talk about in the dream. As best I understand it God is present in every moment urging us toward the best alternative in our particular human situation with all its societal and personal constraints and limitations, like when people at meetings describe their Higher Power as Good Orderly Direction. Not transcendental truth but what's actually doable with a choice in every instant within the parameters of who we are and what's going on. It seems so clear and intuitive compared to what I grew up with—like reading the Four Noble Truths for the first time—but unfortunately my inner Evangelical raised on symbols and sacrifice finds it a little bloodless. (I'm not talking about process theology per se, of course, which I'm in no position to evaluate, but my inner Evangelical battling it out with my inner process theologian.)

You and I talked ad nauseam about my intellectual/emotional split, but this time instead of getting bogged down in fruitless arguments I suddenly discover I don't have to choose. Unlike childhood where there was one right answer it turns out we can both be right, all that and more with meanings exploding off the page. A graced "this/and" like admitting powerlessness in the First Step and working like hell for the next eleven. Everybody's got a piece of the elephant (I hate to picture what mine is) and there's room for everyone at God's table, Anselm and Abelard and Alfred Whitehead too. And that goes double for my internal village (more like metropolis), those I know and the ones I haven't met yet.

You always paid particular attention to emotions in dreams, and this one is actually sort of a thought/feeling, a heartfelt passion of the mind, "a kind of excitement as though opposing perspectives have been bridged." Breaking down categories and blowing open false dichotomies as God and dreams are wont to do. (The boundaries are ours anyhow and don't exist from God's perspective like the picture of Earth from space.) The dream has it both ways, mine and the inner Jennifer's—Christ's atoning sacrifice manifesting in every moment as a guiding presence and relative choice on our part, internal and yet separate from us since we're rooted in God but still relatively separate. I know my unsystematic theology gives you headaches, but (once again) I'm not really talking about theology but my personal relationship with Christianity with all my parts weighing in (a process that looks suspiciously like ahimsa).

The second step in working with emotions in dreams (I hear your voice in my head again, there must be a pill for that) is looking for where the dream feelings pop up in waking life. Which brings me to the whole point of this letter. Do you remember the dream about riding in a car with a young Latinx man who reminded me of my childhood best friend and my sense of Jesus as companion? Turns out it was a preview of coming attractions, the prophetic quality of dreams you talked about. Because that's more or less what's happening now—even if it doesn't look like I expected.

This dream looks back on our journey together from the other direction—or better put, my own journey in your company—a kind of summary bookend (to mix metaphors again). All the stuff we talked about coming together in a scene like a movie clip, me and Jennifer reading scripture together in a back room while a group Bible study goes on out front. It's all there, my inner and outer marriages, the inner Evangelical and the grownup me. Because what goes wrong in my relationship with God is pretty much the story of my marriage, childlike fusion at the expense of adult identity as if entering the Kingdom of God as a little child means becoming a three-year-old. (Just cuz there's something bigger than my brain doesn't mean I can discard it.)

Well it's back, the casual awareness of God's presence I remember from childhood, and it doesn't violate who I am now or require lopping off parts of me. God wants me to be fully me (still hard to believe), and intimacy doesn't have to mean losing myself in somebody else's expectations. The marriage metaphor again, accepting and being accepted (even loved) and meeting on multiple levels, fully functional adults playing together like kids. Letting God be God, as the preachers say and not my father after all—well you know what I mean. What's hysterical is historical, we say in the rooms, but it doesn't have to define us anymore. The best of what I had then with no code-switching or compromise of my grownup self required and I can call on God's help throughout the day without dissonance.

Coming full circle (om again, om again jiggly jog). I realized the other day that my theological quibbles are pretty much gone, like taking Advil and at some point you notice your headache isn't headaching anymore. I'm still totally confused about pretty much everything and know way less than I used to but what do you expect when God is like jumping out of a spaceship? "We walk by faith and not by sight," we sang when I was a kid. Brailling my way like the time I told you about when I got stuck in the mountains on a moonless night and walked out by the feel of the dust of the trail under my boots. Peace isn't just a nice feeling but things as they are, a desert of silence and spaciousness with nothing to bounce off or reflect my image, a chance to escape the hall of mirrors that is my mind for a moment and see something besides my own reflection or maybe even nothing. But there's also a spirit in the woods, as the Tao Te Ching kindly reminds us.

So I guess in a way I found what I was looking for even if it's not as conclusive as I hoped, living the question and all that. Turns out the Christian symbols I grew up with are real after all, once I stop making them stand for ideas, and they're sprouting away like seeds in the night. For all my bitching about Evangelicalism I'm forever grateful it made God real and took the Bible seriously. I'd pick the literal reading any day over turning it into a set of free-floating precepts. But we can have both, that's the point. A this/and way of seeing that doesn't negate the old way (not one jot or tittle) so it's not whether the Resurrection is true but let me count the ways. Because what happened then is happening now, always happening, in here and out there, in me and everywhere. The story reading me into itself like all those cheesy movies about getting sucked into a video game so what's happening in the Gospel narrative is an expression of my own experience of the inexpressible and how that looks in my daily life.

I remember reading a Buddhist folktale where the various gods were betting over who had the most awesome superpowers. One could hear everything (unless I'm mixing it up with the Dr. Suess story), another could see clear through the Earth etc. The Monkey King bragged he was so fast he could jump to the farthest snow-capped peak and grab the pinecone from the tree on top and be back before they knew he was gone and then presto, there it was in his hand. He was busy gloating and counting his loot when the Buddha spoke from the sky, not thundering but with a kind of affectionate chuckle offering to open the Monkey King's eyes for a second so he could see how things really are. I'm sure you see the punchline coming. It turned out the faraway mountains were really just the Buddha's fingers and the poor proud Monkey King had been in the palm of his hand the whole time.

That's how it feels looking back over the last few years, the whole grand journey of me questing boldly into the unknown and it turns out I was in God's hand the whole time (just thankful he didn't applaud). Right back where I started from and knowing it the first time etc. And that as they say is that, at least until the next level of the video game opens up. So once again I've put my muddy theological feet where angels fear to tread (not that God's going to lose any sleep over it) and it's time to sign off. Thanks again for everything and glad to hear you finally replaced that ratty old couch.

Yours in Christ (truly and without irony),

Mark

Bibliography

Alighieri, Dante. *The Divine Comedy: The Inferno, The Purgatorio, and The Paradiso.* Translated by John Ciardi. New York: Penguin Group, 2003.

Alighieri, Dante. *La Vita Nuova (Poems of Youth): Revised Edition.* Translated by B. Reynolds. New York: Penguin, 2004.

Anonymous, *Alcoholics Anonymous: The Story of How Many Thousands of Men and Women Who Have Recovered from Alcoholism.* 4th ed. New York: Alcoholics Anonymous World Service Inc., 2001.

Anonymous. *Twelve Steps and Twelve Traditions.* New York: Alcoholics Anonymous World Service Inc., 1952.

Aronfsky, Darren, dir. *Black Swan.* Los Angeles: Searchlight Pictures, 2010.

Athanasius of Alexandria. *On the Incarnation.* Yonkers: St. Vladimir's Seminary Press, 2011.

————. *The Life of Anthony of Egypt.* New York: Pantianos Classics, 2016.

Augustine. *Confessions.* Translated by Sarah Ruden. New York: Penguin Random House, 2017.

Baring, Anne, and Jules Cashford. *The Myth of the Goddess: Evolution of an Image.* Harmondsworth, England: Viking, 1991.

Barone-Chapman, Maryann. "Gender Legacies of Jung and Freud as Epistemology in Emergent Feminist Research on Late Motherhood." *Behavioral Sciences* 4, no. 1 (2014): 14–30.

Blake, William. *The Complete Poems and Prose of William Blake.* Edited by David Erman. Los Angeles and Berkeley: University of California Press, 2008.

Bernard of Clairvaux. *Commentary on the Song of Songs.* Translated by Matthew Henry. North Charleston SC: Createspace, 2016.

Bolen, Jean S. *Goddesses in Everywoman.* New York: Harper & Row, 1984.

Brewster, Fanny. *The Racial Complex: A Jungian Perspective on Race and Culture*. New York: Routledge, 2020.

————. "Wheel of Fire: The African-American Dreamer and Cultural Consciousness." *Jung Journal: Culture & Psyche* 7, no. 1 (2013): 70–87.

Camus, Albert. *The Myth of Sisyphus*. Translated by Justin O'Brien. New York: Vintage Books, 2018.

Claremont de Castillejo, Irene. *Knowing Women: A Female Psychology*. Boston: Shambhala, 1973.

Clift, Wallace. *Jung and Christianity: The Challenge of Reconciliation*. Pearl River, NY: Herder & Herder, 1983.

Columbus, Chris J., dir. *Harry Potter and the Sorcerer's Stone*. Burbank, CA: Warner Bros, 2001.

Davies, Brian. *The Thought of Thomas Aquinas*. Oxford, England: Clarendon Press, 1993.

Deida, David. *The Way of the Superior Man: A Spiritual Guide to Mastering the Challenges of Women, Work and Sexual Desire*. Boulder, CO: Sounds True, 2017.

Dickens, Charles. *A Christmas Carol*. Morgantown, KY: Tole Publishing Co., 2021.

Dourley, John P. *Paul Tillich, Jung and the Recovery of Religion*. New York: Routledge, 2008.

Downing, Christine. *Myths and Mysteries of Same-Sex Love*. New York: Continuum Publishing, 1989.

Edinger, Edward. *Ego and Archetype: Individuation and the Religious Function of the Psyche*. Boston: Shambhala, 1992.

Eliot, T. S. *Collected Poems*, New York: Harcourt, Brace & World, 1970.

Estés, Clarissa Pinkola. *Women Who Run with the Wolves: Stories of the Wild Woman Archetype*. New York: Ballentine, 1986.

Ferenczi, Sándor. "Confusion of Tongues between Adults and Children." In *Final Contributions to the Problems and Methods of Psycho-Analysis*. London: Routledge, 1994.

Fleming, Victor, dir. *The Wizard of Oz*. Beverly Hills, CA: Metro-Goldwyn-Mayer, 1939.

Fordham, Michael. *Children as Individuals*. London, England: Free Association Books, 1996.

Forman, Miloš, dir. *One Flew over the Cuckoo's Nest*. Hollywood, CA: United Artists, 1975.

Freud, Sigmund. *The Future of an Illusion. Complete Psychological Works of Sigmund Freud.* Edited by James Strachey. New York: W. W. Norton and Company, 1989.

Gaiman, Neil. *American Gods.* New York: Inner City Books, 1981.

Goethe, Johann Wolfgang. *The Sorcerer's Apprentice.* 1797.

Harding, M. Esther. *The Way of All Women.* New York: Putnum, 1970.

Hartley, Linda. *Servants of the Sacred Dream: Rebirthing the Deep Feminine: Psycho-spiritual Crisis and Healing.* Norfolk, VA: Elmdon Books, 2020.

Hill, Gareth S. *Masculine and Feminine: The Natural Flow of Opposites in the Psyche.* Boston: Shambhala, 1992.

Hillman, James. "Anima." *Spring: A Journal of Archetype and Culture,* 1973.

_____. "Anima II," *Spring: A Journal of Archetype and Culture,* 1974.

_____. *The Dream and the Underworld.* New York: Harper & Row, 1979.

_____. *The Myth of Analysis: Three Essays in Archetypal Psychology.* Evanston, IL, Northwestern University Press, 1972.

_____. *Suicide and the Soul.* 2nd Ed. Woodstock, CT: Spring Publications, 1997.

Ignatius of Loyola. *The Spiritual Exercises of St. Ignatius.* Translated by George E. Ganss. Chicago: Loyola Press, 1992.

John of the Cross. *The Collected Works of St. John of the Cross.* Translated by Kieran Kavanaugh and Otilio Rodriguez. Washington, DC: ICS Publications, 1991.

John of the Cross. *Dark Night of the Soul.* Translated by Mirabai Starr. New York: Riverhead Books, 2002.

John of the Cross. *The Essential St. John of the Cross: Ascent of Mount Carmel, Dark Night of the Soul, A Spiritual Canticle, Twenty Poems.* Translated by E. Allison Peers. Radford, VA: Wilder Publications, 2008.

Joseph, Jenny. "Warning." *Selected Poems.* Hexham, UK: Bloodaxe Books, 1992.

Jung, Brennan J. *Revisioning Anima and Animus: A Paradigm of Queer Otherness in the Psyche.* PhD diss., Fuller Theological Seminary, 2020. ProQuest (AAT 28769817).

Jung, C. G. *The Collected Works, Second Edition.* (Bollingen Series XX; H. Read, M. Fordham, & G. Adler, Eds.; R. F. C. Hull, Trans.). Princeton, NJ: Princeton University Press, 1953–1979.

_____. *Aion: Researches into the Phenomenology of the Self, The Collected Works Vol 9ii, Second Edition.* (Bollingen Series XX). Princeton, NJ: Princeton University Press, 1969.

_____. *Alchemical Studies, The Collected Works Vol 13, Second Edition.* (Bollingen Series XX). Princeton, NJ: Princeton University Press, 1968.

_____. *C. G. Jung Letters, 1951–1961.* Vol 2. Edited by Gerhard Adler. Princeton, NJ: Princeton University Press, 1975.

_____. *Dream Analysis: Notes of the Seminar Given in 1928–1930.* (Bollingen Series XCIX). Edited by William McGuire. Princeton, NJ: Princeton University Press, 1984.

_____. *Jung on Ignatius of Loyola's Spiritual Exercises: Lectures Delivered at ETH Zurich, Vol. 7, 1939–40.* Edited by Martin Liebscher. Translated by Caitlan Stephens. Princeton, NJ: Princeton University Press, 2023.

_____. *Memories, Dreams, Reflections.* Edited by Aniela Jaffé. Translated by Richard and Clara Winston. London: Collins & Routledge & Kegan Paul, 1963.

_____. *Mysterium Coniunctionis, The Collected Works Vol. 14, Second Edition.* (Bollingen Series XX). Princeton, NJ: Princeton University Press, 1970.

_____. *Psychological Types, The Collected Works Vol. 6, Second Edition.* (Bollingen Series XX). Princeton, NJ: Princeton University Press, 1968.

_____. *Psychology and Alchemy, The Collected Works Vol. 12, Second Edition.* (Bollingen Series XX). Princeton, NJ: Princeton University Press, 1971.

_____. *Psychology and Religion, The Collected Works Vol. 11, Second Edition.* (Bollingen Series XX). Princeton, NJ: Princeton University Press, 1970.

_____. *Symbols of Transformation, The Collected Works Vol. 5, Second Edition.* (Bollingen Series XX). Princeton, NJ: Princeton University Press, 1967.

_____. *Two Essays on Analytical Psychology, The Collected Works Vol. 7, Second Edition.* (Bollingen Series XX). Princeton, NJ: Princeton University Press, 1967.

_____. *The Archetypes and the Collective Unconscious, The Collected Works Vol. 9i, Second Edition.* (Bollingen Series XX). Princeton, NJ: Princeton University Press, 1969.

_____. *The Practice of Psychotherapy, The Collected Works Vol. 16, Second Edition. (Bollingen Series XX). Princeton, NJ: Princeton University Press, 1966.*

_____. *The Structure and Dynamics of the Psyche, The Collected Works Vol 8, Second Edition.* (Bollingen Series XX). Princeton, NJ: Princeton University Press, 1969.

_____. *The Symbolic Life: Miscellaneous Writing, The Collected Works Vol. 18, Second Edition.* (Bollingen Series XX). Princeton, NJ: Princeton University Press, 1977.

Keating, Thomas. *Open Mind, Open Heart: The Contemplative Dimension of the Gospel.* London: Bloomsbury Continuum, 2019.

Kelley, C. F. *Meister Eckhart on Divine Knowledge.* Berkeley, CA: North Atlantic Books. 2009.

Lauter, Estella, and Carol Schreier Rupprecht. *Feminist Archetypal Theory: Interdisciplinary Re-Visions of Jungian Thought.* Knoxville: University of Tennessee Press, 1985.

Lammers, Ann C. *In God's Shadow: The Collaboration of Victor White and C. G. Jung.* Mahway, NJ: Paulist Press, 1994.

Luibheid, Colm, trans. *Pseudo-Dionysus: The Complete Works.* Mahwah, NJ: Paulist Press, 1987.

Matthew, Iian. *The Impact of God: Soundings from St. John of the Cross.* London: Hodder & Stoughton, Ltd., 1995.

McGinn, Bernard. *The Harvest of Mysticism in Medieval Germany.* New York: Crossroad Publishing. 2005.

_____. *The Mystical Thought of Meister Eckhart: The Man From Whom God Hid Nothing.* New York: Crossroad Publishing, 2001.

McGuire, William, and R. F. C. Hull, eds. *C. G. Jung Speaking.* Princeton, NJ: Princeton University Press, 1977.

McKenzie, Susan. "Gender and Sexualities in Individuation: Theoretical and Clinical Explorations." *Journal of Analytical Psychology* 55, no. 1 (2010): 91–111.

_____. "Queering Gender: Anima/Animus and the Paradigm of Emergence." *Journal of Analytical Psychology* 51, no. 3 (2006): 401–421.

Meister Eckhart. *The Complete Mystical Works of Meister Eckhart.* Translated by Maurice O'C. Walshe. New York: Crossroad Publishing, 2009.

———. *Meister Eckhart: The Essential Sermons, Commentaries, Treatises and Defense.* Translated by Edmund. Colledge and Bernard McGinn. Mahway, NJ: Paulist Press, 1981.

———. *Meister Eckhart: Teacher and Preacher.* Edited by Bernard McGinn. Mahwah, NJ: Paulist Press, 1986.

Milton, John. *Complete Poems and Major Prose.* Edited by Merritt Hughes. New York: Odyssey Press, 1957.

Munitiz, Joseph A., and Philip Endean, trans. *Saint Ignatius of Loyola: Personal Writings: Reminiscences, Spiritual Diary, Select Letters including the Text of The Spiritual Exercises.* London: Penguin Books, 1996.

Nagy, Marilyn. *Philosophical Issues in the Psychology of C. G. Jung.* Albany: State University of New York Press, 1991.

The New Oxford Annotated Bible: New Revised Standard Version with the Apocrypha. Oxford, England: Oxford University Press, 2001.

Perera, Sylvia Brinton. *Descent to the Goddess: A Way of Initiation for Women.* Toronto, Canada: Inner City Books, 1981.

———. *The Scapegoat Complex: Towards a Mythology of Shadow and Guilt.* Toronto, Canada: Inner City Books, 1986.

Plato. *Plato: Complete Works.* Edited by John M. Cooper. Indianapolis, IN: Hackett Publishing Co., 1997.

Ray, Nicholas, dir. *Rebel Without a Cause.* Burbank, CA: Warner Bros., 1955.

Rosenberg, Stuart. *Cool Hand Luke.* Screenplay by Donn Pearce and Frank R. Pierson. Based on Donn Pierce, *Cool Hand Luke,* New York: Scribners, 1965. Burbank, CA: Warner Brothers, 1967.

Rowland, Susan. *Jung: A Feminist Revision.* Malden, MA: Polity, 2002.

Samuels, Andrew. *Jung and the Post-Jungians.* New York: Routledge, 1985.

———. *The Plural Psyche: Personality, Morality, and the Father.* London: Routledge, 1989.

Samuels, Andrew, Bani Shorter, and Fred Plaut. *A Critical Dictionary of Jungian Analysis.* London: Routledge, 1986.

Sartre, Jean-Paul. *No Exit and Three Other Plays.* New York: Vintage International, 1998.

Sendak, Maurice. *In the Night Kitchen.* New York: Harper & Row, 1970.

_____. *Where the Wild Things Are.* New York: Harper Collins, 2012.

Shelley, Percy Bysshe. *Prometheus Unbound.* Los Angeles: Black Box Press, 2007.

Singer, June. *Androgyny: Toward a New Theory of Sexuality.* Norwell, MA: Anchor Press, 1976.

Singer, Thomas, and Samuel L. Kimbles, eds. *The Cultural Complex: Contemporary Jungian Perspectives on Psyche and Society.* New York: Brunner-Routledge, 2004.

300. Screenplay by Zack Snyder. Directed by Zack Snyder, 2006.

Stevenson, Robert Louis. *The Strange Case of Dr. Jekyll and Mr. Hyde.* Mankato, MN: Capstone Press, 2008.

Sturluson, Snorri. *The Prose Edda: Norse Mythology.* Edited by Jesse L. Byock. New York: Penguin Books, 2006.

Tarnas, Richard. *The Passion of the Western Mind: Understanding the Ideas that Have Shaped Our World View.* New York: Random House, 1991.

Teresa of Avila. *Interior Castle.* Commentary by Dennis J. Billy. Notre Dame, IN: Ave Maria Press, 2007.

Tillich, Paul. *The Dynamics of Faith.* New York: Harper & Row, 1957.

Tolkien, J. R. R. *The Lord of the Rings.* New York: William Morrow Paperbacks, 2022.

Twain, Mark. *The Adventures of Tom Sawyer.* Orinda, CA: SeaWolf Press, 2018.

Ulanov, Ann Belford, and Barry Ulanov. *Transforming Sexuality: The Archetypal World of Anima and Animus.* Boston: Shambhala, 1994.

Underhill, Evelyn. *Mysticism: A Study in Nature and Development of Spiritual Consciousness.* New York: Image Books, 1990.

Von Franz, Marie-Louise. *The Problem of the Puer Aeternus.* New York: Spring, 1971.

Wehr, Demaris S. *Jung and Feminism: Liberating Archetypes.* Boston: Beacon Press, 1987.

White, E. B., *Charlotte's Web.* New York: Harper Trophy, 2012.

Whitmont, E. C. *Return of the Goddess.* New York, NY: Continuum Press, 1982.

Winnicott, Donald W. *The Child, the Family and the Outside World.* Cambridge, MA: Perseus Publishing, 1987.

Woodman, Marion. *Addiction to Perfection: The Still Unravished Bride.* Toronto, Canada: Inner City Books, 1982.

Wordsworth, William. *The Major Works Including The Prelude.* Edited by Stephen Gill. Oxford, England: Oxford University Press, 2008.

Yacoub, Ishak Azmy, and John Paul Abdelsayed, eds. *The Strong Saint Abba Moses: Hermit, Abbot, and Martyr.* Los Angeles: Saint Paul Brotherhood Press, 2010.

Yamada, Koun, trans. *Gateless Gate.* Los Angeles: Center Publications, 1979.

Young-Eisendrath, Polly. *Hags and Heroes: A Feminist Approach to Jungian Psychotherapy with Couples.* Toronto, Canada: Inner City Books, 1984.

Young-Eisendrath, Polly, and Florence Wiedmann. *Female Authority: Empowering Women Through Psychotherapy.* New York: Guilford Press, 1987.

www.ingramcontent.com/pod-product-compliance
Lightning Source LLC
Chambersburg PA
CBHW030421100426
42812CB00028B/3055/J